ATTENTION DEFICIT HYPERACTIVITY DISORDER AS A LEARNED BEHAVIORAL PATTERN

A Return to Psychology

Craig Wiener

University Press of America,® Inc.
Lanham · Boulder · New York · Toronto · Plymouth, UK

To my father and mentor,
Morton Wiener Ph.D.

Table of Contents

Preface

Attention Deficit Hyperactivity Disorder as a Learned Behavioral Pattern: A Return to Psychology is a critique of the assertions and explanations that are currently invoked to account for ADHD response patterns. This work is a point-by-point analysis of the biological determinist's position and interpretation of empirical work that is now prevalent. In that we are telling increasing numbers of children (and adults) that they have this genetic delay, it seems important to evaluate the bases of those claims.

ADHD has become the exclusive province of geneticists, neuropsychologists, and physicians. Coursework has been designed to *inform* students, practitioners, and academicians about the neurobiological causes of the behaviors, and the necessity to medicate and more stringently manage the "inflicted" individual. While this general attitude may continue to prosper, there is, meanwhile, increasing concern that we are positing the existence of a medical problem when there exist no biological markers or dysfunctions that reliably correspond with the behavioral criteria.

In this more psychologically-based formulation, biological categories are not disregarded; they are integrated into a framework that places greater emphasis on nurture and the importance of context, situation, and circumstance when understanding ADHD behaviors. A learning paradigm (which has a long tradition in the field of psychology) is put forth as an alternative way to account for the frequency rates of diagnostic responses. This model avoids the many conceptual problems and contradictions that seem evident with the accepted neurobiological paradigm. Since this text is based on the same research as the acknowledged perspective, it is also evidence-based. However, we reinterpret much of the accumulated data.

The proposed alternative intervention has not yet been pursued, but similar approaches have been utilized for many years in order to increase cooperation and work productivity for diverse groups. The final chapter explores the possibility of using these methods with the diagnosed population. Given that there are significant shortcomings associated with the implementation of traditional treatments, we welcome an alternative way to address ADHD problems. While substantial resources have been allocated to support biological determinism, *A Return to Psychology* could lead to a variety of improvements in the way we understand and treat ADHD patterns. If there is a reluctance to explore, we must settle with what we have.

This book owes special thanks to Susan L. Davis for her expert copyediting and outstanding effort in helping to prepare the manuscript.

Craig Wiener, Ed.D.
Worcester, MA
October 2006

Chapter 1

The Current Bias of Nature in the Explications of ADHD Behaviors

The alarming rise in the number of children being diagnosed with Attention Deficit Hyperactivity Disorder (ADHD) is reaching near epidemic proportions. Despite the statements in the DSM-IV-TR (The American Psychiatric Association, 2000) warning that diagnostic classifications are not to be interpreted as if all individuals who are given the same diagnosis necessarily have identical symptoms, signs and behavioral patterns, many mental health practitioners proceed as if an ADHD diagnosis identifies the same problem and treatment for each individual. It is now a widespread assumption that hyperactive, impulsive, and inattentive individuals, as described in the diagnostic manual, have an underlying neurobiological delay.

While ADHD frequency rates may vary with nationality, gender, age, social class, and residence in either a rural or urban setting, it is estimated that from 3% to 7% of children and 5% of adults have this developmental disorder. In that individuals in the population may be assigned a numerical value, there will therefore always be predetermined numbers of persons who function at the lower extreme within a normalized distribution for ADHD, and labeled as such. Similar to other dimensions of behavior that follow a bell-shaped curve, where extremes are seen as delays (e.g., intelligence), the claim is made that diagnosed individuals have a *distinct* neurobiological condition that leaves them at the bottom rung for ability to self-control.

When considering the behavioral continuum, other practitioners have also suggested that individuals might be categorized as borderline when there are sufficient problems in daily living, and full diagnostic criteria have not yet been met. This proposal classifies an additional 9% of individuals (Barkley, 2000). To accept this approach would mean that approximately 16% of the total population could be considered as either borderline ADHD or actual ADHD. It should therefore not be surprising that ADHD currently represents one of the most common reasons that children are referred to mental health practitioners in the United States (Barkley, 2006a). As Diller commented, "One gets the sense that almost everyone who sees a doctor about ADHD walks out with a prescription if they want it" (Sinha, 2001, 48).

As recommended by Barkley (2002), individuals who have never met criteria for the impulsive/hyperactive pattern before adolescence are not included in this current analysis. While it has been typical practice to understand ADHD as having hyperactive/impulsive and inattentive components, most who study this diagnostic category are beginning to see the purely Inattentive Type as a separate and distinct disorder associated with deficient speed of processing information, poor stimulus selection, deficient focus of attention, and/or sluggish cognitive tempo (Milich et al., 2001). ADHD is purportedly related to a diminished ability to inhibit a response in comparison to problems with receiving stimuli.

If an individual qualifies for the ADHD behavioral diagnosis outlined in the DSM-IV-TR, behaviors including intrusiveness, lack of consideration for another's viewpoint, non-responsiveness, immoderation, provocation, and indulgent actions that relate to long-term problems are assumed to be caused by an inadequate physical body. Rather than to describe an individual as lazy, insecure, preoccupied, disinterested, passive-resistive, eccentric, sassy, show-off, spoiled, rambunctious, clownish, entitled, monopolizing, infantilized, pampered, avoidant, egocentric, hedonistic, and selfish, the prevailing trend nowadays is to cluster these behaviors under the category of a fixed biological handicap.

While Hallowell and Ratey's (1995) construct "driven to distraction" is a notable and popular example of a traditional construction to account for behavior by positing neurological determination, it seems increasingly that the majority of practitioners are adopting this way of explaining ADHD behaviors. In fact, in earlier categorizing systems, an ADHD behavioral pattern was identified as "Minimal Brain Dysfunction," which was an even more explicit earlier focus on biological causation.

As a consequence of this trend, there has been controversy about whether too many individuals are being incorrectly labeled as having this biological problem. Some have voiced the concern that many individuals who are given that diagnosis might more reasonably be described as misbehaving, or as simply less competent in mastering tasks. Since stimulant medications are often recommended to help treat the disorder, an increasing number of individuals are worried that individuals are being over medicated when other interventions might be more appropriate.

In that the numbers of ADHD diagnoses are mounting significantly, many are now distressed that individuals are being identified as medically troubled, simply because they do not comply with social expectations or to the requisites of school personnel and family members. There is increasing concern that significant numbers of children are placed on stimulants in order to enhance performance (much like what occurs when athletes take steroids), and/or are urged to take drugs simply to make a parent or teacher's job less difficult. For example, after one diagnosed child told his mother about his above average report card, she replied by saying, "Think how much better you would be doing if you would take the meds!"

While the hope is to identify individuals who show impairment in life's major settings, a major question that we will return to later is that it is not always clear how inattentive or impulsive one must be in order for the diagnosis to be imposed. Still others hold that ascribing the label is always based on the clinician's judgment, especially when problems are not intense or troubling (Murphy and Gordon, 1998). In other words, statements about impairment are almost invariably derived from evaluations of psychosocial events rather than biological categories.

Most would agree that the ways in which we understand ADHD and treat the non-normative behaviors have become a significant social concern. The attachment of the ADHD label has resulted in increasingly larger numbers of people concluding that they have a particular kind of delay, disability, impairment, or deficiency. The ADHD descriptor now identifies a particular infliction, the necessity of treatment to compensate for purported insufficiencies, and the requirement to add to what is missing rather than to simply help individuals learn new behavior. In our current age of biological determinism, behaviors that might have been classified and understood very differently in other times, are now labeled in ways consistent with the traditional biological metaphor that neurology is giving rise to this atypical set of actions.

However, within the context of these assertions, a number of traditionalists are recognizing that ADHD is indeed being diagnosed in epidemic proportions. Pearl et al. (2001) emphasize that evaluators must make distinctions between ADHD and attention problems related to lead poisoning, fetal alcohol syndrome, and allergies to medication, sleep deprivation, emotional distress, epilepsy, and damage to the frontal or parietal cortex. Professionals are urged not to impose a psychiatric account when other accounts are tenable and worthy of investigation. Since inattention is a common symptom of mental illness or distress, one should not make a diagnosis on the basis of inattention alone. Moreover, in that people are increasingly biased in favor of identifying themselves as ADHD, there is now concern that professionals must resist social pressure in order to *not* give an ADHD diagnosis (Murphy and Gordon, 1998).

Traditionalists are becoming increasingly concerned that some individuals might call attention to their posited symptoms as a way to reduce disapproval, required work, and diminish the expectation of competence, since having a disability might solicit more sympathy and thus accommodation from others, and meanwhile further reinforce those behaviors. Because traditionalists encourage greater societal tolerance and adjustment of policies for individuals who show ADHD patterning, qualifying for the DSM-IV-TR behavioral criteria may sometimes produce significant social benefits. Some individuals have attempted to use their own diagnosis in order to avoid personal or legal responsibility (Barkley, 2001).

The result of this bias has been that many more individuals are self-diagnosing and defining their own behavior in ways consistent with the extant traditional view. Traditionalists now find it necessary to address this problem, and fewer self-referring adults are being labeled as ADHD when presenting at specialty clinics (Murphy and Gordon, 2006). It is now more common to require clients to provide hard data to substantiate self-reports. Many traditionalists claim that ADHD patterning should leave a trail of evidence in the hope that this corroborating evidence will weed out some of the suggestibility apparently occurring in our social group at this time. Steps must be taken to guard against the possibility of over diagnosis.

Barkley and Edwards (2006) also recommend that professionals take precautions to ensure that observed behavior is atypical when compared to children of the same ethnic group, in that different cultural groups might reinforce different kinds of behavioral patterning. Since atypical patterning for one group might not apply to another, diagnostic labels are always culturally dependent. Much like what has occurred in other diagnoses, ADHD behaviors may be more or less frequent and severe in relation to cultural parameters. Since some cultural groups reinforce certain behaviors above other behaviors, understanding behavioral frequencies requires understanding the contingencies that maintain those responses within a particular cultural matrix. As noted by Wiener (1991), labeling particular actions as disordered, deviant, strange, or aberrant may frequently be related to socio-cultural designations.

Consequently, even for traditionalists, diagnosis of ADHD requires comparison to a reference group, in that what might be acceptably inhibited behavior for some groups will not be for others. However, if it can be proved that persons are psychosocially conditioned to initiate a typical ADHD-like pattern in some socio-cultural groups, is it reasonable to presume then that persons functioning in *other* socio-cultural groups who respond in an ADHD-like pattern, invariably possess abnormal body functioning?

If one accepts the notion that an ADHD diagnosis is embedded in a cultural relativist perspective, ADHD behaviors may alternatively be understood as a deviation from normative social practice within a particular group. This contrasting interpretation may avoid the additional inference that behavior is necessarily deficit, delayed, disrupted, or disabled. There might then be increased focus on understanding the individual's reinforcement history, and on analysis of the ways in which diagnostic behaviors have been shaped over time in relation to the individual's *culture* or way of living in the world. As Skinner (1953, 97) notes, when people leave one community and go to another "the topography of our behavior may change."

When considering cultural relativism, rather than seeing a person as delayed when responses do not correspond to particular standards, the person could also be seen as conditioned to behave in a discrepant way. He or she could be behaving in ways that are consistent with his or her personal culture. Once it is determined that patterns of behavior are consistent with particular histories of reinforcement, it becomes less desirable to impose the characterization of delay, as this would be suggesting that one socio-cultural group is better than another.

If we adopt this learning paradigm, we examine ADHD behaviors from an historical perspective, and study the contexts, situations, and circumstances in which those behaviors may initially have occurred and been reinforced. After conducting a historical analysis, a learning paradigm often seems more reasonable; outcomes that seem to increase the frequency rates of particular responses may be identified. Behavior that seemed to have been delayed may appear more malleable and cogent when considering the sequence of events occurring after a behavior was expressed. The important point here is that behaviors characterized as disrupted, deficient, troubled, and problematic may become more meaningful, logical, and functional after a person's unique history of reinforcement has been discerned.

While some might consider these interpretations as radical, similar views are espoused by cultural anthropologists, who have urged observers to understand the customs, patterns, values, and traditions of a cultural group before assigning meaning to particular actions. As an observer begins to understand the learning history of an ADHD diagnosed individual, particular behaviors seem considerably less disinhibited or uncontrolled.

For example, rapidly paced behaviors might be reinforced when a social context (e.g., a city) is, for the purpose of our discussion, "impatient." The enactor may be imitating intolerance for waiting. Rapidly paced behaviors may be advantageous, and individuals may indeed learn that moving slowly will result in "missing out," or that moving at one's own pace allows others to dominate or impede. Behaving at an increased rate of speed may also permit uncomfortable evaluative interactions to be completed faster, and finishing first may often be seen as a sign of competence. Despite the high incidence of errors and increased jeopardy that often correlates with rapidly paced behaviors, there are numerous opportunities for that behavior to be reinforced in modern life.

In this view the results of engaging in rapidly paced behaviors may either increase or decrease the recurrence of those behaviors. Rather than understand rapidly paced behaviors as instances of an inability to stop, they could be understood as reinforced behaviors in relation to what happens when they are enacted in certain situations. Instead of arguing that rapidly paced behaviors in the context of an ADHD diagnosis are dysfunctional, delayed, or disordered, they may be better understood as consistent with a learning paradigm to the extent that there is an historical correspondence between conditions and frequency rates.

Succinctly put, if the behaviors occur more or less frequently in relation to what happens, why is it necessary to claim that biological categories endogenous to the individual are causing the problem? Why not suggest that, depending on contingencies of reinforcement, a behavior could be altered, and the incidence of recurrence when similar conditions arise could be changed? Although aspects of the aftermath might not be positive when evaluated from the perspective of a person's ethnic origins, standards of social propriety, family priorities, or task competency, when ADHD actions are understood in relation to the greater involvement and accommodation from others, escape from adversity, and prevention of denial, it becomes increasingly difficult to interpret these behaviors as symptoms of biological determinism. The behaviors might instead be characterized as psychosocial functional responses and dealt with, given that assumption.

Interestingly, DuPaul and Ervin (1996) temporarily break from tradition when they discuss possible functions that ADHD behavior might have for diagnosed persons; in this respect, their interpretation is more consistent with this learning model. For example, they note that ADHD behavior might make it possible for a person to avoid or escape from diligent or challenging activity. They add that ADHD behavior might also increase the likelihood of getting attention from others, and permit individuals more rapid access to preferred activities, including daydreaming. Very similarly, Pfiffner, Barkley, and DuPaul (2006) also encourage a functional analysis of diagnostic responding when devising school-based programs. They claim that certain antecedents and consequences may be perpetuating those responses.

While all of these authors subscribe to a medically-based view, their interpretations nevertheless introduce inconsistencies; for example, by recommending a functional analysis, the implication is that these responses might be reasonably explicated within the domain of psychology. Although other than recognizing that diagnostic responding may be maintained by environmental contingencies, traditionalists are not positing that ADHD behaviors are socially patterned in the same way as more "considerate" behaviors. That is, while traditionalists recognize all socially acceptable behavior as controlled, ADHD behaviors are always seen as unfortunate consequences of neurological delay and diminished self control, even if those responses sometimes result in something positive for the afflicted person, who most certainly would not exhibit those behaviors if they possessed greater self-control.

A further example might help illustrate this point. A child rushes across the room, tramples toys lying on the floor, and then jumps into a toy box to grab a ball. Traditionalists might interpret that behavior as impulsive. It might be inferred that the child could have created less damage (and taken fewer risks) had he inhibited his reaction to the ball (and thought about what might happen). Although the child might receive immediate reinforcement when behaving in this manner, he would not have behaved so energetically were it not for his disinhibited state.

However, when understanding the child's actions within a learning paradigm, a number of conditions come to the fore: getting to the ball as quickly as possible becomes a reinforced behavior compared to moving slowly, given that the game is played within particular conditions (e.g., number of participants, importance of winning, parental reaction, etc.). Under these circumstances, getting to the ball quickly, and jumping into the toy box is cued by the situation, just as stopping or approaching the ball more slowly might be cued for someone who has been reinforced to respond more cautiously in similar situations.

It is not that one child contemplates more than another before acting under the particular conditions in the room or more adequately delaying gratification, but rather that individuals react differently in relation to different reinforcement histories under equivalent circumstances. This same child who jumps into a toy box might be cautious when hiding wrongdoing from a parent, or may move slowly when asked to find a ball to gratify his baby brother. However, since ADHD behavior is inconsistent with sharing, taking turns, caution, courtesy, and conformity, many would believe his behavior is unacceptable because he is biologically less able. Instead of characterizing him as conditioned differently, traditional belief maintains that he *cannot* rather than does not, or has not yet learned to behave in more acceptable ways.

In contrast, a learning theorist might alternatively claim that sometimes we characterize behaviors as non-functional, uncontrolled, and delayed when it is our failure to identify the outcomes that become probable in relation to particular behavior expressed in particular situations and circumstances. Categorizations of impairment may be a function of our limited understanding of which events increase in frequency when those particular actions occur in particular situations. While some behavior might be compared to a "gold standard," positing that a behavior is inadequately inhibited could mean that we have not yet identified the contingencies that reinforce the occurrence of those responses.

If ADHD behaviors were reinterpreted as conditioned responses rather than a result of an under-functioning antecedent biology, more effort could be placed on identifying the sequencing of events that reinforce the continuing recurrence of those behaviors in various contexts and situations. We might alternatively investigate the extent to which loved ones are involved in shaping ADHD responses when they accommodate after the child overreacts, complains, provokes attention, or gives up. There could be greater focus on what might be reinforcing the inattention during particular activities, or confused and overwhelmed behaviors that often occur when others impose tasks requiring mental effort or some other demand. Actions that traditionalists call "failures to inhibit" could be reinterpreted as reinforced behaviors that are better understood in relation to events that take place when these responses are emitted.

However, professionals and parents alike are urged to presume that bodily caused inhibitory deficits cannot be cured. While some discretionary contribution may be afforded to diagnosed teens due to problems related to adolescent independence (Robin, 2006), the notion is maintained that the core problem of ADHD must be treated with medication, systematic external monitoring, contingency management, and a enormous vigilance by loved ones who care enough about the afflicted person to direct his or her actions over time. Even though

DuPaul, Barkley, and Connor (1998) note that 20% of diagnosed individuals may be able to discontinue medication after one year of treatment (without fully illustrating the biological account), individuals are generally informed that they have an embedded lifelong medical problem, and are instructed that medication and monitoring will be necessary throughout their lives.

Diagnosed persons are told that they have a neurological disinhibition that produces difficulties with working memory, verbal fluency, persistence, motor sequencing, and basically the deployment of frontal lobe functioning. They will experience the greatest difficulty when vigilance is necessary to fulfill tasks (Newcorn et al., 2001). Their delay is thought to be on the "output side" of behavior, although a computer metaphor is problematic when applied to organisms, in that all responses, reflexes, sensations, and behaviors apparently include the notion of output. The prevailing belief is that ADHD correlates with less ability to plan, organize, and evaluate (Barkley, 2000). Deficits in response inhibition are regarded as unique to ADHD (Nigg, 2001).

Conventional practitioners maintain that diagnosed persons have a basic neurological delay that will cause them increasing difficulty whenever tasks or activities require a degree of resistance to a powerful reaction that would give them a more immediate payoff. Enduring tedium, or working towards larger more distant future payoffs, requires a well-functioning inhibitory system so that individuals may gain access to executive functions that help them behave in ways consistent with socio-cultural standards. Inhibitory system failure becomes the reason for their pattern of giving up quickly, especially when activities are considered tedious, or when tasks require mental effort.

Diagnosed individuals more often complain of boredom, in that they have greater difficulty recognizing the long range repayments that could occur in relation to carrying out particular required tasks. Rapid reinforcement becomes a necessity in order that activities which increase the probability of future rewards will not seem meaningless, nonsensical, or monotonous.

According to many who study the ADHD diagnosis, regardless of how much a diagnosed person is taught, he or she will not enact the learned responses in the correct situations because of the presumed output delays. Since diagnosed persons are less able to inhibit, they are less able to launch the necessary executive functioning which would allow them to adequately control their future environment. Whatever they learn will not be accessible to them at the moment of performance. Different environmental situations will elicit the destroyed functioning to a greater or lesser extent, depending on the degree to which certain mental actions are necessary to meet the demands of a situation.

Most practitioners agree that diagnosed persons should comply with a regime designed to minimize unavoidable impairments in functioning. All behaviors associated with an ADHD diagnosis result in the person being biologically "unable" to meet age-related expectations. Diagnosed persons may be unable to suppress emotions or comments, and they may be impulsive spenders (Barkley, 1998b). When there is difficulty with self-sufficiency and self-help behaviors, such problems are also interpreted as consequences of this neurobiological limitation (Barkley, 2000).

Conventional ADHD specialists generally believe that an analysis of one's psychosocial history will not likely result in identifying the parameters which lead to significant behavioral change. Altering diagnostic patterns through talk therapy is viewed as an unsuitable endeavor as well. Meaningful treatment is recommended to proceed with the understanding that the primary problem is a biologically caused developmental delay. The lauded traditionalist approach seems intent on dispelling the age-old view that childhood behavioral problems are a result of upbringing.

For traditionalists, parental behavior or other environmental factors may only exacerbate the severity of ADHD behaviors, reduce the probability for remission, stop or allow for an ADHD reaction at a point of performance, and/or increase the likelihood of various secondary problems (Biederman et al., 1996; Weiss and Hechtman, 1993; Barkley, 2000). Currently this is the most acceptable way to understand and solve the problems that many ADHD diagnosed persons show when attempting to complete various laboratory tasks, and when responding to requirements of parents, teachers, and peers. Individuals with competent inhibitory systems can escape the helplessness that occurs when powerful responses dominate behavior, while those with ADHD are less able to resist. To avoid an ADHD diagnosis, it is necessary for the person to block the response that might produce immediate satisfaction, and then wait for mental actions to identify content which subsequently leads to preferential or correct responses.

Rather than respond impulsively, individuals with normal inhibitory systems are able to continue to integrate a wider range of parameters before selecting the response to outwardly enact. Only by operating in this fashion, can individuals organize behavior over extended time frames, benefit from the past, solve complex problems, and maintain persistence without distraction (particularly when activities become increasingly burdensome). While their behavior might seem tactless or irresponsible, this is considered to be an inaccurate interpretation; it is more correct to infer that they are less able to delay their responses long enough to be cognizant of the effect of their actions. These individuals become victims of their limitations, and loved ones should be aware of this when disciplining.

Concerns, Inconsistencies, and Resistance

When questioning the traditional understanding, even if it were the case that most diagnosed persons do more poorly than others when engaged in non-motor preparatory activity immediately prior to encountering a problem situation, accounting for their failure to do those posited actions is still a matter of interpretation. A learning paradigm might still be tenable. We suggest that many diagnosed persons have been conditioned to give up, complain, overreact, and rely on others to relieve, and respond without any preparatory activity when encountering different and complex situations or difficulties. Neurological delay need not be invoked to account for their failure to function in a prescribed fashion.

Barkley (2006, 81) claims that "poor effortful regulation and inhibition of behavior, in fact the hallmark of this disorder, is so substantial that it can be considered a fact." However, the counter claim is that it is only factual in that many people assert the view in order to account for diagnostic patterns. Widespread acceptance does not make the explanatory construct of behavioral disinhibition a "fact." One might just as reasonably assert that diagnosed persons have become conditioned to do ADHD responding in some circumstances. For activities requiring precursor mental responding, one can argue that diagnosed persons have not yet learned to respond in that way, or that they have perhaps learned ADHD patterns instead.

Despite alternative possibilities, diagnosed persons are invariably encouraged to believe that they have an incurably delayed body, and are typically indoctrinated into that neurobiological account. They are told that their root problem is medical, and that they possess a bodily hindrance. This way of conceptualizing their actions essentially shifts the locus of accountability from what they do, to a delayed inhibitory (inherited) mechanism. ADHD becomes something they possess rather than a set of learned behaviors.

Traditionalists espouse the view that ADHD is caused by a predetermined neural biology that the problem occurs prior to birth, and for all intents and purposes, is immutable to environmental influences. Given the entrenchment of that perspective, many or most professionals, diagnosed individuals, and their loved ones are likely to react suspiciously to any attempts to undermine the traditional model. Proponents of the traditional model may fear that interest in a psychosocial account will trigger knee-jerk reaction in the media about over diagnosis and over medication of children. They worry that a learning model might increase skepticism regarding the care of ADHD diagnosed children, and arouse suspicion about who gains financially from traditional treatments. For these reasons, the response to a non-biologically based alternative could very well be unenthusiastic.

Several decades ago, Golden (1984) cautioned that potential harm may occur when individuals use their resources to pursue unproven interventions at the expense of employing strategies that have been systematically and empirically studied. Shaywitz and Shaywitz (1991) have also asserted that public concern about the overuse of medication to treat ADHD is unfounded. These claims have served to encourage those involved with the theory and practice of treating ADHD to proceed tentatively when encountering new perspectives.

We therefore understand how exceedingly difficult it is to alter belief systems after a particular paradigm has been accepted within public and professional communities. The medical community apparently endorses the biological determinist position regarding ADHD; therefore, the information communicated to the general public mirrors this view. Many parents will easily agree when a physician (an authority figure) recommends medication and stringent control over the diagnosed person. Rather than question potential adverse effects, and inquire into other possible ways to address problem behaviors, many parents defer to experts.

However, there are exceptions; we know that some parents disagree to a medication regimen recommended by school personnel and thus encounter strong disapproval. Parents are instead urged to accept that their child is neural biologically *delayed*. By not ascribing to medicinal treatment and contingency management, parents are implicitly categorized as betrayers, as resistant, and negligent. This problem has occurred so often that laws have now been passed to restrict school personnel from recommending psychiatric medications; it is also illegal for school personnel to ban students who decide not to take medication (Whitaker, 2005).

Individuals under social pressure to quickly alter their behavior, or those who risk social consequences such as losing a job, repeating a grade, or succumbing to a divorce might, however, think it is imperative that they take medication and submit to other traditional treatment. For these individuals, it may provoke too much anxiety to endure incremental changes that could eventually benefit them over the course of a time-consuming psychotherapeutic intervention. Following the traditional recommendations becomes a greater necessity under tight time constraints or obvious disapproval from loved ones.

There are a number of ways that diagnosed persons can be persuaded to adopt traditional views upon learning that they meet diagnostic criteria. Practitioners who incorporate biological causation in their explanations of psychological events may be regarded as more scientific than those endorsing other perspectives. When diagnosed persons hear that something inherent to their bodies limits their possibilities for success, framing the problem in this way often means that a psychologically-based intervention cannot adequately deal with existing concerns.

Under these circumstances the possibility of improvement without medication will likely be less attractive to those who suspect that psychosocial intervention is off the mark. Individuals may therefore be unwilling to participate in non-medically based treatment. Many people are susceptible to suggestion, so if a medical professional urges that drugs are needed to treat ADHD, the desire to trust can potentially overrule and avert discussion away from possible alternative treatments. If an individual has been having problems for a long time, he or she may be very receptive to a medication regime that quickly and radically changes long-standing failures.

The underlying issue here is that when a particular view becomes so widely endorsed, attempts to characterize and understand behavior from a different perspective will often be dismissed as uninformed or naive; this is evident when traditionalists recommend that parents show greater assertiveness when they encounter a teacher who does not agree with the traditional view. If this occurs, parents are urged to pressure administrators and place their child in a different class (Pfiffner and Barkley, 1998).

Mainstream understanding of ADHD is embedded to the degree that those who disagree are characterized as wrong-headed and are accused of being ignorant to the "evidence." The model is so widely accepted that only a small minority of people currently question this approach. Blaming parents and teachers, which is seen by critics as ineffective or harmful (Conrad, 1975; Schrag and Divoky, 1975) is not, according to Barkley (1998a), corroborated by empirical investigation. The apparent lack of empirical support for environmental determinism reinforces the notion that ADHD is a medical phenomenon, not a socially derived behavior. Since a wide range of psychotherapeutic interventions have not led to positive treatment results—compared to techniques that specifically alter biology and stringently control persons—traditional belief is fast becoming codified as the only scientific perspective.

Practitioners who do not utilize traditional protocol are also thought to be exceptionally naïve. They are presumed to be depriving diagnosed persons of proper care, or else they use interventions that border on malpractice (Barkley, 2001). If diagnosed individuals or their loved ones disagree with the *disability* formulation, they are also assumed by treating professionals to be in denial.

The category system of the accepted paradigm is regarded as the exclusive way to make sense of the obvious. For example, when adolescents are brought for treatment, clinicians are urged to correct the myths and false beliefs that one often hears about ADHD. Professionals are encouraged to show pictures of positron emission tomography (PET) scans from the Zametkin classic study (i.e., Zametkin et al., 1990), which demonstrate brain functioning differences between diagnosed individuals and controls during continuous performance tasks (Robin, 2006). The rationale is that the individual should realize that he or she has a neurological problem (i.e., much like needing glasses), and thus accept traditional treatments.

Most research currently designed to study ADHD seems to be conducted from the perspective of what I have referred to as the *traditional* understanding, a belief system with the primary and fundamental premise that neurology is the determinate antecedent of the behavioral pattern that evolves. This paradigm forms the present basis of how we treat and understand the behaviors subsumed under ADHD.

While one would hope that diagnosed individuals are educated about their disability, there are no apparent discussions during traditional indoctrinations regarding the failure to replicate Zametkin's findings (Ernst, 1996). Diagnosed persons are also not told that findings might not generalize when subjects engage in other activities, or that neuropsychological tests may not differentiate between expressed behaviors of diagnosed persons and controls, even when such delays are expected (Hervey, Epstein, and Curry, 2004; Frazier, Demaree, and Youngstown, 2004).

We also do not know whether clinicians discuss the problems and limitations of using correlational data to support a casual argument, or if they explain the relative inconsistency of categorizing individuals in group data statistics. Parents and adolescents are also unlikely to be informed about other populations of individuals, such as taxicab drivers in London (BBC, 2000) and musicians, who exhibit differences among individuals and between groups in brain functioning and structure when identical analyses are used to compare non-disabled individuals.

There is also little discussion about the extent of reinforcement of ADHD behaviors in various situations, or how more typical behaviors can be shaped without the use of medication or other compensatory measures that apparently increase one's reliance on the stipulations, efforts, and directions of others. Psychotherapeutic intervention which is *not* based on contingency management techniques is rarely considered. To reiterate, this particular way of thinking about ADHD is so embedded in both the professional and socio/political community that questioning the most basic presumptions occurs infrequently.

We can, nevertheless, observe that scientific endeavor has endured paradigm shifts in the past when new ways of understanding data develop. If alternative interpretations are comprehensive, pragmatic, coherent, parsimonious, and plausible, it is reasonable to give them due consideration. However, during any transition from one paradigm to another, heated debate and resistance are inevitable as proponents of the status quo protect their beliefs. We anticipate the same resistance with those who describe ADHD within a biological deterministic framework. Although it may seem heretical to understand ADHD behaviors as a heterogeneous set of conditioned responses rather than unregulated neurological delay, we proffer this alternative view with the main priority to improve our care and treatment of diagnosed persons.

In order to put forth a tenable alternative orientation, we must also provide a detailed examination of the hypotheses, assertions, assumptions, tacit presumptions, and issues inherent in the traditional perspective. It is also important to contrast the current traditional approach with learned behavior explanations in order to account for the ostensible difficulties attributed to identified ADHD individuals. While this is can be a lengthy process, most of the contentions and disputes about biological determinism might be noted in other diagnostic categories as well. In that sense, the current work may have relevance for researchers interested in other categories of diagnosis.

This current perspective does not attempt to debate the empirical facts within the plethora of ADHD studies carried out over several decades, but instead aims to present a reinterpretation of those findings. With different questions, the same information can lead to very different inferences, conclusions and treatment recommendations. Traditionalists assert, "Show me the data!" when responding to alternative views; however the essential controversy surrounding ADHD is not about the data per se, but rather about the possible ways to interpret data.

In addition to the assertion that identical data may be interpreted differently, it is therefore prudent that we begin to examine some of the non-diagnostic responses of diagnosed individuals *before* being absolutely sure that they possess a coherent biological delay. While many of the examples used in this work to illustrate competent non-diagnostic functioning are anecdotal reports derived from clinical practice, this less reliable data source can be found in traditionalists' reports as well. Moreover, these anecdotal behavioral examples come directly from persons who were rigorously diagnosed from reliable sources, and each diagnosed person was not in a mediated state when demonstrating a particular competency.

Because both traditionalists and skeptics recognize that behavioral patterns of diagnosed individuals are variable, the occurrence of seemingly *competent* responses (anomalies) are a major source of interest and attention for those who oppose a biologically-based disability characterization. In other words, diagnosed persons sometimes behave acceptably and in ways that contradict their assumed functional delay. At times ADHD diagnosed persons are magnanimous, reliable, and diligent such that they are indistinguishable from the control group. While the traditionalists attempt to incorporate apparent inconsistencies into their biological model, the learning approach interprets these exceptional behaviors as evidence in support of a different way to understand ADHD behavior.

For example, children diagnosed with ADHD have been known to cook elaborate meals for their parents. They will set the table in a very detailed fashion, meticulously prepare the food, and anticipate each family member's favorite dish. Similarly, when making up after a conflict, and/or "buttering up" a parent to do a favor, they might complete all their chores without cue or prompt before their parents return home from work. They might be very thorough in cleaning up after themselves, and they might finish their homework prior to the designated time without any intervention whatsoever. While reports indicate that diagnosed children do have trouble completing some of these behaviors, it is nevertheless likely that these same children will show significantly fewer ADHD responses if instead more accommodating and considerate actions will increase the probability that their parents will conform to their requests.

One might also ask how the alleged "constricted working memory" of a diagnosed child might fluctuate such that he *remembers* to remind his mother that the dentist recommended that she brush the child's teeth, but he *forgets* that his teacher instructed him to do his homework on his own. Similarly, it is intriguing that many diagnosed persons remember to keep plans made with friends on the Internet the day before, while consistently forgetting appointments scheduled by others. When these discrepancies are observed, is it that actions differ in their requirements for self-control, or are certain behaviors conditioned in particular ways in relation to particular reinforcement histories?

When characterizing diagnosed persons as medically delayed, it is unclear as to which mechanism allows them to follow directions when assembling a toy, yet be too impaired to follow directions for many school assignments. It is puzzling that it is somehow more difficult (in a biological sense) to remember details pertaining to characters in a collection or a television program, compared to remembering details and information required to achieve in history class.

However, for diagnosed teens who frequently initiate activities pertaining to history (e.g., they watch the History Channel), it is not at all unusual to observe them showing extensive working memory for certain historical periods, battles, aircraft, etc. Similarly, it is not unusual that diagnosed adolescents read for pleasure (e.g., Stephen King novels) without showing *diagnostic responding*, and yet we hear these same individuals complaining about their inability to concentrate when undertaking assigned readings for school (i.e., reaching the end of a page and not knowing what was read).

Very often we observe that when engaged in non-coerced achievements, the procrastination often evident when faced with school work is non-existent. Frequently parents complain that they have difficulty getting them to stop, and at times, it may become necessary for parents to impose rules to quell *intense* interest. If these kinds of activities were to be more socially valued, it would be very difficult to convince people that someone with presumed ADHD had less ability to function over a broad time horizon. Persistence might then be considered as an asset. For example, diagnosed teens might read feverishly about mythical wars and become quite conversant with that material even though they only rarely master facts and details pertaining to an actual war being taught at school.

There are instances when diagnosed persons exhibit deft future management as well. For example, one diagnosed child quickly recognized that his parents would probably not allow him to change schools if he demonstrated that he could function adequately in his current school. He correctly predicted that his parents would not want to "rock the boat" if success were to occur. Similarly, another diagnosed child manipulated his mother to agree to his demand for a new toy, in that he accurately predicted that if he threatened to not attend his after school program, she would be less able to enjoy visiting with her afternoon guest. In another scenario, when reacting to requirements imposed by others, even putting dishes away becomes a crisis for many diagnosed persons, and their pleas of "not knowing how," will be uttered.

Similarly, in another situation where presumed inability is used as an excuse, a diagnosed adolescent tried to convince his brother that he was not able to keep pace with material presented in the classroom because of his ADHD. He felt he should be compensated because of his functional delay, and he was effective in persuading his brother during the ensuing heated banter that he was indeed deficient. However, he failed to recognize that he would not have been able to keep pace with his brother's counter arguments if he actually had the functional limitation he claimed to have.

If we consider the prevailing traditionalist biological determinist view, we must ask what kind of neurological delay enables a person to remember orally-presented codes for a video game in a noisy room, but disables that same person when reciting digits on an intelligence test. What kind of delay disrupts remembering a teacher's imposed rules, but permits one to remember rules to games and hobbies? What kind of delay permits the detailed quoting of a parent or spouse when establishing a point of view (even if these interactions occurred days before), but prevents the recall of a promise to complete a chore? What kind of delay enables a diagnosed teen to accurately draw a war helmet seen earlier in the day at school, and recall information about the soldiers and wars associated with the helmet, but not remember the details of a homework assignment written on the board? And finally, what kind of neurological delay accounts for the unwavering persistence to complete an activity despite being called for dinner?

Parents often complain how difficult it is to distract their diagnosed child when he or she is involved in an activity associated with success and discretionary authority. Contrary to the traditionalist claim, instances of sustained concentration apparently occur even when doing mental actions to solve particular problems, as for example, when they calculate the amount of money owed to them by their parents. However, if it is the case that diagnosed persons are at times resistant to distraction (rather than driven towards it), it is disingenuous to assert that they are less able to resist the urge to escape during executive functioning.

However, as noted, most conceptualizations of ADHD have thus far been variations on the traditional model. It is widely accepted that the condition is a biological disability and must be treated by introducing compensatory remediation. For example, some practitioners have recommended the use of magnets, natural foods, herbal remedies, special diets, and have introduced techniques to help diagnosed persons alter their EEG brain patterning. Even practitioners who oppose the use of prescription medication have recommended compensatory psychological treatments to offset less capable functioning. The prevailing view is that most practitioners regard an ADHD diagnosis as representative of a deficit, disruption, defect, or delay that can only be treated by adding something to that which is missing.

Meanwhile, at the opposite end of the spectrum, there have been attempts to ascribe all behavioral variability to environmental parameters, and to disregard biology altogether. For example, some practitioners focus on attributing the problems to particular child rearing styles, cultural demands, and media influence. These perspectives are usually espoused without the necessary corroborating empirical work to demonstrate the contribution of these singular environmental categories on those who may be eventually diagnosed as ADHD. Ultimately, traditionalists have found these explications fairly easy to dismiss. Moreover, other formulations have been denigrated by counter-claims that alternative efforts are promoting a particular cause, or attempting to induce monetary gain by "scamming" unsuspecting consumers (Barkley, 2000).

In so far as the basic tenets of the traditional model are considered as immutable truths by many in the field, and a cottage industry has emerged, any studies that could bring the dominant model into question are usually overlooked or not taken seriously. A tenacious hold on the traditional paradigm is the norm within professional and lay communities. The treatment approach and medical explanations are buttressed by an interested economic community (e.g., pharmaceutical companies, contingency management devices, etc.). Change or renunciation of the traditional model is exceedingly problematic with so much at stake (Timimi, 2004).

However, various inconsistencies in the traditional model, as we will observe, are apparent enough to warrant fresh questions and different approaches to ADHD. For now, investigations that could be designed to explore inconsistencies, contradictions, and limitations of the accepted explanation model are not introduced as frequently (or conscientiously) as those that more likely produce data consistent with the traditional perspective. Curiously, dogmatic adherence to a set of medical assumptions (even when confronted with contrary empirical data), also introduces the problem of what types and how much empirical data will be persuasive enough to shift entrenched assumptions in order to better serve individuals with behavioral problems. Proponents of an inherent disability model seem more likely to offer extenuating circumstances as the explanation for data that do not fit neatly into the posited hypotheses.

For instance, if a problematic response does not occur, one may argue that the assessment item did not tap into the existing underlying disability. This interpretive tactic is evident when conducting an experiment on impulsivity; analysts speculate that taking extra time to study a picture before selecting the identical picture from a group of pictures is a different sort of impulsivity from the type assessed when a child is asked to draw a line slowly. The child's ADHD may represent a more *specific* underlying form of an inhibitory problem (Barkley, 1998b). Rather than interpret variations in competency on various tasks as contrary to the disability model, it is asserted that some diagnosed persons may have only *particular* kinds of delays in self control. The continual mitigation of circumstances permits the retention of the conceptual framework.

Similarly, in another ongoing attempt to preserve the disability model, traditionalists also argue that it is the nature of ADHD to show greater variability of competency and performance across contexts and settings (Barkley, 2006e). Given that traditional interpretation, it becomes possible to interpret *all* exceptions to neurological predication by incorporating them into the disorder; in other words, biological determinism cannot be refuted. Attributing the non-occurrence of diagnosed responding to the nature of the disorder only makes inconsistencies *inexplicable*, rather than stir doubts regarding the veracity of the biological determinism model.

Moreover, the shift to a new understanding of a problem is also difficult, in that proponents of biological determinism may not always interpret the accumulated data fairly. Biases are inevitable, depending on whether findings are consistent with the paradigm or if they diverge from the accepted belief system. For example, when findings are in conflict with the traditional view, it can be argued that criteria for diagnosis is not rigorous enough (i.e., DSM-IV-TR criteria), or that the study has a too-small sample size and low statistical power. However, criticism seems to occur less often when evidence supports the traditional paradigm.

If we presume a skeptical standpoint, it also becomes increasingly unclear how we decide whether or not an executive act took place in a person diagnosed with ADHD. For example, how would anyone know whether an individual was reactivating and prolonging past sensory events during a response delay (Barkley, 1998g)? We would have to infer that non-observable mental actions occur from the kinds of observable behaviors that are emitted, as well as rely on self-reports of diagnosed persons (including measurements of brain activity correlated with those reports). However, since diagnosed person are allegedly not keenly self-aware, that data may be unreliable.

Moreover, even if it were determined that a diagnosed person did not enact a particular response at a particular time, on what basis could it be claimed that it was due to an inability to inhibit? Might it still be tenable to assert that the person had not *yet* learned to respond in that particular way in that particular situation? On what grounds has it become established that neurological disinhibition has accounted for that failure, or that the non-responding individual was "less able?" Perhaps the individual was simply reinforced to respond differently, and could learn the required mental actions as well as others do—by altering contingencies of reinforcement in systematic ways.

Additional problems arise when contradictory non-diagnostic responses are rationalized by asserting that some content, situations, and conditions can "offset" the occurrence of the neurologically-based symptoms. These offsetting parameters include interest, saliency, external representation, and immediacy of reinforcement. These categories are not seen as indicative of psychosocial parameters, or related to the history a person brings to a situation (i.e., interest) in order to account for *what happens.* Quite to the contrary: those offsetting parameters are regarded as compensating for a condition that remains present but is not expressed. Despite whether the frequency and severity of ADHD behaviors occur in ways consistent with other kinds of explications, the behaviors are always presumed to occur because of a particular non-normative biology.

This form of explanation is apparent in the case example "Vanessa" (Hathaway, Dooling-Litfin, and Edwards, 1998). In this illustration, it is noteworthy that ADHD attention problems are likely to change, depending on the extent to which a task is *interesting.* These authors claim that clinicians can differentiate ADHD from other complications because diagnosed persons might perform better when they are interested. Once again, biological determinism is maintained. If the person does not show ADHD behavior in ways consistent with presumptions, it is only because other factors (e.g., interest) can temporarily hold the determinate delay in abeyance. The person's interest is recognized as a compensating parameter that makes environmental parameters more salient, more meaningful, and more immediately reinforcing.

In our current state of affairs, a disability model may be retained whether or not a diagnosed person outperforms his or her posited disability. Once qualifying for diagnosis, the presumption is that a neurological delay exists whether or not problematic behaviors are evident or consistent. The posited delay is always present and ready to emerge whenever mitigating circumstances do not provide the diagnosed person with something that is lacking, or when interests are not temporarily counteracting that delay. ADHD then becomes a very strange biological problem that can seemingly vanish in certain situations or states of response. Those who possess this biological problem may transcend their bodily limitations as long as they are fascinated by events taking place.

However, when we say that a person has a particular interest in an activity when doing an activity frequently and intently without coercion, and that individuals show greater mastery of material when they often engage in activities, traditionalists will essentially discount obvious non-coerced achievements within the diagnostic population. This point is critical, as an ADHD diagnosis would then be reduced to doing non-conforming, less acceptable, immature responses when cumbersome expectations exist or requirements are imposed by others.

If interest can offset ADHD problems, and all activities competently completed by diagnosed persons are deemed (even on a post hoc basis) compensatory due to interest, one may always assert that the individual is delayed even when functioning relatively well. Since traditionalists claim that the inhibitory system is less taxed under conditions of interest, this argument (as those previously mentioned) permits us to discard non-confirming behavioral events. Each non-diagnostic response might be explained as an instance of extenuating circumstances, and beliefs that posit disability may be maintained, regardless of seemingly contradictory behaviors.

The traditional account is apparently equivalent to saying that if diagnosed persons perform well, it is because their inhibitory system is bolstered by a compensatory event. If they perform poorly, they have an inherent *delay* of that system. When it is acceptable to discount non-diagnostic functioning whenever the diagnosed person seems interested, adequately responsive to conditions (i.e., saliency), or persisting without extra enticements (i.e., the activity must be providing immediate reinforcement), it becomes impossible to posit behavior to contradict that view. Any competent functioning can be explained away by referencing any one of the mitigating possibilities.

If diagnosed individuals show adequate functioning during the play of video games (e.g., they stop the characters, jump at the correct times, etc.), researchers can claim that these tasks do not exceed their ability to self-control (i.e., the tasks provide reinforcement and are externally represented). Even though their tantrums during these games invariably occur because of their inhibitory problems, their own interests may at any time temporarily offset their developmental delay when competency is exhibited.

Within this seemingly convoluted, tautological, and circular explication, activities such as chores and schoolwork (assigned by others and which correlate with ADHD) become the proving ground for the formulation. It may be asserted that imposed activities require the most from the inhibitory system. However, when putting forward that account, traditionalists would also be required to explain why adequate task performance requires less executive behavior (and inhibition) simply because another person does not expect that achievement. That is, the task may require a great deal of competency and management of future contingencies to adequately perform, and yet the diagnosed person will still be managing competently on his or her own.

When belief systems are protected in the aforementioned ways, it then seems possible to identify an environmental variable or the person's *interest* that either exacerbates or compensates for the posited disability. Symptom variations and inconsistency of competency may occur because it is the nature of the ADHD disorder to produce erratic functioning. Environments may sometimes compensate for inner neurobiological delay by providing stimuli that prevent delayed functioning from becoming obvious. Sometimes symptoms and delays in functioning will lie dormant, in that some conditions negate the necessity of having to inhibit and utilize executive functioning to control behavior, and at other times diagnosed people may be inordinately enthusiastic, which can also rectify responses.

For example, some diagnosed children's clinic behavior may be unrelated to the reports that the child's parents provide to the clinician, although diagnostic responding in the clinic usually means that those responses occur in the school setting as well (Shelton et al., 1998). For traditionalists, one can qualify for diagnosis, and enact diagnostic or non-diagnostic patterns of behavior in school, the clinic, and at home in myriad ways, and still be deemed as having the same underlying problem as everyone in the group, even though others might show very different patterns of behavior in the various settings.

It is, however, incongruous for proponents of a learning paradigm to accept that, within a disability model, diagnosed individuals may show functioning presumed to be delayed as long as one can somehow infer that the latent disability is receiving compensation. It becomes unclear as to what disability or biological delay these individuals possess (other than poor functioning) when required to undertake actions deemed (sometimes post hoc) less interesting. Rather than have motivational deficits caused by delayed biology, *the alternative learning model* suggests that diagnosed persons are more likely to have been *conditioned* to express ADHD-like behaviors when they do not initiate and enjoy particular events.

As Skinner emphasized (1953, 72), "one who readily engages in a given activity is not showing an interest; he is showing the effect of environment." A diagnosed person is not interested first, then second able to function in a certain way; he or she is sometimes conditioned to respond in a more participatory fashion, and then able to repeat those behaviors henceforth without coercion. When traditionalists claim that an individual's interests will offset the ADHD, they are simply stating that if a person is conditioned to readily engage in a particular activity that person will rarely express ADHD.

Likewise, it is not that some activities offer less immediate reinforcement than others, but, depending on one's learning history, some contexts and situations will be characterized as negative, uncomfortable, boring, etc.; ADHD responses are more likely to be expressed and reinforced during those times. However, it does not logically follow that these same individuals cannot respond with increased consideration for others, greater self-reliance, less antagonism, and more participatory behavior in other situations and circumstances, or that they cannot learn to behave differently over time.

When *non-diagnosed ADHD persons* show no *interest* in response to a game, schoolwork, or crafts for example, little time must pass before they report tedium, boredom, frustration, and irritation while engaged in such activities. Many of us will show less participatory behavior, an increase in error rates, and problems with pacing our responses when doing those tasks. If we perceive behavior from this perspective, "put ourselves in the ADHD shoes" as it were, we notice that it is not that some activities provide more external representation or immediate reinforcement than others; but rather that diagnosed persons (like the rest of us) are conditioned to respond differently in different circumstances. Whether their ongoing patterns are socially acceptable or not depends on conditioning (not biological limitation) if we assume that ADHD responding is their only problem.

Barkley notes that "there is no ADHD while playing Nintendo" because of the "rapid, ever-compelling, visually complex nature of the video game, and its constant rewards to sufficiently engage the child to rivet attention" (Hallowell and Ratey, 1995, 280). This current learning view focuses instead on the learning of more competent functioning with particular tasks and activities. Rather than claim that certain situations compensate for ADHD motivational delays by providing contingencies to keep the child goal-directed and less dependent on kindling motivation through self-direction (Barkley, 2006f), we argue that individuals are conditioned to behave in particular ways when encountering certain contexts and circumstances.

The view espoused here is that it is unreasonable to assert that a person has a biological delay simply because one has learned to express ADHD behavior more often than most others in response to conditions that less often cue those reactions within the general population. For example, how many parents of diagnosed children show ADHD responding when their child is chattering away or inundating them with information about the latest card collecting craze? How many adults express ADHD patterns when playing video games with their child? How many find the subject matter that engrosses diagnosed persons to be extremely boring or tedious, and thus routinely exhibit severe ADHD responses at those times?

Rather than claim that some people depend more on reinforcement that emanates from an activity, reinforcement really refers to how a person responds to an activity. Those reactions may or may not coincide with what is considered to be inherent in the task. Although video games are designed to appeal to a mass audience, not everyone is keen to play or initiate playing all the time. Positive reactions may occur only for limited periods of involvement, and attitudes (even thoroughly negative responses), may possibly be emitted thereafter by that same person.

Since many diagnosed persons are apparently solving relatively complex problems, and are functioning acceptably when involved in activities they initiate and enjoy, and sometimes they behave in ways that are consistent with a wider time horizon, an ADHD diagnosis starts to lose its coherence. Competent behaviors, which only rarely occur while completing assigned tasks (science fair projects), may be largely evident such that diagnosed persons are seen to function in ways that are indistinguishable from controls. For example, what is inherently more reinforcing (or externally provided) when learning about professional wrestling statistics, or when reading through a video game study guide? Yet many diagnosed persons fulfill those acts competently.

Similarly, there are apparently many diagnosed persons who learn everything they can about baseball, model cars, story lines and details about science fiction films, comic books, or various athletes. Some show an ability to remember song lyrics, and others can recite impressive statistics about sports figures. Some engage in activity associated with these activities, including solving mathematics problems, acquiring materials relative to hobbies, and making schedules—in order to participate more often in preferred activities.

Rarely would anyone suspect ADHD diagnosis while observing these individuals involved in actions related to a hobby, even though hobbies often require the type of planning, working memory, persistence, and organization also necessary for academic achievement. However, it would seem that if one has limited access to one's working memory due to inhibitory problems as traditionalists assert, it follows that this problem should *always* occur—whether or not one is remembering school work or some other material. Even if it is confirmed that the inhibitory system corrects itself during periods of interest (or arousal), ADHD would then be assigned to an inherited disorder which causes a person to be galvanized by highly personalized content. It is therefore unreasonable to claim that diagnosed persons are biologically delayed when they do *not* respond typically with all other tasks and activities, because myriad factors in their histories can influence how they achieve and react to the requirements they encounter.

If a diagnosed person functions in non-diagnostic ways in some situations and exceeds posited limitations when they are interested, it is difficult to accept the assertion that biology is the limiting parameter that thwarts the expression of particular behaviors. What other developmental delay allows one to transcend posited limitations in functioning in relation to interest, once that posited limitation has been delineated, and rehabilitation has not yet taken place? It would therefore seem that if someone has a biological limitation in working memory or interference control, then that person would be unable to show competency in that specific function (e.g., if one is color blind, one is always color blind).

However, Barkley (2001) asserts that some activities do not tax the inherent delays of the diagnosed person, that diagnosed persons will only have difficulty maintaining symptom-free behavior when they must rely on internal representations and delays in offered reinforcements. Symptoms will sometimes not be evident because some activities are relatively simple, or they provide immediate reinforcement (Barkley, 2006f). Task completion at those times requires little executive functioning.

As task complexity increases, and when more planning, organization, and mental preparatory activity is required, the more diagnosed individuals will differ from others (Douglas, 1983; Luk, 1985). Here is where the traditionalists find no contradiction in the relatively normative functioning often apparent when diagnosed persons are engaged in self-initiated actions; those accomplishments purportedly require less mental effort.

Traditionalists contend that when individuals play games or watch television, they need not be self conscious, nor is it necessary that they motivate themselves. The presumption is that most forms of self-initiated play will *not* elicit ADHD delays because the activities can be performed with ease, or they are very interesting. Similar to a mentally deficient individual doing a non-challenging task, or a crippled individual treading water in a pool, no one suspects a limitation unless task difficulty exceeds a defined deficiency.

In this fashion, traditionalists maintain that symptoms do not *always* occur because some environmental situations provide adequate external compensation for delayed individuals to function normally. Under those conditions it might not be possible to identify differences among individuals, since compensatory support is provided: solitary play, washing and bathing, and father at home, for example, are conditions less likely to provoke diagnostic responding.

Conversely, when diagnosed children have to complete chores, when their parents are busy with phone calls or guests, or when functioning takes place in public places; ADHD responses are more likely to occur. Diagnosed children tend to deviate whenever demands exceed their capacity to maintain attention, restrain impulses, delay gratification, endure waiting, or whenever planning for the future is required (Barkley, 2000; Barkley, 1998b; Anastopoulos, Rhoads, and Farley, 2006). For traditionalists, it is not that diagnosed children show ADHD responding when in public because there is an audience and their parents are more limited in the discipline that might be imposed, or that the child must follow the parent's agenda, or that the child is unhappy about parental involvement elsewhere. Due to inhibitory delays, the diagnosed child is presumed to be less aware of future consequences of actions, which allegedly gives rise to the more delayed behaviors in public places. As noted, symptom occurrence is always presumed to depend on whether or not situational demands exceed the capacity of the individual to maintain self-control (which seems to reduce to the posited amount of inhibition and executive functioning necessary to meet situational requirements).

Empirical data which measures the relationship between amount of inhibition required and diagnostic responding in particular situations is, however, not currently available. Practitioners of the status quo simply assert that circumstances differ based on the demands placed on the inhibitory system. This view is maintained without providing a single measurement of anyone's inhibitory capacity apart from their expression of ADHD, and without any independent measurements pertaining to the level of inhibitory stress in a particular environment.

Despite apparent shortcomings, traditionalists believe that continuous fluctuations in environmental demands relate to the amount of inhibition and executive function required to aid in performance. Questions about the veracity of the disability model do not arise when variations take place. Traditionalists seem unconcerned that sometimes diagnosed persons behave exactly like everyone else; but instead believe that events are at times so salient, externally represented, interesting, and immediately reinforcing that motivational delays become irrelevant and executive behavior is unnecessary; only for those reasons do diagnosed persons appear normal some of the time.

Given the aforementioned conditions, diagnosed persons are able to function adequately even without stimulants or external management (although stimulants may also enhance non-assigned performance). While diagnosed persons might report enjoying non-assigned activity without external management, they typically report enjoying managed rewards and avoiding managed punishments whenever they are added to induce participation during traditional interventions.

Environmental parameters such as individualized attention, mothers vs. fathers, immediate vs. delayed feedback, early in the day vs. late in the day, etc., are comparable to prescription drugs in that they ease expression of the posited underlying biological problem. Invariably, it is held that these conditions reduce the load placed on the inhibitory system; they are compensatory parameters which allow reinforcements for behavior to be instantaneous. They diminish the motivation requirement necessary to fulfill a task, or facilitate the neurological system towards functioning without becoming depleted later in the day. By offering an external and immediate feedback loop, a diagnosed person has a greater chance of functioning as others do. This arrangement will more frequently offset the poorly developed inhibitory and executive systems that are less able to help the diagnosed person see the benefit of engaging in activity organized around future outcomes. The traditional remedies help merely to stimulate interest.

Traditionalists' assertion of a common underlying disability persists, despite that diagnosed persons show highly discrepant patterns of behaviors, qualify for diagnosis at various points in childhood, and fail to demonstrate consistent problems on psychological tests specifically designed to cull their posited functional delays. Those claims continue despite the absence of behavioral markers, or biological tests that could produce accurate hit rates in order to clinically diagnose individuals (Barkley, 2000; Gordon and Barkley, 1998). In other words, no one has yet identified a functional delay that aligns itself with the behavioral criteria in a sufficiently consistent way, even when studying diagnosed persons during assigned tasks.

Traditionalists therefore emphasize that diagnosis should not be based on any psychological or biological test. The use of neuropsychological tests is an ongoing problem that often results in classifying children as not having ADHD when in fact they qualify for the behavioral criteria (i.e., false negatives) (Gordon and Barkley, 1998). While this type of test can accurately categorize individuals as ADHD when low scores are achieved, many individuals qualifying for the behavioral criteria still function quite adequately on any of the currently developed competency tests.

There is relative agreement that categorizing individuals based on merely one method of data collection (i.e., including molecular biology and executive functioning), is likely to lead to highly unreliable results. For example, while Weyandt (2005) reports that problems with executive functioning may occur within the diagnosed population, similar problems with executive functioning are found in other diagnostic groups as well. This type of functional problem is not unique to ADHD.

The disorder is proclaimed to be "too heterogeneous" for any one measurement "to function as a 'litmus test' or 'gold standard'" (Gordon, Barkley, and Lovett, 2006), although it is meanwhile asserted that diagnosed persons possess a singular inhibitory problem. The view of a coherent functional delay is upheld, despite that up to 50% of diagnosed individuals can function competently on many kinds of neuropsychological tests, including those specifically constructed to assess executive functioning and goal persistence (Barkley, 1998g). Interestingly, simply assessing a child's behavior during a testing session seems to show greater diagnostic power than the tests designed to cull particular functional deficits (Gordon, Barkley, and Lovett, 2006). In our current state of affairs the assessment and identification of ADHD relies on integrating data from a variety of less-than-perfect sources (Gordon et al., 2006).

Despite the observation that there exist no biological characteristics or test findings reliable enough for diagnostic purposes (as with other psychiatric disorders), traditionalists claim that, given more sophisticated ways to assess, and by fine tuning diagnostic criteria, current limitations will be rectified. Rather than question the biological account or the view that diagnostic behaviors are caused by a particular kind of underlying biogenetic delay, it is widely held that the inadequacies of the medical model can be ascribed to deficiencies in how we categorize, including the need to find more specific genetic codes, and to develop increasingly sensitive biological and neuropsychological tests.

While the traditional perspective satisfies many, the curious fact remains that approximately half of the diagnosed population may function adequately, even when responding to tests assessing executive behaviors. It seems reasonable to ask why diagnosed persons—with allegedly less ability to provide the responses that these tests are designed to measure—can function so competently. Why isn't there a better one-to-one correspondence between these tests and ADHD diagnosis, as with sugar levels and diabetes (an analogous disorder)?

A Different Path

We are presently labeling individuals as having a particular neurological limitation when their problem is very likely that they have *learned* to do intrusive, non-normatively paced, and inadequate participation that has arisen from haranguing and excessive directing, emotional upheaval, negative insinuations, demeaning treatment, disapproval, dismissal, or social exclusion. If that is the case, how does behavioral inhibition *differ* from the notion that some people learn to respond to particular kinds of adversity in specific, less acceptable ways: to participate less, respond too quickly or too slowly, to disrupt others, or inordinately rely on others to complete work.

In the light of such scientific inexactitude, a learning perspective could therefore account for the vicissitudes of ADHD patterning during day-to-day living with greater precision than traditional biological determinism, and that particular environmental changes reinforce different behaviors. If diagnosed persons function within situations that cue non-diagnostic reactions, it is reasonable to argue that they have been reinforced to respond in those ways.

It is unnecessary to impose managed contingencies (or any other traditional compensation) in order to increase considerate, self-reliant, normatively paced, and persistent on-task behaviors as long as diagnosed persons have been conditioned to respond non-diagnostically. A manager is less often required to introduce or supply structure, excitement, and coaching in order for adequate achievements to be observed; non-diagnostic functioning has already been reinforced. Tasks are more likely to be completed without simplifying them by providing external representations, in that diagnosed persons have learned to function very differently when circumstances are less disapproving, less exclusive, restrictive, or associated with failure.

While procedures such as explicitly directing the actions of the diagnosed person, contingency management, and medication may help increase participation and more measured responses when those behaviors have not been conditioned with particular activities, again, rather than insist that these behaviors compensate for inner delays, one could claim that these interventions are changing conditions in ways that evoke different reinforced responses. Giving stimulants, making tasks easier, offering rewards, and threatening punishment essentially changes the context and circumstances so that more acceptable behaviors are likely to be emitted.

Despite more acceptable behaviors being emitted, these behavioral changes seem no different from what happens when many of us are exposed to traditional training techniques and "state" altering stimulant medications. For example, this kind of performance enhancement was evident when methylphenidate was given to military personnel or professional athletes. Individuals generally behave compliantly, eagerly, and productively when their worlds or bodies are manipulated in highly specific ways, and many of us revert to previous functioning when those specific social and pharmacological treatments are withdrawn.

In other words, it does not seem that traditional intervention differentiates something unique about diagnosed persons compared to those without an ADHD diagnosis. It is baffling as to why it is necessary to posit neurological delay when performance improves with traditional remedies. It seems that many people function better when environmental parameters are made more discernable, when attention states are altered with amphetamines, when people are enticed with rewards, when tasks are made easier, and when people are provided with increased external representation (e.g., reading vs. spelling, doing math with and without a pencil and paper, etc.). Most significantly, if biology were the driving force of ADHD diagnosed persons, why do symptoms seem to vary with changes in context, situation, circumstance and subsequent happenings? Doesn't this indicate that living in the world accounts for the frequency rates that occur, and that particular sequences of events increase or decrease the occurrence of ADHD responding?

There are profound differences between ADHD and other biological problems. For instance, offering a reward or punishment will not shift the behavior trajectory of an epileptic seizure as can occur for ADHD responding. Persons with brain cancer typically do not phase in and out of lucidity based on situation or circumstance as do those diagnosed with ADHD. It seems that biological problems change in direct relation to biological categories (e.g., blood pressure, sugar level), while ADHD problems change in relation to environmental parameters and consequences.

Anecdotally observed variations in functioning for ADHD diagnosed persons also differ markedly from what happens with other pervasive developmental delays such as intellectual deficiency or autism. With the exception of particular instances of *savant* behavior, it seems that persons showing pervasive developmental delays show functional impairment on chores, school assignments, and when playing cards and board games when their impaired competency is required for adequate task completion. Their identified limitations in functioning are more consistent and predictable than that which is usually evident within the ADHD population. They will typically not surpass their denoted and defined limitations in response to a bribe; their deficiencies in functioning remain the same irrespective of who assigns the task or instructs the action. Traditional ADHD remains a peculiar neurological problem without a biological marker, or a consistent limitation that one can ascribe to those qualifying for the behavioral criteria.

Since *consistent* dysfunction is not apparent, it might be more reasonable to explore alternative ways to account for the variability of competency, and entertain the possibility that diagnosed persons' biology may not be encumbering functioning in the presumed ways asserted by the biological determinist account. In that many diagnosed persons can function more calmly, carefully, and attentively at one time or another, adequacy of response seems more related to context, situation, and circumstance rather than locked into inherent biological categories.

While in general no one debates that diagnosed persons do ADHD behavior *on average* more often than others, it is unclear how that statistical assessment translates into *having* an ever-present neurological problem. Even though the disability model implies consistency to the presenting problem, it seems that the delays shown by diagnosed persons fluctuate widely; sometimes they seem to form relatively complex category systems when organizing certain of their personal belongings, although they are also messy and irresponsible with other items. At times they handle objects very carefully, and strive to ensure that particular possessions are not misplaced. At other times even prized expensive possessions are left behind or put in unpredictable places (to their parents' chagrin). They might negotiate a trade that depends on knowing the value of objects, but on other occasions (in an ill-fated attempt to "buy" a friend or provoke a drama), they might exchange an expensive toy for a worthless object. They may remember objects missing from their collections while forgetting undone chores. There may be times when they take impressive precautions to prevent parents from discovering their non-compliance, while at other times, they will engage in risky behavior. They will, however, exhibit reliable and responsible behavior with friends (increased punctuality), or when they remind parents about a trip promised earlier in the week. They may notice that a sibling has touched one of their toys, or recognize that others deny, manipulate, or trick them into a particular action; but not notice that they have not cleaned to their parents' standard.

Given the aforementioned situational irregularities, it is therefore problematic to ascribe a coherent limitation in functioning to ADHD diagnosed persons. The occurrence of non-diagnostic responding is inconsistent with biological determinism, and the discrepancies between ADHD and other organically-based impairments raises significant concerns about traditional views. Moreover, even when some diagnosed persons report more consistent ADHD responding (e.g., forgetting with both friends and authority figures), it might still be reasonable to account for that patterning without invoking a disability model. Let us posit that some diagnosed persons are reinforced (in a more diverse set of conditions) to not keep commitments. Perhaps some diagnosed individuals consistently learn to not accommodate to others; perhaps some are conditioned to placate others more often by telling them what they want to hear, and then learn that nothing terrible happens when they do not follow through. Perhaps some diagnosed persons are conditioned to show less concern for a range of perspectives, or are socially patterned to be less obliging when competing interests arise. We suspect that when people are regularly socialized in any of the aforementioned ways that which is remembered or forgotten, and whether one is punctual or tardy, is likely to be very different when compared to individuals who learn to respond more conscientiously with others.

While we might sometimes observe consistency in diagnostic responding across situations and settings for a subset of diagnosed individuals, it is generally anticipated (within the biases of this learning paradigm) that non-diagnostic functioning will be more frequent when diagnosed persons (without comorbidity) undertake achievements they initiate and enjoy. Instances of persistence, immersion, self-reliance, and thoughtfulness are expected to be more evident when diagnosed persons initiate, as compared to functioning that more often occurs when the same individuals are required to conform to expectations of others. Diagnosed persons will respond non-diagnostically more often when they initiate and do not encounter hindrance or failure. This very prominent situational variability of ADHD symptoms has been noted for decades (Douglas and Peters, 1979; Routh, 1978). Over the years, many parents have asked why their child can concentrate so well on chosen tasks, but cannot on other activities (Barkley, 2000). In this way ADHD deviates from a medical model.

Despite the concerns raised here, diagnostic responding has not yet been thoroughly studied in relation to a derived history of reinforcement. Nor have the behaviors of diagnosed persons been adequately evaluated during assigned and non-assigned responding. Most often, descriptions of diagnosed persons are based on how they have responded to the initiations of others, and the extent to which they meet family and school expectations. In that regard, ADHD responding is simply one of the many different ways that children and adults learn to respond to requirements, stipulations, itineraries, and preferences of others.

When functional weaknesses or attention problems are assessed, those competencies are typically measured as the diagnosed persons function in relegated situations. Given the restricted ways in which diagnosed persons have been evaluated, we could infer that they have attention problems when responding to coercion, assignments, imposed discomfort, and the directives of others. However, it has not been established that diagnosed persons have attention (or inhibitory) problems in a more generalized sense.

Traditionalists do not explore the behaviors that are apparently contrary to their disability model; instead they tend to focus on identifying differences in functioning between groups of diagnosed individuals and controls. Statements about atypical functioning almost without exception are derived from empirical work on the actions of aggregates of diagnosed individuals when instructed to operate in particular ways. Although we acknowledge that diagnostic responding is most frequent when actions pertain to responsibility (Barkley, 2000), and that stimulant medication shows its most significant effects during assigned tasks

(Werry, 1978; DuPaul, Barkley, and Connor, 1998), an underlying neurological delay is nevertheless promoted and asserted by most who study this problem.

It is within this backdrop that the approach described here departs from the biological determinism model when we interpret accumulated ADHD data. We can reasonably incorporate patterns of diagnostic and non-diagnostic responding into a consistent, coherent, and more parsimonious view, assert that symptoms are reinforced only in relation to particular situations and circumstances, and not be quick to posit a disability model until functioning is assessed under more varied conditions (including assigned and non-assigned situations).

Because both anecdotal observation and traditionalists' own reports confirm the notion that quality of performance and symptom expression vary widely in relation to such parameters as discretionary authority and the particular history the person has with the activity, it is increasingly difficult to insist that ADHD behavior (apart from comorbidity problems) is a result of a posited lesser ability. Even staunch traditionalists note that many diagnosed persons show few symptoms when conducting self-selected tasks without external pressure. It is therefore incumbent upon them to account for the extensive symptom variation within the confines of biological determinism. While Lawrence et al. (2002) have observed problematic responses when diagnosed children are required to perform various tasks during a visit to a zoo and when required to play a particular video game, there have been few inquires into the functioning of diagnosed persons during non-assigned tasks *as well as* self-initiated activities that they enjoy.

For example, some diagnosed individuals routinely work out at the gym. Although they forget to do assigned chores that are equally routine, it is unnecessary to intervene in order for them to maintain an exercise regime, or ensure that assigned activity does not interfere with their workout schedule. Their time horizon is broadened because they continue to work for relatively distant future goals, in this case maintenance of a particular body weight and muscle mass.

If these individuals are able to be so self-controlled and organized that they can coordinate this pattern over time and still qualify for behavioral diagnosis, it is unreasonable to argue that a neural biological delay explains their failure to meet such daily responsibilities as completion of homework assignments, missed orthodontist appointments, and forgetting to take out the trash. While Fingerman and Perlmutter (1994) note that time horizons may be lengthened if consequences are salient, in this current alternative vernacular their findings indicate only that people may be reinforced to behave in ways that range across broad spans of time, if subsequent actions (known to markedly influence their behavior), are introduced. But the length of one's time horizon very much depends on one's learning history (presuming that they are intellectually competent).

The problem is not that they are less able to manage time effectively, but rather that they do not manage time as others implore. Since the instances of non-diagnostic functioning mentioned here are inconsistent with traditional disability assertions, it is important to empirically test whether diagnosed persons are actually as limited as traditionalists claim. We can begin to more systematically evaluate their organizational competencies and management of future contingencies when considering both coerced and non-coerced response patterns.

The Problem of Quantifying "Inhibitory" Control

As a way to study this problem, we can first identify parameters that relate to variations in reliability, conformity to scheduling, and complex problem solving. It may help to identify the individual's priorities, values, pre-occupations, and emotional reactions during investigations. After the personal history is integrated with present behavior, we anticipate that it will be easier to predict how the diagnosed person will respond when confronted by difficulties and time-structured scenarios under varying circumstances. For example, it would be interesting to know if diagnosed children are as likely to miss an appointment with a peer who will lend them a toy, compared to what might occur when they make an appointment with the same individual to return the toy. If different patterns emerge, it does not seem that a neurological explanation can account for the variations of time-related functioning.

Similarly, we can ask whether the same posited shortfalls in controlling the future—coupled with a lack of persistence—occur when diagnosed persons attempt to persuade others to follow their directions. At these times, do diagnosed persons still differ from controls in the same ways apparent during school work or other activities stipulated by teachers and parents? For example, how frequently do diagnosed children complain that "you didn't let me finish," if they instruct that a particular task be done, compared to making the same statement when taking instruction from others?

If variations in functioning do occur, it is reasonable to claim that ADHD behaviors are learned acts that occur in response to particular conditions rather than via a fixed developmental impairment. Positing that immediacy of reinforcement or saliency compensates for their ADHD only informs us that, under certain conditions, diagnosed persons will respond in conscientious ways; but the explication adds no new information about whether compensation for a disability has occurred.

While variations in diagnostic responding might be high or low, depending on the individual, we anticipate that in many instances simply determining whose agenda is being enacted will predict whether ADHD responses will take place. The limitations traditionally assigned to the individual could actually be contingent upon changes in context and situation. More acceptable competency may be evident for each identified delay noted within the traditional empirical work, depending on the conditions under which that person operates. Divergent patterns of functioning likely occur, depending on whether the individual initiates or answers. Minor environmental changes may also alter the frequency with which ADHD behaviors are expressed for particular diagnosed persons, such as whether others are in the room, previous remarks, difficulties encountered, the anticipated future, tone of voice, content of interaction, and so on. For example, a diagnosed child might play a video game and not respond to conversation, but if the same child makes mistakes while playing, he might blame others for being too noisy.

Given such a diversity of response, it might be interesting to examine whether excessive immersion in a hobby will sharply reduce if the activity is made mandatory (i.e., the quickest way to dampen an interest is to make it a chore). It would be noteworthy if ADHD behaviors increased in frequency after making the non-assigned task seem more like an assigned activity for persons who have been conditioned to respond in diagnostic ways. That is, what might happen if diagnosed individuals (who frequently play video games on a non-assigned basis) were required to play for a certain time period, forced to achieve a certain outcome in one sitting by imposing contingency management, and also be subjected to constant monitoring, including point of performance directing that instructs the child about how best to play?

Would ADHD responses prevail when operating under such conditions? To what extent might their behavior mimic what happens when they complete typical school assignments? Would changing video game playing to an assigned activity increase instances of ADHD behaviors even though traditionalists believe that the activity or game is giving them constant and immediate reinforcement, or in conventional parlance, "compensating for ADHD?"

We predict that diagnostic behaviors will increase when imposing conditions that seem to evoke reactions (e.g., forced participation, stipulated time parameters, harassing to increase achievement, and frequent evaluation). Other experiments might vary exposure to failure, disapproval, unsolicited advice, and other intrusive exchanges in order to observe whether ADHD behaviors increase with the introduction of aversive social patterns. Especially for individuals already reinforced to respond with ADHD patterns, activities which were previously symptom-free and classified as play might become replete with ADHD behavior simply by changing situational parameters. Even by making winning too easy, it may be possible to markedly increase instances of ADHD responding during particular tasks.

While the possibilities for investigation are extensive, the point is that the behavior of the diagnosed population may be reasonably understood as contextual, situational, and circumstantial. What seems like a biologically-determined disability may be a reinterpreted as particular response patterns occurring under particular sets of conditions. In that traditionalists' own empirical data reveals no particular functional delay to predict who will qualify for the DSM-IV-TR diagnosis, this alternative interpretation of ADHD empiricism is consistent with that data as well. We anticipate that non-assigned activity may quickly become disrupted by interference or interjection from others. Loss of discretionary authority may rapidly occur, and ADHD responding may be reinforced in numerous subtle ways.

For example, these problems seem to frequently occur when parents worry about how their diagnosed child handles and organizes trading cards. At these times, it is not unusual for the child to revert to the more typical patterns evident during their assigned activities. A number of these children rely more on their parents to monitor their collectibles, and they might be reinforced about their importance when their parents worry about the objects. Some children will spitefully stop doing these previously non-monitored tasks when they become angry with their parents, or resist doing the activity in response to the usurping of their discretionary authority, over protectiveness, and on-going evaluative responses. There could be increased ADHD responding when previously, these children had behaved fairly self-reliantly, independently, persistently, and competently prior to increased parental involvement.

A very similar shift of response pattern seems to occur when previously un-diagnosed children initially ask to play a musical instrument. Instead of keeping the activity under the child's discretionary authority, playing the instrument quickly becomes externally instructed and associated with pestering and failure to meet expectations. Rather than reinforce the instrument playing by way of positive responses whenever the child wants to demonstrate her playing, the parent instead begins to encroach, monitor the activity, and introduce contingency management on practice time. The child then responds as if playing a musical instrument is solely the parent's agenda, and thus will stop responding in a positive manner. For many children who function under these conditions there is often a sharp increase in diagnostic responding when situations pertain to playing the musical instrument.

However, we find an opposite shift in patterning in various other instances. Actions that were coerced by others may become reinforced without parental involvement, and diagnostic responding could become significantly less prevalent at these times; for example, on occasions when diagnosed young adults return to high-school after dropping out, and they start to function more acceptably. To the extent that this kind of shift in response patterning occurs, why is it then reasonable to locate the problem in an individual's neural biology as a fixed delay?

Sometimes very subtle changes in conditions significantly alter the frequency rates of diagnostic reaction. For example, a child might observe slight facial movements in the parent's face (eye rolling), or a parent might begin to direct or attempt to convince the child to behave in a particular way, thus instigating diagnostic behaviors to promptly ensue. Much like what often happens when individuals are coerced to eat ice cream and are evaluated while doing so, behavior that becomes conditioned contrasts with the times when a child initiates the very same ice cream eating.

However, when carrying out these experiments, we anticipate that it will be easier to realize an increase in ADHD behaviors with individuals who already

ADHD respond frequently under different sets of conditions, in that response generalization is often easier to accomplish, compared to shaping new response patterns. These studies will help us identify which parameters are reinforcing ADHD responding and thereby test the traditional views.

Traditionalists maintain that self-initiated tasks require less executive functioning than typical homework assignments, and that some games provide greater reinforcement than other activities. But until empirical work confirms those assertions, one of the most important and basic concerns raised in response to the traditional view, will be ignored: why do diagnosed persons sometimes behave in seemingly unimpaired ways? Parents of diagnosed children have also voiced concern about the disability interpretation when confronted by the noteworthy competencies seen within the diagnosed population. They frequently observe their diagnosed child behaving competently when doing self-generated activities. Other than not doing symptom-free behaviors at preferred times with preferred content, the child seems reasonably capable of not expressing ADHD.

With the adoption of the learning paradigm, increased response rates of particular behaviors in particular situations are explicated by referencing a derived biopsychosocial history. Each individual's current status becomes a function of this biopsychosocial history, and we anticipate that particular sets of conditions will not receive identical responses from one individual to the next. Conditions that are negative to some individuals will be attractive to others. This problem can be illustrated by a person with a history of trauma who is threatened by precise conditions that have no negative effects whatsoever on most people. There is nothing inherent in these consensually benign events to account for negative reactions, but the trauma victim's peculiar responses are more understandable when his history with similar threatening conditions is elucidated.

Often it seems that traditionalists' views only indicate that diagnosed persons will sometimes behave normatively, organize their behavior over extended time frames, show no attention or motivational problems, and/or persist adequately, as long as they are not burdened by adversity, or required to conform to an agenda that departs from that which they initiate and enjoy. The traditional account frequently narrows to the assertion that ADHD diagnosed persons will less likely conform to what others initiate unless enticed by additional rewards and punishments, asked to do easier and/or little work, and/or given stimulant medication to increase productivity and achievement for tasks imposed by others.

Although it is generally agreed that self-initiated activity does not tax the executive system to the same extent as the typical school assignment, traditionalists have not yet been explicit enough about the criteria used to confirm assertions. Picture card games, Internet exploration, and knowledge of sports franchises may require competencies equivalent to a number of school assignments. Moreover, the skill required to sift through the menu of a cell phone or basic video game requires executive functioning that is comparable to many homework requirements that immediately instigate diagnostic behaviors.

In order to carry out a systematic inquiry into how much inhibition and executive functioning various tasks require, we must first quantify the amount of working memory, tedium, and interference control, responsiveness to feedback, time organization, reconstitution, hindsight, and/or forethought a particular task necessitates (whether assigned or non-assigned). By engaging in this inquiry it may be possible to determine the extent to which the traditional view predicts instances of diagnostic responding. Rather than bow to traditional assertions, it is important to find a way to *measure* the categories that are imposed to explicate ADHD from a biological determinist perspective *prior* to observations of performance, and allow for the evaluation of non-stipulated achievements to be part of this inquiry.

If this kind of scaling were to take place, it could be found that many diagnosed individuals function in non-diagnostic ways that are not as simplistic as now presumed. A number of their accomplishments may require the same amount, extent, and degree of thought, working memory, patience, and coordination of present responses with long-term outcomes much like some of the assigned activities that are riddled with ADHD behaviors. We might discover that diagnosed persons are not as limited in capability as is assumed by the traditional disability model if their functioning is evaluated on both assigned and non-assigned tasks.

Criteria for making these determinations would have to be imposed, such as number of steps anticipated, rehearsed, and imagined, number of simultaneous discriminations necessary to respond correctly, units of information that must be remembered, etc. An inquiry of this kind will help to operationally define and rank order tasks in relation to their inhibitory and executive requirements, thereby investigating claims of both the traditional and the current learning approach more systematically.

However, because expressing ADHD frequently and severely for many years has potential generalized consequences on skill development, the probability remains that not all behavioral differences will disappear when diagnosed persons are observed under varied sets of conditions. ADHD patterning may indeed interfere with practicing and learning more acceptable, competent alternative responses on assigned and non-assigned tasks. Given that caveat, and despite the possibility that diagnosed persons may be "interested" and functioning less diagnostically under some conditions, they may still not function as well as others, even if we factor out other co-occurring problems often confounded by an ADHD diagnosis.

Although regardless of whether some diagnosed persons consistently show ADHD responding on various assigned and non-assigned tasks, we nevertheless cannot presume incurability or fixity. Current functioning does not rule out the possibility that very different responses might be shaped in response to new forms of training. It remains likely that some or many diagnosed persons will learn to respond with fewer ADHD patterns from exposure to new sequences of events.

Since the scaling problem noted above raises a crucial concern that has not yet been examined systematically, it nevertheless seems important to introduce greater conceptual diversity. That is, in which alternative ways might we account for the non-diagnostic responding of diagnosed individuals when they enact some activities? Does biological determinism and the categories of actions discriminated by the traditional model do an acceptable job explaining all instances?

Unless a relationship between symptoms and the amount of inhibition required prior to an act can be demonstrated, traditionalists' interpretations will always be post hoc and hypothetical (i.e., if the person had trouble, it was due to inhibitory failure). Traditionalists could argue that signs and symptoms vary due to certain changes that alter the amount of required inhibitory control, but this must be specified ahead of time. There has to be a way to determine a rank ordering of tasks, activities and situations in terms of the degree of inhibitory control necessary for competency. After identifying how much inhibitory control is associated with particular actions, it then becomes necessary to see if that quantification allows us to predict when a diagnostic response will be enacted, and whether it identifies persons qualifying for DSM-IV-TR criteria.

A proper assessment can focus on competencies that are believed to be less possible for diagnosed persons, such as how well they recombine variables and predict the future. For example, if a diagnosed person is a wrestling enthusiast, we might ask him or her to predict what specific wrestlers are likely to do in order to win a competition. Whether or not diagnosed individuals can make astute predictions remains to be seen, although their knowledge about the subject can be evaluated for consistency and coherence when compared with wrestlers' past competition outcomes. Similarly, for picture card devotees, we can gauge their competency in imagining and recombining possibilities when asked questions pertaining to the trade value of particular cards, and ask them what might happen if the various characters depicted on those cards were to use their powers in battle.

If diagnosed individuals can show adequate command of a game or activity requiring knowledge of facts, rules, and an understanding of future probabilities, it is difficult to argue that they are delayed in their ability to become competent in those ways. Similarly, if adequate working memory, and their understanding of strategy, rule violations, and correct responses to hypothetical possibilities is evident without having to provide physical representations for any of these responses to occur, we cannot reasonably make the traditional inference that they have problems holding mental representations "in mind" so as to permit recombination and hypothesizing. Many diagnosed individuals may not have an undermined neurological ability to imagine, to identify future possibilities, or to engage in particular kinds of mental actions such as non-vocal verbal responding at all points of performance. But rather it may be the case that those responses have not yet been reinforced to occur frequently enough through the use of socially important content.

For example, we have observed that when a particular diagnosed child builds a tree house in the backyard, he avoids all diversions and immediately begins work on the project. While this same individual rarely does chores or homework with such focus, he coordinates the entire tree house building project from start to finish without prompting or point of performance intervention from others. He often reports that he thinks about the project, and there was evidence of organization and planning in ways that departed dramatically from what occurs during assigned projects. No cues are necessary for him to maintain the tree house work schedule. Instead it is the parent who is reminded by the diagnosed child to not forget building supplies from the hardware store. Although father's tools are left out (despite father's protests) for ready use, the entire project is orchestrated and completed without tightening any external controls. These non-compulsory tree house building behaviors differ starkly from that which occurs when the child is asked to comply with parental instructions; the child exhibits all the behaviors he is *purportedly* minimally able to achieve. He has therefore demonstrated enough organizational ability to remember and work on his science project to be assigned during the school year.

While it is recognized that many diagnosed persons may also express other difficulties and complications in functioning, such as lower intelligence (Rutter, 1989; Frazier, Demaree, and Youngstrom, 2004), motor coordination problems (Kadesjo and Gillberg, 2001), and speech problems (Barkley, DuPaul, and McMurray, 1990), which potentially impair functioning, we predict that if the behavioral sampling is expanded to include activities the diagnosed person initiates and enjoys, instances of diagnostic responding will decrease. History of reinforcement rather than a posited biological inhibitory mechanism may reasonably account for instances of diagnostic responding.

We argue that much of what diagnosed persons can do is ignored if evaluations are limited only to assigned work. Often it is not discerned whether a diagnosed person's difficulties relates to conformity, lack of practice, inconvenience, or incompetence. For example, some diagnosed individuals are apparently orchestrating relatively complex schemes to obtain and sell illicit drugs. Sometimes the math involved (e.g., determining price and quantity per sale) is equivalent to (or more complex) than what is required to balance a check book: something they insist they cannot do because of their ADHD.

Similarly, it is also not unusual for many diagnosed children to engage in extremely repetitive non-assigned activities (e.g., arrange piles of objects, count play money, observe an insect trap, etc.) that most of us might find utterly boring and tedious. They conduct these non-assigned tasks with ease; they persist and are able to avoid distractions. In that these kinds of non-diagnostic responses occur with activities classified as boring by the majority, we argue that it is unreasonable to posit that certain kinds of activities and tasks provide compensation for inner problems; and that ADHD, as understood by traditionalists, has no empirical coherence.

If diagnosed persons (without comorbidity) can engage in the posited delayed behaviors in increasingly acceptable ways (i.e., persistence, time management, interference control, resistance to distraction, control of future contingencies, and working memory, etc.), as long as their discretionary authority is maintained and adversity is infrequent, we can alternatively regard ADHD behaviors as solution responses rather than delayed behaviors. We can accept this formulation, even if the individual eventually becomes delayed as a result of engaging in patterning that persistently and severely departs from socially expected behavior over very long periods of time.

While traditionalists argue that a lack of sustained effort is a consequence of having neurological ADHD, it could also be claimed that lack of persistence during required activity is reinforced behavior. The more an individual gives up, the less failure and discomfort there will be, and in some instances, the more the outside world will accommodate. However, the more an individual engages in these behaviors over time, the poorer the individual's eventual functioning on a spectrum of tasks and activities will be. The individual's resources are simply not being developed. For example, if a diagnosed person frequently blames a teacher or a video game when losing instead of figuring out viable solutions, his skill development will remain frozen. Generally speaking, a continuous lack of success reinforces an increase in instances of diagnostic responding, which progressively makes matters worse.

Adopting the Learning Paradigm: Context, Situation, Circumstance

Given the failure of ADHD empirical analyses to uncover a consistent functional delay, it also seems that the traditional model limits its attempts to explain symptom variations under fluctuating conditions. Instances of non-symptomatic behavior where individuals wait patiently, manage the future, sustain attention, abide by a schedule, and remember substantial amounts of material do not fit easily into their disability model. Diagnosed children do not always show symptoms when parents speak on the telephone, when out in public, and when asked to do chores. The parameters designated by traditionalists cannot fully account for these instances of typical functioning. Although diagnosed children may behave diagnostically more often when a parent focuses elsewhere, or when they are asked to accommodate or be inconvenienced, this is not always the case.

Instead of proffering a neurobiological delay to account for ADHD behavior while the parent talks on the phone, for example, symptomatic behaviors can alternatively be characterized as reinforced actions which increase the probability that the parent will end the phone call and get involved with the child. The frequency of these diagnostic behaviors may also relate to other available persons, what happened prior to the phone call, and what might happen after the phone call. Since a parent's attention is often diverted from the phone call to a child's ADHD behavior, it is claimed that subsequent conditions (i.e., outcomes) often maintain the frequency rates of the ADHD responses when equivalent conditions recur. On those occasions when the child's bedtime can be put forward by the phone call, there may be few or no diagnostic responses that would hasten the end of the parent's phone conversation.

We suggest that the behaviors mentioned above relate to a history of reinforcement. Because the child does not always express ADHD behavior, it is important to examine instances of non-symptomatic behavior as a way to refine prediction statements about what parameters (i.e., current, recent, past, and anticipated) may or may not cue either a diagnostic or non-diagnostic response. If an activity such as waiting for a parent to finish a phone call can exceed the capacity of the diagnosed children's ability to inhibit, perhaps ADHD behavior will occur not only when diagnosed individuals are required to exert mental effort or manage the distant future, but also when they encounter almost any problem. Simply having one's own concerns negated may be enough to exceed the capacity for self-control. However, if that is the case, it then becomes difficult to distinguish between ADHD and what can only be described as self privileged or extremely insecure behavior.

When adopting the learning paradigm to account for instances of ADHD behavior, the question of whether conditions exceed the ability to self-control is averted; if a child shows ADHD while the parent talks on the phone, it is not that the situation exceeds the child's ability to self-control, but (significantly) that the situation cues a particular reinforced behavior. ADHD responding becomes psychosocial action, and we need not posit terminology such as "inhibitory capacity" when that parameter has not independently been established. While it is generally anticipated that there will be a relationship between ADHD behavior and conditions that are blaming, interrupting, negating, and excluding, diagnosed individuals could indeed be engaged in reinforced behaviors rather than suffering from a lesser ability.

While not as overtly negativistic as individuals who behave defiantly, diagnosed persons generally do not conform, complete assignments, or accommodate to external instructions any more than individuals who behave in more obviously contrary and argumentative ways. It seems that diagnosed persons impinge on those around them by complaining and behaving in ways more characteristic of much younger persons. Diagnosed persons will typically underproduce when required to please others unless they receive extra compensation or inordinate assistance. The behaviors may often keep the diagnosed person socially focal, and those who attempt to coordinate their actions with them are often disappointed, disrupted, and exploited. We observe that the diagnosed person is often the least inclined to change.

However, when diagnosed persons respond within conditions less associated with adversity, frequency rates of diagnostic responses can plummet. Conditions such as having a positive relationship with an instructor, a history of success with assigned content, and instances of success prior to exposure to the directive or assigned task can potentially reduce the discomfort associated with particular tasks and diminish the frequency rates of diagnostic responding. Consistent with this view, Winsler et al. (2000) report that young children at risk for attention and behavioral problems began to show increasing silence (and perhaps more private speech) as success occurred with a task over time.

Context, situation, and circumstance are reasonable ways to account for the changes in functioning often seen in the diagnosed population. For example, the possibility that someone with ADHD can resist powerful responses associated with focusing on a computer game, and *abruptly* begin working on homework before the parent can identify the transgression—when the traditional account makes the case against such a turnaround—therefore puts the traditional model in a conundrum.

While the traditionalist might counter argue that a prepotent response manifests in not getting caught by the parent, it seems that one can always justify inconsistencies in this way; one can always discount non-confirming events. However, we observe that the diagnosed person *can* adequately stop some actions in some contexts, situations, and circumstances, and shift to another behavior that coincides with a more positive sequencing of events (i.e., it is more advantageous for the parent to *not* discover his failure to do homework), then we cannot interpret the meaning of a statement that an individual is limited in self control or ability to manage the future. He is simply managing the future differently. His total concentration on a computer game, combined with avoiding parental interference, could mean that he is effectively controlling the future, although the upshot is that the outcomes being managed or increasing in frequency are not socially preferred or acceptable to those in authority.

In this current analysis ADHD patterning may instead be portrayed as non-preferred, disruptive, and socially-difficult set of conditioned behaviors that describe individuals who infringe upon others too often, and who accommodate and defer less often to the preferences, instructions, and limits of those around them. Instead of being indicative of self-regulatory problems, these behaviors could be understood as occurring in predictable ways with particular results. A diagnosed individual's primary delay would thus be that he does ADHD in response to restriction, obligation, evaluation, disappointment, social exclusion, failure, insecurity, berating, or when others direct or act as a "taskmaster." ADHD then seems like a peculiar neurological delay that reacts predictably to what happens while living in the world.

Although traditionalists might respond to these interpretations by saying that only persons with neurological ADHD will respond to adversities by doing diagnostic behaviors with such frequency and severity, they have only established that *some* people more often respond to particular adversities by doing ADHD. The explication of the data remains open to scrutiny. It has not yet been refuted that some people may be more likely to *learn* ADHD responding when adversity occurs due to their biopsychosocial circumstance (including lower intelligence), or that, due to their biopsychosocial circumstance, more conditions are likely to be characterized as adverse or disquieting, and thus increase the likelihood of learning diagnostic responding.

Given that many of us behave similarly to ADHD responses when we are excluded, are likely to fail, be disapproved of, or be subjugated or denied, diagnosed persons may actually not be a unique sample. ADHD empirics may only reveal that diagnosed individuals frequently enter into these situations, or respond as if the situations they encounter have those characteristics.

Interestingly, in an interview with Egerton (1973, 41) Kamin notes that "social scientists, like everybody else in the world, have their biases and their prejudices," while "they say they have hard evidence," the evidence "reflects their preconceptions." "If you ask who is going to go around studying monozygotic twins, or correlation coefficients of uncles and aunts and siblings and grandchildren, you find that it is people by and large, who from the outset were convinced that there ought to be a genetic determination." Conversely, "if you ask what happened to the psychological scientists who had the opposite point of view," "they didn't investigate that kind of question," they were "more likely to work on such problems as the kinds of teaching and training programs that will maximize the performance of kids." Put another way, most often researchers invoke categories of explanation from their domains of concern and may not properly investigate instances where anomalies arise.

Consistent with Kamin's view, most genetic studies of ADHD will start with the assertion that the behavioral pattern is genetically controlled or determined; disappointing findings in genetic studies are also invariably explicated such that initial presumptions are protected. The preponderance of evidence, not surprisingly, therefore supports the view that ADHD is a biological (and ultimately) a genetic event, although as Kamin indicates, bias is a factor of those doing the accumulating research and interpreting data.

As we have observed, biological determinism as an explanation for ADHD is the entrenched view at this time, but it is important not to inadvertently reinforce conformity at the expense of more comprehensive empirical work. While some have raised objections and concerns about the tenability of the ADHD syndrome over the years (e.g., Gardner, 1987), there is apparently much less receptivity to non-medically based explications.

However, the alternative formulation is that many diagnosed persons might have problems meeting socio-cultural expectations for many reasons. ADHD behavioral acts can be understood as a set of reinforced behaviors that are more probable when socialization is complicated by developmental delays, indulgences, deprivations, etc. In this view, there is nothing inherent in the external event or activity (i.e., saliency, providing feedback) that benefits the neurological system of the diagnosed person when non-diagnostic responding is evident. It is merely that certain acceptable behaviors have been reinforced within those situations.

The expectation is that this alternative account will consistently integrate empirical data accumulated thus far, and also impose a reasonable and parsimonious account when diagnosed persons apparently exceed their posited functional limitations in some instances; this is particularly important, in that many find the disability formulation contradictory. Many have found it quite perplexing that neurologically delayed individuals can show so few symptoms when doing something that they enjoy. The existence of contradictions and exceptions to the rules of biological determinism are too numerous to ignore.

There is evidence worthy of further concerted investigation indicating that differences in symptom occurrence for ADHD diagnosed persons relate to conditioning not internal delays. Symptom variations may be interpreted to mean that the individual has been conditioned to behave differently at particular times. Diagnosis could be used only as a descriptive label for individuals who express a set of non-preferred behaviors more severely and frequently than others in contexts and situations often encountered, and we might drop the label "neurobiological delay." By understanding symptom occurrence and non-occurrence as related to conditioning, the post hoc mitigating factors that are unceasingly imposed to account for contradictory responding can be avoided.

We propose that we address ADHD behaviors in terms of their functionality rather than as impairment. When ADHD behaviors sequence with other people accommodating or becoming more involved, or when those behaviors permit a rapid escape from adversity and disappointment, and permit more time for self-initiated acts, we can begin to understand these patterns of response as serviceable in a multitude of ways.

Given the apparent diversity of both acceptable and undesirable diagnostic responses for persons qualifying for the ADHD behavioral criteria, the actions of diagnosed and non-diagnosed persons can be studied in terms of differences in conditioning rather than differences in inherent ability to do certain non-observable antecedent actions. The alternative paradigm may be more appropriate in its ability to capture the inconsistencies of ADHD behavior in a more comprehensive way. If nothing else, we hope that these efforts will inform individuals who are interested and concerned about the impact that a diagnosis can have on their own children, entire families, and the medical profession in its treatment of ADHD.

Chapter 2

Considerations Essential to the ADHD Diagnosis

In order to evaluate the premises found in traditional ADHD literature, a number of important concerns are introduced in this chapter. Our proposed interpretation of ADHD as a conditioned set of responses reinterprets what is known as "attention difficulty" as *non-participatory* behavior. We abandon terminology that supports most medical categorizations used today that purport genetic disability.

Traditionalists generally ignore any attempts to formulate ADHD as a reinforced problem behavior. Barkley and Edwards (2006) indicate that the clinician should pay attention to certain "red flags" indicating a burgeoning neurological problem. If teachers describe the child as an immature individual who does not complete work, shows unacceptable organizational skills, touches others frequently, and does not fulfill homework requirements, a neurological delay is purportedly the reason. Parents are asked about the child's pattern of meeting expectations in different settings, whether the child conforms to rules, and whether the child demonstrates self-control consistent with his age group when away from adults. The kinds of problems related to meeting expectations become grounds for inferring neurological disability.

However, a learning model could equally account for the aforementioned behaviors in that ADHD may be a particular class of non-normative behaviors that some individuals learn in response to expectations, rules, and limits. While traditionalists offer neurological delay as the reason for greater difficulty meeting the contextual demands of various situations (Landau and Milich, 1988; Whalen, Henker, Collins, McAuliffe, and Vaux, 1979), for disturbing the reciprocity of conversations (Clark et al., 1988), and for being generally more controlling and uncooperative during social interactions (Cunningham and Siegel, 1987; Cunningham, Siegel, and Offord, 1985; 1991), these patterns can be interpreted as reinforced by contingencies. Although traditionalists might argue this as preposterous, since ADHD correlates with so much dysfunction, in so far as we know, proponents of the traditional view do not study ADHD behaviors in relation to a detailed reinforcement history.

In the view espoused here, the probability is that more intrusive, careless, non-normatively paced, and non-participatory behaviors will increase when conditions are associated with losing and denial, or are incompatible with that which the diagnosed person has historically initiated and enjoyed. ADHD responses are more likely to be triggered when constraints are imposed by others, when accommodation does not occur, or when there is a failure to meet socio-cultural expectations. Most often individuals with various functional impairments and histories that disrupt growth towards self-reliance and accommodation to others will more likely learn ADHD behaviors.

We expect that many diagnosed persons will respond with ADHD patterns when others limit, deny, brow beat, pressure, disapprove, and lecture in ways that are difficult to comprehend. Diagnostic responding is likely to be frequent when others instruct actions that are associated with negativity and failure, or when the child is jealous, distracting others, or prevented from enjoyment. Although we are not saying that others are "teaching" ADHD, the point here is that children are being reinforced (absorbing as in osmosis). The more the child reacts in accordance with ADHD, the more corrective and disenchanted will be the social response, and those reactions can effectively perpetuate the conditions that increase diagnostic responding.

ADHD patterns may be coherently understood as a set of conditioned actions that are continuations of behaviors more often enacted by chronologically younger individuals. There is an inordinate reliance on assistance from others (e.g., who continue to remind, accommodate, etc.), frequent non-participatory behavior (e.g., non-completion of assignments, irresponsibility, non-responsiveness), and fewer instances of sharing and sense of perspective (e.g., driving accidents, divorce, and other forms of self-indulgence). However, provocation and intrusiveness via *movement* usually subsides over the years, as older diagnosed individuals are more often seen as lazy or avoidant rather than hyperactive during adolescence to adulthood.

In the learning model view, ADHD responses have not been adequately predicted under traditional category systems, even in the case where frequent and severe expressing ADHD means that one is less likely to learn substitute responses in order to increase acceptable outcomes and achievements. Diagnosed individuals are likely to have fewer opportunities to learn alternative ways to effectively manage contingencies when they rush to finish, give up quickly, or avoid situations altogether. But rather than assume an inherent delay, one could consider that when learning to do ADHD, there are numerous functional consequences—even if ADHD behaviors are more likely to be learned when one has functional delay.

One might also assert that diagnosed persons do not have problems with "an ability to pay attention," since those having so-called "pure" ADHD adequately pay attention in many diverse situations. But rather, these persons depart from paying attention to what others deem appropriate, correct, or acceptable. While some individuals may indiscriminately show a lack of attentional continuity, non-persistence of response, or perseverative responses, those diagnosed with ADHD demonstrate those behaviors within some but not all contexts, situations, and circumstances.

It is therefore unreasonable to presume that their behavior is analogous to other pervasive functional difficulties including specific types of brain damage, or to reject outright the possibility that diagnosed persons express particular reinforced responses in particular conditions. Traditionalists have not yet established empirically that diagnosed persons are permanently delayed in their ability to focus or concentrate, react efficiently to environmental cues, or sustain awareness. It still remains tenable for this population of individuals that it is possible to condition their responses in acceptable ways, especially when it is observed that many are already showing competency some of the time.

Assigned vs. Non-assigned Conditions

An alternative to the traditional approach starts with the attempt to discern between compulsory actions assigned by others and non-assigned actions initiated by the diagnosed person without coercion or appraisal. This distinction is important, in that non-assigned actions often permit greater discretionary authority for the actor, compared to assigned activity. There is typically less judgment or comparison with others, and individuals often learn to rely increasingly on their own resources when completing non-assigned tasks; the actor typically reports enjoying and wanting to participate. There also seems to be a higher level of safety associated with events whenever discretionary authority is maintained, because the individual continues when adequately prepared, and when he or she feels confident that success will be achieved. Having access to non-assigned activities where impressive achievements are often observed frequently becomes the reward for compliance with requirements summarily imposed by others; ADHD responding is seldom observed at those times.

Diagnosed persons will usually show their most acceptable functioning during self-selected tasks. At these times they are most likely to have a history of success with particular activities, and ample opportunity to be self-sufficient without involvement from concerned others. While diagnosed persons might quickly say, "I can't," or request help on a homework assignment, they may otherwise persist independently if confronted with a complex dilemma pertaining to an activity (such as assembling a toy) that they have performed many times without coercion, interference, or contingency management.

However, there is nothing inherently compensatory about non-assigned task activities; the individual's history under those particular conditions may have been influential in shaping patience and persistence. Under conditions of self motivation without disapproval, direction, or constraints imposed by others, ADHD behavior fades. With the exception of limitations imposed by objects and/or rules of a game, etc., individuals can retain greater discretionary authority; in this way ADHD behavior correlates with discretionary control rather than chaotic responding.

Traditionalists, meanwhile, continue to recommend medication, simplification, and contingency management—primarily to increase their compliance with assigned agendas associated with adversity. While traditionalists claim that their delays necessitate medicinal intervention in order to increase required achievements, non-assigned achievements are not ordinarily managed in the same way. Surprising competencies have been reported when diagnosed persons achieve on non-assigned tasks. What we observe is that even if the diagnosed individual is required to organize, increase the probability of future outcomes, remember significant amounts of material, derive solutions to complex problems, and respond effectively to environmental cues, competency in those functional areas may increase under non-assigned conditions for diagnosed persons whose only problem is ADHD.

We know that not all differences between diagnosed persons and controls will disappear when observing them during assigned vs. non-assigned activity, but there might be significant differences in functioning worthy of investigation when we inquire into *whose* agenda is being enacted. If diagnosed individuals master the parameters of a non-assigned activity, event sequences will less likely include interference or judgment from others. They need not consider the preferences, moods, and opinions of those around them. This is important, in that ADHD behaviors may become reinforced when individuals have not learned to resolve problems with others in mutually-acceptable ways.

When assigned activity becomes associated with negativity, it is more probable that diagnostic responding will be learned. It may often be more reinforcing to *not* try than to try and fail, and to be abrupt or avoidant, rather than be vulnerable and friendly and risk being rejected. Those frequent negative responses contradict the adage, "It is better to have loved and lost than to never have loved at all." Traditionalists assert that negativistic patterns may develop because of the frustration of having a neurological condition; however, in our view, persons are labeled as ADHD when they express these patterns.

We note that diagnosed persons show exceptional difficulty when exposed to failure. For example, Hoza et al. (2004) found that diagnosed boys often perceive themselves as better than their actual performance (i.e., illusory bias) when functioning in a particular domain is impaired. Diener and Milich (1997) earlier posited that those responses could be self-protective, in that illusions help them to cope. Brown (2000) noted that diagnosed children more often exhibit lower self-esteem, and Bussing et al. (2003) found this to be the case primarily when diagnosed persons behave aggressively.

These problematic responses can occur in non-assigned situations as well. Despite the improved functioning often evident when diagnosed persons engage in non-assigned activity, it is not always the case that non-assigned tasks are completed without snags and drawbacks. A diagnosed person could overreact to his disappointment and failure to understand material even while immersed in hobbies, because repetition of conditioned ADHD behaviors increases if adversity occurs. Therefore, on some occasions when non-assigned tasks result in dissatisfaction and failure, the same behavior can result as that emitted with formally assigned activities.

Diagnosed persons may still give up easily, linger, rush, obstruct, and antagonize others when conditions are believed to be troublesome; they might externalize blame for unsatisfactory outcomes more often than non-diagnosed persons—even when involved in non-imposed or coerced activity. For example, video games impose limits, restrictions, and delays, and do not always meet the player's expectations. Diagnosed persons are still likely to differ to some degree from a random sampling during the completion of leisure pursuits, in that not all of the conditions encountered will be fully satisfying. Although even with this diverse responding, symptom patterns evident during low demand situations can still be accounted for within a learning paradigm: that is what the person has *learned* to do in similar situations.

Interestingly, this interpretation is consistent with the small number of studies that focus on diagnosed children and leisure activity. For example, Landau et al. (1992) found that diagnosed children spend less continuous time observing television programs when toys are available. Traditionalists try to dispel the notion that ADHD is simply a non-cooperative social pattern by alluding to these findings. If diagnosed persons are *also* distracted when watching television, then there indeed must be something congenitally wrong with them.

But the findings mentioned above may be consistent with a learning model that correlates a history of reinforcement with particular responses. The more distracted pattern during television viewing might be cued when disappointment, failure to comprehend, or discomfort arises during viewing. Some children may be conditioned to look elsewhere when dissatisfied with a show's content, or significantly, it could be less enthralling for some diagnosed children to watch television programs when interactive play is available.

Moreover, whether diagnosed or not, it is expected that individuals who exhibit language and intellectual delays will also have trouble understanding the content of the television program. This may account for the inattentiveness during television viewing for many diagnosed children who have such problems. Patterns of distraction may have little to do with decreased ability to inhibit off-task behaviors. In fact, some parents report that their diagnosed child can become so immersed in television that they must often go to great lengths to unglue the child from it. Diagnostic children do not always have a greater propensity for distraction when watching television.

So rather than to interpret empirical findings on television viewing as indicative of neurological delay, it might be worthwhile instead to investigate when diagnosed children ignore television. Do distracted responses occur more often with some shows compared to others? As we gain knowledge about a child's history of conditioning with television and other activity we will then be better able to predict patterns of attentive and distracted behavior in recurrent situations. For example, are distractible responses more likely for particular diagnosed children during self-selected television viewing than when listening to programs imposed by others? Because many diagnosed children may have become conditioned to escape when required to sit still, television viewing might be on par with sitting at the dinner table and enduring the constraining circumstance. Thus it is worthwhile to investigate whether highly *motoric* individuals (in general) are less interested when faced with sedentary activities.

These analyses can help us determine which parameters cue distractible or sustained responses for each diagnosed individual. For example, we can observe patterns of distraction during a lecture given by a teacher or parent. We might investigate whether distractible responses occur less frequently during interactive play such as block building, video games, playing with miniature figures, or during verbal exchanges in which participants volley conversation, compared to when diagnosed children must passively absorb information while having little discretionary influence.

There are advantages to studying diagnosed individuals not only when they enact an imposed agenda, which occurs during typical laboratory experiments, school, responsibilities, parental directives, chores, etc., but also when they do *non-assigned* tasks (challenges) that do not require obligation or external evaluation. Knowledge of parameters such as who is involved, what happened prior, and what may happen afterwards, will likely yield insights. There are many occasions when a difficult or time-consuming assigned task provokes an ADHD reaction, but if presented at another time, that same task or challenge yields little to no diagnostic responding. For example, after receiving an award for an accomplishment, or when a peer is observing, ADHD behavior may seldom be emitted.

Conversely, instances of ADHD responding can occur when completing self-initiated tasks, simply because a parent makes negative comments after the occurrence of a mistake. The point here is that diagnostic responding will fluctuate with sometimes subtle changes in conditions, and more careful charting of diagnostic responses can help us better understand what is problematic for each diagnosed person (e.g., disappointment, exclusion, evaluation, reduced discretionary influence, loss of social importance, coercion, condemnation). If one presumes that ADHD behaviors are particular ways to deal with adversity, we need to understand the conditions under which each diagnosed individual is likely to enact those particular responses. If we pursue a psychological account we may discover that it competes favorably with the explanations usually put forward by biological determinists.

Interestingly, an example of a repetitive ADHD behavior during leisure activity (apart from a restrictive setting such as school) is noteworthy when many diagnosed children play team sports (e.g., soccer and baseball). Anecdotal observations of diagnosed children during team play often show that symptomatic behaviors are more probable when the opposing team has the ball, when their team is losing, during delays and time outs, or when the coach speaks to the team as a whole (i.e., similar to whole group instruction at school). One could ask if their neurology disables their ability to wait and adjust to these conditions, or whether these children are *reinforced* within group activity to show impatience, non-participation, and less tolerance when functioning under conditions of greater exclusion, less discretionary authority, greater disappointment and feelings of insignificance.

Additionally, diagnostic responses may be learned during social interaction with their usual first objects (i.e., parents), as well as when responding to inanimate objects. For example, a tantrum is just as likely when interaction is not reciprocated, as when attempts at schoolwork, video games, and operating a computer are disappointing. When these individuals experience disappointment, the patterned solution during both social and solitary activity is to externalize blame and overreact. To the extent that this behavior results in increasing other reinforced events (i.e., others' help, self-belief about competence is increased, relief of tension takes place), the problematic behaviors are triggered to repeat in social as well as non-social conditions.

Therefore, if diagnosed persons learn to overreact and become frustrated when they lose, if they typically give up when disappointed (i.e., if you cannot do something right don't do it at all), outbursts and resentment will likely occur more frequently whether activity is assigned or non-assigned when these conditions present. Not surprisingly, some parents report that their diagnosed children will alter rules or overreact during both school work and video games.

ADHD responding is thus concluded to be more probable when conditions are irrelevant, disappointing, admonishing, scrutinizing, or exclusionary. However, while ADHD behavior may nevertheless be evident under some conditions during play or non-coerced activity, more often than not, more trials will be necessary in order to extinguish non-diagnostic patterns of behavior that have already been reinforced. There is usually a learning curve associated with extinguishing conditioned responses, whether they are ADHD or non-diagnostic functioning. For example, a diagnosed child may concentrate longer when trying a challenging new video game, compared to his less persistent approach to a new reading assignment if reading has historically been problematic for him, and success has been more frequent when playing video games. Moreover, depending on one's reinforcement history, there may be occasions when diagnosed individuals are more disturbed than usual during self-instructed actions. For example, showing intense reactions towards a video game may be perceived as safer than expressing those same emotions towards parents.

Given that behavior can be reinforced in sometimes subtle ways, it is more heuristic to consider context, situation, and circumstance when accounting for which behaviors will occur, rather than rely solely on the more obvious *assigned vs. non-assigned* task dichotomy. However, it must be said that this dichotomy can be useful in identifying competencies within the diagnosed person's current behavioral repertoire. For example, it is interesting to compare instances where acceptable behavior occurs in the car while enroute to a friend's house, but rambunctious behavior often occurs in the car while on a family errand.

In a related matter, there have been numerous attempts to distinguish between *work* and *play* in psychological literature. As proffered here, ADHD behavior occurs predominately in work-related circumstances (as with much assigned activity), while ADHD behaviors seem to occur less often during playful activity. Not surprisingly, Barkley (1998a) has commented that when situations change from task-oriented to playful, much of the conflict between parents and diagnosed children dissipates.

Piaget (1962, 150) notes that "play begins as soon as there is predominance of assimilation," and that more "accommodation" is required during the completion of work. In that following instructions from others requires more accommodation when compared to one's own initiatives, assigned activity will therefore be perceived as work whereas non-assigned activity will not, all else being equal within Piagetian construction.

Interestingly, Piaget also claims that work is frequently distinguished as an activity requiring added contingencies (managed by self or others) to be reinforced, while activity we call play is repeated without extra contingencies. If one accepts that view, traditional intervention accomplishes what is usually necessary for most people when work-related activity is imposed. Piaget also notes that distinctions between work and play are often thought of as a continuum rather than as two discrete behaviors. That same conceptualization can be applied to the assigned vs. non-assigned dichotomy as well. Conditions correlated with each kind of activity could occur, regardless of the source of the instruction to express the behavioral sequence.

However, before proceeding further, it is also important to note that the functioning of diagnosed persons can be influenced by other problems that affect competency and diagnostic responding more consistently across contexts, situations and circumstances. For example, diagnosed individuals showing lower intellectual functioning might more often respond with ADHD patterns while completing a wider range of tasks, regardless of discretionary input. For these lower functioning individuals, more situations might be perceived as difficult and unsavory.

In a similar way, diagnosed persons showing brain damage may also exhibit diagnostic responding more consistently irrespective of who is instructing an activity. Persons diagnosed as ADHD who are preoccupied by trouble, depression, and despondency could ostensibly be distracted not only in school, but also during play. Tense and anxious diagnosed persons might also show atypical pacing of responses during instances of work and play. However, for the majority of diagnosed persons, we expect that marked shifts in the occurrence of diagnostic responding will occur depending on context and circumstance. The assigned vs. non-assigned dichotomy is seen to yield the most marked changes as diagnosed persons operate in their worlds.

That ADHD is highly-correlated with assigned activity seems consistent with the traditional claim that homework problems occur almost invariably for diagnosed persons. For most traditionalists, if an adult does not identify a history of difficulty with homework, a diagnosis of ADHD would be in doubt/dubious (Murphy and Gordon, 1998). However, homework assignments are one of the best examples of the dichotomy between assigned and non-assigned action. Playing vs. doing schoolwork when not in school, and having to arrive home from a work environment and then be required to continue working, is certain to generate conflict.

When understood in that light, it is not surprising that ADHD behaviors are most likely to be evident with homework assignments. Homework introduces a polarization between the impositions of others and that which the child initiates. Because the child has many other possibilities at home, to endure assigned school work would only heighten frustration and make ADHD patterns likely to occur, especially since finishing quickly, doing less, and avoidance will be reinforced.

If we understand that within the home context, assigned schoolwork, coupled with frequent monopolizing of the parent's time in the evening, and greater possibilities to sneak, lie, and avoid, it is not surprising that homework problems correlate with an ADHD diagnosis. However, as noted by Bruns (1993), difficulty with homework may also relate to problems related to separating from parents, difficulty working alone, and problems taking on personal responsibility (i.e., a socio-cultural account). Inhibitory failure as posited by conventional practice is not the only way to understand homework difficulties.

Similarly, Talbot (2003) describes how middle class parents often dedicate a great deal of their time to their children's activities, including homework. Although sometimes regarded as a burden that interferes with other cultural activities, homework is nevertheless usually monitored closely. As with other of the child's activities, homework for these parents is an integral way to prepare the child for middle-class life. Problems with homework can become particularly troubling within this socioeconomic group, and thus intensify diagnostic responding as situations pertaining to homework become increasingly adversarial to the child.

ADHD: Delayed or Situational Behavior?

A noteworthy point in this discussion is that diagnosed persons may respond with ADHD patterns in many circumstances (particularly with homework), but *also* show impressive responding, which is antithetical to ADHD in other situations. For example, it seems paradoxical that many parents and spouses report that diagnosed individuals will pester and nag incessantly, and show great determination in attempts to convince others to abide by their wants and desires. On some occasions they are relentless, and they show much less difficulty anticipating future possibilities in order that others will yield to their preferences. Rather than rely on others, they apparently initiate intervention so that parents do not forget a particular action at a particular time.

When distracting a parent from other concerns, they can also engage in persistent questioning, which essentially monopolizes the parent. Despite the parent's reply, there is contention or fault finding which sometimes prevents the interaction from ending. The child talks for example about a controversial topic that is certain to provoke extreme reaction and lengthy debate. These strategies are often effective in derailing any agenda the parent may have had (e.g., getting the child into bed). In these ways, diagnosed persons can be very persistent.

Under some conditions, the so-called "motivationally delayed" diagnosed person is clearly adept at implementing past learning and showing persistence. ADHD behaviors rarely occur when diagnosed persons are maintaining discretionary authority during a social interaction. One illustrative example of this competence is evident when a diagnosed child articulates a plan which enables his parents to stop at a store that sells his collectibles. He might derive this plan in such detail that he not only buys his collectibles, but also figures how his parents can pick up a sibling at a friend's house, and still have ample time to complete homework when arriving home. The child's plan is derived and executed without external representation, and he anticipates the parents' concerns. The impulsive, overreacting, forgetful, easily-distracted individual now becomes a diplomat who competently outlines an event sequence, which includes compromise, in order to persuade his parents. Moreover, when his parents comply with his requests, he then seems better "able" to conform to what his parents stipulate in the interim. The adult no longer has to repeat incessantly because the child is now pleased with the adult's accommodation.

Likewise, in some instances their *posited delays* disappear when convincing others that they are correct, or when guessing what "surprise" a parent has bought for them. On these occasions it is not unusual that diagnosed individuals can identify a variety of insightful possibilities, as well as talk with their parents in socially typical ways such that this historically increases the likelihood that parents will continue to listen. However, if they neglect to get the desired results, more emotionality can ensue, particularly if that escalation has been reinforced by parental acquiescence in the past. Although traditionalists claim that this occurs due to interest or saliency, or some other compensation (usually identified post hoc), which inconsistencies would they accept as non-confirming data?

Conventional practice dictates that if diagnosed persons do not protest explicitly (which would be considered oppositional behavior), failure to comply is often interpreted as biologically-determined motivational shortcomings, not reinforced responses (once diagnosis is established). Practitioners point out that after the child convinces his parents to go to the store, because of ADHD delays there will not be appropriate follow-through. They assert that neurological ADHD will subsequently impair this child when conditions are less salient and interesting. While the child appears competent when *immediately reinforced* to effectively manage, he or she will be too disinhibited and non-future-oriented to function non-diagnostically when conditions are less exhilarating after returning from the store.

However, do we account for failure to behave as others prefer by positing disability, or might the case be that this diagnosed child is reinforced to derive the plan to go to the store, and also to conduct different behaviors (other than conformity) when returning home later in the day? For example, although he might not fulfill his homework as promised, he will be less likely to forget that he told his friend at school that he would be playing a video game on the Internet at a predetermined time.

Because some schedules *are* kept, traditionalists must claim saliency, interest, and immediacy of reinforcement whenever instances of competency or adequate time organization are demonstrated in order to maintain the integrity of their assumptions about ADHD behavior. This seems to make the traditional account equivalent to saying that competency cannot be ascribed to an individual once he or she has been diagnosed. A learning paradigm can instead be utilized to account for the improved performance of diagnosed persons on tasks that they have chosen, compared to tasks that are required; statements about delayed neurology are therefore unnecessary.

ADHD behaviors are instead regarded as non-normative ways to respond to conditions characterized as problematic. By so doing we are able to explicate symptom variations across contexts, situations, and circumstances, and avoid contradictions and conceptual problems evident in the traditional model. For example, Barkley (1993) once described diagnosed children as manipulative, but if we accept the traditional view that they have delays in forecasting the future, we should not expect them to be very adept at manipulating situations as described above.

When ascribing to the learning paradigm, the evaluation of the presenting problems will proceed much differently. We infer that context, situation, and circumstances cue the behavior, and subsequent events influence their recurrence the next time equivalent conditions take place: this matter is investigated as a first priority. Of note, while this category system is a construction applied to observations, there are no presumptions of ontological status. There is not the assumption that diagnosed individuals are "trying" to be socially disruptive in order to obtain reinforcement in a rehearsed or pre-planned fashion. The responses of diagnosed individuals may be referred to as reinforced, but there is no indication that their behavior is premeditated.

The expectation is that subtle environmental parameters may influence the frequency rates of particular diagnostic responses. The necessity to observe behavioral patterns over extended periods of time before influential contingencies are identified is consistent with the traditional recommendation not to diagnose from limited behavioral samples. One analyzes how diagnosed persons coordinate and adjust in order to deal with various kinds of expectations. In that ADHD behaviors are likely to be more frequent under conditions characterized as unsavory, this inquiry will focus on instances where difference of opinion takes place, or where there is a history of difficulty meeting certain requirements and expectations, which is primarily when ADHD behaviors are likely to become frequent. We anticipate that this approach to ADHD will subsume the diverse and heterogeneous patterning of the diagnostic category into a useful and coherent conceptual framework.

In contrast, the commonly used ADHD Rating Scale IV from the University of Massachusetts Medical Center (based on DSM-IV-TR criteria), does not distinguish situation and circumstance with much specificity, and some questions blur the assigned vs. non-assigned dichotomy. For example, one question asks if the individual has "difficulty sustaining attention in tasks or fun activities." Given the construction of this item, the individual might be functioning non-symptomatically during "fun" but nevertheless obtain a score indicating problematic behavior.

Individuals receive a total score without the attempt to discern whether symptoms vary in relation to self-initiated functioning or that which is stipulated by others. A more precise designation of the context, situation, and circumstance that correlates with ADHD responses is not required when responding to these rating scales. Diagnosis is largely based on the total score, and potentially very important discriminations related to the assigned vs. non-assigned dichotomy are ignored.

Moreover, it is not possible to know how many false positives and false negatives will occur if these scales are disseminated to the general public. While these questionnaires may be useful within professional settings in which problematical situations are already known, the outcomes of discriminating impairment (however defined) may be poorly executed when given to a randomized population.

The consequence of the usual diagnostic procedure is that individuals are being identified as having a neurological problem, even if they only express the problematic behavior when reacting to instructions and assignments imposed by *others*, and perhaps rarely at other times. Meanwhile, psychosocial events that could reinforce those behaviors remain clouded and thus are not identified; the situations and circumstances that correlate with those behaviors will often not be

specified. Without such discernment and specifications, we could reach the conclusion that individuals exhibiting this heterogeneous assemblage of behaviors
are all delayed in precisely the same way, even though their ADHD patterning is
dissimilar.

Of further concern is that, while the University of Massachusetts rating
scale *does* ask if the child has "difficulty engaging in leisure activities or doing
fun things quietly," the question does not highlight the nuanced conditions that
occur and correlate with the noisy behavior. For example, does a child become
louder when her point of view is ignored, or if it is somehow beneficial to disrupt others? The question does not allow respondents to specify when a lack of
quiet might typically occur during enjoyable or leisure activities.

Even if it is the case that the child is incessantly loud and difficult during
leisure and fun activities, can we presume that the child is neurologically delayed—or has she learned those particular behaviors in a wider variety of situations? We might also observe whether the child imitates important adults who
are loud in similar situations and circumstances. Designating that a child has
difficulty engaging quietly in fun and leisure activity tells us very little about
how psychosocial categories such as monopolizing, imitating, or reacting to loss
of discretionary influence can, conversely, reasonably account for the high frequency of noisy behaviors. Again, neurological disinhibition need not be our
only explication.

However, the most typical ADHD rating scale items seem to be written
such that they are consistent with traditional conceptualizations. For example,
one item asks if the person seems "driven by a motor," and another asks if the
person "blurts" out answers. Characterizations of behavior in these questionnaires are subtle reinforcements of a particular notion: that diagnosed individuals react to something *they cannot control*. Seldom is it investigated whether an
individual does *not* "blurt out" or intrude, or whether a diagnosed child can behave considerately and courteously.

Because these behavioral checklists also assign equal weight to each item,
other concerns arise as well. Scores are subdivided into patterns of inattentiveness and impulsivity/hyperactivity, but variations within the general subtypes
are not recognized. Individuals thus might be classified according to the two
major subtypes, obtain the same total score and subtype classification, and yet
there may be wide discrepancies that go unnoticed. In that behavioral patterns of
individuals with the same total score can be highly discrepant, it is problematic
to perceive the condition as a coherent category, much less one that emanates
from the same underlying neurobiological substrate. This problem is not unique
to ADHD, as the criteria for Major Depression are also fairly heterogeneous
where individuals describe opposite types of symptoms, such as eating and
sleeping too much or too little, yet still qualify for the same diagnosis.

We can ask if a person who "talks excessively" is enacting the same pattern
as someone who "fidgets with hands or feet or squirms in seat." While these
items are consistent with the hyperactive subtype, they could describe very dif-

ferent psychosocial patterns and ways of living in the world. The total scores for both individuals might qualify them for diagnosis, but overall differences between them could actually be greater than their assumed similarity. Loquacious individuals could be verbally adept such that their behavior invites involvement from others. Whereas those who "fidget and squirm" may not be verbally skilled; they might pattern more frequently in order to *reduce* social contact, and show a higher incidence of ADHD behaviors under conditions of physical constraint, or when others are domineering.

Perhaps diagnosed persons who have "difficulty waiting turn" or who "interrupt or intrude on others" will also manifest a very different psychosocial patterning when compared to individuals qualifying for diagnosis and who function in more considerate ways. Similarly, it seems that persons "blurting out answers before questions have been completed" may be patterning differently compared to those who often "don't follow through on instructions" and "fail to finish work." The variations are extensive; therapeutic intervention could differ and therefore be contingent upon the psychosocial patterns endorsed by each diagnosed person and his or her family. The failure to discriminate differences among diagnosed persons is an important issue worthy of address, since heritability studies could treat diagnosed persons as identical even when their behavioral patterns are diverse.

Of additional concern is the notion that all diagnosed individuals have a common neural biological delay, despite that these inferences are drawn from group data merely showing average differences between aggregates of diagnosed individuals and controls on a variety of measures pertaining to biological characteristics and particular aspects of functioning. Genetic or biological characteristics of most diagnosed persons are not evaluated directly. The explication of inherent biological delay is predicated on data that: some diagnosed individuals show different biological patterns than a comparable non-diagnosed population; that on some laboratory tasks group differences are evident; and that diagnosis runs in families. Traditionalists use this group data when making assertions about biological causation for each presenting individual.

Since the set of individuals showing ADHD behavior is larger than the set showing the biological peculiarities and ADHD, this methodology seems flawed. There are many diagnosed individuals who show no differences in biology compared to controls, and there are many controls showing the same biological patterns as diagnosed individuals.

In order to avoid being trapped in a scientific dead-end, the current perspective posits that ADHD is a descriptive label for a heterogeneous set of atypical (unacceptable) social behaviors, which are more characteristic of how chronologically younger children typically behave. Diagnosed persons do not reliably show a specific impairment or biological anomaly apart from qualifying for the heterogeneous behavioral criteria. Observations based on small samples of behavior in the natural environment or during psychological tests have been unreliable. Tests designed specifically to identify posited delays in functioning during the evaluative process show low predictive value, and there is no independently shared problem (i.e., behavioral or biological) that diagnosed persons demonstrate consistently. The variability of functioning for this diagnostic population is exceedingly high. Many diagnosed individuals will qualify for diagnosis but simultaneously *not* exhibit the correlated biology or associated delays and problems noted for the aggregate; this includes size variations in brain structure, instances of low performance on working memory tasks, and problematic functioning when estimating time intervals.

Using group statistics to make predictive statements about individuals can be problematic. While actuarial data has been the best available way to make diagnostic predictions (Meehl, 1954); this method can result in prediction failures and incorrect categorizations. Cohen (1994) illustrates this problem when he notes that 60% of individuals may be categorized as false positives even when a test has a 95% accuracy rate in positive diagnoses, and 97% accuracy in declaring normality when the population base rate for a diagnostic condition is 2%. While the number of assigned false positives will depend on the exact statistical parameters, it is clear that misclassifications are likely when using differences between groups as the benchmark for making inferences about individuals.

However, it is now conventional practice that a diagnosis of ADHD carries the implication of a problematic biology. All diagnosed persons are given this characterization even if they lack entirely the characteristics correlating with group assignment—often including large numbers of persons with lower intelligence, pre- and post-natal injuries, learning, language, and motor delays. This approach is truncated, as the behavioral criteria listed in the DSM-IV-TR tells us nothing about the presence or absence of any other functional problems or biological anomalies.

Once the ADHD diagnosis is given presenting individuals are often told that they probably have smaller brains, are unable to handle dopamine efficiently, and are inept at time management and interference control. When a person qualifies for the behavioral criteria, they are often informed that a variety of functional limitations and bodily characteristics are the root causes of their ADHD behavior, despite that the person may in fact be dissimilar to group averages. Diagnosis has many ramifications, the most obvious of which is an enormous impact on how these individuals regard themselves and how they are treated by others.

However, since many diagnosed persons are also showing other complicating problem conditions, it is important to consider the correlated problems before informing them about the devastating effects of having ADHD. Unless these other problems are noted when assessing the functional impairments of particular diagnosed persons, less will be understood about the extent to which ADHD is distressing to long-term adjustment outcomes, and how much the co-occurring problems are undermining the functioning of diagnosed persons over time. For example, when considering the usually least disrupted sampling of clinic-referred adults, approximately 2/3 will at least have attended college, and their achievement and IQ scores are typically within the average range, even though they may not be functioning as proficiently as controls in other ways (Murphy et al., 2002).

While it has only recently become more common to take co-occurring problems into account when studying ADHD delays and deficits (e.g., Murphy, Barkley, and Bush, 2001; Weyandt, 2005; Fischer, Barkley, Smallish, and Fletcher, 2002), there has historically been less emphasis on controlling for correlated problems when interpreting data. A past example of this problem is evident in Abikoff's (1987) overview of Cognitive Behavioral Therapy for ADHD individuals. By and large, the studies included in his review did not account for the presence or absence of co-occurring problems. Diagnosed children and adolescents with a wide range of problems and behaviors were typically grouped together. As long as everyone in this heterogeneous diagnostic group expressed ADHD behavior, conclusions were drawn on the benefits of Cognitive Behavioral Therapy.

Hence when it was reported that diagnosed persons did not benefit from imposed Cognitive Behavioral Therapy treatments, the extent to which outcomes were related to statements about ADHD, language difficulty, learning problems, oppositional behavior etc., remained unanswered. The diagnosed group could have differed from controls in numerous ways *in addition to* qualifying for the ADHD behavioral criteria. For this reason, it is essential to study outcome data along with comorbidity, and analyze the extent to which treatment effects may be influenced by other co-occurring problems correlated with the diagnosis. We observe, however, the assertion—in contrast to recommendations provided here—that some of the correlated problems such as lower intellectual functioning, encoding difficulties, or fine motor problems are actually consequences of the disorder. For that reason, it has been urged that co-occurring problems should not be factored out of most analyses, as these problems are symptomatic, and thus indicate what it means to suffer with ADHD (Barkley, 2006c).

We can counter-argue that problems correlated with ADHD increase the probability that the behaviors will be learned, and that once a child has learned to do ADHD behavior, they become more likely to learn other troublesome behaviors and not develop their resources in positive ways. The explication for the correlated problems with diagnosis has to do with how one perceives ADHD.

We might also posit that when ADHD behaviors are learned, not only is it more probable that other non-normative behaviors will be learned (e.g., oppositional behaviors), but that one's biology will also likely pattern in atypical ways. Different brain structure and function may indeed develop, and other medical problems might increase as well due to living in a particular way. For example, in some instances a child patterned to do ADHD behavior can potentially suffer lead paint poisoning, in that the child may learn to test limits and provoke others by repeatedly putting foreign objects into his mouth. Consistent with this assertion, Barkley and Edwards (2006) have noted a higher than usual rate of poisoning for diagnosed children.

Subtleties to Reflect On

To disregard the influence of biology would be irresponsible, because biological *factors* can increase the probability of learning ADHD. Although one need not conclude that biology is antecedent and seminal to ADHD; theories based entirely on biology (similar to theories based solely on environment) have not produced criteria to adequately predict diagnosis. Statements about biology are relevant in discussions about behavior, although in our view, biology does not determine the changes in frequency rates of certain behaviors when certain scenarios are reencountered.

Even though it has been observed that the parent-child interactions between diagnosed persons and their primary caregivers are frequently negative and directive (Keown and Woodward, 2002) thus leading to poorer outcomes (Webster-Stratton, Reid, and Hammond, 2001), our model proposed here does not attempt to fault either the parent or the child when ADHD diagnosis occurs. Focus is given to how each participant reinforces the other's behavior in specific ways. By employing this perspective it may ultimately be more productive to learn how behavioral sequences potentially derive solutions for all involved. We reject the idea that one individual causes the other to behave in a non-normative fashion, or that either shared or unique environments cause ADHD.

Traditionalists have noted that attempts to categorize and evaluate parental behavior as an influential factor in the development of ADHD have not helped to account for the behavioral patterning (Barkley, 1998c). This failure to adequately account for ADHD patterning has subsequently been used to support the notion that ADHD is outside the realm of psychology, and that social explanations for ADHD should no longer seriously be considered (Barkley, 1998e). Parents of diagnosed children are instead encouraged to focus on gaining compliance from the "disinhibited" child, and not be concerned about the extent of democracy in the home (Barkley, 2000).

However, when considering those assertions, we suspect that general classifications of parenting style lack the specificity necessary to identify patterns of conditioning that may be increasing the frequency rates of ADHD behaviors. We have seen that very different, and even opposite, parenting behaviors may relate to the reinforcement of the same ADHD responses. Showing poor stimulus control by maternal commands (Willis and Lovaas, 1977), over stimulating the child, or parental psychological problems (Barkley, 1998e) may or may not correlate with ADHD child behaviors, depending on other parameters.

General descriptors of parental behaviors will not necessarily correspond with learning histories that shape ADHD patterning; ADHD may be conditioned early and in relation to the myriad styles of parenting. For instance, children in permissive families can become conditioned to behave intrusively, in that limits have not been designated to help the child shape considerate behavior; waiting and turn taking may be neglected within that kind of patterning. Some children in permissive households can also learn how not to participate by having family members who are avoidant, inconsistent or neglectful. However, depending on many other parameters, another child in the same family might be encouraged or reinforced to be conscientious, in that other family members respond favorably when he or she assumes family responsibilities that others ignore.

Given the complexities of what is possible within families, it is unlikely that generalized categories such as parenting style will effectively predict the more specific kinds of behaviors being learned over time by particular children. A parent might show various kinds of psychological problems, negativity, permissiveness, positive adjustment, strictness, or possibly be overly critical, and ADHD may be reinforced often or infrequently in relation to general statements about these parental behaviors. Much like the heterogeneous ADHD behaviors where persons do the extremes of intrusiveness or disengagement, parents may often act out the extremes of excessive protectiveness or detach-ment, and diagnostic patterning will still be reinforced.

Moreover, since investigations carried out by traditionalists have often relied on parental report, inquiries into the extent to which ADHD behaviors may be reinforced have not been reliable or informative; many adults are unaware about how their actions reinforce others to behave in particular ways. For example, anecdotal evidence tells us that a parent with a self-professed democratic style may nevertheless be reinforcing the child's ADHD behaviors by over-accommodating, making idle threats, not adequately instilling self-sufficiency, or not resolving problems in mutually acceptable ways, despite qualifying as a democratic parent. These same parents might excessively pressure their child towards acceptable behavior in one situation, and in other situations acquiesce to or infantilize the child, rather than promote greater self-reliance and cooperation when differences of opinion arise.

Therefore, even a democratic household cannot necessarily tell us the extent to which some family members unwittingly reinforce ADHD patterns rather than forge what they believe to be mutually acceptable interactions. Parenting types, moreover, cannot identify the frequency with which the child is being conditioned to rely on his or her own efforts, or what happens when problems remain unresolved through "democratic" means. Nor can we know how often the reported "democratic" collaborations occur to solve difficult problems, and how individuals attempt to stop exploitative behaviors.

Given those shortcomings, the focus of the methodology used here is on social interaction and event sequences. We study the course of events following ADHD behaviors in particular situations and circumstances and how these behaviors either increase or decrease when equivalent conditions recur. ADHD behavior is understood as an *adaptive response* to various contexts, situations, and circumstances encountered by the diagnosed person despite the maladjustment that often occurs in relation to a socio-cultural standard when expressing ADHD behaviors.

Parameters such as social class, environmental stimulation, parental criticism, attachment problems, parenting style, fast-paced cultural tempo, and insufficient or excessive parental attention or supervision (DeGrandpre, 1999; Block, 1977; Ross and Ross, 1982) will not likely account for ADHD frequency rates very well. We doubt that any environmental parameter which neglects factors pertaining to the respondent who interacts continuously with the environment will adequately or fully articulate the complexities of human behavior.

It is not surprising that ADHD does not correlate consistently with any particular child or parental categorization or biological characteristic because the social exchanges shaped over time are a function of parameters that interrelate in subtle and diverse ways. Characteristics ascribed to participants cannot predict how others will behave; the psychosocial interactions are not a function of one parameter acting upon another. Diagnostic patterning is not solely a result of something internal or endemic to the diagnosed person, nor is it caused entirely by parents or culture.

Focusing strictly on characteristics pertaining to individuals or environments has thus far not been very productive when making predictions about diagnostic responding. While ADHD patterning may correlate with fine motor coordination problems, negative early temperaments, and accident proneness (Taylor et al., 1991), not all individuals with those characteristics will evolve an ADHD pattern. Similarly, not all individuals showing poor performance on selected psychological tests show ADHD, and not all individuals with specific genetic material, or particular brain structure and function will show ADHD patterning, even if those patterns correlate with diagnosis to some degree.

One might reasonably presume that various correlates simply increase probabilities, or are consequences of having learned to do ADHD responding more frequently and severely than others. There are numerous possible combinations of parameters under which atypical patterning such as ADHD can become conditioned, the same as certain people will become astronomers rather than astronauts.

However, repetition of what we learn in different situations can instigate other problems. There is often a cost/benefit ratio associated with our actions. In this sense, the impairments and complications in adaptive functioning noted by traditionalists are examples of what happens when we learn to respond in particular ways, and then repeat those behaviors in different settings and circumstances. We are not suggesting that ADHD behaviors are delayed, but rather that doing those behaviors frequently results in social, health, academic, and work-related delays throughout life, even though the behaviors may also be reinforced. While we accept that other complicating factors can shape the type and intensity of behaviors for some diagnosed persons (e.g., low intelligence, neurological problems), frequent and severe ADHD behaviors nevertheless usually result in a failure to meet the expectations of others (even when those other complications are absent).

While the correlated complications with ADHD behavior are noteworthy, they are not unique to ADHD. Part of the human condition is that we repeat patterns of behavior learned under particular sets of conditions when encountering equivalent situations and circumstances, given the prospect of varied and unknown consequences that can occur in relation to our repetition. One illustrative example is an individual who is initially reinforced to eat everything on his plate; but when engaged in this pattern as an adult weight gain is the potential result. While it is healthier to not overeat, the reinforced pattern is to not waste food. Once this pattern is conditioned, new behavioral conditioning is necessary in order to reduce the frequency of particular eating behaviors that are resistant to extinction after years of repetition.

The current methodology identifies what happens when ADHD behaviors are emitted in various situations. The account identifies parameters that seem to reinforce ADHD responding. Thus we need to specify that which has previously occurred and what is likely to occur later as family members interact over time. To focus piecemeal on typifying molecular biology, the discipline used at home, on social class, parents' education, nutrition, parental beliefs about child rearing, marital satisfaction, and descriptions about the qualities of the parent/child relationship weakens our potential to better understand the processes of ADHD.

We anticipate that ADHD diagnostic responses are reinforced in numerous ways. One illustration is that of a diagnosed child who asks a question that she can easily answer (e.g., is that a clock?). These immature behaviors can potentially prod others to shift and accommodate. The adult can inadvertently reinforce the presenting incompetence by suddenly stopping a discussion with other adults in the room and answering the child. When patterning in this way, diagnosed children do not learn to occupy themselves when parents are busy, nor do they learn to effectively utilize their resources without quickly asking for assistance.

Diagnostic functioning can also be reinforced when the diagnosed child is reprimanded, or when others introduce content that is uncomfortable or awkward. At these times the child might do some other diagnostic act or repeat the same behavior in objection to being corrected or limited. A continuance of unacceptable responding can prevent the adult from establishing discretionary authority, and a string of diagnostic responses can distract and incite the adult, thus reinforcing the responding.

In the same way, after hitting a sibling and being reprimanded, a diagnosed child can launch into his own reprimand towards his mother about her not buying something for him. This diverts the parent away from the child's initial wrongdoing and instead focuses her attention on how she was so mean to have said "no" to him. The interaction began with a parental reprimand, but the tables quickly turn. Similarly, diagnosed persons are likely to introduce non-sequitur responses during emotional struggles; they can become easily reinforced if they successfully interrupt or derail aversive social exchanges, including when other family members are bickering.

Traditionalists would regard the aforementioned diagnostic actions as disinhibitions, but it appears that the succession of ADHD behavior also directs the adult's actions. Each new transgression or peculiar response can distract or sabotage adult authority. ADHD behaviors can thus be interpreted as determining or controlling the content of an interaction rather than allowing for an imposed agenda. But if we accept this, how can we support the notion that the child is delayed or under-controlled when those behaviors occur?

As we have seen, given the numerous reinforcement possibilities, it is necessary to study the interactive patterns of families in greater detail across a wide range of conditions. Investigators can try to ascertain clearly what takes place when there are problems coordinating events within the family, and how the child is reinforced to achieve autonomously and contribute to family functioning. Those areas of concentration might reveal numerous instances where ADHD responding is reinforced.

The current learning paradigm offers another way to account for the differences in behavior observed for those diagnosed with ADHD. The categories imposed are not located within the individual, family members, loved ones, or in any other parameter, but rather that ADHD patterning is reinforced. Statements about people, their biology, and the situations they encounter are considered within a contextual matrix. Traditionalists continue to discount ADHD theories based on characteristics of parents, patterns of care giving and management, and any other social patterns within the family (Barkley, 1998e), but it is premature to rule out an approach that examines a diagnosed person's history of reinforcement. Child management procedures that seem acceptable may also be reinforcing ADHD patterning in subtle ways. As noted by Diller (2005, 60), who "suspects" that stimulant medications may be helpful to children during mandatory schooling, "longer-term outcomes are far more affected by learning problems that have roots in family and community factors."

However, traditionalists seem to discount environmental parameters when it is observed that they correlate with ADHD. For example, trends which indicate increasing frequency of diagnosis within lower socioeconomic groups (Trites, 1979; Boyle and Lipman, 2002) are regarded as instances of non-random mating rather than a result of social factors. It is claimed that people from similar educational backgrounds are more likely to meet and mate (Barkley, 2000). Since having ADHD lowers educational attainment and socioeconomic status, traditionalists assert that social parameters may often correlate with diagnosis for biological reasons. Individuals from lower class groups are also claimed to be more likely to be exposed to environmental carcinogens, to experience difficult pregnancies, and be susceptible to other environmental deprivations that could also cause neurological disruption. This is how correlations with psychosocial parameters are incorporated into a biological determinist's genetic model.

Moreover, traditionalists have questioned whether ADHD correlates at all with social class, as suggested by some empirical work. For example, they observe that much of the correlation between ADHD and socioeconomic status (SES) seems to relate to the stringency with which an assessment of ADHD is made. When required that altogether parents, teachers, and physicians must agree on a diagnosis, ADHD is less correlated with social class. Instead it is emphasized that ADHD seems to be equally distributed across economic groups (Lambert et al., 1978), and that when instances of comorbidity such as conduct disorder are statistically controlled for, the prevalence of ADHD in lower class groups is no longer significantly different from those with higher socioeconomic status (Szatmari et al., 1989).

While traditionalists may concede that socioeconomic status can affect the severity of ADHD symptoms (Barkley, 1998f), under no circumstances do they suggest that the initial occurrence of ADHD is related to an individual's life history. Instead, they assert that "pure" ADHD presents very consistently in all socioeconomic groups (Barkley, 2006b). Social variables are seen as a possibly worsening adaptation, but are never capable of adequately accounting for the origin of ADHD behavior. Correlations between diagnosis and social class may occur because of non-random mating or other health impairing reasons, but ADHD delay can genetically affect anyone.

The traditionalists, however, seem to overlook the possibility that those same data can also be interpreted within a *learning paradigm*. For example, while ADHD may be learned in all socioeconomic classes, it might also be claimed that one is more likely to learn ADHD patterning if hindered by a particular functional problem. Lower class groups are likely to comprise greater numbers of these individuals. Similarly, when living in difficult social circumstances, there is also the increased likelihood that individuals will learn many different kinds of implacable behaviors.

Researchers could also explore the possible ways in which ADHD (and other problematic behaviors) may be reinforced when individuals live under restricted economic conditions compared to other socioeconomic levels. For example, lower SES may correlate with increased difficulty accessing resources, and future events are less predictable when individuals live in precarious financial circumstances. Less reassurance about future resources could mean that individuals are reinforced to function within a more compressed time horizon. Doing behaviors that are coordinated with distant future events cannot be envisaged to payoff as frequently. Behaviors that are consistent with one's seizing available opportunities may be reinforced more often rather than adopting a cautious approach, believing that better things will happen by deferring.

One could indeed argue that if the world is primarily characterized as a depriving, unreliable place, the more probable it becomes that behavior that is organized around immediate payoff will be reinforced. With limited available resources, there is the decreased likelihood that waiting will result in benefit. Traditionalists claim that ADHD actually *causes* behaviors organized around relatively immediate events, but our alternative psychosocial account suggests that the increased frequency of ADHD behavior in lower socioeconomic groups relates to the biopsychosocial conditions under which people learn to operate.

While there are numerous individuals and families living under economically repressive circumstances patterning *without* ADHD behaviors, limited knowledge about how to interact collaboratively can also contribute to the higher probability that lower SES individuals learn to express ADHD behavior. For example, Bernstein (1961) claims that lower class groups tend to solve problems through the use of physical strength or coercion compared to middle class groups that more often incorporate reasoning when problems occur. It is possible that middle class patterning helps to integrate the child's perspective into the social exchange, and thus reduce the probability of learning ADHD behaviors. The author explicitly notes that lower class patterning is also likely to correspond with a narrowing of time concerns, and the urgency for immediate outcomes; these behaviors are consistent with ADHD as well. It may be that the conditions of lower SES increase the frequency of learning the behaviors subsumed by an ADHD diagnosis. For example, Bernstein notes that in lower socioeconomic groups:

> The specific character of long-term goals tends to be replaced by more general notions of the future in which chance, a friend, or a relative plays a greater part than the rigorous working out of connections. Thus, present or near present activities have greater value than the relation of the present activity to the attainment of a distant goal. The system of expectancies, or the time-span of anticipation, is shortened, and this creates different sets of preferences, goals, and dissatisfactions. This environment limits the perception of the developing child of and in time (p. 297).

This psychosocial account is remarkably consistent with the traditional description of what purportedly occurs with diagnosed persons for biological reasons. For Bernstein, social condition rather than genetics and neurology is the culprit. Patterns of reinforcement are seen to influence the occurrence, shaping, and repetition of behaviors that seem analogous to ADHD.

However, since ADHD patterning occurs very early (some traditionalists do allow until puberty), and often tends to generalize quickly and pervasively, the behaviors are more typically understood as endemic and inevitable in relation to an unfolding, independent biological process that operates while the child interacts with surroundings. This traditional interpretation contrasts with explications of non-normative patterning in later development, as well as the more transient and circumstantial patterns.

For example, sometimes individuals depart from typical behavior only in specific relationships, in reaction to specific content (e.g., performing poorly on only some academic tasks), in very rare or awkward circumstances (e.g., speaking to a large group), or when angry, anxious, or sad. When these kinds of responses are observed, most of us would not consider that the person has a developmental delay. Likewise, if she returns to more normative functioning after a reasonable period of time, and after changes in psychosocial parameters, any subsequent problems are not typically ascribed to an unremitting biological substrate.

When non-normative behavioral patterns are less generalized, there are likely to be fewer negative reactions when emphasis is placed on psychology to account for those non-normative responses. For example, it seems easier to accept the claim that failure to comply is related to fear of criticism in a particular situation rather than be attributed to a neural biological delay—if noncompliance occurs in particular when criticism has historically been apparent. Similarly, a learning paradigm is generally readily accepted if individuals put themselves in jeopardy, if they overreact to injury, or exaggerate sadness and suffering *only* in limited sets of conditions such as when their mother is witness to the occurrence of those behaviors.

Comparably, if individuals get angry very quickly when blamed or restricted *only* when interacting with particular people, there might be more agreement that overreactions are reinforced. The "walking on egg shells" atmosphere may encourage the individual to continue to respond with angry patterns. If atypical behavior takes place only *some* of the time with *some* content and with *particular* people, we would be disinclined to impose a biological determinist account.

Inordinate self-indulgent patterns may also be reinforced when individuals behave as "princes" and princesses," and others frequently acquiesce to them. While not necessarily behaving immaturely, ineptly, or recklessly as is often the case with diagnosed individuals, they might only accommodate to others or extend themselves in tightly controlled ways when functioning across a wide variety of contexts and circumstances. However, if there is reason to think that these people could function in more accommodating ways, few would argue that a biological limitation impedes the extent to which they fulfill the requirements of others.

Therefore, whenever non-normative patterns appear to be more circumscribed, or when it seems that the individual could adequately meet requirements (if inclined), a psychological model is usually retained and patterns are not seen as medically-based problems as is the case for diagnosed persons. Most practitioners would agree that these less ambient behavioral patterns are learned or acquired. However, when individuals are hyperactive, impulsive, or inattentive over long periods, and across behavioral settings, the interpretation changes. Those behaviors transform into a pernicious non-normative behavior and are believed to emanate from a deficient biology that has created a developmental delay to disrupt functioning (unless held in abeyance).

While most seem to follow this interpretative pattern, we still suspect that behaviors can repeat frequently across a wide array of situations, can run in families, become evident early in development, change positively in response to medication, and show bodily correlates (including molecular biology), and still be environmentally-conditioned behavior. As long as we can establish that subsequent events alter the frequency rates of the behaviors when equivalent conditions recur, the behaviors coincide satisfactorily with a learning model, even though the behaviors are repetitious and pervasive, difficult to extinguish, and the contingencies of reinforcement are subtle. The behaviors can start early and continue, although many patterns understood to be "conditioned" may exhibit similar characteristics as well (e.g., eating disorders).

However, by recognizing that the ADHD "medical" diagnosis is often assigned too liberally, traditionalists urge diagnosticians to first consider whether other medical conditions might be responsible for symptoms that seem to be ADHD. For example, Murphy and Gordon (2006) note that stress can make individuals appear to have the condition. They claim that the ADHD diagnosis is only meant for those who are significantly inattentive and poorly self-controlled throughout their lives. Diagnosticians should ensure that presenting problems are not more reasonably accounted for by other diagnostic categories and problems.

When following this traditional protocol, diagnosis should be reserved only for those showing ADHD behaviors over the course of at least one year, relatively early in development (i.e., prior to adolescence: ages 10-12), across more than one major setting, and when other diagnoses are less tenable. Clinicians are also urged to combine their observations with other materials (e.g., school records, psychological tests, and interviews with teachers and family members) before formulating a diagnosis. ADHD is assumed not to be caused by family dysfunction; problems should present as atypical developmental patterns, and not occur in relation to psychosocial trauma (Barkley and Edwards, 2006).

Although when conforming to those criteria, if a young child begins to do diagnostic responding in a currently stressed family, and his older brother also qualifies for an ADHD diagnosis, the evaluator is saddled with the task of determining whether the younger brother is simply imitating the older brother's behavioral pattern, or is disinhibited in a neurological sense. While traditionalists may presume that such distinctions can be reliably established, they have not clarified how one can accurately make a differential diagnosis in that case. This seems to be especially thorny if the younger sibling enacts diagnostic behaviors when quite young, and maintains the patterning over the required year.

At this juncture it seems prudent to ask other important questions. How many empirical studies are being carried out by traditionalists to examine early interactive patterns between children and parents that could help to identify possible histories of reinforcement that correlate with the behavioral criteria? How many investigations observe how parents of atypically motoric toddlers can possibly reinforce risk taking and other diagnostic responses? What inquiries are taking place to identify ways that parents shape self-reliance and family contribution—or perhaps more immature patterning—when a child shows a developmental delay and fine motor and encoding difficulties?

Moreover, if diagnosis cannot be assigned when there is evidence of family stress (even if DSM-IV-TR criteria are met), it is unreasonable to suggest during an epidemiological study that the absence of psychological problems in diagnosed families supports biological determinism. In other words, if investigators exclude those who fit the diagnostic criteria and have been exposed to stressful circumstances, they cannot use the *absence* of an atypical psychosocial history to substantiate the view that ADHD is biologically determined.

Because medical tests are not employed during the process, doubt can arise about the veracity of the diagnostic decision. Diagnosis is a clinical judgment, which relies heavily on interpretations of others, and is therefore susceptible to a wide array of distortions (Gordon and Barkley, 1998). The heart of the evaluation centers on the reports of loved ones, particularly when individuals do not self-refer. Often these family members complain that the person is distracted and often unwilling to follow their instructions (Barkley, 1998f).

However, when relying on such reports, a medical diagnosis based on the ways that a person reacts to the requests, demands, requirements, and preferences of loved ones in daily functioning is put forth. If individuals (typically children) are regarded as too active, impetuous, and non-attentive when conformity to an agenda is required, an ADHD label may be ascribed; and very often it is the individuals living with these persons or teaching them in school (authority figures) who are responsible for making these assessments.

Other problems arise, given that an ADHD diagnosis is permissible as long as the behaviors are evident in a minimum of two settings. However, when adopting such criteria, we can also argue that, although school and home are usually regarded as unique spheres, they are not as independent or distinct as one might think. Children interact continuously with parents about school topics, and teachers and parents discuss school performance, which in turn influences the relationship between child and parent. Repetition of particular behaviors both in school and at home is therefore not surprising; the two settings are not mutually exclusive.

Moreover, when functioning in school is given significant weight in assigning diagnosis, it further emphasizes that ADHD patterning is a set of behaviors that occur in response to expectations, instructions, and other forms of social constraint. While parents observe their children's behavior in a wide array of contexts and circumstances, teachers normally observe children's behavior within the confines of the classroom, which is imbued with expectations. For that reason, it seems that a teacher's participation in the evaluation is even less likely to yield data about the child's non-assigned actions, yet information from school frequently tips the decision when assigning diagnosis.

While traditionalists urge evaluators to base diagnoses on functioning in more than one major setting, to the extent that school performance is frequently one of those settings, we see that inordinate emphasis is placed on how the child responds to instruction from others (compliance) compared to the child's behavior within a more self-determined agenda. The classroom behavioral sample is restricted, and is thus unlikely to enlighten us about the child's behavior when he or she maintains discretionary authority, and functions independently from comments about the adequacy of a response.

Other problems can also occur when individuals who assess do not always agree on how to describe the diagnosed person. Failure to obtain consensus not only occurs between the diagnosed person and evaluators, but also between primary caretakers and teachers. For example, Achenbach et al. (1987) indicate that parent and teacher reports show a relatively low average correlation of approximately 0.30.

Similarly, a relatively large scale longitudinal study called the Milwaukee Follow-up Study, found that only 3% of the subjects would qualify for a diagnosis if assessment were based solely on the diagnosed person's self-report (Barkley, 2002). However, when parents of these individuals were interviewed, Fischer (1997) noted that 42% would have qualified for an ADHD diagnosis. Given such data, it would seem that depending on which reports are used, diagnosis may or may not be assigned or be consistent over time. Moreover, no data is available on whether parents in general change their opinions about their children's behavior regardless of whether or not they qualify for an ADHD diagnosis.

In many ways the ADHD category of behavior is erratic. Behaviors can be expressed in school for one time period, with some teachers, and not at other times. The diagnosed person can show intermittent ADHD behavior within the family and still qualify for diagnosis. He might also function acceptably at school as well as home for substantial lengths of time and yet possibly qualify for diagnosis. Given this variability of scenarios, it is difficult to justify a diagnosis when there are relatively long periods when symptoms do not occur in any setting whatsoever. Traditionalists insist that none of this should dissuade us (Barkley, 2006b), but these problems are crucial to the assignment of an ADHD diagnosis.

Learning: A Substitute for Traditional Explication

Traditional interpretations abound in comparative observations between diagnosed individuals and controls when operating in society or the laboratory. For example, Barkley (1998g) claims that diagnosed individuals will initiate the inhibition of a response at a slower rate than others. He claims that they are less able to disengage when responding, and shift to more productive responses when signaled by others during task completion. This account is presented as if it were a factual rendition, although it is based on Barkley's assumptions and tacit presumptions about human behavior. His data do not indicate that individuals have a slower initiation of response inhibition or an inability to disengage; that is Barkley's construction and interpretation.

While there is consensus that diagnosed persons do not stop as quickly as controls, or shift task as rapidly when instructed to do so, there is no independent basis on which to decide if this is because the posited inhibition did not occur. There are a multitude of reasons that can account for the patterns. For example, the individual might have been reinforced to follow self-initiations, and to not respond to directives from others during most daily interactions. Those learned patterns of behavior could be repeating. Inability to control oneself is not the only explanation. MacCorquodale and Meehl (1948, 97) make a similar claim when they emphasize that "one can deduce empirical laws from sentences involving hypothetical constructs, but not conversely."

Moreover, it is noteworthy that traditionalists apparently invoke what Mac-Corquodale and Meehl call a "hypothetical construct" when they infer that inhibitions occur under some circumstances of behavior, and that the failure of this inhibitory response accounts for the discrepant behavior of persons diagnosed with ADHD. According to MacCorquodale and Meehl, hypothetical constructs pertain to the "hypothesization of an entity, process, or event which is not itself observed" (p. 95). It appears as if traditionalists' usage of the term *inhibition* is consistent with this meaning. For instance, in an attempt to concretize the inhibitory mechanism, traditionalists identify certain brain structures as the physical representation of this inhibitory apparatus, in that damage or injury to these biological structures correlates with impaired actions believed to require an inhibitory response (Barkley, 1998g).

Although it is not yet an empirical fact that an hypothesized inhibitory process is a necessary prerequisite for the development and enactment of behaviors we identify as self-regulated (Barkley, 1998g), this hypothetical process is for now the traditional and most accepted way to account for the different behavioral patterns between diagnosed persons and controls on some tasks, and the particular interactions often evident between diagnosed individuals and other people under some conditions. However, despite the apparent consensus, there could be myriad other possibilities that would reveal consistency with empirical observations. As MacCorquodale and Meehl have indicated, empirical findings cannot be used to deduce a hypothesized construct; the debate is seldom about data, but rather is centered on the *meaning* ascribed to the data.

Traditionalists rely on laboratory findings as proof that an inhibitory problem caused by neurological delay gives rise to behavioral discrepancies, and that all responses—apart from the most basic prepotent reactions—require an inhibitory step as a preliminary first occurrence. Diagnosed individuals allegedly commit errors because they are less able to control themselves due to this posited delay; they are also unable to access executive functioning in order to behave appropriately. Executive functioning cannot be supported and protected from interference, and "the generation and execution of the cross-temporal goal-directed behavioral structures . . ." that develop from the executive functions will also not occur (Barkley, 1998g, 229).

Traditionalists posit all of these inner processes and insist that their views are the most scientific, but it is unclear how their presumed inhibitory response adheres to scientific criteria. It is not possible to know if the *hypothetical unobservable inhibitory process* was or was not occurring, whether or not it was protecting and supporting, and whether or not it performed those duties so that other hypothetical constructs called "cross-temporal goal-directed behavioral structures" could take place. This mentalist construction merely highlights the observation that diagnosed persons sometimes behave differently from controls.

In contrast, a *learning paradigm* can account for differential behavior between diagnosed persons and controls by elaborating a reinforcement history through a model that coordinates frequencies of particular behaviors with present conditions and past events. The explanatory system relies on what Mac-Corquodale and Meehl have called "intervening variables." This variable is defined as a "construct that merely abstracts empirical relationships, and it does not suppose an entity or process not among the observed events" (p. 95). The mentalist constructions of the traditional inhibitory model are therefore avoided, and the "intervening variable" labeled as reinforcement history is offered as a substitute formulation.

This "intervening variable" is not given ontological status, nor is it presumed that something extra happens within the person when we say that the person has been reinforced. The terminology is used to help us discuss the relationships between present conditions, past sequencing of events, and the frequency rates of behaviors. An "intervening variable" does not identify particular inner workings; it merely coordinates these parameters. We regard this approach as a viable way to explicate the numerous instances and severity of ADHD behaviors for particular persons with particular histories and present circumstances. The current model posits that ADHD social responding and atypical functioning on various laboratory tasks may be reasonably understood within a psychologically-based account. ADHD reactions in the lab and during social interactions are interpreted as conditioned responses rather than evidence of neurological delay.

For example, if it is frequently the case that not responding to directives is reinforced, in that non-responsiveness sequences with avoidance of *assigned activity* (often associated with failure and disapproval), increased soliciting and accommodation from others, or that not responding permits self-initiated actions to continue, we can then predict that low responsiveness will be observed in the laboratory when directives are imposed. The person has become conditioned to be less responsive, and those behaviors repeat under various conditions within and outside the lab. Decreased responsiveness to requirements (initiated by others) could generalize to include a wide variety of content, people, and settings (also the laboratory). If laboratory behaviors are understood as samples of reinforced reactions rather than as the pathway to inhibitory delays, it is reasonable to alter circumstances to detect whether more adequate responsiveness to feedback is the result. Thus we can determine whether acceptable responses can be shaped through a systematic altering of the individual's history of conditioning. We might try this intervention before concluding that a fixed delay is operative.

While ADHD behavioral extremes can be problematic, dangerous, and unsettling, greatly upset social relationships, and lead to failure in life's major arenas, one may still be reinforced to behave in those ways. All of the behaviors subsumed within the diagnostic category can *reasonably be understood as conditioned* in relation to the sequencing of events that occur when they are emitted, and characterized as functional from that vantage point. The behaviors increase the frequency rates of particular outcomes, even if those outcomes are not considered appropriate or acceptable.

We often observe that the reinforcements are so strong that siblings are jealous of the attention their brothers or sisters receive (Barkley, 2006e). If ADHD patterning is not reinforced, why then are diagnosed persons often the least likely to respond positively when others indicate that they want them to change? When considering the payoff, ADHD often seems like a peculiar condition that does not interfere with efficient responding when the child is asked if he or she would like to take a turn, but *does* interfere with efficient responding when the child is told that his or her turn is over.

By observing events that seem to influence the frequency rates of ADHD responses, we can argue that behavioral control is different rather than delayed for diagnosed persons. Rather than something being amiss, the behaviors could be understood as coordinating with a different *sequencing* of events. While some of these event sequences are clearly not beneficial from the perspective of normative practice, it is also possible to identify how those behaviors coordinate with outcomes that could be described as advantageous for the enactor. A similar claim could be made in relation to smoking cigarettes, working excessively, and frequent shopping; these are behavioral acts that also often result in negative long-term consequences. As noted, since diagnosed persons can at times adequately follow instructions, persist and achieve over time, and share responsibility under certain conditions, it is problematic to argue that they are less able do these behaviors given their biological limitations. The problem becomes explaining the reduced occurrence of these behaviors when it is socially important to do so; we invoke utilizing history of reinforcement in order to accomplish that end.

To illustrate the difference between the two approaches, we can focus on how each perspective accounts for patterns of disorganized behavior. For example, Barkley (1998f) discusses how others must often reorganize the diagnosed person's belongings in order to help them achieve at school. Often their lockers, notebooks, and desks are in disarray. These behaviors, according to Barkley, are a result of an underlying neurological limitation that prevents better control of future consequences. However, the alternative view is that it is possible to account for the disorganized behaviors by exploring how being less tidy and organized are reinforced.

For example, others will tend to clean the mess for the diagnosed child. There is also the possibility of increased concern and assistance from others when they perceive a lack of competence. Unwanted articles can be discarded at an accelerated pace; or perhaps the extra time and effort required to help the diagnosed child put his belongings away in a more conscientious fashion also inadvertently reinforces the child to continue the neglectful patterning. Such reinforcement is not likely to develop a behavior of routine and orderly placement of objects.

There may be numerous other possible reinforcements when messiness is observed. For example, perhaps diagnosed children are repeating behaviors that occur more often when they handle trash. When doing those repetitions, their disorganization enables them to rid themselves of school-related objects more quickly by haphazardly throwing them into lockers or desks. Not seeing or retrieving schoolwork is thus reinforced, compared with taking time to examine the objects and carefully situate materials (i.e., out of sight, out of mind).

Moreover, to the extent that disheveled clothing and misplaced essentials are often replaced or organized by others, we think that disorderliness can be reinforced for some children in many ways. From this vantage point we are therefore unable to know whether diagnosed children are less able to organize, or if it is instead the case that they have not yet been shaped to do those more acceptable behaviors in particular situations due to the confines of their reinforcement history. While some of the consequences of ADHD behaviors might coincide with such annoyances as losing papers, ruining clothing, frustrating others, or not doing certain assignments, we detect that other sequences of events continue to reinforce the repetition of the ADHD responding. This seems particularly evident when the child has a history of failure with the expected tasks, or has learned to respond in less accommodating ways when others arbitrarily impose limits and requirements.

These views can be corroborated, moreover, if we see that these same children can exhibit careful and organized behavior when handling other objects in other contexts and situations (e.g., new toys, collectibles). Their haphazard placement of certain objects could easily be construed as conditioning that often occurs with school-related materials, or belongings that adults value, or to avoid requirements imposed by others. The events that sequence with these behaviors may account for their frequency rates, and the messy school desks and lockers can be understood as reinforced patterns that occur in response to particular social constraints, stipulations, and compensations. To claim that these individuals are less able to "acceptably" organize their belongings, whereas when in other areas they are fully capable of organizational behavior, highlights the problem of how to intervene on the child's behalf.

More succinctly, intervention may simply be a matter of shaping the child's more careful handling of school materials and personal belongings in precisely the same way as that same child protects a valued personal possession. For example, when a diagnosed child does not want a sibling to locate a particular possession, its placement is more conscientious and coordinated with the distant future outcome that the sibling will not find it. Intervention is simply a means of getting more acceptable behaviors to repeat more often in different contexts and circumstances.

However, the conventional view is that these more acceptable behaviors occur only because of environmental compensation or lower situational demands. Because of those beliefs, Anastopoulos, Smith, and Wien (1998) urge parents to make consequences more meaningful and varied in order to ensure that the ADHD individual is kept interested, since boredom is likely, unless special precautions are taken to offset the lurking inability to access executive functioning.

There is, on the other hand, no requirement to invoke a failed sequence of inhibition and executive function to account for the occurrence of ADHD behaviors, if traditional views are not endorsed. For example, a bored response can be "conditioned" when others do not do what the child wants, or when the child realizes that others will try to accommodate or please when displeasure is expressed. Thus, when complaining of boredom, it becomes the parent or teacher's fault for not doing enough. To the extent that reinforcing outcomes occur (e.g., parent or teacher satisfies the child), the frequency rates of stating or showing boredom are likely to increase.

Generally, complaints of boredom prevail when diagnosed persons must endure another's agenda, when others do not follow their initiatives, if they are limited or insufficiently indulged, when unsuccessful, when variations (especially during assigned activity) are infrequent, when tasks are extremely easy, or when their efforts are required to please someone else. In some instances, complaints of boredom are presented as justification for outlandish, idiotic, and self-indulgent action. All of these event sequences may reinforce persons to complain of boredom; it is not necessarily the case that they have less access to executive functioning that would otherwise stimulate them.

In the same way, when required tasks are simplified (Barber and Milich, 1989) and made more palatable by offering more intense less delayed reinforcements, many diagnosed persons begin to respond more acceptably (Luman et al., 2005). But this does not establish that their inhibitory delay is being temporarily rectified. Diagnosed children also become more excitable in response to rewards, and also more visibly frustrated when past rates of reinforcement decline (Douglas and Parry, 1994; Wigal et al., 1998). However, this empirical finding may only mean that diagnosed individuals have been conditioned so that others increase rewards (i.e., do more for them) when they are enthusiastic or frustrated in particular situations and circumstances. Overreactions can increase the frequency of others accommodating to them. These responses can be seen as an example of reinforced behaviors rather than indices of delay or less controlled responding.

On balance, if one accepts the possibility that ADHD patterning can be coherently understood within a learning paradigm, the notion of neurological delay need not be invoked to account for every behavioral anomaly exhibited by diagnosed individuals, despite that some diagnosed people may have neurological delays and other functional problems. If we are to shape diagnosed children to be more tolerant of situations that are not to their liking, we might condition them to be more accommodating to what others want, and become less reliant on something or someone else to relieve their dissatisfaction. We expect that the constant search for novelty will decrease as the child learns how to transform activities and situations by using personal resources.

Although no singular social pattern will account for the majority of cases, it is worthwhile to investigate how ADHD behaviors may become more pervasively reinforced. In some cases these reinforcements may occur when children recognize that parental or adult prodding and pleading to behave "for their own good" is a form of caring. Others may learn that diagnostic responding can compel people to do more for them. Some may learn that not following instructions can reduce requirements, keep expectations low, or help to avoid failure. Some learn that people will frequently accommodate them if they act difficult to please, are sensitive to disappointment, or act vulnerable. Still others may learn that rapidly paced behaviors will prevent others from impeding their efforts or constraining them, and at other times, learn to react lethargically, thereby making it more difficult for others to stipulate or coerce.

Not surprisingly, hyperactive behaviors occur more frequently in younger children, as motor responses are the first human behaviors. The only requirement for enacting hyperactive behaviors is to move and magnify. Hyperactive behaviors change conditions rapidly, and often increase excitement and stimulation, and eliminate loneliness. In contrast to remaining sedate or introducing variation by engaging in skillful manipulations, the behaviors are less intricate or difficult to enact. Like throwing confetti into the air, lighting fireworks, or rocking back and forth in a chair, variation and enjoyment are produced through movement, and ADHD hyperactive behaviors can be reinforced whether the child is alone or with others.

In that hyperactive behaviors are more likely to be enacted by those with a limited behavioral repertoire, it is not surprising that it takes several years to identify children in relation to hyperactive behaviors. Relatively young children are usually more motoric and show less language facility, which would otherwise permit alternative forms of engagement and coordination of action. Since younger children often orient towards physically active and tactile involvement, any behavior that goads others to chase can become conditioned across different situations.

Hyperactive silliness and ineffectuality also seem to be reinforced when a child's attempts to achieve have not been successful. For children with a history of failure and disapproval when responding to parental and teacher expectations, inane hyperactive behaviors can be conditioned frequently, in that these children avoid the unwanted event sequence of trying and failing. Hyperactivity protects them from their fear of failure. This problem can sometimes occur when the diagnosed child is also struggling with fine motor, language and learning problems, or encounters perfectionism in others, for example. Hyperactivity in this case allows for the child to avoid the disappointment of not meeting the expectations of others. As noted by Zentall, Cassady, and Javorsky (2001) and Matthys, Cuperus, and van Engeland (1999), diagnosed children often show less optimism and generate fewer responses when responding to problematic social situations.

But rather than to characterize hyperactive behaviors as out of control (e.g., pouring pails of liquid onto their clothes, not away from their bodies), the behaviors are understood as immature and demanding, in that they increase attention towards themselves and require little practice or skill. Instead of making the case that these children have difficulty inhibiting and then anticipating future distant eventualities, the behaviors are framed as showing off, rambunctious, or clownish, and are reinforced by the contingences that take place. However, if a child patterns in this way, sitting quietly, waiting, and behaving in more acceptable ways will be difficult to condition. The requirement to be sedentary might be associated with restriction, and therefore escapist behavior is likely to occur in a wide range of situations.

Hyperactive responding may be characterized as loosening the control of self by others, in that for the child, risk taking becomes the consummate form of breaking free from imposed constraints much like when younger children engage in fantasy activity. The behaviors may be understood as relatively extreme ways of disregarding and defying boundaries and establishing ownership of extraordinary capability. Hyperactive behaviors can foment crisis and drama, and it often does not matter whether others approve (i.e., the squeaky wheel gets the grease). If he receives only mild reaction, the child will continue until a stronger reaction is evoked. The behaviors can be reinforced by the excitement, which becomes its own reward.

Other social agendas become increasingly difficult when children behave in extreme ways. The more a child engages in fearful or undesirable behaviors, the more a parent worries, and attends to the child. Rarely is there time for anything else, including other family members, leisure activity, or employment. These sequences of events can influence hyperactive behaviors, and account for the high frequency rates of many ADHD actions.

Hyperactive patterning can be compelling, as not only does the child usurp and monopolize family resources, but because hyperactive behaviors also make it less probable that the child will be denied. Reckless treatment of objects, or increased instances of placing oneself in personal jeopardy almost invariably lead to focused attention from loved ones. Many children also learn to incite others by making outlandish verbal statements (e.g., "I wish rocks would fall on the school."). While it is important to protect everyone involved, this kind of hyperbole is often reinforced by the commotion that ensues. As soon as troublesome statements or hyperactive behaviors occur, all heads turn; discipline is directed towards the individual who may not have been the center of attention prior to doing the unacceptable actions. Hyperactive behavior is generally within the repertoire of most extremely young children and toddlers. The more chaos, turmoil, and pandemonium there is the greater is the probability that important adults get involved.

Moreover, hyperactive patterns can become relentless when the behaviors elicit inconsistent responses from adults. If a parent is negative, the child can pout and become angry. If the parent then becomes conciliatory, there is the possibility that the child will increase the frequency of similar hyperactive behaviors in other situations. Similarly, a parent can reinforce the child's rambunctious behavior by smiling during one instance (as if the behavior is cute), and at other times responding negatively. The variability associated with these parental responses adds to the difficulty encountered when trying to extinguish those actions. Likewise, if the parent defends the diagnosed child when others react negatively, that pattern can also reinforce the child to continue the irritating actions.

Diagnostic responding could also become more frequent under conditions of social propriety, that is, when patterns of interaction are impatient or focused on others. When diagnosed children are intrusive and obnoxious in public places, this patterning can effectively provoke the parent who is concerned about social decorum. In the case where the parent is also a role model for similar behavior (e.g., disapproving the child in front of others or invading the child's privacy), the child is also more likely to imitate that behavior.

Although changing any pattern requires great tenacity, the difficulty associated with eliminating a behavior tells us *nothing about its source*. Repetitions of behaviors can be advantageous or detrimental depending on circumstances, and behaviors that are problematic can nevertheless be reinforced in many different ways. However, despite the fact that we all learn at different rates, the ADHD debate has never been about intellectual prowess or delays in rates of learning. We are concerned about whether the frequency rates of ADHD behaviors relate to lifestyle categories or to a biological problem. Currently, the debate seems to be whether a delayed inhibitory system prevents some individuals from doing executive behaviors, or whether some people (due to their biopsychosocial circumstance) simply *learn* to enact ADHD behaviors more frequently and severely than others due to the long-term reinforcement of those same behaviors.

Given that numerous different unacceptable behaviors (including ADHD) can be frequently reinforced, it is not surprising that medication and increased structure are the most common ways to induce change; those interventions above all can get relatively ubiquitous troublesome behaviors to stop more rapidly. For this reason few people choose alternative approaches. However, clinicians often address problems related to response generalization when doing psychotherapy, and many encourage their clients to change present conditions in different ways so that new responses might be elicited, and help their clients explore alternative ways of responding to old situations that continuously recur so that new event sequences will take their place. Although psychotherapeutic intervention can be time consuming, long-term results can nevertheless be impressive for many participants.

Chapter 3

A Critique of the Traditional Biological Argument

In this chapter we discuss the weaknesses and inconsistencies in each of three arguments used to promote biological causality for ADHD diagnosis: that behavior runs in families (Smalley et al., 2000); biological differences correlate with diagnosis (Yeo, 2003), and special conditions (including medication) must often be introduced to achieve desired results. Taken altogether (Pliszka, Mc-Cracken, and Maas, 1996), these arguments are presented as grounds for the existence of a biological delay. However, none of the arguments has effectively established that ADHD behaviors are not also learned behaviors.

High heritability quotients do not disprove the impact of the environment on behavior. Additionally, the studies carried out thus far neither includes data on the diverse learning histories of participants, nor any evidence of a systematic effort to identify possible confounded environmental effects. Second, it may be that links between patterns of biology and diagnosis only demonstrate a coincidence of biology and behavior rather than provide unequivocal proof for biological determinism. Third, the fact that medication can reduce ADHD behavior does not inform us about the etiology of the ADHD diagnosis. Medication may alter ADHD behaviors, but it also does not refute the notion that ADHD behaviors are also learned.

Over the years debate has been jangling about the extent to which behaviors are attributable to nature (biology and genetics), or to nurture: the acquisition of behavioral patterns as a function of events occurring in everyday life. Psychological studies of behaviors have thus far emphasized behavioral events, but there is also concerted emphasis on finding relationships between behavior and biology. Currently, most investigators believe that nature *and* nurture each play essential roles in behavior, with the exception being reflexive reactions. There are now more investigations that attempt to *quantify* the relative importance that nature and nurture have for particular classes of behavior. The main struggle underway seems to be between investigators who attempt to quantify behavior they deem inherent, and investigators who adopt the view that largely, behaviors are learned and shaped by ongoing experiences.

Bonham et al. (2005) note that in our "Genome Era" many professionals (including psychologists) are increasingly emphasizing nature or genetics to account for some differences among individuals for some kinds of behaviors. For example, Berry et al. (2003) report an association between certain genes and schizophrenia. Ryu et al. (2004) offer a genetic explanation for depression. Lam et al. (2004) identify relationships between genetic material and panic disorder. Dick and Foroud (2003) find genetic co-occurrences with alcoholism, and Bespalova and Buxbaum (2003) observe genetic co-occurrences with autism. Similarly, Ebstein et al. (1996) have investigated possible genetic influences with novelty seeking behaviors, and Caspi et al. (2002) with antisocial behavior.

The finding that identical twins are the most likely to show concordance for various kinds of mood disorders, psychotic disorders, substance abuse disorders, as well as ADHD, is seen to support the view that nature is more influential than nurture with regard to many atypical behaviors. While those studying heritability generally recognize that developmental outcomes are not inevitable or predetermined (i.e., canalization), once it is established that a trait shows high genetic loading, many scientists infer that the condition is highly fixed and is essentially acting on the individual.

ADHD, for all intents and purposes, has been characterized as impervious to environmental effects. Although Barkley (1998e, 175) states that ADHD symptoms are still "malleable to unique environmental influences and non-shared social learning," he also claims that it is only the "severity," "continuity," types of "secondary" problems, and/or eventual outcome of ADHD that is "related in varying degrees to environmental factors." Similarly, Faraone et al. (1992, 272) argue that while "environmental factors are necessary for the gene to be expressed as ADHD," they also maintain that "a single major gene may be etiologically involved in the familiar transmission" of the troublesome patterning.

Traditionalists emphasize that it is possible to predict (with some confidence) who will show the behaviors by using genetic models. To the extent that this is possible the behaviors are recognized as innate. For instance, Biederman et al. (1995) report that if a parent has the disorder, then 57% of the time their offspring will show the condition. This data has generated plenty of excitement, even though a value of 57% is not significantly different from 50%, which can be translated as a random probability of prediction of a genetic match or a non-match.

Understandably, individuals who are informed that they are inherently inferior become offended, discouraged, and outraged by such a definitive conclusion of permanency (Frontline, 2001). It is therefore not surprising that those who object to such negative designations argue that there is greater environmental control over the trait being studied than suggested by biological determinist's interpretations. Their counter argument runs that changes in behavior could likely occur if they were given more access to resources, more opportunities to learn, and greater exposure to helpful advice.

Individuals who think that their opportunities have been limited by external agents, and are considered to be "unable" to perform well, will also resent the implication that they are constitutionally less capable. They may continue to insist that environmental changes can affect behavior. The conclusion that the quality of their performance is primarily inherited is taken as a pernicious decision resulting in inequities that further impede achievement. It is therefore not surprising that those identified as functioning poorly neither agree nor accept the defeatist interpretation that their behavior is fixed and beyond their own control.

We have also seen cases in which individuals and groups interpret conclusions about the relative importance of nature or nurture as demeaning to their ethnicity, race, or culture. Their reaction often provides the impetus to review findings and inspect data for mistakes and limitations (Egerton, 1973). Weaknesses are highlighted, inferences from the data are debated, and alternative interpretations are discussed and posited.

However, the idea that ADHD is a fixed, inherited condition has not stimulated the same outcry that occurs when assertions are made about the inheritability of intelligence, variations between racial groups that account for different social positions (Gould, 1996), or that males are inherently more capable than females in certain kinds of functioning. While Barkley (2000) notes that individuals can react adversely and suffer a "grief reaction" when they hear that they have the incurable ADHD condition, we notice a very peculiar response from a large subset of diagnosed individuals. Often people approach professionals hoping to convince them that they actually *have* the limiting condition.

Since ADHD is explained as biological delay, it then becomes easier to accept that failure and disruptive behaviors are inevitable and beyond one's control, thus they need not feel guilt or blame. Shockingly, the trend is so widespread that many individuals are relieved to receive an ADHD diagnosis assigned in their case. They readily accept the view that much like what is described in discussion about "action potential" and "firing of neurons," ADHD persons are spiked more easily by the outside world, and their bodies (specifically, their inhibitory mechanisms created by their genes) cannot prevent motor reactions that lead them into difficulty. Murphy (2006) notes that it can be encouraging and helpful for diagnosed persons to hear that their underachievement, frustration, and missed opportunities are largely a consequence of problems with neurobiology rather than with character. While diagnosed individuals may appear to be impolite, tactless, irresponsible, or obnoxious, Murphy believes that diagnosed individuals can feel liberated by knowing that many of these interpersonal problems stem from a biological condition that has not been adequately managed.

Although concern is rising about the increases in labeling individuals with ADHD, Barkley (2000) insists that the higher numbers of diagnosed individuals relate to more effective identification and treatment of previously unclassified persons. He insists that the base rate of the condition within the general population remains essentially unchanged even though greater numbers of people are being identified as having an ADHD diagnosis and are accepting that conclusion.

Moreover, when data are presented indicating that base rates may be changing, those upholding biological determinism invariably attribute those changes to genetic factors rather than psychological variables. For example, Barkley (2002) speculates that any increase can be due to better medical care, thus infants now survive that might otherwise have died. The result of medical improvements is that more impaired individuals enter the population. However, the counter claim is that the same improved medical care can also limit the number of individuals who *would* have been impaired due to less sophisticated medical intervention. Given that possibility, it is not crystal clear as to how improvement in medical care is increasing the number of *impaired* individuals.

Whatever the reasons for any possible changes in base rate, the frequency of diagnosis is highly dependent on the population sample, as well as the criteria and methods used to assign the diagnostic label. For example, if criteria are selected that identify a fixed percentage of people (i.e., seven percent), then there will always be this proportion of individuals with the "condition" despite what occurs in the general population. The criteria are designed to adjust to population shifts similar to what occurs when there are changes in the distributions of scores in intelligence testing (Kanaya et al., 2003).

Additionally, we could argue that the increased identification of the disorder relates to labeling and discrimination within a traditional framework, while excluding other possibilities. For example, with the emphasis given to genetic causality for the ADHD disorder in the media, suggestibility can encourage individuals to channel their observations of behavior into a category system consistent with popular belief. While traditionalists agree that some individuals are resistant, reluctant, or unwilling to be labeled as ADHD, or they make concerted efforts to shun the categories on the rating scales, we observe that many others (especially teachers and parents) are increasingly tending to describe and classify disruptive behavioral patterns in ways compatible with a model of disinhibition and biological determinism.

The Genetic Argument

ADHD is understood by a majority of the U.S. population to be a biochemical condition caused by a particular type of genetic constitution. Many are attempting to locate the ADHD gene or constellation of genes that essentially cause the disorder which permanently induces "behavioral disinhibition." For example, Barkley (2000) remains optimistic that molecular research will eventually quell the controversy, and thus validate the view that biologically-based factors are the driving forces behind ADHD behavior.

When alluding to the inhibitory system, traditionalists posit two systems (i.e., biological and mental). The first system is the biological inhibitory system that refers to brain activity and structure, or to categories pertaining to neurology. Traditionalists then attempt to identify how biology correlates with ADHD behavior. For example, investigators try to determine whether manipulations or alterations of these structures correlate with ADHD behavior, and whether the size or any other characteristic of the biology correlates with diagnosis. Since some empirical work has shown relationships between ADHD behavior and particular biology, the conclusion is that aspects of biology account for (and cause) the observed behavioral acts. It is then posited that this biology facilitates the occurrence of certain kinds of mental activities (regarding self control). Behavioral disinhibition is seen as the consequence of having delays in this biological system, which allows for some people to do certain mental acts at particular times. As Barkley (2006a, 31) notes, environmental causes for ADHD have been undermined as evidence accumulates "for the heritability of the condition and its neuro-anatomical localization."

The biological determinists also posit that diagnosed persons have a "genotype" (information inscribed in the two meters of coiled DNA in each cell) that produces relatively poor inhibitory functioning. While genotype was merely a hypothetical construct before the advent of molecular biology, it is now possible to actually observe the biology associated with this term. As Lewontin (1994) points out, genotypes relate to an internal state, while phenotypes pertain to external manifestations.

While it is now possible to correlate actual genes with particular traits or characteristics, we notice that the concept of genotype has historically been embedded in a theory of how traits occur from generation to generation. For example, Lehrman (1970) states:

> When a geneticist speaks of a character as inherited, what he means is that he is able to predict the distribution of the character in an off-spring population from his knowledge of the distribution of the character in the parent population and of the mating patterns in that population (p. 22).

To establish the biological basis or heritability status of ADHD, investigators must first identify the individuals who show the disorder, and then study their immediate and extended families in order to determine whether the behavioral pattern is consistent with the pattern predicted in a genetic theory. If ADHD occurs in a pattern within families similar to that anticipated by the model, the trait is considered to be inherited.

Genetic determinists are saying that biological processes aptly explain the occurrence of ADHD because inherited criteria are being met. Some claim that the heritability of ADHD resembles that of eye color and height; aspects of our biology that rarely, if ever, vary as a function of changes introduced by personal sociological variations. For example, Stevenson (1994) has reported that studies thus far indicate that the heritability of an ADHD diagnosis is approximately .80.

Moreover, with the advent of molecular genetic research, physical genes can now be studied and identified. These biochemical structures are correlated with the development of other physical structures, diseases, and behavioral patterns. For example, the dopamine transporter gene (DAT1) has been found to coincide with the occurrence of an ADHD diagnosis in some studies (Cook, Stein, and Leventhal, 1997). Likewise, the DAT2 gene has also been linked to ADHD (Blum, Cull, Braverman, and Coming, 1991), although not consistently (Fisher et al., 2002).

Another gene known as DRD4 has been found to be over-represented in the 7-repetition form of the gene in some diagnosed children (LaHoste et al., 1996). Many have been excited by this finding, because this gene has been associated with individuals who express high novelty seeking behavior. Since novelty seeking is remarkably consistent with the behavior of many diagnosed people, this finding is given particular significance. It is now believed that this gene can identify a reasonable number of diagnosed persons (Faraone et al., 2001), and can even help account for the higher activity levels and greater impulsivity of some diagnosed children (Langley, et al., 2004). In fact, Barkley (2006d) claims that by having this gene, an individual's probability of diagnosis may increase by 50%. Proponents of biological determinism are thus hopeful that genetics will eventually fully provide accurate predictions about the different sorts of behaviors associated with an ADHD diagnosis.

However, it is now crucial to highlight that these investigations have found only limited results. For example, the D4 receptor gene 7-repeat allele occurs in approximately 29% of the ADHD samples (Barkley, 2006d). If one were to extrapolate from the findings regarding the over-representation of the DRD4 repeater gene, 710 diagnosed individuals out of 1000 cases would not be showing the over-representation, and would nevertheless qualify for diagnosis. Given this relatively low percentage, many false categorizations are bound to occur were this gene to be used as the basis for diagnostic prediction. Thus, it seems reasonable to say that it has not yet been the case that, by observing particular constellations of genetic material, adequate predictions about behavioral patterns such as ADHD have emerged.

Moreover, depending on the base rate of the over-representation in the general population, the percentage of non-diagnosed persons in the population who would show the over-representation, but not the ADHD behavior is still unknown. While some will argue that diagnosed persons *without* the correlated biology are not truly ADHD sufferers, and that non-diagnosed persons *with* the correlated biology have "latent ADHD," or have somehow overcome their disorder, this scenario seems merely to be another way to justify data and muddle observable anomalies.

Thus far, results of studies on the relationships between a diagnosis of ADHD and various genes thought to give rise to particular neurotransmitter systems that allegedly comprise the pathophysiology involved with an ADHD diagnosis are neither consistent nor conclusive. Relationships have sometimes been reported with varying kinds of genetic material, but not always. For example, Frank et al. (2004) report no significant association between dopamine D4 receptor gene alleles, Novelty Seeking traits, and a diagnosis of ADHD as defined in the DSM-IV-TR. Moreover, the case could be made that if enough experiments were attempted with enough genes, we would expect (by chance alone) that five experiments out of 100 would show significant correlations when following accepted statistical procedures. At this point it does not seem diagnostically helpful to rely on genetic material to determine diagnosis. Molecular biology is not producing reliable correspondence with the eventual development of the DSM-IV-TR disorder, and in that respect, biological determinism is limited.

However, in order to maintain the idea of purely biological determinants for ADHD, some investigators assert that the aforementioned imperfect findings nonetheless indicate the existence of variant conditions, or more homogeneous phenotypical subgroups. For example, Gottesman and Gould (2003) adopt the construct "endophenotype" (i.e., the posited bio-behavioral abnormalities that evolve from genes and neurobiology and are expressed in reaction to living in the world) as a way to account for the failure of specific biology to show a one-to-one correspondence with psychiatric disorders. In that view, persons can possess certain "endophenotypes" that occur in high frequencies for particular diagnostic categories. Given the very broad diagnostic categories commonly used in psychiatry, groups of persons with sometimes different "endophenotypes" will be subsumed under a singular inexact category.

There is a tenacious hold on the biological determinist's formulation, along with much anticipation that further investigations will better coordinate biology with behavior, and locate new genes (and gene combinations) that will ultimately increase ADHD prediction accuracy. With numerous reports that researchers are identifying different genes that correlate to some degree with the occurrence of the behavioral pattern, there is hope that the root cause of ADHD behaviors will be embedded in the microscopic domain of biology. A problem with this telescopic view is that anomalies can appear that do not fit the supposed model; these anomalies could provide insights but are nevertheless set aside. One such example is that of the learning histories of individuals who have the particular genetic constitution for ADHD, but *do not show* the correlated behavior.

For genetic determinism to become a tenable approach, proponents must offer indisputable proof in support of their hypotheses. Individuals having a different molecular biology must consistently show corresponding changes in the diverse behavioral patterning subsumed by the diagnostic category. It should also be possible to account for individuals at the opposite end of the behavioral continuum—those who show excellent self-control—by delineating their differences in molecular biology as well. Without evidence of correspondence, it is scientifically and ethically problematic to regard genes as the primary determinate of the behaviors categorized as ADHD in the traditionalist model.

Moreover, even though diagnosis does sometimes occur in ways anticipated by genetic models, it is nevertheless unreasonable to conclude that the behaviors are fixed, inevitable, or resistant to the influence of learning. Although such inferences are often drawn about "innate" or "inherited," these frequently-used concepts can be interpreted to mean something very different.

Lehrman (1970) notes that people less familiar with biological interpretations of terms such as innate and genetic interpret the concepts as an "unchangeable unraveling." He notes that students and non-geneticists in general think that the words mean "developmental fixity." That is, the organism is impervious to environmental effects during development, and thus must develop characteristics that are pre-organized regardless of environmental rearing. In contrast to using the words innate and inherited in this fashion, Lehrman understands these terms as meaning *controlled by selected mating*, which simply states the similarities between generations of related individuals. When conceptualized in this way, one cannot rule out the possibility that other characteristics can become evident when environmental conditions change. Inherited does not mean predestined, in the genes, or fixed.

For Lehrman, the terms *innate* and *inherited* are associated with what has happened historically for generations of related persons within particular tested environments. New variations are possible with the introduction of new conditions or new opportunities for learning. Within that conceptualization, one must consider that environmental context can influence and modify the frequency and severity with which a person might do a particular class of behaviors such as ADHD patterning. The rejection of the null-hypothesis is not tantamount to saying that ADHD diagnosis cannot be influenced by environment.

In this regard, Sternberg et al. (2005, 53) note that "the coefficient of heritability does not tell us the proportion of a trait that is genetic in absolute terms, but rather the proportion of variation within a specific population." Although genetic models of prediction seem consistent with those who receive diagnoses, it does not negate the possibility that new kinds of learning can introduce new variations, or conclude that ADHD behaviors will not change in appreciable ways when new conditions are introduced. Sternberg et al. add:

> Heritabilities are like snapshots of a dancer. They will not tell us either what the dance is about or what is coming next in the dance. The true genetic nature of humans is far from being defined. But what is absolutely clear is that genes

do not act in a vacuum; they act in environment, and their actions can be altered by the environment (p. 55).

The inferred similarities in the behavioral patterns among collateral family members may also be a function of the kinds of learning that have occurred, including similar parenting, culture, gender, and emphases during socialization. The extent to which biologically-related individuals teach each other and incidentally reinforce each other to live in the world in similar ways might also influence commonalities among collaterals (something which may not be statistically controlled for to a sufficient degree).

As a way to resolve this possible confounding of variables, investigators (who are often pursuing biological causes), focus on relatives (especially identical twins) who live separately. These investigators have tried to determine the extent to which environments contribute to the development of ADHD. The degree and kinds of environmental differences evident in these studies has always varied, and as noted above, environmental effects are not systematically investigated when no evidence of concordance is apparent.

Despite emphasis on instances of high correlations, the challenge for biological determinists is to account for instances of discordance. This is especially important, in that we do not yet know the degree to which similarities of identical twins are attributable to conditioned parameters such as learning, even though their differences can be assignable to environmental parameters. Until the influence of conditioning is fully accounted for, there is the likelihood that certain environmental influences occurring throughout a lifetime will be ignored.

It is also problematic that traditionalist methods to derive environmental effects are based on mathematical models, but they neglect to draw from direct observation of individual learning histories. The precision of their accounts rests solely on the extent to which these mathematical models can adequately delineate environmental influences. The end result can potentially yield overestimations of biological or genetic effects.

An illustration of the confounding of the effects of learning and genetics seems evident in the following example. A little boy is observed behaving much like his father despite never having met him. While similarity is predicted by genetic theory, it seems that a learning paradigm could also account for the correspondence of behavior. This can occur even if the primary caretaker (or adopted caretaker) also knows nothing about the biological father. To the extent that the child is reinforced when behaving in ways analogous to the biological father, a behavioral pattern similar to the father may increase in frequency. For example, if the boy's mother selected the boy's father in terms of some relationship to her own psychosocial patterning, behaviors consistent with the father can be conditioned as the boy interacts with the mother over time, even without the father's presence. By the same token, in that many boys might under achieve when abandoned by their birth fathers (who may also have been abandoned), this same boy's lack of accomplishment in school can also be viewed as a genetic predisposition that matches his father's maladaptive functioning.

Moreover, a further consideration is that maladaptive functioning can increasingly occur if the primary caretaker knows about the birth father's negative or positive behaviors, and begins to react in predictably reinforcing ways when those behaviors occur. While anyone who knows the boy's father would agree that the child must have genetically inherited the father's personality, we can also understand how a learning paradigm can account for the boy's patterning reasonably well.

Therefore, while a behavior may be attributed to inherited or innate influences, from the standpoint of predictability from genetic theory, we need not conclude that the patterning is immutable or immune to environmental shifts or different modes of learning. Lehrman (1970) illustrates his concerns regarding the hardening of these concepts when he wrote:

> Geneticists have dealt with this problem by restricting the concepts of "heritability" and "environmental influence" with respect to any given character to an estimate of the amount of actually observed variability in that character that can be attributed to variations among the different genomes actually tested, and to the amount that can be attributed to the variety of environments in which organisms with those genomes have actually been raised. They thus do not preclude the possibility that other genes than the ones tested might have an effect upon the character, or that environments other than the one tested may cause unpredictable changes in the phenotypic appearance of a given genome (p. 23).

Of additional importance is the fact that when investigators assign a value to how much a particular trait or behavior is inherited, they designate a number based on statistical analysis. While this kind of analysis enables the investigator to discuss a category such as heritability, as if it has a separate status apart from all else, it is merely a statistical artifact without empirical status—and should be recognized as such—because the inherited category always includes *a range of tested environments* or particular reinforcement histories. The problem, as ever, is a desire for simple explanations. People conceptualize "inherited" as something with independent existence and power to cause subsequent events which are entirely disconnected from environment or learning. The attraction to statistical analysis is that it provides a number to give the impression of a separate explanatory entity, but this is not the case.

Instead of asserting biological causality, we presume that all behavior is a function of both environment and biology. For variables that seemingly occur independently from living in the world (e.g., molecular biology, early negative infant temperament, etc.), we assume that these parameters simply increase the probability that certain behavioral acts and socialization patterns will occur, and that when those patterns of lesser functioning become evident, they may also limit the possibility that other learning will take place. For instance, if people respond in circumscribed ways to individuals showing particular characteristics, and these individuals also learn that their actions lead to similar consequences (e.g., failure, receiving extra help, rejection, and disapproval), a circular system evolves in that little variability is introduced into how these individuals are trained to live. In this way there is the likelihood of a confounding of learning history with specific bodily characteristics or functional problems that occur independently from lifestyle patterns or conditioning. It is then not surprising that some people eventually decide that ADHD must be a fixed genetic model.

While few people would contest that genes reliably account for variations in tissue and body organization, sensations, and even rates of early learning as long as environments are not extremely deleterious, the debate is whether genes are as influential in determining which behaviors are learned in particular situations, what happens biologically as the individual learns, and what changes, if any, occur in the frequency rates of particular behaviors as various situations are encountered over time. It is in that context that biological determinism does not adequately account for the frequency, severity, and heterogeneity of the behavioral acts (symptoms) used to diagnose ADHD.

As we have seen in chapters 1 and 2, diagnosed persons do not always express ADHD behaviors; they do not incessantly "intrude on others," "leave seat in classroom when seating is expected," or "talk excessively." These behaviors are known to occur in predictable circumstances, such as when those behaviors sequence with increased attentiveness from others or when desiring to avoid responsibility and failure. Quite often the frequency rates of these behaviors can be altered by introducing new conditions or contingencies of reinforcement such as when diagnosed persons are preoccupied with a solitary activity that they historically enjoy and initiate.

Although biological characteristics of individuals increase the likelihood that certain behaviors will be learned, *what* is learned and *when* particular behaviors are emitted apparently depends on which conditions are encountered. For example, an individual must be able to see in order to make visual discriminations, but what is eventually identified and responded to at particular times becomes a function of which response has been conditioned. These *responses* in particular situations are not determined by variations in tissue structure, functioning, or sensory possibilities, but instead are related to what has transpired historically. The issue foremost here is not whether biology is involved in an organism's acts, but rather to *account for* situational actions or patterns of behavior associated with specific biological events and characteristics.

Vangelova (2003) raises an analogous issue in the context of discussing the problem of cloning an extinct species, in that cloning taps into the great "nature-nurture quandary," and the belief that the science of cloning will fix everything. To what extent will genetic material actually *recreate* the animal? As Vangelova notes in his article, cloning an extinct organism may permit us to maintain the recreated animal's biology, but without the recreation of the species' learning history, we have no basis for understanding whether the cloned animal will behave precisely as the original animals had behaved. Every species is the product of its history and its biology, not one or the other.

Rather than give ADHD precursor status within one's biology, the current learning model gives more credence to identifying the patterning of learning that may influence the frequency rates of the diagnostic responses. This approach is taken, even for individuals showing particular genes, reduced blood flow in the striatum, early negative temperaments, and coordination problems etc. that have been correlated with the behaviors. Since there has never been a one-to-one correspondence between these parameters and an ADHD diagnosis, it is unreasonable to assert a causal relationship.

Despite the finding that genetic models seem to best predict the distribution of the disorder for related individuals, there has not been a consistent 1.0 correlation even for identical twins that share the same genetic constitution. The fact that discordance occurs for identical twins, indicates that environments can be introduced that preclude the development of ADHD. Given such data, it makes more sense to investigate instances of discordance and discriminate (wherever possible) the conditions that seem to be influencing whether or not ADHD behaviors will occur. However, when traditionalists have carried out twin studies, greater attention was paid to concordance rates, not in exploring discordance.

Those asserting biological determinism have simply embedded instances of discordance into their explanatory model. For example, in the Sharp et al. (2003) twin study, they note that a very low rate of discordance for monozygotic twins was reported. When discordance was evident, it appeared to relate to biologically compromising events, such as a breech delivery and to one twin being physically smaller. Traditionalists understand this data as showing biological determinism at work, even though it could also be argued that monozygotic twins are unlikely to have different reinforcement histories unless something atypical occurs to set them on a different course. For example, had the smaller twin been treated and raised very differently, or if one of the twins was less functional, he or she would likely have learned diagnostic responding.

Some data generated by twin studies could also be interpreted in ways that *bolster* an experiential model rather than biological determinism. An example of this trend is evident in Goodman and Stevenson's (1989) twin study. While this study found that the underlying genetic differences appeared to account for "30 to 50% of the inter-individual variation measures of childhood hyperactivity and inattentiveness" (p. 704), those percentages only account for *less than half* of the total identified cases. One can reasonably use the same data to support the claim of nurture effects.

More specifically, even though half of the variance may be accounted for by genetic differences, Goodman and Stevenson also note that when using a "broad category of hyperactivity, proband-wide concordance was 20/39 (51%) for MZ twins and 18/54 (33%) for same-sex DZ twins" (p. 699). With those limited data, it appears that even when probands were raised in the same households (suggesting that they share more commonality of environmental settings than if they had been raised in different environments), approximately 50% of the identical twins showed discordance for hyperactive symptoms. When viewed in this light, the relatively modest numbers ascribed to heritability are less than convincing for biological determinism.

These authors further note that when mothers gave reports about their child's hyperactivity, "the combination of high correlations for MZ twins and zero or negative correlations for same-sex DZ twins is hard to explain on genetic grounds alone, and again those kinds of data are suggestive of expectancy effects" (p.703). That is, since DZ twins share half of their genes, there should be at least some correlation between DZ twins if hyperactivity is inherited, yet a correlation of this kind was not at all evident. Goodman and Stevenson conjecture that the mothers must have been expecting, and/or cueing the greater than predicted behavioral discrepancies between dizygotic twins. This outcome is a further demonstration of significant experiential effects, and apart from maternal expectancy effects, there are ostensibly many other psychosocial events that also relate to dizygotic twins developing different behavioral patterns.

Sherman, McGue, and Iacono (1997) also found an analogous problem in their twin study. While concordance rates were 67% for monozygotic twins, there was a 0% concordance rate for dizygotic twins. Traditionalists may point to these findings as supportive of biological determinism, but the reported data is highly consistent with an experiential explanation as well. That is, since it is currently emphasized that the risk of diagnosis to siblings is 32% (Beiderman et al., 1992; Beiderman, Keenan, and Faraone, 1990; Levy and Hay, 2001; Faraone and Doyle, 2001), a finding of zero concordance for dizygotic represents a noteworthy discrepancy. Utilizing data from the Sherman et al. study, one could claim that the environment is powerful enough to be entirely protective against the occurrence of an ADHD diagnosis if one is lucky enough to have a fraternal twin who responds with ADHD patterns.

While investigators have attempted to compensate for effects such as parents' overestimation of the similarity of identical twins by deriving mathematical models to control for expectancy effects, this is clearly a persistent problem in studies of this type (Scarr, 1968). Other analogous environmental contributions, such as behaviors identified by the twins themselves, may either exaggerate or minimize differences between them, depending on the personality patterns of each. In addition, even if investigators incorporate mathematical models purporting to adjust for expectations (i.e., deviations from predictions based on shared genetic material), identical twins could nevertheless be entirely alike both in relation to expectancy or other environmental effects, and in relation to their genetics.

The question remains as to how well these studies parcel the sources of variability. Because environments can introduce subtle influences not always anticipated or controlled for, how reliable or believable are the statistical data now being generated? For example, McGuffin and Huckle (1990) warn that traits understood to be entirely non-genetic and related to cultural variables may also occur in patterns consistent with Mendelian systems. To the extent that cultural patterns show this kind of correspondence with genetic theory, conclusions can be highly misleading.

Despite the higher probability of introducing even more confounding variables, studies of both monozygotic and dizygotic twins cited in the traditional view to establish the heritability of ADHD are usually based on twins reared *together* rather than apart (Barkley, 1998e). The necessity has therefore been to rely solely on mathematical models called "Structural Equation Models" (Heath et al., 1989; Jinks and Fulker, 1970; Neale and Cardon, 1992) to estimate genetic and environmental influences on behavioral variations. Environmental effects are often subdivided into shared or common environmental effects (i.e., what creates similarity among family members, such as collective experience, SES, family nutrition, general child rearing approaches, etc.), and unique or specific environmental effects (i.e., what tends to make family members different from each other, such as individual events that shape a life). Although when considering the usage of these models, Faraone et al. (1992, 267) warn that "any segregation analysis must be interpreted with caution."

While it is generally asserted by proponents of biological determinism that heritability correlations are high for ADHD, and that unique environments rather than shared environments typically have a greater impact on whether diagnosis occurs (Levey and Hay, 2001), these studies are methodologically more complex (i.e., more confounding variables to consider) compared to the classical approach of studying twins reared apart. Twins reared apart are more likely to yield data from different environmental contexts, which is more discrepant than investigations of twins reared together. Environmental effects evident in typical heritability studies of ADHD might therefore not be the same as what might occur when extensive environmental variation is introduced. In this regard, Sternberg et al. (2005) have anticipated that as more environmental variations are introduced when studying a trait, heritability quotients are likely to plummet. In a strict theoretical sense, exposing individuals to a singular environment (although impossible) means that all variations between individuals must be attributable to genetic factors (Herrnstein, 1974).

Although studies that accumulate data from identical twins reared apart and unrelated children raised in the same family are likely to help us factor out genetic and environmental effects, Lewontin (1970, 296) emphasizes that these studies are also difficult to depend on when making inferences. For example, "twins separated from birth are nevertheless likely to be raised in families belonging to the same socio-economic, racial, religious, and ethnic categories." Similarly, "unrelated children raised in the same family may easily be treated differently than biological sibs." One can say that these investigations are less reliable than proponents of genetic explanation believe.

Lewontin (1970, 295) claims that many problems are encountered when one attempts to establish the heritability of a trait. He cautions that "estimations of heritability of a trait in a population depends on measuring individuals of known degrees of relationship to each other and comparing the observed correlation in the trait between relatives with the theoretical correlation from genetic theory." He further states that these measurements can be highly inaccurate, in that "the exact theoretical correlation between relatives, except for identical twins, cannot be specified unless there is detailed knowledge of the mode of inheritance of the character." He notes that while "a first order approximation is possible," it is "based upon simplifying assumptions, and it is usual for this approximation to be badly off." When considering these remarks, it is likely that Lewontin would be very skeptical of the heritability estimates being put forth nowadays in the ADHD literature.

Studies showing the inheritability of a trait depend on the premise that environmental parameters that could influence a particular trait are being adequately accounted and controlled for. Because relatives are likely to share similar environments and socialization, it is important to take those commonalities into account when internal factors such as genetics are used to explain such commonalities. If one infers that environmental parameters are not introducing variability, commonalities among relatives are then subsumed within a genetic similarity explication.

If environmental variables are not fully examined, it is more likely that investigators will presume that commonality of traits or behavioral patterns under scrutiny can be ascribed to genetics. As noted by Skinner (1974):

> One unfortunate consequence is that genetic sources sometimes become a kind of dumping ground: any aspect of behavior which at the moment escapes analysis in terms of contingencies of reinforcement is likely to be assigned to genetic endowment, and we are likely to accept the explanation because we are so accustomed to going no further than a state of the organism (p. 44).

According to Skinner's claim, it is our own limited understanding of environmental effects that is the cause for more variability being assigned to genetics. Consistent with that account is Lewontin's (1970) exemplar of a plant experiment where differences between plants were ascribed to genetics by interested investigators who were unaware that the soil from one group lacked nitrates and zinc. After discovering the absence of nitrate, the presumption remained that differences were still genetic, because the plants continued to exhibit differences after correcting for the nitrate. However, all along, the "culprit" had been the undetected missing zinc. Extrapolating from Lewontin's example, if related individuals show correlated patterns in the ways they condition offspring to live in the world (i.e., patterns that reinforce ADHD behaviors), and these relationships are influential but are not considered, then we assume that similarities are genetic; but they could just as readily be attributed to environment.

In order to competently consider the relative importance of genetics and environment, we must also rule out preconceived notions, if any, associated with the finding that ADHD "runs in families." If children and parents are not diagnosed independently from one another, we cannot accurately assess expectancy effects from the diagnosticians themselves. For example, when a clinician with genetic causality beliefs is diagnosing a child, we would expect the clinician to presume that the parent also has or will have that diagnosis. Given the belief of co-occurrence, we can anticipate that both have ADHD after either one has been diagnosed.

Consistent with this interpretation, Crawford (2003, 29), in an interview with Kathleen Nadeau, notes that "One of the most common pathways to a woman being diagnosed is that one of her children is diagnosed." Similarly, Barkley and Edwards (2006) note that strong family histories of ADHD will lend weight to an ADHD diagnosis, especially in doubtful situations. While it is possible to safeguard against possible expectation effects, and generate diagnostic data for parents and children independently (a requirement in *any other controlled experiment*), on most occasions, such an experimental procedure is not followed when diagnosis is established within families.

Numerous investigations indeed show that the more an individual is biologically related to another individual, the more likely the individuals will share the same form of atypical ADHD patterning. But if individuals are aware of these relationships, there is always the risk that a self-fulfilling prophecy or an "expectancy bias" will occur. For example, Barkley and Edwards (2006) suggest obtaining a full history of psychiatric disorders in the family during the assessment phase of therapy, since the presumption is that ADHD is inherited. They emphasize that a history of ADHD in biological relatives supports an ADHD diagnosis. However, if we follow this approach logically and consistently, we see that presumption or bias in the diagnostic process yields more claims of heritability.

In a pattern that can also tip the scales to a biological viewpoint, Barkley and Edwards (2006) also recommend that clinicians should rule out family stress as a causal determinant for the child's problems. Their system of categorization may then lower the probability that subsequent empirical work will uncover correlations between the disorder and family dysfunction. Since diagnosis does not occur independently from information gained about relatives and environments, the deck is stacked in favor of finding high heritability quotients and less influential environmental contexts when data is later accumulated.

Although in an attempt to provide further evidence for genetic effects, biological determinists have tried to understand environmental effects by studying whether adopted individuals' behavioral patterns are more similar to those of their adopted parents or their biological parents. The hope is that these studies will obviate more confounding variables compared to studying offspring reared with biologically-related individuals. While correlations seem significantly lower, given the reports of a 20-54% possibility that a child with the condition will also have a birth parent with the same condition (Barkley, 2000), these studies are important.

Adoption studies such as those performed by Sprich, Biederman, Crawford, Mundy, and Faraone (2000), Cantwell (1975), Morrison and Stewart (1973), and van den Oord, Boomsma, and Verhulst (1994) are cited to counter the view that children are affected by exposure to parental behaviors and induced by those environmental experiences to manifest ADHD behavioral patterns. For example, Sprich et al. (2000) found that the adopted families of diagnosed children did not have elevated patterns of ADHD in their extended families, while non-adopted diagnosed children did show elevated patterns of ADHD in their family lineage.

Despite the trends in favor of the view that ADHD is better explained by biology than socialization, the heritability correlations in adoption studies are below those that occur when individuals are raised with birth families. For example, van den Oord et al. (1994) report that genetic models of prediction account for 47% of the variance. This indicates a greater environmental effect (53% not accounted for), and less than the number when studying children living with birth families. These statistical tendencies indicate that, as more environmental variations and opportunities for new patterns of learning are introduced, the less possible it is to predict diagnosis by relying on presumed biological relatedness to other diagnosed family members.

There are other reasons not to interpret the data in adoption studies as definitive for biological determinism. For example, the "Attentional Problems Checklist" was used in the van den Oord study rather than the DSM-IV-TR criteria. While this measure is associated with an ADHD diagnosis, it does not meet the agreed DSM-IV-TR criteria that traditionalists recommend (Barkley, 1998e). Additionally, the Cantwell and Morrison investigations were retrospective inquires, and the biological parents were never actually assessed (Pauls, 1991). Similarly, the Cadoret and Stewart (1991) adoption study only provided information about whether a birth parent was delinquent; it was never determined at all whether the parent was diagnosed with ADHD. Given these problems, the methodology used in these studies is unlikely to yield reliable findings.

In addition to concerns about unreliability, it is also worth noting that Hallowell and Ratey (1995, 197) report that "if you are adopted, that itself is a significant finding," in that "ADD is much higher among the adopted than among the general population." If Hallowell and Ratey's assertion is reliable, and if ADHD follows a similar course, the base rates for ADHD will be higher for adopted children than for non-adopted children. For instance, there might be a greater likelihood for over-accommodating parental behaviors, such as unusual pleasing, assisting, and rescuing. There may be more barriers against trust, increased worry about what could go wrong, higher incidence of attachment problems, and more concerns about mutual acceptability between parent and child. There could also be a higher probability that the child will also show functional problems that could lower success rates for expected achievements.

These hypotheses can be further investigated by assessing whether adopted children from birth families without ADHD also show a higher incidence of ADHD compared to the general population. Similarly, it might be heuristic to assess base rates of diagnosed children living with non-diagnosed biological parents, and determine whether those base rates differ for diagnosed children living with non-diagnosed adoptive parents. Perhaps those kinds of inquiries can shed light on how being adopted might influence an ADHD diagnosis.

It might also be fruitful to investigate the extent to which diagnosed adoptive parents show the same ADHD base rate for their adopted children as do non-diagnosed adoptive parents, and explore the extent to which non-diagnosed adoptive parents show the same base rate with children genetically predicted to show ADHD, compared with diagnosed birth parents raising their own children. This kind of data might help to determine whether the degree to which being adopted (i.e., environmental effects) changes the probability of being diagnosed.

We can also explore whether there is anything different about adoptive parents who raise non-diagnosed adopted children despite that these children come from birth families with a prevalence of ADHD. What factor(s) account for these genetically predicted adopted children to *not* show the atypical behaviors compared to adoptive families who show outcomes consistent with genetic predictions? The current notion is that these concerns permit an analysis of the learning or environmental effects that could indeed have significant influence.

One could also inquire into whether there is an increased incidence of ADHD for adopted children when they or their adoptive parents have information about birth parents (including whether a parent was diagnosed). Such an inquiry could shed light on expectancy effects, or the idea of a self-fulfilling prophecy related to children resembling their parents. For example, one adoptive mother indicated that she often overreacted to any lower extremity pain reported by her adopted son, because she knew that her son's birth father had a hip disorder. She also recalled that when her son was 18 months old, she anxiously approached her pediatrician to find out when she should begin to give him medication, because she had been told that her adopted son's birth father also had an ADHD diagnosis.

Other parameters in adoption studies can be examined; for instance, does the age of the diagnosed child at the time of adoption influence outcomes? Does contact with the child's birth parent(s), type of early training and care prior to adoption, and the increased incidence of various problems change the frequency rates of eventual diagnosis? Perhaps these factors significantly influence behavioral patterning throughout childhood, and increase the probability of learning ADHD behaviors.

There might also be some value in determining whether extended family relatives are raising the adopted diagnosed child. This scenario could mean less environmental variation than would be the case, given that psychosocial patterning could be similar within extended families. We would then explore whether base rates of ADHD change for adopted children in relation to whether they are raised by extended family or unrelated persons.

Consistent with these concerns, Alberts-Corush et al. (1986) reported that biological relatives of ADHD children do poorly on standardized measures of attention compared to adoptive relatives of ADHD children. While traditional-ists utilize these findings to secure their biological account, this finding could mean that extended families learn to behave similarly. This finding does not establish the degree to which attention patterns in families are due to environ-mental or genetic influences.

Moreover, if it is presumed that many people react similarly to particular childhood behaviors that include negative infant temperament, atypical motor and language encoding behaviors, and various health problems, it might not matter whether diagnosed individuals grow to adulthood with a biological or non-biologically related caretaker. It is more probable that evolving social pat-terns will play out in predictable ways. Empirical work seems to characterize environmental factors as discrepant in adoption studies, but they may be similar in ways that relate to shaping ADHD behaviors.

A case could also be made that both an environmental and biological ac-count can predict that diagnosed adopted children will likely match their bio-logical parents when ADHD behaviors are evident. Because most ADHD teen pregnancies result in diagnosed teens not keeping their babies due to incompe-tence (Barkley, 2000), and the majority of adopted parents are pre-selected for their normative functioning, it would be predicted that adopted diagnosed chil-dren will likely match their biological parents if adoption and other complica-tions associated with adopted children increase the probability of learning ADHD behaviors. The correlations that seem consistent with genetic explana-tions can also be a function of environmental parameters.

In any event, when discussing relationships between heritability quotients and environmental contexts, Benson (2004, 44) refers to a recent study by Turk-heimer and colleagues at the University of Virginia showing that children among poor families tend to have similar IQ scores regardless of genetic similar-ity. Approximately 60% of the variance was accounted for by environment, while genes "contributed almost nothing." Conversely, "among affluent fami-lies, the reverse was true," as monozygotic twins "tended to have much more similar IQ scores than dizygotic twins, regardless of family environment." We see that those data demonstrate how, depending on the environments examined, very different conclusions are reached regarding the heritability of a trait.

Given these possibilities, high genetic loading does not mean that it is im-possible for new or different environmental patterns to profoundly influence development. Perhaps the limited variation of techniques to socialize children who show characteristics associated with ADHD can account for the findings thus far. Consistent with this interpretation, Lewontin (1970, 299) notes that "even though no environment in the normal range has an effect on the character, there may be special environments, created in response to our knowledge of the underlying biology of the character, which are effective in altering it."

Rather than respond with a sense of futility to high heritability quotients, Lehrman (1970) suggests greater effort in identifying environments that can influence the behaviors in question. He states:

> That I regard an experiment that shows an effect, during development, of any
> treatment, as a contribution to the illumination of a process of development,
> while a study which succeeds only in showing that some types of manipulation
> have no effect upon the outcome seems like a challenge to follow the problem
> to an earlier stage of development, or to a more intricate level of physiological
> analysis (p. 30).

To take Lehrman's recommendation seriously, it is important to explore environmental interventions that could demonstrate environmental effects in the development of ADHD. It could be interesting to *not* assume that ADHD is antecedently "in the genes" (Barkley, 2000), that certain individuals are "predisposed" to have ADHD (Barkley, 2006e), or that they are incited towards more familial conflict (Robin, 2006; Elkins, McGue, and Iacono, 1997).

We recommend less pessimism about the relatively high heritability correlations, as well as a refusal to accept that the condition is unavoidable. Instead we might search for a way to deeply affect behavioral patterns. However, when we undertake this task we are likely to realize success if we do not focus exclusively on either parental or child characteristics and instead examine the *interactions* between parent and child with special attention on how symptomatic behaviors are reinforced—regardless of whether a parent is critical, warm, appreciating his or her spouse, or reporting malaise (as stressed in the Goodman and Stevenson twin study). We do not presume that any of these parental patterns can predict the child's learning of diagnostic responses. Unless an investigation identifies which behaviors are being learned and reinforced, it is unlikely that data will show environmental effects, even though traditionalists continue to use non-positive data to support inheritance as an explanation for ADHD.

Thelen (1995, 94) also does not assign biological causality when high heritability quotients are evident; she rejects the approach of looking for pre-existing genetic instructions that "direct and prescribe the performance." In Thelen's view, "each component in the developing system is both cause and product." There is no apparent way to know an ultimate cause "if task motivates behavior while behavior enables new tasks." She wonders:

> At what point, then, can researchers partition causality into genes versus environment, structure versus function, or competence versus performance? Rather, the new synthesis sees everything as a dynamic process, albeit on different levels and time scales. Even what psychologists usually call "structure" —the tissues and organs of the body—is a dynamic process. Bones and muscles are continually in flux, although their changes may be slower and less observable than those in the nervous system" (p. 94).

In this more dynamic view outcomes are seen as dependent on context whereby the influence of any gene depends on other genes present *and* other events. Events that happen over time are inextricably linked to the conditions that the system encounters. Phenotype is not imbued in the genes; it is actually a consequence of development which always includes genes and environment. As noted by Lehrman (1970):

> It is not true that each structure and character in the phenotype is "represented" in a single gene or well-defined group of genes; it is not the case that each gene refers solely, or even primarily, to a single structure or character; and it is not the case that topographical or topological relationships among the genes are isomorphic with the structural or topographical relationships among phenotypic structures to which the genes refer (p. 34).

There is no presumption in this conceptualization that an individual is predisposed, or that environments mediate the extent to which a previously occurring ADHD shows itself, nor is there any implication of something latent or inherent in the developing system. Environments are not compensating, offsetting, or controlling something with *a priori* status. Statements about heritability become predictive statements about event sequences; they do not infer that a diagnosed person is predestined to show ADHD or is born with ADHD, but that he or she is *more likely to show* particular behavioral patterns if particular temporal sequences of biological and learning events occur.

As noted by Lewontin (1994, 24), "different genes and different environments through unique interactions, give rise to unique organisms." The eventual outcome (phenotype) always depends on characteristics of the individual's genes and the sequence of subsequent events. *Inherited* always retains the implication of being an evolving pattern within a range of tested environments where each environment is unique to the extent that we are all unique transducers.

Moreover, Lewontin (1994, 19) emphasizes that we don't know the possible variations that are possible for the "human psyche" in relation to the introduction of new environmental contexts. He maintains that it is a typical "norm-of-reaction" in most empirical work with other species that "norms cross each other" as new conditions are introduced. Rank ordering frequently shifts markedly, and Lewontin anticipates that changes in conditions "will produce very surprising results." He asserts:

> The metaphor of innate capacity is a problematic wrong metaphor. There are differences among genotypes, with different consequences in different environments, but there is no apparent way to generalize for different environments, or to rate those innate or intrinsic properties as 'bad' to 'good,' 'high' to 'low,' 'small' to 'big.' There is complete environmental contingency (p. 19).

Past studies have only described that which occurs in the range of conditions tested; therefore instances where outcomes are inconsistent with biological determinism must be more avidly explored. Thelen (1995) makes a similar point when she concludes:

For developmentalists interested in providing effective and appropriate intervention for children who are at physical, emotional, or social risk, knowing that a particular trait is 25% heritable is of little use. Instead, the therapist needs to know the history of the system in all its richness and complexity, its current dynamics, and how the interventions can disrupt the stability of the current dynamics to allow new and better solutions to emerge (p. 94).

Since there have been occasions where a trait shows a high genetic basis, and environmental shifts have produced miraculous changes, this option remains viable. For example, individuals who have the disorder PKU (Phenylketonuria) will develop the condition only if they eat certain substances; if their diet is altered to be phenylalanine-free, they proceed to develop normatively. If we extrapolate from this example, it may be that children showing certain kinds of early problematic functioning require careful socialization so that ADHD behaviors will not be learned. Unless these sorts of measures are taken, ADHD behaviors are likely to continue to be conditioned with great frequency for those persons.

The Biological Differences Argument

There is yet another observation that seems to warrant continued belief that ADHD is primarily a biological disorder. Despite inconsistencies in some of the studies, there is general agreement that a disproportionate number of diagnosed persons show differences in brain biology on various examinations. They exhibit differences in biochemistry, in the ways their brains operate, and size and symmetry of certain brain structures (Zametkin et al., 1990; Frazier, Demaree, and Youngstrom, 2004; Halperin et al., 1997). It is believed that the ADHD disorder creates the biological differences that develop over time. Structural formations and brain events are purported to become the necessary conditions for the advent of competent behaviors, not necessarily the consequence of previous or concurrent acceptable responses.

Barkley (1998e; 2006d) writes that these inquiries indicate that certain brain structures thought to relate to behavioral inhibition and executive functioning, such as the right frontal region, cerebellum, and certain pathways connecting prefrontal regions to the limbic system by means of the striatum, are different for diagnosed individuals compared to controls. These findings have been instrumental, and often sensational, in helping to convince professionals and the wider public that ADHD is a biologically caused problem.

Neuroimaging studies do not show signs of brain damage in any identified structures for diagnosed persons, but the regions thought to be related to ADHD are often smaller than those typically observed (e.g., prefrontal cortical regions, caudate volume). Many of the implicated structures are less likely to show the expected "asymmetry in size between the right and left frontal regions (or those of the caudate and globus pallidus)" (Barkley (1998e, 168). Castellanos on

Frontline (2001) similarly notes that the posterior inferior vermis of the cerebellum has also been correlated with smaller size for diagnosed persons. However, since many pathways link this structure to the frontal regions, and since injuries to this structure can mimic frontal lobe impairment (Barkley, 2000), these findings are presumed to be consistent with the behavioral delays evident with many diagnosed persons.

These summaries and conclusions coincide with previous reviews indicating that explicit brain damage occurs less than 5% in diagnosed individuals (Rutter, 1977; 1983); it is apparently the case that size matters. Barkley emphasizes that differences in brain structures are probably the consequences of "abnormal" brain development within "particular regions" "probably under genetic control," since "genes control in large part the developmental construction of the brain" (Barkley, 1998e, 168).

Not only do some diagnosed individuals show less activity in certain parts of the frontal brain areas (Barkley, 1998e), but they also show differences in the structures of their brain cells compared to controls (Barkley, 2001). For example, Belkin (2004, 27) reports that dopamine receptor density has been found to be greater in the brains of diagnosed persons. He notes that there are also differences in "prefrontal cortex glucose metabolism in people with ADHD."

These striking findings are interpreted to mean that ADHD has a biological basis or cause, and that diagnosed individuals are going to be delayed in the rate that they develop adequate inhibitory behavior. The inference is that their brains must be less able to perform certain functions, in that biological examination indicates structural and functional differences in the areas of the brain thought to be associated with self-control. For example, Castellanos on *Frontline* (2001) also notes that while the cerebellum can be removed without producing terrible effects, this part of the brain functions much like a "co-processor." He sees ADHD as a "disorder of inefficiency," in that diagnosed persons generally perform less well than others. Moreover, when answering the question whether parents cause ADHD, Castellanos (2003, 128) points to a study conducted by the National Institute for Mental Health, which found that the brains of ADHD children were 3 to 4% smaller than controls. He adds that the study suggests that the smaller the brain, the more severe the disorder.

Despite these sensational and provocative findings which have been disseminated to the public, rarely are standard deviations between groups reported. The public is also not informed about any co-occurring conditions such as learning and developmental delays that could also be factors influencing the functioning of participants. Neither is the public informed about the number of false negatives and positives that occur in relation to using the specified criteria. Most importantly, the general public is unaware that correlational findings do not establish causality. Public awareness is also scarce about how living in the world also correlates with differences in activity, cell density, and structural development within the brain.

More precisely, instead of interpreting findings to mean that ADHD causes these brain anomalies, we could argue that when a person functions less well than others, it is more likely that he or she will learn to do ADHD acts. Once a person learns to behave in ADHD kinds of behavioral patterns, he will generally continue to function less well than others, and identified brain changes may in fact be the consequences of those defining patterns of ADHD individuals.

Yet we notice that biological determinism is posited when findings report that a sample of diagnosed persons has more of a specific protein called dopamine transporter compared to non-diagnosed persons (Aoki, 2001). This seems consistent with genetic research indicating that certain genes correlate with the later measures of cell sensitivity to the neurotransmitter dopamine. Barkley (1998e) also emphasizes that this cell sensitivity is important, in that a person might engage in novelty-seeking in reaction to how the body processes dopamine.

Barkley (2000) also ascribes to the view that certain genes are purportedly determining the quality of the dopamine transporter system, which can rob the cells of dopamine too quickly if the system is too active. When this occurs, the person slips into a disinhibited neurological state. Barkley (1998e, 169) asserts that evidence points to a "selective deficiency" in the availability of the neurontransmitters dopamine and norepinephrine. This view coincides with Elia et al. (1990), who report that stimulant medications block the reuptake of dopamine and norepinephrine into the presynaptic neuron, as well as help release these neurotransmitters into the extraneuronal space.

However, for this scenario to adequately account for a continuum of behavior such as ADHD, these parameters would also have to predict the opposite biology for individuals at the other extreme of the normal curve. For example, the implicated structures would have to be larger or more asymmetrical for individuals showing a highly-evolved pattern of inhibition and executive control over their behavior. There would also have to be a consistent relationship between cerebral blood flow in certain pathways, and greater availability of dopamine and norepinephrine, and the extent to which ADHD behavior occurs from high to low frequency rates. However, the specific biology being identified in traditional inquiries has not yet accounted for the continuum of behaviors noted in ADHD individuals.

Moreover, it is unknown what a behavioral pattern at the "high" end of the inhibitory continuum looks like, since it has never been identified by traditionalists. For example, would individuals behaving markedly different from ADHD behaviors show patterns similar to an obsessive pattern? Would this opposite extreme be more socially desirable than doing ADHD? Do persons identified as obsessive manage more effectively when mulling over details in relation to their overly developed inhibitory systems?

Individuals who take excessive amounts of time to mentally rehearse, who worry about distant future events, who check and recheck, and who second-guess when interacting socially or when completing tasks, also encounter social difficulties and much personal discomfort. When conceptualized in this fashion, obsessive patterning much like ADHD can be problematic and "delayed" relative to a standard, and associated with numerous benefits and detriments.

Similarly, might we consider individuals to be neurologically enhanced when they diligently self-sacrifice to meet very tedious requirements, or zealously save money to retire early? Would an analysis of their neurobiology indicate that their brain structures and functioning are discrepant in predictable ways relative to controls? Are individuals patterned to conform (often at their own expense) revealing biological evidence of an extremely advanced inhibitory system? While those patterns seem diametrically opposed to ADHD behavior, it is not our usual practice to characterize these individuals as neurologically gifted.

When excessive conformity occurs there is a greater probability that those behaviors will be explicated by referencing psychosocial parameters such as learning. We maintain that these persons are conditioned to *not* increase the probability of disapproval, despite that this metaphor of understanding is abandoned when individuals function at the opposite end of the continuum (e.g., ADHD). However, since we do not interpret obsequious or celibate behavior as caused by an enhanced biological substrate, why should we impose that same account when persons displease others or appear to be more self-indulgent?

If it is posited that ADHD is related to certain kinds of biology (e.g., smaller brain structures, lack of asymmetry, and cell sensitivity to dopamine), it would logically follow that the biology associated with the disorder would have to account for the entire behavioral spectrum in a consistent fashion including why a person shows some symptom behaviors but not others. While the traditionalists speculate that it is only a matter of time before a biological account can predict ADHD behavior in this fashion, especially since it is already being found that some genes correlate primarily with impulsivity and not distractibility (Barkley, 2000), this is not the current state of affairs. Until biological analysis can show a consistent correspondence with behavior across the entire range of analogous behaviors, it is difficult to understand how the posited variables account for the posited delays. Other than showing average group differences between controls and diagnosed persons, no biological variables (including genes) have been adequate predictors of the continuum of ADHD behaviors.

Those ascribing to biological determinism must also contend with the problem that biological differences identified in ADHD also occur in varying degrees in other diagnostic categories. For example, this problem has surfaced during discussions about the neurotransmitter dopamine, a chemical implicated not only for ADHD, but also in Obsessive Compulsive Disorder (Rauch and Jenike, 1993) and Schizophrenia (Davison and Neale, 1998) as well. While there is a corresponding theory about the role that dopamine plays in producing symptoms for each disorder, and the areas of the brain that seem most relevant, the neurotransmitter is often the same for each condition.

For example, it has been hypothesized that schizophrenics have a variety of problems with dopamine in different areas of the brain. Some propose that these individuals have problems with dopamine receptor sites. Davis et al. (1991) theorize that excess dopamine may be occurring in the mesolimbic pathway, which could account for positive symptoms, while dopamine neurons in the prefrontal cortex may be under active and thus fail to exert inhibitory control over the dopamine neurons in the limbic area, thereby accounting for negative symptoms.

We observe that very similar scenarios regarding dopamine in the frontal portion of the brain are being put forward for negative symptoms (e.g., lack of persistence in completing tasks) for *both* disorders. However, is the symptom "lack of persistence" the same behavior when it occurs in someone diagnosed as Schizophrenic, as it is when occurring within an ADHD behavioral pattern?

Further attempts to establish the biological difference argument appear in a recent newspaper article by Aoki (2001), entitled "Brain Chemical Linked to ADHD; Study Raises Hopes for a Diagnostic Test." The study concludes that the chemical compositions of ADHD brains are discrepant from non-diagnosed persons. The article indicates that 20 diagnosed adults were found to have a significantly higher level of a protein called dopamine transporter than the 20 non-diagnosed people. This finding was exciting to both the researchers and the underwriters of the study, in that the biotechnology company was hoping to market an agent called "Altropane," which could detect the amounts of dopamine transporter protein in the brain. While the article did mention a recent concern about whether diagnosed persons are being over medicated, investigators were enthused that it might eventually be possible to identify ADHD biologically in relation to "Altropane."

However, these kinds of findings can also be interpreted quite differently. The fact that there could be chemical correlates to patterns of living in a particular way does not require the inference that chemical differences are causing the behavioral pattern, or that chemical treatment is necessary to resolve the problem. For example, if one were to compare 20 individuals who exercise daily with 20 people who do not, it is probable that an analysis of muscle tone and percentage of body fat would clearly put individuals into their appropriate groups. Although in this case it would likely be argued that exercise accounts for physiological discrepancies: Bodily differences would *not* be seen as the cause of the more active behaviors.

In the same way while some regard the relatively high frequency rates of "insensitivities to punishments" as a sign of a deficient neurology that causes a lack of response to adverse consequences, it is important to know about the person's reinforcement history prior to such an assertion, especially if other complications do not impede responding. We may see that a less responsive pattern has been conditioned over time. For example, are workaholics and anorexic individuals insensitive to conditioned punishment when they continue their patterning—despite the sometimes severe disapproval from others, and the extreme adverse biological consequences of such behaviors? Perhaps "insensitivities to punishment" for the ADHD group are simply reinforced patterns that make it more difficult for others to deny or impose limits, despite negative biological and social results.

A Frontline program (2001), called *Medicating Kids*, which shows a diagnosed boy playing a video game without atypical behavior, seems to demonstrate the power of circumstance when accounting for diagnostic responding. The same child is shown later in the program responding lethargically and unhappily while completing an assigned activity (also on a computer), which was part of an evaluation to test him for ADHD (i.e., persistence, error rates, etc.). Although the activities were diverse, different patterns of arousal (and sensitivities to consequences) were evident in the two circumstances. If diagnosed children are frequently languid when reacting to social expectations, we would expect that their patterns of neurological arousal will be shaped in unique ways.

As pointed out by Eberhardt (2005), brain response research shows that changing social context and altering a participant's immediate processing goals will produce definite changes in brain activity. Over time, patterns of varying responses may well have significant effects on the biological parameters being measured. Given that possibility, when Ernst et al. (2003) reported that diagnosed adults are less likely to activate their hippocampal and insular regions (i.e., they activate the right anterior cigulate instead), is this due to their brains being inherently delayed, or have they learned to respond in ADHD patterns, and now their brains show the co-occurrences and consequences of that patterning?

We suggest that these biological co-occurrences simply mean that if behavioral patterning is of a particular sort, then biological correlates may be observable. Instead of contending that these findings mean that something else is causing a reduced ability to recognize the importance of appropriately fulfilling environmental demands (Barkley, 2000), we again proffer that diagnosed persons have learned to respond differently across an array of situations and circumstances, and their brain structure and function reverberates those differences.

It is in this sense that our brains are likely to reflect how we often pattern (e.g., volumetric changes in the brain, differential patterns of activation during color/word sorting tests, etc.). Studies upholding the status quo have only provided us with biological observations performed after living in the world has taken place. Those studies do not inform us about how a person's way of life may influence biological development.

Since molecular biology (which occurs prior to birth) has not been particularly efficacious in predicting diagnosis, thus far biological inevitability for ADHD is not proven. Moreover, even if molecular biology could accurately predict diagnosis as well as the patterns of brain structure and function evident within the diagnosed population, we still would not know the extent to which diagnosis and bodily characteristics can be changed by altering environment and learning patterns.

We observe the propensity for people to believe that the brain has a relatively fixed status that subsequently determines observed behavioral problems—rather than as a changing system shaped by events and situations transpiring over time. For example, Castellanos et al. (1996) posit that the impairments in the development of the brains of diagnosed people (especially in the prefrontal-striatal regions) are likely to have occurred during embryological development. They hold that those impairments existed prior to birth. However, this interpretation has not been empirically established, as we do not know what the brains of diagnosed persons looked like during the embryological stages, nor has it been established how much change is possible in these areas of the brain over the course of a lifetime. As noted by Skinner (1953, 118), "a small difference in early instruction may make a big difference in the eventual result," and this is relevant for both biological and psychological status.

In a study that demonstrates such effects, Robertson-Souter (2001, 3) in an interview with Teicher, reports that children with histories of abuse often develop significant differences in how their brains operate; this seems to be a direct result of the environmental events they encountered. These influences include "limbic system irritability that is often seen in temporal lobe epilepsy," "twice the incidence of clinically significant abnormal EEGs," "a huge difference in the left hemisphere cortical development," and notable differences in the activated areas of the brain, depending on whether memories are neutral or disturbing in content. Similarly, Erickson et al. (2003) and Hull (2002) have shown that stress will frequently translate into discernable changes in brain neuroimaging findings. Given these findings, it seems that environmental factors —such as how a person lives in the world—can significantly impact on brain development, organization, and functioning. No currently available brain data establishes a causal relationship between the observed biological discrepancies and an ADHD behavioral pattern, as has been inferred by many in the field.

Nevertheless, the view that the brain is relatively fixed early in development persists despite growing evidence that the brain is flexible, and that it changes and responds to individual behavior. Much like any other organ and body system, what happens over time influences the structure and function of the brain's appearance. Thelen (1995) writes:

> Neural diversity arises from dynamic neuroembryonic processes and means that there can be no genetically determined point-to-point wiring in the brain. Rather, the diversity provides the raw material—the rough palette—for experience-dependent selection, that is, the strengthening of certain connections (groups of neurons) through use (p. 90).

Perhaps we will not be surprised to learn that accountants show different brain patterning compared to professional artists. In fact, research by Gaser and Schlaug (2003) and Knox (1995) shows that musicians have a different brain structure when compared to non-musicians, and the kinds of discriminated differences are similar to our discussion of the analysis of the brains of ADHD individuals. These investigators have noted that during gestation a structure called the "planum temporale" forms between the 29rd and 31st weeks and is larger and more asymmetrical for musicians compared to others. When considering this data, it is clear that environment counts when investigating functional and structural differences between classes of people who may live very differently in the world.

Interestingly, Hynd, Semrud-Clikeman, Lorys et al. (1990) have studied size differentials in the planum temporale for diagnosed children as well. They note that children with both ADHD and a learning disability will show smaller right-hemispheres relative to controls, and that only children with a learning disability will show smaller size in the left planum temporale. Although as noted above, are these differences *causes* or *consequences* of behavioral acts?

When addressing this concern for musicians, Gaser and Schlaug have asserted that brain differences between musicians and controls seem to represent structural adaptations in response to long-term skill acquisition and the repetitive rehearsal of particular skills. In a report that is consistent with Gaser and Schlaug's assertions, both Draganski et al. (2004) and Maguire et al. (2000) track the remarkable ways in which brain function and experience may significantly influence brain structure.

Since these kinds of changes are being uncovered, we have not yet found evidence for the kinds of biological variations that possibly occur for diagnosed persons if behavioral patterns are changed early and frequently over a lifetime. Whereas in the Maguire et al. study noted above, the hippocampus (a brain structure instrumental for navigational behavior) apparently grows and adapts as cab drivers in London recall the intricate routes necessary to weave through the city.

In a statement consistent with the view that biological differences between groups does not certify that biology has caused those differences, Barkley (1998e, 164) notes that "neurochemical abnormalities that may underlie" ADHD have "still proven extremely difficult to document with any certainty." He adds that although "evidence is converging on a probable neurological site or network for ADHD," "most findings on etiologies are correlational in nature." These findings "do not permit direct evidence of immediate and primary causality." However, despite these explicit statements, an individual who qualifies for diagnosis is nevertheless usually informed that he or she cannot control symptom behaviors, and that these behaviors are due to a constitutional delay.

Conversely, if biology is understood as co-occurring event with behavior, it is reasonable to presume that differences in brain tissue and functioning evolve over the course of a person's life. We could suggest that these co-occurrences are present for all behavior, and that this is a function of the ongoing interaction between biology, behavior, and a range of other influential variables (i.e., a dynamic process). Even if much of the brain's structural development occurs early in the embryological process, we do not yet know how much change can be introduced by behavioral variations over time. In this sense the biological differences between diagnosed and non-diagnosed persons is "a chicken and egg" problem.

While traditionalists recognize the above claim "in principle," their interpretations imply that genetics creates biology, and that these parameters have an antecedent status in relation to behavior. They hold that biology unfolds in a relatively set pattern (genetic predisposition), which is *not* dramatically influenced by environmental events (such as parental influence) as long as minimum standards are met (Barkley, 2000; Scarr, 1984; Scarr, 1983; Scarr; 1992). They assert that parents cannot "reengineer" their children, but they can at most only provide "indirect" influences on their child's behavior (Barkley, 2000).

However, Baumrind (1993) responds very differently to the view that environmental effects are relatively limited if certain minimal standards are met. In Baumrind's opinion, many children in contemporary society seem to be troubled both psychologically and behaviorally. Parental intervention may not be good enough to address ADHD behavior effectively. Rather than argue that environmental effects are not significant, one could argue that we have not been insightful about how we attempt to change ADHD behavior. Not finding effective ways to alter ADHD using the kinds of psychosocial interventions already tried does not negate the possibility that a relearning methodology can in principle yield reasonable treatment effects. As Kolb (1989) indicates, early enriching experiences can also aid the brain in its recovery from milder injuries and physical insults by helping it "rewire" itself.

There are plenty of instances where non-biological treatments have produced notable biological changes. For example, Baxter et al. (1992) indicate that some individuals diagnosed with Obsessive Compulsive Disorder (OCD) show reduced metabolic activity in the right caudate nucleus either by taking fluoxetine or by preventing the compulsive response. Further, only persons demonstrating positive clinical improvement produce this kind of change in their brain activity as measured by PET scans. We see that both the drug and the behavioral change can produce similar effects on the biological system. Similarly, Mayberg et al. (2002) report that depressed individuals will show similar metabolic changes in the brain when treated with either a placebo or fluoxetine. These results also illustrate the possibility that changes in one's biological system can be attributable to changes in behavior.

If we accept that behavior can change biology, we may also find that brain wave patterns occurring during vigilance tests (El-Sayed, Larsson, Persson, and Rydelius, 2002) will change as new learning takes place. For example, it is already being reported that diagnosed individuals can be trained through biofeedback to control a video game based on the kinds of brain waves they emit (Wright, 2001). It was possible for diagnosed children in this study to be conditioned to alter certain patterns of brain functioning by shaping procedures, thus revealing that their former brain activity was not fixed.

These studies seem to show that biology and behavior are inextricably linked and mutually influential. For the children in Wright's study, the observed biological patterns reflected or corresponded to behaviors being emitted and learned over time. Thus, it does not appear that ADHD empiricism has established the extent to which diagnosed persons' patterns of brain activity and behavior alter in conjunction with new learning, nor has it established the degree to which this newly-evolving biological substrate and history of reinforcement relates to the diminishing of ADHD responding.

We might therefore investigate whether a treatment approach emphasizing new skill development leads to altered brain structure and functioning in some or many diagnosed individuals. Perhaps over time as patterns of living in the world change, subsequent behavior changes will remove, or at least ameliorate, biological differences that were found in some studies. For example, while stimulants seem to increase dopamine and norepinephrine in the area of the synaptic cleft (Solanto, 1998) it has also been found that dopamine levels increase with positive and novel experiences (Schultz, Dayan, Montague, 1997; Wickelgren, 1997).

If we presume that biology is continuously changing and flexible, we can approach biological correlates and ADHD from a very different vantage point. For example, Thompson and Nelson (2001) indicate that even the adult brain is capable of "functional plasticity." They note that the formation of new neurons continues throughout much of the lifespan in the dentate region of the hippocampus and in the parietal and prefrontal cortex regions as well. Differences in the frontal lobes of diagnosed persons could therefore be understood to be highly affected by environment rather than as a genetic fixture.

However, we cannot overemphasize the need for ADHD diagnosed individuals and those who frequently interact with them to consider the value and necessity of developing personal autonomy, and to therefore facilitate this process. For example, Scheibel et al. (1985) found that infants' self-produced experiences enhance the development of the right side of their brains faster than the left. We might argue that this finding is consistent with the view that the brain develops very differently in relation to the frequency with which self-reliant functioning occurs, in contrast to responding to other peoples' directives. Succinctly put, if the person is not doing and practicing behaviors that contrast with ADHD responding, how can the correlated brain activity occur and develop in normative ways?

We can surmise that if ADHD children are within a psychosocial pattern that coincides with others reminding, arranging, and anticipating during daily functioning, they are not expressing the behavior that potentially elicits increasing activity levels in certain brain areas. Their living patterns of *minimal personal responsibility* could indeed impact on how their brains organize and function over time. Moreover, interventions that tend to compensate for *presumed* ineptitude may not help these children show so-called normal growth and development of brain structure and function, especially when contrasted with interventions that foster greater initiative, self-direction, and inventiveness.

It therefore would be interesting to see what happens to the brain biology of early identified diagnosed individuals who are reinforced to largely use their own resources and rely less on other peoples' solutions. A comparison of biological developments between individuals with self-initiative and personal responsibility training, and those trained in the traditional regime of medication and external control will undoubtedly give us insights into this issue.

However, given the dependency that develops over time, coupled with a lack of self-reliance training, it is not surprising that when the drugs and outside assistance are removed, diagnosed persons typically return to their previous patterns and symptom severity. They have not yet learned to do the kinds of activities that would permit them to function adequately to the point of autonomous reflective reinforced response. Conventional practitioners might argue that their return to previous functioning further supports their perspective, but it could be that the treatment was the wrong choice of intervention. There as yet seems to be no way to establish the extent to which atypical biological structure and function found in the ADHD population is the cause, consequence, or concomitant of behavior over time.

The Medication Argument

Because taking a drug (e.g., methylphenidate) often improves functioning both behaviorally and biologically (Amen, 2001), this finding is often interpreted to mean that the source of the problem has always been biological. Their logic suggests that problematic biology is the cause of the behavioral dysfunction, since the addition of medication (that alters biochemistry) ameliorates the dysfunction. Those who ascribe to this view often assert that the problem is a "chemical imbalance," in that the plethora of research shows that most diagnosed persons exhibit fewer problem behaviors when taking prescription medication (i.e., usually amphetamines).

The presumption that medication offsets biological weakness is significantly bolstered when individuals who show improvement while taking medication regress to their dysfunctional patterns if they miss even a single dose. Conventional practitioners have typically characterized medication to have such positive effects that the diagnosed person reverts to previous (poor) functioning without it. So it is not surprising that they continue to posit that medication is correcting something that is biologically amiss.

Drugs are understood to alter, compensate for, or rectify delays in biology that are a function of the person's physical composition. In conventional practice, medication helps return the inhibitory system to competent functioning. In that non-diagnosed individuals sometimes show a less profound reaction to medication, traditionalists emphasize that they do not have a biological delay; the medication will therefore (as expected) have less influence.

However, this interpretation has a practical flaw. For example, it would be unreasonable to insist that aspirin corrects an endogenous chemical imbalance or a genetically caused delay when it merely helps relieve headache pain. We would also not make those inferences simply because non-headache sufferers report no observable effect from ingesting aspirin. Since there are also occasions when a medication does not have the predicted effect on a diagnosed person, or it actually alters the behavior of a non-diagnosed person in a profound and noteworthy way, these conventional arguments are weak. When these events are observed, we neither insist that the non-diagnosed individual must have ADHD simply because the drug is so influential, nor do we say that the diagnosed person must have been improperly categorized.

We conclude that it is therefore problematic to infer the presence of a particular biological delay merely because a medication correlates with positive behavioral changes, or that we can note differing responses to the medications. Moreover, while some diagnosed children show different growth hormone and prolactin levels in blood plasma when taking methylphenidate (Shaywitz et al., 1986), depending on whether they are the combined or inattentive type, we still do not know how those responses are attributable to psychological patterns that may have shaped biology in different ways.

Furthermore, it is not always the case that diagnosed and non-diagnosed persons differ in their responses to ADHD medications. It is known that both diagnosed and non-diagnosed individuals ingest stimulants to aid in studying, particularly when preparing for examinations or completing term papers, in that increased productivity is required. This indicates that stimulant drugs can be advantageous irrespective of whether diagnosis is assigned. Both diagnosed and non-diagnosed individuals can exhibit similar reactions to medications used to treat ADHD, including increased concentration, better encoding, and work productivity. Stimulant medications in general have frequently been used to improve functioning on work-related tasks for many people.

Ackerman et al. (1982) also report that reading-impaired non-diagnosed children will show significant improvement during attentiveness tests when taking Ritalin; and Gittelman et al. (1983) report that Ritalin also helps non-diagnosed subjects perform better when doing arithmetic during an 18-week treatment program. Similarly, the drug Modafinil has improved the cognitive functioning of healthy individuals (Baranski et al., 2004), as well as helped improve task performance of diagnosed persons in several different ways (Turner et al., 2004), in addition to helping individuals with narcolepsy.

The relationships between behavior and medication can also be markedly inconsistent. For instance, some individuals show initial improvement immediately after taking a medication, but then revert to former patterns of behavior after a period of time. Others experience a worsening of problematic behaviors; some show changes in their behavior only in specific situations even with the medication. Given the possible wide variations, we can reasonably assert that people react differently to particular medication at different times, and that people behave differently both on and off medication. However, none of these observations establishes that ADHD is determined by an antecedent biological delay.

Furthermore, we know that several different kinds of medication can produce beneficial changes for individuals with the same posited biological problem, as well as for people with different posited biological problems. For instance, Tricyclic Antidepressants may help individuals diagnosed with both ADHD and/or Depression, and Wilens et al. (1996) found that most adults taking Tricyclic Antidepressants improved so much that they no longer met the diagnostic criteria for ADHD. Similarly, in their review of 31 studies, Spencer, Biederman, and Wilens (1998) report that close to 90% of the studies show noteworthy improvement when diagnosed individuals ingested Tricyclic Antidepressants. Not only did these medications produce behavioral improvements in 68% of individuals compared to 10% of placebo participants, but many subjects were helped after they had not responded positively to stimulant therapy.

Several other medications have also produced positive results for diagnosed persons. Bupropion (antidepressant) has shown effectiveness (Conners et al., 1996; Wilens, 2005), and atomoxetine (a norepinephrine reuptake inhibitor) has yielded such impressive results that it is now considered an ADHD front line medication (Spencer et al., 2001; Adler et al., 2005). Furthermore, Clonidine (which also impacts noradrenergic output to the central nervous system), has also been used successfully with diagnosed persons (Connor, Fletcher, and Swanson, 1999). Moreover, Haight (2003), in a relatively offbeat approach, reports that 158 mg a day of caffeine, which activates adrenaline production and helps to release sugar into the bloodstream, may also help to relieve ADHD symptoms for some diagnosed children.

When outlining the many seemingly different drugs that relieve ADHD symptoms, we must emphasize that the medications that usually work effectively with ADHD typically influence the catecholamine reuptake system in one way or another (Spencer, 2005). Wilens, Spencer, and Biederman (1998) note that Tricyclic Antidepressants (much like stimulants) seem to impede the reuptake of dopamine and norepinephrine. Although the drugs are designed to treat different conditions, there is a commonality to the neurotransmitters that are influenced. Tricyclics might be designed primarily to manipulate norepinephrine and serotonin for the treatment of depression (Spencer, Biederman, and Wilens, 1998), but they also change the way the body uses dopamine. Not surprisingly, ADHD symptoms are at times altered in positive ways by both medications. It is now generally believed that the medication that produces the most significant relief from ADHD symptoms (for the most people) will influence the transmission of dopamine and norepinephrine (Zametkin and Rappoport, 1987; Wilens and Spencer, 2000).

However, the results of various studies can also be dissimilar, depending on the study; and sometimes medications do not produce anticipated effects. For example, some studies of Tricyclic Antidepressants have shown consistent improvement for up to two years (Biederman, Gastfriend, and Jellinek, 1986; Gastfriend, Biederman, and Jellinek, 1985; Wilens et al., 1993), while others report a 50% dropout rate due to intolerance of side effects, and indicate less positive long-term benefits (Quinn and Rappoport, 1975). Sometimes tricyclic medications outperform stimulants in some trials, even though it is more often the case that stimulants perform better (Spencer, 2006). At times it is expected that a drug will have a particular effect on cognition or other symptoms, given its biochemical properties (e.g., clonidine, amino acids), but these effects are not guaranteed to occur (Connor, 2006; Prince et al., 2006).

But if ADHD is a singular biological delay, why not prescribe the same biological treatment for all "pure" diagnosed persons? We know that this is an absurd proposition because some individuals respond to one ADHD medication and not another; some show benefits from combining medications (Ratey et al., 1991; Gammon and Brown, 1993; Connor, 2006), and some do not respond at all to medication. Given such diversity of medication response, it is disingenuous to assert that all diagnosed persons have the same neurobiological delay simply because medication therapy can be efficacious.

Instead of viewing ADHD medication as correcting an inherent delay, medication could ostensibly be regarded as a quick and easy way to induce behavioral and biological change compared to the intensive work required to change biology and behavior psychotherapeutically over the longer term. However, when utilizing psychological intervention, we know that problems can occur for many people when they try to stop a psychotropic medication, because they have become accustomed to living in the world while under medicinal influence. Since the world is very different to medicated individuals, those who are ADHD diagnosed do not have the opportunity to learn acceptable behaviors without the aid of medication. All participants are truly at the beginning of their learning curve when drug remedies are removed.

We have discussed in this chapter the three basic pillars of biological determinism: studies of heritability, differences in biology, and medication effects. Each argument is limited in its capacity to establish biological determinism for ADHD. Biology is of course included as a parameter for psychology, but other variables outside the realm of biology also affect which behavior will be emitted under particular conditions.

Conventional practitioners acknowledge that more acceptable responses are within the typical behavioral repertoire of most diagnosed persons, and consider ADHD to be a problem of *not being able to perform* what one knows. The crux of our debate therefore rests on explicating the increased occurrence of ADHD responses within a variety of situations and circumstances. To that end, a learning paradigm can show greater precision and scope when compared to biological determinism.

We know that specific limitations evident in particular species (e.g., humans cannot see some frequencies of light) can reasonably be ascribed to biology, but the greater dilemma is how to account for individual differences in the spectrum of possible behavior within a species. Biology *is* influential and should not be expunged from any psychological data, as even with individualized training regimes designed to maximize performance, some people will outperform others. However, conditioning over time can produce remarkable results in changing the distributions that are noted. One never knows prior to intervention the kinds of changes that occur as new conditioning is introduced.

In the view proposed here, diagnosed persons are conditioned to enact the behaviors we call ADHD more often than other people, although it may also be the case that many diagnosed persons possess a body that is likely to increase their probability of learning diagnostic patterns. While traditionalists claim that significant environmental influences have not yet been empirically demonstrated, the counter claim is that a learning paradigm has not been sufficiently evaluated by work in the field thus far.

Chapter 4

A Critique of the Traditional
Inhibitory Mental Mechanism

The predominant view about ADHD behavior is that it results from a decreased ability to inhibit immediately gratifying responses. The individual is mechanically deprived of the information that executive functioning would otherwise have provided in order to lead behavior to long-term success. We critique this mental model here, and argue against the traditional mentalist account's series of untenable claims. We also suggest that the case may instead be that patterns of not performing "what one knows" are due to *conditioning* rather than a lesser functioning inhibitory mechanism.

We support a learning paradigm as an alternative approach to account for the supposedly dysfunctional kinds of behaviors of diagnosed individuals in some contexts, circumstances, and situations, which have become the cornerstone for assigning the ADHD diagnosis. An individual's unique learning history with its contexts and situations can provide credible (and repetitive) evidence to assist mental health practitioners in their understanding of ADHD. We would argue that the assertion of a biological delay underpinning has diverted researchers from plausible alternative explanations of ADHD patterning. For example, that the atypical and inappropriate responses emitted by diagnosed individuals can *also* activate different loci in the brain as well as influence biological development. The danger is that discrepant brain functioning will be put forward as the *cause* rather than the *result* of relentless conditioning of ADHD behaviors.

Our perspective incorporates a commitment to individual differences in the exploration of patterns of behavior, as well as reliance on experimental psychology principles and data. We presume that people engage in particular sequences of behaviors in particular circumstances, and on some occasions behaviors are given the characterization or descriptive label of ADHD. Diagnosis only implies that those kinds of actions occur with greater frequency.

The Traditional Mental Model

Wakefield (1992; 1997) takes a very atomistic view in his assertion that all individuals have a mental mechanism which permits one's control over the future; this construct is the cornerstone of the traditional ADHD formulation. Diagnosed individuals are purported to suffer with a condition called *disinhibition*, a weakened or delayed biological inhibitory mental mechanism that disrupts behavioral output. Not having an operational inhibitory mechanism means that executive functioning (rational decision making capacity) is hindered. The less executive functioning one has, the less is the probability that he or she will develop future adaptive behaviors.

The accepted traditionalist view also seems to rely primarily on the formulations of Bronowski (1977) and Fuster (1997). These theorists describe a mental inhibitory process that purportedly occurs when persons engage in goal-directed or intentional behavior. In their account, in order to respond in effective ways that are future-directed, one must be able to first *inhibit* the initial response to an event. Second, they must *maintain a delay* so that they can decide about a course of action. Third, they must *protect* the mental actions that occur during the delay from disruptions created at certain times by competing events and responses. When a person has a competent inhibitory system, she can stand outside immediate events, figure out a strategy for the longer term, and be less inundated by immediate circumstances (Barkley, 2006f).

When competent time-organized behavior is evident, traditionalists presume that the observable behavior has been preceded or governed by a private inhibitory activity that has also enabled the participation and guidance of other mental activities called *executive functioning*. These functions permit distant events to factor into the action taken, which then enable individuals to produce responses that facilitate future events. The hidden mental machinations also enable individuals to internalize a "sense" of time that helps one to organize behavior. The individual is better able to anticipate changes in the environment and more likely to recognize what may lie ahead.

Traditionalists maintain that inhibition plus executive functioning are necessary antecedents (and sometimes concurrent) of normative behavior. They argue that ADHD individuals are competent only when acceptable functioning entails a response to current, physically-represented stimuli. Traditionalists have developed this mental model to depict what happens in the mind to account for the delayed behaviors we call ADHD. This model is presumed to work in an isomorphic fashion with our biological inhibitory system.

We suggest instead that acceptable behaviors are continuously enacted *without* the posited requirement that inhibition must precede or co-occur with executive functioning. We contest that acceptable behaviors can be differentiated from ADHD behavioral responses by their characteristics, not by the absence of so-called co-existing mental actions. If we understand the traditional mental model correctly, a person apparently has to know prior to inhibiting that a delaying response—imbued with executive functioning—is required. This mental exercise would require executive activity *prior* to the inhibiting response (not afterwards) as asserted by traditionalists.

One can easily detect that the inhibitory mental model is rife with problematic assertions, and offers little if no apparent explanatory value. For example, Robin (2006, 505) explains to his adolescent clientele that ADHD hampers the ability to control behavior or the "urge to act before thinking," but it goes unrecognized that his formulation requires the inhibitory mechanism to know ahead of time that the impending action is problematic. However, if that is the case, which agency informs the person about that possibility if executive functioning has not yet been accessed?

According to traditional perspective, individuals are more motoric during childhood, and inhibitory problems will initially take the form of hyperactivity and recklessness. However, by adolescence, diagnosed children typically become less motoric (Hart et al., 1995), and functioning shifts its orientation more towards language and its private forms. We then begin to rely on executive functions for effective behaviors as we age, and delays in attentiveness and time management difficulties become more pronounced as diagnosed persons enter adulthood.

Barkley (2006f) claims that people must have an inhibitory response in order to competently access the executive functions that control motor responses during goal accomplishments. While diagnosed persons may be able to function much like anyone else, they are supposedly less adept at carrying out actions or behavioral patterns that they already know how to do because of their ADHD delay. The result is that the individual is less likely to stay focused or will stop altogether during the performance of behavioral sequences.

Problematic behaviors include poor emotional control, impulsivity, inadequate resistance to distraction, and lack of persistence for non-physically represented consequences. Diagnosed individuals are said to have relative difficulty moderating and detaining responses. While most individuals manage to invoke more control over their actions, diagnosed individuals are consistently less adept at managing themselves, especially over broad time spans. It is for these reasons that traditionalists have designed elaborate ways for others to counteract ADHD impairment, in that diagnosed persons are less able to manage themselves (or enact what they know) whenever ameliorating conditions do not occur.

From a normative standpoint, we purportedly develop increasing inhibition and ability to delay responding to the immediate environment, and a corresponding ability to modulate behavior in our response to changes over time. As individuals become capable of delaying their responding, it is possible to consider greater numbers of environmental parameters. Behaviors evolve in order to meet the demands of situations, and to skillfully control future contingencies. When conventional practitioners convey the notion that diagnosed individuals fail to utilize their executive functioning (an essential component for motivation, intention, and intelligent action), they seem to be asserting that some executive (biological) activity is not taking place because the failure to do another biological activity (i.e., inhibition) is limiting the individual to the realm of initial (impulsive) responses.

Traditionalists' claim ADHD individuals have difficulty initiating socially acceptable responding without immediate and obvious consequences because they do not delay long enough to identify important future contingences. Diagnosed individuals are governed by the moment; therefore, responses to future or remote circumstances are essentially disconnected events. It is almost as if intelligent actions are absent much of the time. The concern is that without responses to enable this "self-regulation," the person is relegated to living in the moment with all of its pitfalls and dangers.

Barkley (2006f) holds that self-regulation may only take place with the inhibition of prepotent responses, or by stopping responses that produce ineffective outcomes. In his view, diagnosed persons could motivate for longer term events if they had a *normal inhibitory system* that allows mental processes to operate and influence behavior. In Barkley's (1998g, 249) conceptualization, diagnosed individuals do not prepare at all, or only begin to when events are poised to happen and are thus often in "chaos and crisis." They dissipate their energies by dealing with urgent situations and are confined to live in the present when "forethought and planning" might have lessened problems in significant ways.

Normative behavior, according to traditionalists, is such that individuals (in general) go from behavior governed by the moment to behavior that involves the "not here and not now." People typically integrate broader spans of time into their responses; this tendency is presumed to maximize survival. Most individuals increasingly free themselves from momentary pressures, temptations, and concerns, to think about the future and modulate behavior in order to change distant outcomes. Diagnosed individuals cannot maximize the use of their resources, in that previous experience that would likely have assisted them in solving current problems cannot be accessed or incorporated into present decision-making. In order for hindsight to help a person be more creative in her environment, she has to rekindle past sounds and images and maintain the sensory events that have been active during the occurrence of a response delay. Failure to effectively do this will limit the extent to which history helps direct subsequent responding (Barkley, 1998g).

To better manage the future, individuals must compare current events with events represented in the working memory. Comparisons will inform the individual when it is best to emit particular responses. If the individual receives information about errors during an enactment, he may continue to self-regulate by temporarily holding the feedback in mind, and then change and fine-tune plans so that preferable states can be achieved (Barkley, 1998g). A person cannot do any of these actions *without* an intact inhibitory mechanism.

Over time, individuals with competent inhibitory mechanisms benefit: they may become increasingly skilled at controlling the future, in persistence, and ability to resist distraction. They will become more proficient at evoking the kinds of responses that lead to achievement, and to compete more effectively with others when vying for limited resources. As inhibiting, moderating, and self-regulating become sophisticated, problem behaviors can be avoided. Dilemmas requiring multiple steps can be solved. Comprehension can become more generalized, greater amounts of information can be integrated, and events and contingencies can be factored into decision-making. The individual's behavior is no longer governed by the moment, but instead relates to long-term learning resulting in: sophisticated intentionality that incorporates inner activity, subsequent future success in the environment, adequate completion of a range of tasks, and socially preferred behavior.

Barkley (2000) also notes that a developmental shift usually occurs over time that finds people reverting from public behavior to private behavior as they mature. This shifting has the advantage of protecting individuals on many occasions. For example, if others cannot see covert activity, they cannot "steal" that information in order to outmaneuver. Since diagnosed persons are delayed in their ability to keep responses in thought form, they are presumed to be losers in a competitive race; they inevitably show weakness in suppressing maladaptive emitted responses. While most individuals first learn to talk out loud, and then learn to talk privately to themselves by suppressing the earlier learned more public behavior, diagnosed persons are less able to suppress their musculature or motor systems in normative ways. This is why they have less control over what becomes public, and what is kept private.

The end result of this delay is that private behaviors are often expressed publicly. Inhibitory problems are believed to deprive them from being able to react to their own thoughts, images, emotions, and creativity. The individual is at increased risk for all kinds of social maladjustment. They may fail to fulfill obligations, and will often make public displays before responses are adequately censured for appropriateness and safety. Not only do they have difficulty competing with others for long-term rewards, but they also have trouble maintaining cooperative relationships. Ultimately, they are less likely to share and take turns, since such behavior requires thinking in longer time frames (Barkley, 2006f). Their behavior will also often appear to lack morality because they have difficulty holding in mind information about a presently occurring action, and the "rule against which it must be compared" (Barkley, 1998a, 4).

Inhibitory problems are particularly unfortunate because individuals with the necessary skills and information to succeed cannot enact *what they know*. They are biologically (and therefore mentally) less able to initiate and maintain a controlled, regulated state. Failure to adequately inhibit becomes the essential and primary weakness of ADHD individuals, and it accounts for the maladjustment and lack of sophistication often seen in their behavioral patterning. They cannot easily withhold a response long enough to plan, anticipate, reconstitute, and synthesize so that their eventual responses will be appropriate and successful.

In sum, while it is not clear how traditionalists establish that inhibition and other mental activity takes place during goal achievement, it is presumed that executive function activity has to occur for behavior to be freed from the immediate or prepotent responses; it is the enabler for individuals to respond to long-term events in their environment. Along with an inhibitory reaction, the executive functions have to be operative for coordinating current behaviors with future contingencies. Individuals must necessarily "formulate and hold in mind the goal of the task and the plan for the future . . ." to produce longer term future achievements (Barkley (1998g, 246). When there is failure to show continuity of behavior over time, the inhibitory mechanism is to blame: diagnosed individuals are reacting too quickly to present circumstances.

If one accepts this conventional formulation of the processes of human thought and behavior over long-term frameworks, one also accepts the belief that people have biological/mental mechanisms. A diagnosed person's failure to realize long-term achievements indicates that his or her brain mechanism does not operate normally, and that that person has difficulty holding in mind future goals and steps necessary to complete them. This formulation is the explication for ADHD-associated impulsivity and lack of future orientation. One also has to presume that behaviors such as persistence in achieving goals require us to inhibit a prepotent response, and continue that inhibition long enough to construct a mental template for the necessary behaviors to achieve those long-term goals.

Conceptual Problems with the Inhibitory Model

To counter such mechanistic characterizations, Ryle (1949) points out that what distinguishes behaviors known as intelligent, skilled, thoughtful, motivated, voluntary, goal-directed, etc., is not that these behaviors are preceded by mental events or processes, but rather that the characteristics ascribed to the behaviors, information about the individual's history, and understanding the context of the behavior are the bases upon which those categorizations are established. He states, "When I do something intelligently, i.e., thinking what I am doing, I am doing one thing and not two. My performance has a special procedure or manner, not special antecedents" (p. 32). Ryle further claims:

> The chess player may require some time in which to plan his moves before he makes them. Yet the general assertion that all intelligent performances require them to be prefaced by a consideration of possible alternative propositions seems to be an implausible demand, even when it is conceded that the required

consideration is often swift and may go quite unmarked by the agent. I shall argue that demands of a precursor intellectual action is untenable, and that when we describe a performance as intelligent, it does not necessarily entail the two operations of considering and executing (p.29).

Ryle takes the view that it is indefensible to assert that a series of covert narratives must occur "in mind" just prior to enacting behaviors regarded as intelligent, rule-abiding, goal-directed, and intentional. Ryle states that this construction of behavior presumes:

That the operation which is characterized as intelligent must be preceded by an intellectual acknowledgment of these rules, or the application of criteria; that is, the agent must first go through the internal process of avowing to himself certain propositions about what is to be done (maxims, imperatives or regulative propositions as they are sometimes called); only then can he execute his performance in accordance with those dictates (p. 29).

Ryle finds this formulation problematic, in that there seem to be many occasions when a person shows intelligent behavior, but has no understanding of rules, canons, or maxims that might have been followed. For Ryle, it is more often the case that "efficient practice precedes the theory of it" (p. 30). A practical example of this seems to occur when a musical theorist analyzes the solo work of a jazz musician who has no knowledge of music theory, and demonstrates how the solo piece fits into traditional ways of comprehending music. Comparably, many therapists might not be immediately aware of criteria that are consistent with their case formulations, and yet they may nevertheless create remarkable insights.

Ryle suggests that persons do not follow a set of previously derived formulations in order to produce competent behaviors, but rather that we impose a particular format on the behavior *after* it has been produced. Very similarly, rather than claim that a future goal (or consequence of an action) is first identified by executive functioning and then acted on, Skinner (1953, 87) also asserts that it is not that "a man behaves because of the consequences which are to follow," or that "behavior is under the control of an incentive or goal which the organism has not yet achieved." In Skinner's view, people do particular behaviors at particular times "because of the consequences which have followed similar behaviors in the past." This understanding has been called the Law of Effect or *operant conditioning*.

A computer program must be very complex in order to generate a chess move, but we observe that that same move can be enacted effortlessly and without prior rehearsal by an experienced player. It is not a *fact* that the chess player had to delay, inhibit, or undergo specific antecedent steps in order to produce the skillful chess response. A particular information processing model (Sergeant, 1995) or category system attempts to formalize the chess maneuver by imposing a construction (as in a computer chess model), but the inclusion of a number of discrete interrelated steps does not prove absolutely that the chess player is actually mentally noting and proceeding through a series of actions and contingencies when playing chess. Even during such complex activities as these, there are occasions when an experienced player moves very quickly, reports that the response "just seemed right," and indicates no awareness of planning or visualizing a scenario of patterns that might happen as a result of the move prior to taking the action.

Moreover, if claims about mind data are predicated on societal traditions, or are derived from inferences of observations of brain activity, the bases for these inferences also do not seem reliable. The only apparently reliable basis of mind activity are the reports given by the individuals themselves (reports of categories of action such as thoughts, ideas, fantasies, and other imaginings). However, if this is the case, how are we to interpret the apparently short-sighted behavior of individuals who also report that they have indeed experienced such categories of action? Similarly, what do we do when individuals act in well-organized ways in relation to future events and are responsive to environmental shifts, and yet do *not* testify to any prior or accompanying mind activity during the sequence of actions? For example, when driving home from work, we undergo a highly complex sequence of organized behaviors, but we may not report having done any particular mind activity whatsoever to accomplish the goal of arriving at home. Once routines become learned we enact complex behavioral sequences and coordinate with the future (e.g., take a vitamin in the morning) without the inhibitory/executive process highlighted by the traditional view.

There is also the question of why it becomes necessary to inhibit or suppress one behavior for another behavior to occur. For example, if an individual begins to respond, and then stops before resuming his/her response, what is the basis to the claim that the person did or did not inhibit or suppress before and during the non-response interval? All that has been denoted is that the person did offer a partial response followed by a further response. It is not clear how we are to decide that the behavioral sequence includes an instance of inhibition prior to and/or during the interval between responses as posited by the accepted theory. Similarly, when non-diagnosed individuals continue particular behaviors without shifting or stopping, there seems to be no way to establish that they had to exert interference control or any other covert activity to account for the persistence of behavior.

It seems that all the traditional controlling mechanisms are not independently discriminated from the observations that particular kinds of acceptable or unacceptable behaviors are occurring. These accounts seem to add no explanatory value. That is, when individuals do not stop when they should, or do not report having done certain mental actions when they should have, it *must* be that they have not inhibited. Moreover, in that no apparent data have been offered to demonstrate that posited intervening inhibitory function is not the same for different non-appropriate response events, what is gained by its introduction?

Conversely, if we presume that behaviors may change or stay the same without also positing a regulatory or inhibitory step, it seems that the aforementioned problems are avoided. History of reinforcement can be imposed to account for the instances of shifting or continuing as one encounters different situations. While traditionalists might consider the shifting or failure to shift to mean that an inhibition has or has not occurred, one may alternatively presume that behaviors can occur in an ongoing succession with continuations, reengagements, and pauses without the requirement that a particular intermediary biological/mental event must occur for the sequencing to maintain conformity to a standard.

In this learning view, if an individual were to introduce a temporal interval in what seemed to be part of some longer response, and then (privately) introduce further content and/or subsequent information about possibilities; those kinds of response patterns can be characterized as distinct behaviors in a sequence without claiming that some unobservable inhibition had to occur to account for the interval or subsequent addition. The explication for the stopping, and/or the identification of future possibilities is derived from past learning opportunities.

Moreover, when traditionalists claim that some actions have the benefit of being controlled by the executive functions, while others do not, and that the controlling actions have a status independent of observations and descriptions of the particular current behaviors of the person, they are engaged in what Ryle (1949, 15) has called "the dogma of the Ghost in the Machine." As a way to avoid this hazard, we say that behaviors are labeled as controlled when patterns of organization are consistent with particular standards or criteria; persons are not doing and also controlling.

In our alternative usage, the label of being "controlled" is a descriptive statement of a sequence of actions characterized as increasing the probability for acceptable future outcomes; there is no need to invoke a driver or an additional event to explain why the pattern of satisfactory behavioral organization or outcome has occurred. When a subsequent behavioral action can be characterized as if it were a relational consequence of a prior action, we impose the description of control. We expect that this alternative approach will avoid the thorny problem of proving which mechanism drives the driver. When addressing this matter, Ryle vehemently states:

> The crucial objection to the intellectualist legend is this. The consideration of propositions is itself an operation the execution of which can be more or less intelligent, less or more stupid. But if, for any operation to be intelligently executed, a prior theoretical operation had first to be performed and performed intelligently, it would be a logical impossibility for anyone ever to break into the circle (p. 30).

It seems that circular and regressive thinking is recycled whenever a conceptual model of behavior is predicated on temporal relationships between antecedent mind agencies that purportedly govern and direct, as proposed by the conventional view. A learning paradigm, however, posits with regard to a child's ability to self-control, that behaviors are emitted, and either conditioned to occur more often, or shaped to diminish in frequency. Persons do not control and behave, they simply behave. The assessment of control is assigned after behavioral sequences occur when those sequences show certain acceptable characteristics. For example, I might say that my actions are controlled when I achieve a particular standard, and I am no longer surprised by what I accomplish. What is understood as lack of control depends on the criteria imposed by those representing the events. That is, if an outcome is seen as unwanted or incorrect, the behavior is characterized as under-controlled; we have no independent information about whether some people have more adequate drivers.

In this view, while certain behaviors might be described as inhibited or disinhibited, we are not discerning an inhibitory action when we make distinctions; we are simply commenting on the *characteristics* of the aforementioned behaviors. Even when we say we *exert* control, we are observing a behavior that we identify as potentially increasing the probability of a particular outcome. When that sequence of actions results in fully meeting certain criteria, we say that we have controlled. *Control* is a characterization that we impose on behavior.

When applying this formulation to our current concern, we suggest that diagnosed children are often very much in control when they do ADHD. If, for example, a child touches objects that are dangerous, valuable, or fragile, we still do not know whether these actions indicate less self-regulation and executive functioning compared to the child who only touches toys. We might presume that the child who only touches toys is controlling the future exceptionally well, but there may be other issues involved. For example, the child who touches the objects that are "off limits" gets noticed more often than the child who only touches toys. The irksome behavior includes the additional discrimination that adults in the area are likely to become aroused and annoyed. When seen in that light, the "off limits" touching behaviors is seen as a means of controlling the future, albeit in a different way. Furthermore, during parents' phone calls for example, it is the *parent* who is usually the most uncomfortable with the situation, and often stops or shortens a call in response to such behavior. Likewise, if asking permission allows others to say no, diagnosed persons may be more effectively controlling future contingencies when they do not stop and ask for clearance.

Ryle (1949, 16) also says that when a behavior is identified as controlled (or intelligent, skilled, methodical, etc.) a "category mistake" is introduced when it is presumed that these descriptors mean that a different category of actions is added to the event. Ryle illustrates this "mistake" when an individual looks at various buildings, classrooms, and libraries etc., and then asks, "But where is the University?" Ryle emphasizes that the category "University" does not denote or describe yet another "collateral institution," "laboratory," or "office." University is a category of the totality of particular collective activities that takes place in the various locations. Anyone looking for another "building" in order to find the "University" is committing a category error.

Analogously, when a jeweler opens a watch to observe the working of its "mechanism," he will see various parts in certain relationship to each other. However, the term "mechanism" is not an additional component or a particular aspect of any part or of the observed parts. It is a statement of the integration and interaction of the parts' operation, not an aspect of the parts.

Extrapolating from Ryle's analyses, when behaviors are typified as impulsive, disinhibited, or uncontrolled, it is not because some other set of actions has done a poor job at managing, but rather because the characterizations are of the observed behaviors. Similarly, when persons operate in ways that increase the probability of greater numbers of socially acceptable future events, this does not tell us whether inhibition or other mental guidance took place. The behaviors are characterized by their coordination with the more distant events; not because particular antecedents or other actions have operated. Comparably, while certain behaviors might be characterized as selfish, mistaken, inappropriate, and short sighted, the terms are categorizations of behavioral events. Certain behaviors might be enacted more carefully (i.e., slowly and accurately) or more thoughtfully (i.e., efficiently), but this does not mean that the person is doing two activities simultaneously (i.e., behaving and executive controlling). The descriptors of the behavioral acts do not become an additional component or aspect of the behaviors (i.e., category mistake in Ryle's terminology).

Similar to Ryle's claim that characteristics of the behavior within a context deem it intelligent (i.e., not an additional mental process), we say that behavioral sequencing is self-regulated when it shows the characteristic of being successful. It is not that some other mental events are being identified. When we say that a person is wary, vigilant, focused, or more precise in responding, this indicates only that he or she is behaving in a particular way. Likewise, when a person behaves attentively and is not diverted by stimuli deemed irrelevant, we *describe* his action as showing interference control.

Peters (1960) also discusses the problem of positing antecedents when accounting for certain behaviors; he says that people are "motivated" when their behavior is directed towards a goal. "Anything is called a goal if we can see that behavior varies concomitantly with changes in the situation which we call the goal and in the conditions necessary to attain it" (p. 46). Motivation, according to Peters, is associated with the characteristics of a behavior (i.e., changes that occur in relation to a posited end state) rather than to its being caused by "some inner spring of action" (p.38).

Given his conceptual stance, he would summarily discard the mental model proposed by traditionalists to account for ADHD behaviors, and avoid the "ghost in the machine" metaphor. Peters does not interpret motivation as a "process of private, self-directed actions" that produces the "power that provides the drive, and in the absence of external rewards, fuels the individual's persistence in goal-directed actions" (Barkley, 1998g, 239).

Hofstadter's (1941) perspective of "objective teleology" is another instance in the tradition of Ryle and Peters, where behaviors are understood as goal-directed when predictable relationships between behaviors, circumstances, means, and posited end states can be shown. Hofstadter asserts that observables —not inner events—distinguish goal-directed actions from other behavioral sequences. Within Hofstadter's teleology, longer term goal-directed behaviors are similar to immediate goal-directed behaviors in every way except the temporal proximity of the posited endpoint that is coordinated with the behaviors. While behaviors might differ in terms of the analysis imposed on it (e.g., it changes predictably in relation to an endpoint closer in time or later in the future), it does not differ in relation to antecedent inhibition and private machinations associated with those behaviors.

Much like Ryle, Peters, Hofstadter, and Skinner, other theorists have questioned how traditionalists characterize intentional behavior. For example, Bargh and Chartrand (1999) discuss the problem of positing mechanisms and internal processes to account for these kinds of actions. They claim:

> Models that acknowledge the role played by higher-order choice or "executive" processes do exist. However, the authors of these models generally acknowledge that the lack of specification of how these choices are made presents problems for the models. For example, Neisser in his (1967) seminal book Cognitive Psychology, describes the "problem of the executive," in which the flexible choice and selection processes are described as a homunculus or "little person in the head" does not constitute a scientific explanation (p. 463).

Others have also questioned constructs that require individuals to keep information "in mind or on line in order to control a subsequent response" (Barkley, 1998g, 235). For example, Kirsch and Lynn (1999) write that behaviors are instigated in a more automatic fashion. They depart from the construction that prior covert processes have to occur in order for intentional behavior to take place. These authors claim that if a "supervisory attentional system" provides control over intentional behavior (as proposed by authors Norman and Shallice, 1986) it would resemble the postulated "ghost in the machine." These kinds of precursor demands would repetitiously violate "the law of conservation of energy," and entail the conclusion that "the operation of precursor supervisory attentional system" would also have to be "governed by prior automatic processes" (p. 508).

In Kirsch and Lynn's view, an infinite regression of prior supervisory attentional responses would have to be invoked. One would have to posit that each supervisory system must be governed by another system to ensure adequate functioning. For example, if we presume that motivation can only occur when other private acts imbue the behavior impetus and power, how do the private acts have those characteristics and what motivates them? In this regard, Peters (1960) contends:

> Psychology's advance, at any rate towards conceptual clarity, would surely be more rapid if it were admitted that it is only the directedness of behavior that is entailed when saying that it is motivated, not any specific causal conditions, of "drive" or anything else (p.42).

It seems that these alternative views about behaviors identified as goal-directed are particularly cogent for traditional claims and explications about ADHD. For example, Hathaway, Dooling-Litfin, and Edwards (1998, 316) assert that ADHD behaviors stem from problems with inhibitory failure, rather than from "intentional misbehavior, coercive defiance cycles, or deliberate aggression associated with ODD." However, a challenge for traditionalist construction is how they distinguish between behaviors that are christened by inhibitions and executive functions (i.e., deliberate), and other behaviors called ADHD, which are not. While the aforementioned behaviors are distinguishable from their characteristics, no one is yet providing data that highlights that they are different in their accompanying mind behaviors. Moreover, when ascribing to this posited view, we are also left with the problem of deciding whether certain mind behaviors are "deliberate" or disinhibited as well.

While "metaphor" seems essential to human comprehension, it is crucial that we remember that our imposed understandings are representational. The unfortunate intellectual problem brought about by traditionalists is that the metaphor "driver," for example, has been used so often that it has attained literal status. We acknowledge the heuristic value of analyzing complex behaviors, but the traditionalists' mental model now has ontological status; the presumption is that people "have" inhibitory responses and governing actions. There is the entrenched belief that one actually experiences a myriad of internal responses when behaving in ways characterized as "intentional."

An example of this kind of reification is evident when Barkley (2006, 304) says that for a person to have self-control, "some neuropsychological or mental faculty must exist . . ." that enables a person to produce behaviors that are organized in time despite lapses in the occurrence of contingencies. Traditionalists are explicit in that these additional mental acts are actually occurring when we observe actions organized over time. The person must have thought about, envisioned, and analyzed past and present events in order to have operated so effectively.

The alternative premise is that even were the behavioral response to contain content consistent with increasing the probability of long-term future events, it is not presumed that the behavior includes other special biological/mental operations. It is essential that we avoid changing an observable descriptive statement such as "behaviors show a particular organization" to an explanatory statement asserting that "behaviors are organized *because* of particular governing activities." From our alternative view of ADHD, when a behavior is labeled as under–controlled, the observer is not identifying the relational consequences which account for the occurrence of the behavior. It is not that the observer has any information about the insufficiency of steering mechanisms. By excluding a biological controlling causal agent, which implies that *something else* is doing the organizing and controlling, the observer's characterization of the behavior does not get reified and given physical existence within the person.

This alternative conceptualization seems workable even in situations where people behave *as if* talking to themselves before (and during) enacting motoric behavior, or are attentively observing their own actions. Rather than claim that the more private actions are controlling what the person is doing, we are merely describing particular behavioral sequences, which occur primarily during initial learning, or when extra precision or caution is required in a situation. It is therefore unlikely that individuals are given an ADHD diagnosis based on the frequency with which these behavioral sequences occur for most people during daily life.

Hence, rather than insist that non-diagnosed people prepare non-vocal verbal actions or imaginings more often than diagnosed persons before speaking aloud when they do talk appropriately, we can instead say that they are conditioned to talk acceptably. Our expectation is that this reinterpretation of the reified mental model will avoid the apparent conceptual confusion of characterizing events and positing agents to account for their origins. We drop the idea "that for an operation to be intelligent it must be steered by a prior intellectual operation" (Ryle, 1949, 32).

While people may at times learn to hesitate, react by doing non-vocal verbal behavior, or behave as if imagining something before manifesting other behaviors, it is unreasonable to presume that these actions *must* always occur, or that they are invariably necessary to protect, generate, and control the enactment of acceptable and appropriate behavior. We accept that these kinds of responses are more likely to be conditioned when individuals first learn new tasks (e.g., playing a new song on a musical instrument or when performing a new math skill, etc.), when individuals are preoccupied with unresolved problems, impeded by obstacles, or apprehensive about the consequences of an action, but we argue that, given repetition and familiarity, achievements eventually occur effortlessly, with less preparatory behavior, and with less self-observation.

Moreover, since parents are generally less critical and more tolerant of unacceptable acts when children first learn how to respond to new contexts and circumstances, the assignment of an ADHD diagnosis is likely to occur when children *repeatedly* behave in unacceptable ways. That is, when children continue to behave non-normatively even though "they should know better," such as when not to interrupt or touch certain objects, and the importance of completing chores and schoolwork. Although if that is the case, then the situations requiring the least precursor executive functioning will most often determine the assignment of diagnosis.

Additionally, since there may be countless instances in which people think extensively prior to doing very unacceptable acts (i.e., what we call premeditated crime), or that the content of one's thinking increases the probability of such behaviors, it seems that one could act either appropriately or tactlessly independent from how much or what kind of thinking occurs in relation to future consequences. There is no empirical evidence to establish a definitive relationship between the frequency of mental actions and an ADHD diagnosis. Nor have traditionalists empirically established that certain mental responses are less able to occur because of the absence of another biological response (i.e., an inhibition). Given the current state of ADHD empiricism, we can argue that some people are simply conditioned to do diagnostic responding.

Empirical work supporting these alternative assertions is reported by Locke and Latham (2002, 707) in their investigation of goal-setting. They report that people "automatically use the knowledge and skills they have already acquired that are relevant to goal attainment" when responding to familiar tasks. However, "if the path to the goal is not a matter of using automatized skills, people draw from a repertoire of skills that they have used previously in related contexts." It is only when an assigned task is new to a person that they are more likely to engage in "deliberate" (another categorization of acts) explorations of strategies in order to attain the designated outcome.

If one accepts Locke and Latham's interpretations, it seems that preparatory vocalizing, or doing non-vocal verbal activity or any other non-observable mental action prior to doing other goal-oriented behaviors seldom occurs, and then only under limited sets of conditions. Although it is more appropriate to take turns, permit someone else to be the center of attention, and not intrude on others, one can claim that diagnosed children enact their typical patterning as most of us do: without taking preparatory mental actions (itemized forethought) first.

Even if empirical evidence eventually proves that non-diagnosed individuals more often enact what traditionalists call non-verbal or verbal working memory, internalization of speech, self-regulation of affect/motivation/arousal, and reconstitution prior to other responses more competently, then each of these so-called mind events can also be considered discrete acts without presuming that they have controlling power over more observable behaviors. They are simply behavioral sequences that people may learn to do given particular histories of reinforcement. Self-reported non-observable activity is simply given the same status as any other behavior in terms of how much control any behavior contributes to subsequent acts.

A learning paradigm does not discount the report of mind behaviors. It is understood that individuals may respond in observable ways or in ways reportable only in the first person. However, increased correspondence between a behavior's frequency rate and particular conditions is explained by invoking a history of reinforcement regardless of whether actions are motoric or mental. That is, whatever happens when the behavior is emitted either extinguishes or increases its future frequency rates under equivalent conditions.

If the views of Ryle, Peters, Hofstadter and others are adopted, we can give each behavioral event independent status and interpret the situation within a stimulus/response paradigm. Individuals may indeed be conditioned to show varying rates of behavior, including differing frequencies of non-vocal verbal responding as well as imaginings. However, we need not invoke a "driver" or protection mechanism before doing behaviors that are valued (and not ADHD). Behaviors that increase the probability of short or long-term outcomes can be expressed *with* or *without* executive behaviors, talking to oneself, imagining future possibilities, or remembering past events. Regardless of whether we emit an overt or mental behavior, those behaviors can be understood as a part of a behavioral succession cued by circumstance (which includes the possibility that the person is reacting to previous mental or overt actions and environmental parameters).

Moreover, while preliminary mental action can be helpful, such behavior can at times also interfere with effective action. For example, I might sometimes attentively observe my own actions or think to myself about a sequence of behaviors in the future, but this mental exercise may not ultimately help me accomplish my goal. There are many instances in which people report thoroughly contemplating what to say at a given moment but later express disappointment at sounding too rehearsed. And very often events transpire starkly different from what we have mentally envisioned. As the expression goes, "life is what happens while you're making plans."

Similarly, some people report that when they pay close attention to themselves while walking (or other physical movement), it is increasingly difficult to walk in a coordinated fashion. Behaviors can become stilted, clumsy, and imprecise if one is overly self-conscious. Baseball pitchers sometimes have difficulty throwing strikes if they become too intent on aiming or steering the ball. Meanwhile, some individuals also report that they think better while taking a walk or when sewing. Are we to believe then, that the function of motoric behavior is to control, protect, and guide the thinking behavior, given these kinds of reports?

Of additional concern is that even if it is determined that diagnosed persons do not engage in particular mind behaviors when required to complete a complex task for school, or when responding to laboratory test items, they may be engaged in effective executive problem solving when figuring out how to have more play time, when mastering a self-selected task, or when carrying out a self-initiated agenda. Once we gain a greater understanding of the mental actions they are doing, we may indeed discover that the frequency rates of various mind behaviors are not very different from control groups. Perhaps it is the case that the content of the mind responses, and the situations where they do executive problem solving and pausing are different.

If, however, we find that diagnosed persons consistently do less effective problem solving, we still do not know if this is because diagnosed persons are less able to inhibit, or whether they have not yet learned to respond in those ways. One's learning history may still be the best explanation rather than assuming a fixed constitutional delay. ADHD empiricism has not established that diagnosed persons have a diminished capacity to learn more acceptable behaviors including non-observable mental actions, nor has that empiricism established that those particular learning curves adequately account for who will or will not be diagnosed.

We must ask ourselves what is gained from the traditionalist's assertion that inhibition and executive functioning, or more appropriately antecedent brain activity (i.e., data derived from neural resonance observations) give us the control needed for adequate completion of goal-directed behavior—when alternative theories are available. By dropping the inhibitory step and the proposed link between this mental mechanism and other mental actions that allegedly permit behavioral control, we think that many conceptual problems can be avoided. For example, when it is posited that executive functioning requires an inhibitory response in order for those actions to occur, *what* response determines whether or not to activate the inhibitory response? How does the brain (or person) know it is necessary to inhibit, if one has to inhibit *before* the executive functions can operate? What mechanism has to be invoked when it is preferable for an individual to *not* delay, or when prepotent functioning would be more advantageous? Are individuals with incompetent mechanisms at an advantage at these times? For example, in battle, it is said that "he who hesitates is lost." If we presume that there are occasions when people would have performed better had they *not* thought too much or hesitated before acting, then a continuous censuring of responses can become a significant disadvantage in certain situations.

While Barkley (1998g, 233) maintains that "behavioral inhibition delays the decision to respond to an event," and that the "self-directed actions occurring during the delay in the response constitute the executive functions," again, what enables a person to know whether to delay or not? Which mechanism determines whether to impede or allow for an external reaction without executive functioning? If it is presumed that non-diagnosed persons sometimes do prepotent behavior, it seems that one would have to posit that there is an additional mechanism that would first determine that it is preferable *not to delay* under some conditions. However, if that is the case, does this action also require an inhibitory step prior to its occurrence so that the necessary ruling can be made? If so, then all of those additional actions remove the opportunity to react without inhibition.

The learning paradigm side-steps the problem of introducing a delaying system that sometimes stops behavior and sometimes allows behaviors to proceed; it is not inhibitory delay that allows for the executive functions to make a particular determination, but more coherently, the executive information has to occur *before* the posited inhibiting takes place. Moreover, not only is this response not discriminated independently from the observation that behavioral change or behavioral continuation is occurring, but it is also not obvious how one can claim whether the person's decision to halt takes place the moment it occurs or after the posited inhibitory response.

As a result, it is reasonable and less problematic to argue that particular situations cue a continuance of behavior or pausing responses (which may or may not be followed by other mental actions). If that is the case, diagnostic responding is not attributable to a faulty inhibitory mechanism as described in the traditional model. If diagnosed persons are not pausing, persisting without diversion, or doing other mental actions when those responses might be helpful, it is because they have not yet learned to respond in those ways.

We could alternatively presume that behaviors occur continuously and in the absence of an inhibitory step, and that acceptable behaviors do not necessarily require antecedent and concurrent mind actions to show particular characterizations. We might account for the frequency of certain behavioral acts of both diagnosed and non-diagnosed person by discriminating patterns of reinforcement associated with certain behaviors.

For example, people with competent inhibitory mechanisms are not better able to refrain from speaking or refrain and then effectively suppress the urge to talk. But rather we suspect that some people learn to do the behavioral act *refraining from speaking* (i.e., one behavior, not two). This act is conditioned the same as talking aloud, and similarly, may be enacted in socially normative or inappropriate ways, according to context and interpretation. We expect that this alternative explication will circumvent the numerous conceptual problems apparent when the metaphor of an inhibitory mechanism and a governing agency called executive functioning are invoked to account for whether or not behavior is deemed less controlled and ADHD.

A person's history of reinforcement (which includes biological influences) is used to make predictions about future behavior within particular contexts, situations, and circumstances, including behaviors traditionalists call executive functioning. We do not presume that imaginings and various non-vocal verbal responding are always more influential on subsequent actions; those responses are simply less motoric. While our overt actions are less silent and more public, they are also influential on subsequent actions, and in many instances, they seem to be profoundly influential on the sequence of behaviors that are emitted. For example, the behavioral changes that occur when a spouse finally expresses resentment that has been held quietly for a number of years, or the benefits that occur when talking out loud about a troublesome problem.

It need not be imperative for us to presume that all diagnosed persons are less able to privately censor in mental form before expressing publicly, they might be *conditioned* to do particular kinds of non-preferred, inappropriate, disadvantageous, incorrect, and/or unacceptable responses called ADHD instead. The probability of being conditioned to do these behaviors can increase when other problems or bodily characteristics are also evident, such as certain kinds of molecular biology, lower intelligence, memory problems, fine motor problems, depression, single parenthood, negative infant temperament, etc. But we maintain that history, rather than delayed neurobiology is a reasonable way to account for the severity and frequency with which particular ADHD behaviors occur whenever equivalent situations and circumstances are reencountered.

Recurring acts depend on an individuals' particular historical behavior reinforced within equivalent situations. Rather than assert that diagnosed persons are invariably disinhibited, one only has to think about the difficulty that occurs when attempting to get a diagnosed person to *admit* wrong doing, and *not* remain quiet under some circumstances. Given the occurrence of wide-ranging behavioral diversity, the traditionalist's alternative that necessitates a fixed delay in being able to inhibit as the root cause of ADHD, introduces more problems than it solves.

In this alternative learning paradigm, each behavior occurring in the sequencing of longer term goal accomplishment can be understood as the one that has been most reinforced in that time frame or circumstance; this inference is derived from an analysis of what happened historically when similar behavioral accomplishments occurred in the past. That is, behaviors that have helped to increase the probability of the goal accomplishment are reinforced. What happens after the behavior is emitted will determine its frequency rates when similar conditions recur. Behaviors that help to accomplish certain results (longer or shorter term) may be reinforced by their temporal association to other behaviors that have increased the probability of reaching the goal. Both diagnosed and non-diagnosed persons might be seen as doing behaviors cued by particular conditions, even if it is the case that non-diagnosed persons are conditioned to emit particular kinds of mental responses more often in some situations compared to diagnosed persons (although this has not been empirically established).

However, in order to support the notion that people *actually* inhibit themselves whenever covert activity is enacted, traditionalists attempt to tangibly demonstrate an instance of inhibition by noting that the motor system is not active during observations of brain functioning when a person is asked to think rather than talk. Barkley (2000) refers to these experiments to corroborate the view that inhibition of the motor system occurs during the enactment of the thinking behaviors.

In response, one could counter-argue that this finding only indicates that the area of the brain correlated with motor behavior does not show activity when the individual is non-motor. We do not know how this translates into evidence for the inhibitory model, which implies holding back rather than inactivity. Traditionalists posit that the motor system is being restrained, but we can neither confirm nor deny whether an inhibition has occurred during the time a person is thinking rather than motor functioning. The only discrimination made is that brain activity rates change, depending on which behaviors occur, and the inhibitory step remains a hypothetical construct. The observation of brain *inactivity* does not indicate inhibition, or that the shift from activity to inactivity requires an intermediary inhibitory event.

Consequently, even though the frequent occurrence of ADHD kinds of behaviors has led some to believe that a developmental delay (caused by a relatively poor functioning inhibitory mechanism) is the reason for the high frequency of these behaviors, there does not seem to be any way to establish that faulty suppression or inhibition is the culprit. Behaviors such as suppression and inhibition can be defined, discriminated and denoted just like any other categories of behavior, but we do not know whether these particular actions occur more often for those who are *not* diagnosed with ADHD. Nor has it been established that these actions occur when individuals do what traditionalists call executive functioning, or that these actions are necessary prerequisites to prevent ADHD behaviors.

As a way to address the problem of introducing a presently unknowable hypothetical concept when accounting for behavioral differences between diagnosed and non-diagnosed persons, one can use the categories self-regulation or disinhibition only to describe a non-normative response patterning. In other words, we would say that a person is disinhibited when he or she reacts in a particular way, not that he or she reacts in a particular way *because* he or she is "disinhibited."

We could also, for example, drop the hydraulic or mechanistic construction used by conventional practitioners to account for impulsive behavior, and instead label it as a descriptive term for instances of mistakes attributed to behavior occurring in a short time interval when we presume that the respondent has the behavioral repertoire to function more acceptably. Impulsive behavior can be understood as different conditioned responses, but it is the *characteristics* of the behavior (i.e., incorrect, hurried, and under-achieving) *not antecedents* that determine its categorization as impulsive.

An individual's behavior can also be characterized as more public or private, organized around longer or shorter term goals, more or less socially preferred, or more or less competent in relation to a specified standard response pattern. Whether a behavior is recognized as being controlled, self-observing, intelligent, thoughtful, unacceptable, or motivated, depends on the attributes ascribed to the behaviors. Diagnostic and non-diagnostic behaviors can alternatively be distinguished by *observable* characteristics rather than by posited antecedents or faculties that permit acceptable or controlled behavior to occur.

Moreover, while traditionalists claim that diagnosed persons would engage in more acceptable behavior if they were to inhibit and gain access to "what they know" through executive functioning, they have not made clear how they have determined that this is the case. The diagnosed individual could still offer an unacceptable response despite full awareness that others will disapprove. For example, most obsessive personalities are aware of that others have difficulty with their actions, yet they continue to respond rigidly in social situations. Most shy individuals too, can mentally envision possible assertive responses, but they continue to behave less assertively. However, we are not claiming that they are not inhibiting sufficiently to gain better access to their executive functions in order that their actions might result in positive evaluations and outcomes.

Evidence of those behavioral patterns supports the claim that it is not obviously necessary to explain ADHD behaviors as a special case of being unable to access important information. When we explicate the behavior of highly accommodating individuals, we are unlikely to identify them as neurologically enhanced. On the contrary; we would more often be concerned that they have learned to be under-assertive, or exceptionally submissive.

Typically we do not believe that biology is the preeminent cause of rigid punctuality, the reluctance to indulge, or the reason for obsessive adherence to social agreements. We do not infer that their high degree of consistency is possible only because they have a better equipped neural biological system. Instead we inquire into how their behaviors may have been shaped in relation to life experience. Similarly, when we observe the typical "obsessive personality" where one leaves one area in the house totally disorganized, we investigate the history of that behavior rather than insist that those actions represent a breakdown of the inhibitory mechanism.

No one debates that all behavior has co-occurring biology, but again, biological categories have not adequately accounted for either ADHD behaviors or social patterns at the opposite extreme. We alternatively propose that ADHD is another way to say that some people have learned to do what they initiate and enjoy if others do not intervene to prevent them from it. ADHD becomes the "flip side" of consistent conformity to the instructions of others, and can be explained within the domain of psychology.

Problems with the Construct "Prepotency"

A diagnosed person, according to convention, cannot protect, stop and delay other mind activity or motor responses when it is adaptive to do so, and because of their delayed mechanism, he or she has disorganized mental activity and disinhibited behavior. Traditionalists hold that neurologically weakened individuals will do prepotent behaviors (that are often socially inappropriate) when particular conditions arise, unless they are subjected to outside remedial assistance to compensate for their biological disinhibited state, and their reduced access to executive functions.

Traditional interpretations rest upon the distinction between prepotent and non-prepotent responses. Non-diagnostic behaviors are discriminated from ADHD behaviors in that non-diagnostic behaviors include inhibition and executive functioning. Prepotent responses are those responses for which immediate reinforcement is available (or has previously been available for those responses). Non-prepotent responses are coordinated with distant future outcomes and larger rewards.

But if we argue in favor of this dichotomy, we must demonstrate a reliable and predictive framework in the form of the prepotent response prior to its occurrence for each individual for particular circumstances. Otherwise, the explanation is always post hoc. Since many different behaviors might be prepotent for a particular set of conditions in relation to past history of reinforcement, a detailed formulation of an individual's learning history is required in order to argue that a prepotent response is *not* occurring, or that diagnosed and non-diagnosed persons differ along these lines. It also seems that this kind of analysis is necessary in order to determine *what response* is being "held back" by the inhibitory mechanism so that executive functioning will help the person derive an even better or socially acceptable response for current conditions.

Moreover, the notion that prepotent responses must be "held back" gives them an ontological status when these responses could otherwise be understood as markers for further predictive statements. That is, when we identify a response as likely to occur (based on an individual's reinforcement history), we call it prepotent. This ascription is our *prediction* about what will happen; it does not assert that the behavior is embedded within the person and must be restrained. A *probability* statement should not be reconfigured into fact.

We could also potentially avoid a host of problems if we presume that all emitted responses can be characterized as prepotent when they increase in frequency in particular conditions. That however the biopsychosocial system responds to particular situations *is* the response that has been primed (or prepotent), given the organism's current status or state. Observable and self-reported unobservable behaviors alike could be understood as prepotent, depending on which behavior had been reinforced to occur within the presented context or circumstance for an individual. All behavior including activity directed towards oneself, as well as pauses, could be conceptualized as prepotent (or cued by conditions). People do not inhibit and then act; people are reinforced to act differently; and sometimes it may be prepotent for some people to pause and consider in some situations.

We argue to eliminate the two classes of responses in the traditionalist system (i.e., one set of responses considered as prepotent, and the other presumed to have arisen appropriately from the inhibition and executive functioning). Both sets of response behaviors can be characterized as prepotent, related to situational cues, and conditioned reactions derived from the individual's history of reinforcement. All claims of executive action or ostensible awareness of one's own behavior to control future responses would also be understood as a function of conditioning within particular contexts and situations encountered in one's earlier history (perhaps in ways resembling how prenatal stimuli apparently have a post-natal effect).

Since the definition of prepotency allows for variation of behavior between individuals depending on learning history (i.e., associations with immediate reinforcement for a particular situation), prepotent responses can vary markedly from one individual to the next, depending on history of conditioning. For example, some have a history of being reinforced when saving money; it might be prepotent for these individuals to say no to spending money in the vast array of situations where they choose to either save or spend. Conversely, others have a history of spending money in the same circumstances, and this may also be an immediately reinforced prepotent reaction, given their history of conditioning. Both the saving and spending behaviors would be prepotent responses, and we need not presuppose that either pattern requires more antecedent mind actions in order to identify content on the consequences of spending *or* saving money in the distant future when the responses occur.

In the same way, some people might be immediately reinforced by staying quiet when angry or disappointed, while others yell or pitch a tantrum, depending on learning history or reactions when those behaviors were expressed. For some it might be prepotent to jam schoolwork haphazardly into a book bag much like the way garbage is handled. But the prepotent response for others could be to place the papers carefully as when handling valued property. Any pattern that occurs frequently under particular sets of conditions is immediately reinforced, and all reinforced responses are characterized as prepotent. Depending on learning history, each behavior (overt or mental) may be immediately associated with positive or negative events. It is incumbent on the investigator to decipher how the learning history coordinates with the different patterns and continuums of response.

Both other-person observable and first-person observable responses may become prepotent reactions (i.e., cued by context and circumstance). Repetition of these behaviors can either be helpful or detrimental, depending on the conditions under which they occur. For example, in some situations and circumstances ADHD patterning yields the greater reinforcement, whereas in other situations a carefully, yet over-scrutinized approach might correlate with less future reinforcement, such as waiting for the opportune moment to ask someone for a date, only to discover that the individual has already met someone else.

A person may be reinforced to react more quickly, slowly, loudly, or quietly than others in particular situations without being functionally delayed. For example, quickened responding can be reinforced in relation to avoiding struggle, knowing answers before others do, suffering less by finishing sooner, moving quickly to the next activity, or lowering expectations as error rates increase. A multitude of learning histories might relate to increasing the frequency of various prepotent responses that are also ADHD.

Failure to show persistence, not preparing, or not taking action to solve assigned problems is not a consequence of a diminished neurological ability to self-control. These same responses can be attributed to conditioned reliance on others to help reduce expectations and demands, desire for easier alternatives, and non-conformity to specific social expectations in order to avoid doubt and failure. Those conditioned responses are disruptive to problem solving, but we need not presume that persons "have" a delay when they respond in those prepotent ways.

A case in point occurs when some individuals enter a testing laboratory with a history of having been reinforced not to respond to directives from others (i.e., that response has made it probable that they will avoid hardship or continue with what they initiate and enjoy). Non-compliance may be identified as the prepotent reaction. Its recurrence is likely to be evident during the investigation. Numerous errors are bound to be evident when instruction to follow is required in the laboratory, and it is likely to be concluded that the person has great difficulty inhibiting responses or responding efficiently to feedback (in the traditional view). When compared to another individual with a history of being reinforced to follow instruction, functioning will seem depleted and the individual will likely be characterized as delayed in self-control.

Still others react to the testing situation with a prepotent reaction of finishing as quickly as possible, while some give up quickly and/or react with hopelessness. Some behave to please the examiner; some react cautiously, and others worry about committing errors. However, in all instances, each reaction can be understood as prepotent for each individual (and unrelated to inhibitory delay). Each pattern of prepotent responses has different consequences when repeated in different situations or circumstances (including laboratory experiments).

In this light, it could be informative to investigate the ways in which prepotent behaviors change for particular individuals as conditions change. For example, what happens if subjects are asked *not* to follow directions? What happens when individuals are observed as they get involved in self-initiated tasks which permit greater discretionary input and are less evaluated by others? Would observations and attitudes change with regard to interference control, persistent behavior and error rates?

In this regard, we already have a large database of many diagnosed individuals functioning adequately on a variety of psychological tests designed to assess sustained attention, interference control, and adaptability to feedback. When some diagnosed individuals are subjected to a testing procedure (i.e., working one-to-one with the examiner in a novel setting), their behavior alters so much that many of them end up functioning in normative ways, despite that the tasks are *explicitly* designed to elicit evidence of the posited ADHD functional delays.

It therefore becomes difficult to accept the notion that a fixed or consistent delay exists. It is imperative that we not diminish the importance of *situation* when explicating ADHD behaviors rather than focus on the presence or absence of mind activity. For example, if borrowed video tapes are near the door, they are more likely to be returned, regardless of whether a person thinks about returning them prior to seeing them in the doorway.

Moreover, even if a number of diagnosed individuals respond differently as a function of the proposed kinds of delays claimed by traditionalists, it may still be possible for some or many of them to function more adequately, if they learn to verbalize the content audibly more often in daily life. They might then have the same results as those of us who purportedly can suppress well enough to keep content non-audible (thus non-observable). If diagnosed individuals have difficulty modifying verbal content by means of the executive functions in their non-motoric form, then perhaps acting increasingly vocally may be all that is needed to attain competency in many instances. Traditionalists make this recommendation as well when they argue for putting relevant content in a more externalized form.

While it might be tiring and less efficient to verbalize that content (e.g., reading aloud as opposed to reading silently), there may be instances when doing executive functioning vocally may help *even more* than doing those same actions non-vocally. Improvements of this kind seem evident when people write journals or deal with concerns in psychotherapy, as compared to keeping problems or concerns to themselves. Similarly, there are occasions when a child's silent reading comprehension may improve simply by helping the child learn to read to another person in a voice that more closely approximates the way in which the child normally speaks.

In that benefits might be derived from using vocal or non-vocal forms of verbal content, diagnosed individuals may not be at such a disadvantage as long as they can learn to do helpful vocal behaviors rather than less acceptable motor behaviors when encountering certain problem solving situations. That is, if vocal language behavior can help the diagnosed person solve problems (as it might for most people), then even if diagnosed persons are less competent with non-observable verbal content they may ably control the future as well as anyone in some situations, except that they will have to learn to feel comfortable verbalizing their thoughts and ideas. The only drawbacks would be a loss of privacy and its social consequences, as well as greater movement of one's body.

However, an opposing view might be that as long as diagnosed persons continue to be conditioned to behave in their old ways, we may find that it remains difficult to get them to make these vocalizations at the required times. Often the greater difficulty may lie in helping diagnosed individuals be less persistent in their avoidant, hurried, neglectful, or non-participatory responses when receiving instruction from others, or when assigned complex problems. As we stated earlier, it is more problematic to help them respond with ease to activity that has in the past been cumbersome, tested, stipulated, and associated with failure.

ADHD empiricism has not ruled out the possibility that new interventions will promote very different patterns of behavior. Perhaps diagnosed persons can, with, practice, learn how to make private the more vocal problem solving responses, and thus close the performance gap with their peers. Even if diagnosed individuals do not respond with the inhibition to help them think of other possibilities, outcomes, and consequences prior to motor actions, the question remains: why aren't they attentive to alternatives, and are traditional assertions about biogenetic delays in inhibition providing a reasonable explanation?

ADHD Emotionality/Impulsivity

Traditionalists claim that failure to react in an emotionally appropriate way is a sign of regulatory failure. Screaming inappropriately and more rigidly inattentive behavior are presumed indicators of the same neurobiological delay. However, if that is the case then any non-preferred behavior can be regarded as an instance of an inhibitory problem, and that explication becomes irrefutable. The conventional account is somewhat contradictory if it asserts that both the screaming and the non-responsive behaviors are caused by the same failure to inhibit adequately. Greater consistency could be realized by presuming that one's history of conditioning accounts for whether people learn to scream or close down in response to circumstance.

Traditionalists, however, maintain that diagnosed persons are at a clear and permanent disadvantage since they are biologically less able to modify their reactions by doing self-directed behaviors. Because diagnosed individuals are not doing these non-observable deliberations in more typical fashion, they end up making inappropriate public displays. Non-delayed persons are better able to counter initial overreactions with other images that may allow them to emit more acceptable responses (Barkley, 1998g).

Non-diagnosed persons avoid the problems often encountered by diagnosed people, in that "negative emotions" are particularly important to inhibit and self-regulate because of their social consequences (Barkley, 2000). Diagnosed persons will more often do socially unacceptable behavior, as their responses will be emitted through a deficient censoring process. They will more often release responses without doing self-directed behaviors that might calm and soothe (Barkley, 2006f). While non-diagnosed persons are more likely to refrain from responding until the longer-term consequences of their reactions can be evaluated, diagnosed persons are more likely to disgorge hyperemotional reactions.

However, in response to the above conventional claims, emotions are not inherently positive or negative; we know that social context and circumstance more often determine appropriate behavior. For example, laughing is regarded as rude, insensitive, and very cruel in many situations. This ostensibly "positive" emotion can result in negative consequences for individuals. So we can say that it is not the *kind* of emotion expressed, but rather the social acceptability of the emotion under the particular conditions in which it occurs that determines either its suitability or its adverse consequences.

In another example, a pause before telling someone that they are loved can lead to negative consequences. When that kind of social exchange takes place, one might reasonably claim that individuals are behaving impulsively when they hesitate, in that it is not uncommon for people to interpret hesitation as a sign of reluctance. The future anticipated events might have less probability of occurring simply because the enactor did not respond immediately. By the time the person's response is emitted, the conditions of social exchange and presenting problem have already altered (i.e., "all bets are off"). In this case, the mental responding was of little or no help at all, and those behaviors seemed to increase the probability of negative social consequences that might not have otherwise occurred.

No one can always be absolutely sure that one's public or private responses will be admissible, correct, satisfactory, or appropriate. While traditionalists argue that some executive behaviors are preferable to none, this is not always the case. There are countless instances where people over-analyze, spoil their work, miss out, or for some reason or another are too afraid to take action.

However, in cases where people engage in behaviors that *work out well* in the long-term, no one is concerned about antecedent delays because outcomes have coincided with societal preferences. The proverbs "strike while the iron is hot" and "good things happen to those who wait," have enormous value in American culture. We know that sometimes it is more advantageous to behave with urgency, and at other times it is better to delay gratification. But one can never be absolutely sure, regardless of "executive functioning" what approach will work out favorably until events begin to unfold.

Thus, despite widespread acceptance of the traditional view, it is difficult to accept their posited scenario of what occurs during social interactions. Social exchanges and day-to-day responding are not actually as stilted or pre-meditated as described in their model. As noted earlier, while there might be conditions under which it is more probable that people will hesitate, scrutinize, imagine different possibilities, mull over, and silently practice and rehearse, the precursor activities (presumed to prevent one from doing ADHD) are not expressed in high enough frequencies during day-to-day living to adequately account for ADHD patterning.

Even on those occasions when individuals start to emit a response, and "catch themselves" before emitting or completing that response overtly, these kinds of self-interrupting responses occur infrequently. One need not hesitate in order to function acceptably, even if those reactions are conditioned to occur more often when new learning is taking place, when responding to novel questions, and when conditions are inordinately restrictive, evaluative, troublesome, or ambiguous. However, if pausing and thinking were the exception rather than the rule for most of us, we can hardly determine this as the basis for differentiating diagnosed persons from controls. Usually after enough practice and under typical circumstances, behaviors can be emitted effortlessly. Hesitation is a unique behavior likely to occur under certain conditions.

Moreover, in our view, "catching oneself" and hesitating can also be understood as conditioned responses that occur in relation to a history of reinforcement for particular situations. It is not unheard of that diagnosed persons sometimes respond in those ways, in for example, the high frequency with which they hesitate, pause and catch themselves before saying something incriminating, which could reveal that they have been sneaking; whereas at other times these same people may "blurt out" and be intrusive.

It is also noteworthy that the conventional construct "failure to inhibit" is used to account for instances of negative or socially unacceptable behaviors, but they do not offer a counter phrase to describe appropriate behaviors. Either it is tacitly presumed that the person is doing positive mental action, or it is only when failures occur that we "post hoc" presume that the person did not perform the necessary antecedent actions.

For example, if a person is doing an acceptable response, and then shifts to a less acceptable response, the view is that he "failed to inhibit." However, if the person could function better by changing to a different response, he is labeled as perseverating, and *also* is viewed as suffering from inhibitory failure. The key issue here is that a person can change and commit a mistake or maintain the same behavior and make a mistake. The conceptual problem is that the assignment of inhibitory failure is a function of the outcome of the response; nothing is discerned about mental antecedents.

We therefore maintain that perspective and situation have more to do with impulsive characterizations than the amount of precursor thinking prior to behavioral enactments. For example, when a diagnosed child demonstrates to others during a rain storm that he can fill a water bottle with the rain dripping from the roof, is he not thinking enough beforehand that the roof water is too dirty to drink? Or was he *reinforced* to show others his "insightful" idea? Was the water's cleanliness irrelevant from his vantage point (despite whether he knew the water might be dirty)? Moreover, had the situation been different, and there was no access to any other source of water, that same behavior (regardless of thinking beforehand) would have been regarded as insightful rather than impulsive by thirsty companions, who would be willing to drink unclean water if they were incredibly thirsty.

Similarly, it seems unlikely that we would label an adult as inadequately suppressing when that adult shouts to his or her spouse who is across the street as a way to establish location. However, if a third individual thought that it might have been more acceptable and considerate for the person to have walked across the street and signal more quietly, that third individual might claim that the person should have been more inhibited, or thought more about what he or she was doing before being so loud and intrusive. Of course, the person doing the yelling might also insist that the third individual was impulsively jumping to a conclusion, as that person would surely be more tolerant if only he or she would think more about the situation and recognize how important it was for the couple to locate each other.

As is evident from these scenarios, the traditional formulation of inhibitory failure does not identify an instance of an inhibitory problem that is independent of the behavioral response and its social acceptability, correctness, or appropriateness. These assessments may often relate to the values and perspectives of the individuals doing the evaluating rather than the perspective of the enactor when behaviors are characterized. For example, when a child is doing an acceptable response (e.g., cleaning his room), or one that has to be completed from the viewpoint of the evaluator, then any "distraction" response is identified as a problem of interference control and seen as indicative of inhibitory failure. However, when the child is putting away a possession when the family has to leave the house (and is not being distracted at all), this may also indicate inhibitory failure. The tacit inference is that the child is perseverating, or not responding quickly enough to external feedback. Given that claims of inhibitory delay may be confounded with the suitability of a response from the perspective of an evaluator, it seems that individuals may be labeled as having a biological problem simply because their actions do not frequently enough coincide with the expectations of those who evaluate.

In conclusion, our bodies and histories of reinforcement influence how skillfully we behave, including non-vocal verbal responding, walking, talking, and imagining. However, we support the proposition that changes in the frequency rates—of either mental or more observable behaviors in response to particular conditions—are adequately explicated through a learning paradigm. The relatively high frequency rates of ADHD behaviors in contrast to typical responding in particular situations can be reasonably accounted for by invoking a metaphor of understanding that focuses on past sequences of events.

However, we also acknowledge that the longer ADHD responses occur, the more diminished the diagnosed individual's possibilities for new learning will become. For example, some diagnosed persons have learned that extreme emotional responses are highly correlated as others begin to conform to their demands. If conditions are judgmental, then highly-charged emotional responses could be more effective than a calm or more sedate response pattern in the desire to increase the probability that others will console, acquiesce, or leave them alone. In this way, extreme emotional patterns get reinforced, in that they result in loved ones' responding in predictable ways under certain circumstances.

Even if over-reactive patterns began very early and seemed to carry on from negative infant temperament, it is nevertheless presumptuous to assume inhibitory failure when such emotionality is evident. Many infants show negative temperament but never qualify for the ADHD diagnosis, so it is untenable to claim that negative temperament is evidence of incipient ADHD. We maintain that ADHD are learned behaviors that manifest in relation to contingencies of reinforcement that shape behavior over time, even if early patterns of infant temperament tend to increase the probability that ADHD patterns will in some cases evolve and persist.

However, as long as diagnosed individuals continue to react in these kinds of ways (instead of responding to difficult, complex or intriguing problems as *opportunities* to enjoy the pleasure of successful resolution), they are unlikely to interact amicably with others or recognize the value of expected achievement. It is therefore not surprising that these individuals have difficulty functioning comfortably and competently when they are conditioned to be frustrated, whiny, angry, and distressed in response to societal requirements. Until parents, teachers, and others introduce role models of problem solving behaviors for those who manifest negative histrionic reactions on a frequent basis, it is likely that diagnosed individuals will continue to show adjustment problems and realize fewer achievements that others would like to see them accomplish.

Chapter 5

Explicating ADHD without the Inhibiting and Executive Response

The diagnostic category of ADHD as a set of conditioned responses implies nothing more than the expression of the behaviors designated in the DSM-IV-TR within some contexts and circumstances prior to adolescence, and with such frequency that social problems occur. We do not incorporate in our hypothesis an antecedent neurological disinhibition, and we maintain that that hypothetical construct adds no additional information or explanatory value, significantly because "inhibition" has not been independently verified.

What we can acknowledge is that diagnosed people sometimes pattern biologically differently from controls. However, we suspect that differences could be the result of having learned to do ADHD responding rather than the *cause* of the behaviors; and some patterns of biology may simply indicate an increased *probability* of learning ADHD behaviors. In this view, if people do particular mental behaviors prior to other responses in some situations, instead of positing that they have a better inhibitory system, we hold that they have been reinforced to behave that way.

In juxtaposition to the learning model is the more common assertion that individuals have a biological delay in self-control when they express three kinds of behaviors excessively. The first is *hyperactivity*, which represents a high frequency of unacceptable overly-active behaviors leading to mistakes attributable to responses enacted too quickly. The second is *impulsivity*, which implies in its historical or customary usage that individuals do not engage in some prior thought before enacting a particular behavior. The presumption is that those persons "could have" functioned more adequately had they acted consciously before the mistake was committed. That is, had they thought about the situation, integrated past information, and planned conscientiously, they would have produced an acceptable response. The third is *inattentiveness*, which implies that a person is *not* doing a required action. This individual is often described as non-participatory in relation to an externally defined correct response pattern. Inattentive responses occur during social exchanges, and during autonomous completion of tasks requiring particular responses at particular times.

Inattentiveness often only comes to the attention of others when one must demonstrate comprehension. It is a *lack* of conformity to a required standard that cues the descriptor of inattentiveness; labeling is always done from an observer's perspective in relation to which behavior should occur. Facial cues are often the means of determining that a person is inattentive. Failure to sustain eye contact, failure to acknowledge others, a tendency towards distraction, or staring into space all lead to the label of "inattentive," especially when their pattern of comprehension is insufficient. In the context of an ADHD diagnosis, persons are deemed neurologically delayed when they do not respond appropriately, but have the capacity to do so, and have not explicitly indicated an unwillingness to respond. Often the behavior is described as "not listening" or "not focusing." Were these individuals better able to self-regulate, according to the conventional view, they would indeed respond appropriately.

Failure to participate often leads to negative social consequences. Relationships become strained if instructions are not followed or assignments are not completed. Negative responses such as nagging and repetition often occur in relation to these behaviors. Traditionalists assume that negativity evolves due to an inborn inability to pay attention. However, it may actually be the case that diagnosed persons respond to the negativity of others, or have trouble accepting that they could be wrong, and thus learn to do ADHD distractibility. One could also argue that when uncomfortable interactions occur, non-participatory behavior is reinforced.

As the child gets older, the hyperactive pattern usually decreases (as most people shift from motoric behavior to more sedentary behavior, and the inattentive/distracted pattern gradually becomes evident in middle childhood through adolescence (Hart et al., 1995). Problematic behaviors shift from errors of commission (e.g., behaving too rapidly, provocatively and intrusively), to errors of omission where slower paced and avoidant behaviors become prominent (e.g., failure to keep appointments).

When accounting for this shift, rather than endorse the unverified biological account, we could easily counter-claim that the shift to greater inattentiveness indicates that the person is changing from being reinforced by the acquisition of others' input to being reinforced by a decline of social responsibility. Put another way, there is a shift from "I'm not getting enough" to "you want me to do too much."

If one accepts that events reinforce diagnostic responding, it is not surprising that very young diagnosed children often behave so that others approach them, or require that others accommodate to them; only later do they begin to distance themselves from others. As children develop a larger behavioral reper-toire and function adequately apart from other people, more disconnected behavior increasingly becomes reinforced. Non-participatory responses can escalate as external expectations rise. At these times, diagnosed persons shift from behaving in order to keep the social agenda oriented around them, to acting in order to prevent others from imposing their own requirements.

Inattentive behaviors also occur if one learns that perseverance rarely increases positive outcomes. In this regard, Rucklidge and Kaplan (2000) note that diagnosed women are more likely to show learned helplessness reactions to negative situations. These diagnosed women seem to more often than men believe that they have fewer opportunities to influence their surroundings. Once this kind of response pattern is conditioned, dropping out increases in frequency, since it is thought that completing work, persevering, and struggling (even minimally) will not affect outcomes.

While this pattern is more common with diagnosed women, it is evident in both genders. Less participation, for example, is highly likely for many of us if we do not fully grasp a situation, if we have not realized many successes, and when negativity is associated with conformity. Inattentiveness can have the effect of distancing the enactor from particular events.

However, that kind of reinforcement is not exclusive to inattentiveness, as similar kinds of reinforcement can also occur with more rapid responding. For instance, if individuals are required to participate in an activity associated with failure or negativity, such as disapproval, anger, and impatience from others, they may learn to respond more quickly than usual, since each rapid response will bring them closer to the end of their discomfort. When success is infrequent, preparatory behaviors such as planning and considering possibilities before responding will be less probable, since individuals are not reinforced to respond positively and conscientiously if they are continuously defeated. However, whenever individuals respond without the persistence necessary to adequately solve problems, a vicious cycle can further reinforce ADHD patterning: the more errors committed, the more individuals are vanquished by their futile efforts.

Inattentiveness, lack of perseverance, and other diagnostic responses can also correlate with learning histories where individuals are over-indulged during child rearing. Within that reinforcement history, the individual's likes and dislikes are typically accommodated, and take precedence over the concerns and needs of others. Being side-tracked easily, not completing work assignments, lacking motivation, and non-conformity to the schedules of others can be seen as generalized patterns of early learning where others have made the necessary adjustments.

These persons are reinforced that their own initiatives are more important than others', and so conforming behaviors are rarely shaped. Self-motivation and persistence on required tasks might not get reinforced very often, because that individual is patterned to operate under extremely accommodating conditions. A lack of urgency when instructions are imposed can signify that there are few, if any, consequences to non-conformity or completion of a task. The individual has been reinforced to be relatively carefree, unconstrained, and non-responsive to others.

Inattentive responses can also frequently occur in situations where there is excess worry or concern from others (similar to hyperactive responses). These behaviors can result in others approaching and helping more. Being lost, disengaged, and non-responsive cues the additional assistance and concern rather than divisiveness, which can occur in other situations. Much like the game of hide and seek, non-responsiveness can be reinforced when those behaviors sequence with increased intensity and involvement from others. Instances of inattentiveness may cue the speaker to repeat, clarify, simplify, reiterate, and assist. Individuals may gain extra opportunities to succeed, obtain additional help, and more allowances from others regarding the imposed agenda.

To the extent that a wide range of conditions might correlate with increased frequency rates of diagnostic behaviors, it is not surprising that singular classifications of parental behaviors or social patterns have not been found to be predictive of the frequency rates of these response patterns. For example, an inattentive pattern might occur when responding to conflicts, invidious or derogatory remarks, intrusiveness and coercions from others, unpleasantness, or in situations that seem depriving. However, the same behaviors may also occur when conditions are simplistic and repetitious, when parents are indifferent, disengaged, or inaccessible, or when the individual is preoccupied.

Although rather than being caused by an insufficient inhibitory response, it is the context and situation of the behaviors that determines either their acceptability or the ADHD designation. For example, it is socially appropriate to respond inattentively when being teased by a peer, but the same behavior is unacceptable when it occurs during an adult's reprimand. Even though the behavior is identical (even in a biological sense), the first is seen as the mature behavior of a person in relation to not reinforcing the harassment or taunting, while the other is thought to be a mistake and a sign of biological delay within the person.

When a behavior is understood as acceptable we label it "aloof," but when a behavior is regarded unacceptable, it is "inattentive," despite that no prior antecedent is being discriminated in either case. The *social acceptability* of the response determines its origins, and it may go unnoticed that the allegedly delayed diagnosed child shows frequent inattentiveness during parental reprimand, yet has difficulty *not* focusing and *not* forgetting every single annoying word a peer said earlier in the day. These less acceptable patterns of response can continue even when the child is repeatedly encouraged to show inattentiveness when being teased by peers, and pleaded with to listen attentively to other adults.

While it is commonly believed that frequent inattentiveness relates to neurological delay, the presented alternative recognizes the occurrence of the behaviors as reinforced (i.e., frequency rates changes in relation to subsequent events). For example, when parents usurp a child's discretionary authority or impose an aversive agenda, to not respond could easily be understood as a response that eases discomfort. The parent might give up or go away if no response is forthcoming, and children can in turn learn how to ignore their parents when their parents frequently ignore them.

However, when these patterns of interaction begin to occur too often across a spectrum of conditions, and result in significant problems such as not responding to a homework assignment, suspicions arise that a neurological delay may be the cause. When the behaviors sequence with major problems in life's important settings, the probability of an ADHD diagnosis appears, and if assigned, the person is no longer seen as repeating what he or she has learned to do. Although the pattern of behavior might be reasonably understood in relation to reinforcement history and correlated with various event sequences that appear to reinforce the repetition of those behaviors, these individuals are characterized as having "less control" once it is evident that significant adjustment problems are occurring, and diagnostic criteria are met.

Since this does not seem very different from excessive shopping or creating significant debt, we can avoid a medical diagnosis here too. For example, is not completing a school assignment an inhibitory problem that diminishes one's ability to organize behavior over time, or might this error of omission also relate to increasing other eventualities such as reducing the discretionary authority of others? While authority figures may assign the work, a lack of follow-through protects one from the chore of doing the work, risking that the teacher will dislike the work, and in some instances, instigate worry from others when work is not completed. Diagnostic responses also get reinforced frequently when individuals learn to rely on people to remind them to fulfill responsibilities, and we expect that they will forget when reminders are not given when patterned to live in the world in that way.

When considered in this light, it is not surprising that with extra contingencies and encroaching deadlines, diagnosed persons (and most others) participate and achieve acceptably. The conventional claim is that these conditions offset inherent delays (i.e., immediacy of reinforcement, saliency, etc.); but an alternative notion is that these changes reinforce more compliant responses by increasing assistance, urgency, threats, or rewards. Diagnosed persons are not less able to self-regulate, but rather, their particular non-participatory behaviors are no longer reinforced when the consequences of participating change, that is, when it is more worthwhile to conform, persist, and join in, and not do ADHD responding.

The coherence of a functional delay is lacking in the conventional view. Diagnosed individuals learn to *not* participate under adverse conditions, but these same individuals learn to be engaged and immersed to such an extent at other times that it is impossible to distract them. Our alternative interpretation is more tenable than traditional assertions, in that sometimes diagnosed individuals show adequate participation, persistence, organization of behavior over time, and resistance to distraction even if no reward is given, or when parameters no longer seem any more externally-represented than instances when inattentiveness is frequent.

ADHD Impulsivity: Problem with Antecedents or Consequences

Traditional conceptualization of diagnostic responding seems problematic in many other ways as well. For example, it is not clear how is it determined whether or not preliminary action did or did not occur in relation to the ADHD action that was taken. For example, if a diagnosed child "in jest" trips and hurts his younger brother as he walks by, the action can be characterized as impulsive. It might be inferred that if the diagnosed older brother had thought more about the possibility of the younger brother getting hurt, he would not have behaved so roughly.

While this framing of the problem tacitly (or even explicitly) indicates that the diagnosed child did not mentally prepare to misbehave beforehand, it is possible that the child had thoroughly planned, imagined, or rehearsed prior to enacting the prank. Such preliminary actions could have increased his probability of performing the unfortunate behavior rather decreasing it. Rather than characterize the impulsive behavioral act as an instance of under-control, that response could be seen as a very controlling action, in that the whole family may be involved. Hurting the brother could be a reinforced behavior contingent on the particular relationship between diagnosed child, his younger brother, and his parents. The diagnosed child could have been angry with his parents for continuously blaming him when his younger brother complains, tattles, or feigns injury in order to get him into trouble. It could also be that he resents that his parents spend so much time with the sibling.

Hurting the brother may increase in frequency in relation to this history. The action becomes reinforced behavior rather than deficient behavior that occurs because of an insufficiency of prior mental actions. While the behavior is a mistake when viewed from the perspective of what loved ones accept, the behavior might not be a mistake at all when viewed from the perspective of the diagnosed child, given the event sequences that occur when that behavior is enacted. Injuring the brother is reinforced in that it punishes others.

Another scenario might also help to illustrate problems that arise when accounting for problematic behavior by positing the absence of antecedents. For example, if a parent sternly commands a child to "Go to the bedroom!" and the child stumbles while going up the stairs, we hold the parent accountable for the outcome, especially if the tone of voice was excessively harsh. We are less likely in this instance to characterize the child as impulsive. However, if the parent in a reasonable tone of voice, tells the child to "stay put" and "listen," and the child rapidly ascends the stairs and subsequently falls in an apparent attempt to escape to his or her room, we say that the child would not have suffered had he or she been less impulsive.

We can therefore see how context, situation, and circumstance influence our account of the child's actions. Similar outcomes can be perceived as either impulsive or merely a response in relation to a confluence of socio-cultural parameters, individual mood, and event sequences. The criteria used for determining whether there was more or less inhibition and executive functioning prior to ascending the stairs and then falling is not usually specified by those asserting traditional views.

However, according to traditional beliefs, individuals behaving impulsively often get into difficulty, in that they seem to act without first considering the longer-term consequences of their actions. They purportedly have less ability to postpone gratification and inhibit prevailing prepotent responses. They will often react before instructions have been fully stated, and not appreciate what is required within a particular setting before they act. They will frequently commit errors which could have serious consequences (Barkley, 1998b).

The traditional meaning of impulsivity is that individuals are not delaying the urge to act; the individual's inhibitory system is *developmentally* less able (in comparative terms) to pause and allow executive functioning to come forth. Hyperactivity is the motor variant of this inhibitory problem, although all ADHD is thought to be caused by the same underlying problem. Problems are expected to arise for diagnosed persons whenever prepotent responses are not the best options, as problem solving insights that would otherwise occur do not. During continuous performance tests, it is mistakes of commission that define impulsivity (Barkley, 1998b), because the presumption is that a failure to notice details (which takes time) accounts for the occurrence of these committed errors.

When assessing impulsivity parents and teachers are asked to evaluate whether the child "blurts out answers," "has difficulty waiting in turn," or "interrupts or intrudes on others." If the child shows such behaviors frequently, they are then labeled impulsive. The inference is that they can avoid inappropriate behaviors, mishaps, mistakes, and unfortunate consequences if only they would first inhibit their reactions and allow themselves the necessary time to consider alternatives that will help them control the future in a socially acceptable way.

Due to their presumed functional delay, diagnosed persons' behavior is organized around maximizing the occurrence of the most quickly obtained reward. Longer term consequences exceed the scope of their response repertoire at the time of performance. They are presumed to be less able to consider long-term possibilities in the shortened time interval available before responses are released. The tacit presumption is that less time is needed to respond in order to maximize the probability of reward within moments, rather than within hours, by tomorrow, next week, or in a few months. However, data showing the relationship between the amount of time necessary to control the future, and the amount of time that is being controlled, is not provided by those who support this conceptual model.

Brown and Quay (1977) define impulsivity as a pattern of rapid, inaccurate responding to tasks, while Barkley (1998b, 59) defines impulsivity as "poor sustained inhibition of responding, poor delay of gratification, or impaired adherence to commands to regulate or inhibit behavior in social contexts." The presumption is that these individuals know what to do and would behave more acceptably, if only they were better able to stop other responses from being emitted. The enactor has the *skill* to respond correctly, but nevertheless commits errors because her inhibitory constraint is insufficient. Contingency management helps these individuals because the required behaviors are within their repertoire. Otherwise, added rewards or threats would be of no help whatsoever to persons whose primary problem is not knowing what to do.

When individuals do not have the required skill to enact the correct or appropriate behaviors, it would seem more reasonable in the traditional view to characterize these persons as ignorant or incompetent rather than impulsive. Taking additional time in those circumstances, or holding back prepotent responses would matter little. For traditionalists, skill deficit may be grounds to defer an ADHD diagnosis, in that individuals can be identified as deficient or defective rather than suffering from inhibitory problems.

Similarly, it is unlikely that persons would be labeled impulsive if they *appear* to hesitate and consider before acting, even if incorrect outcomes occur (unless of course it is decided that they still did not take enough time to prepare). Under those circumstances, one would infer that they were enacting what is known (i.e., traditional vernacular), in that they did the necessary antecedent activities to perform adequately. They just didn't know what to perform. Likewise, if a correct response is enacted quickly, it is also unlikely that the person would be labeled impulsive, as in these instances, the person would likely be characterized as inordinately adept, masterful, or intuitive.

It seems that a person may be labeled as impulsive only when the outcome is negative on the basis of the presumed competency of the enactor. When an ADHD label is affixed to an individual who exhibits pervasive competency limitations, the assumption remains that this individual might still function more acceptably if it were not for his or her additional inhibitory delay.

As a viable alternative, we assert that the characterization of impulsivity is simply a statement about *presumed competency, time intervals and outcomes*, which may in fact have nothing to do with the occurrence (or not) of an inhibition or executive function. Their behavior yields an incorrect outcome when expectations are higher, the action displeases others, shows lack of consideration, or does not coordinate acceptably with longer term event sequences important to those who determine the labeling. In the context of an ADHD diagnosis, the ascription has little to do with whether or not particular mental actions took place prior to the behaviors in question.

The appraisal derives from characteristics of emitted behavior within particular conditions and we presume that the individual could do better, not that particular neural biological antecedents or mind behaviors did or did not occur. While the label also carries the presumption that persons could have functioned effectively had they utilized more of their resources, it has not been empirically confirmed that individuals not doing the diagnostic behavioral acts engage in more antecedent mental actions (i.e., inhibitions and executive functions). Nor has it been determined that less antecedent mind activity in particular situations will result in those behavioral acts.

Conventional practitioners assume that ADHD diagnosed children are less able to *not* dash into the street after a ball (because their inhibitory systems cannot easily quit the running response long enough to "think" about the danger). The learning model, however, inquires into past episodes when the child's ball had gone into the street: What is the social significance of getting to the ball first in that situation, and what has occurred when the child crossed streets in the past (e.g., power struggles, overreactions, disagreeable coercions). For example, we ask whether others frequently accommodate when competing interests are present, and whether the child has been conditioned to believe that cars will always stop and defer.

Reinforcement history in equivalent situations and circumstances is an alternative way to account for whether risky or cautious behavior will occur as the child approaches the curb. In this view, both the cautious and dangerous pattern could be enacted without the necessity for prior mind enactments. Similar to persons who learn to make others wait while they more leisurely walk, it is not surprising that the child would rush into the street without modulating actions to correspond to traffic, given a particular history of reinforcement. Moreover, if the child is also reinforced by any ensuing hysteria, we can also expect repetition of similar behaviors as a result of those outcomes as well.

When examined from different angles, it is difficult to believe that diagnosed children are delayed when they engage in hazardous behaviors. Some of these children have learned that others will adjust to their initiatives in many situations (including darting into the street). Not abiding by parents' rules to maintain health and safety can also factor into their behavior, as that social pattern frequently provokes worry about cuts and bruises and other reinforcing parental responses. However, when conditioned to behave in these seemingly egocentric less conciliatory ways, even though many onlookers might judge the behavior as dysfunctional and impulsive, we think that past history can nevertheless reasonably account for the greater risks that some children take when not checking for safety, not waiting for cars to pass, or running into the street without looking to retrieve balls.

In this perspective, when children stop at curbs instead of chasing balls into streets, it is not that they are necessarily doing more antecedent mental action compared to children pursuing balls in a more risky fashion. The learning model asserts that stopping behavior is *cued* by the conditions of arriving at the street curb. That behavioral act has been reinforced for that situation. Given that children who race into streets in pursuit of balls can stop exceptionally quickly under different sets of conditions, such as when parents "catch" them misbehaving, it is problematic to claim that neurology is the root cause of their failures to stop in other settings and circumstances.

We argue that the social circumstance of particular behaviors influences our diagnostic labeling rather than a presence or absence of antecedent mind actions. For example, in some cities drivers in congested traffic areas must learn to drive aggressively. Often they may dart into intersections with narrower spaces between cars, because waiting for a "safer" time to enter into a traffic lane correlates with intense honking of horns. Cautious behavior in this case is both non-adaptive and unacceptable; the preferred social pattern here is to be more audacious. It is in this sense that history of reinforcement can adequately account for assumed impulsive behavior in other settings. Insofar as most people behave in particular ways, labeling shifts from delayed to typical, and we are unconcerned about delays.

Another illustration of this problem is when a crowd attempts to board a bus with limited space. Many people will push and shove in order to secure a seat. This scenario would be totally inappropriate in non-competitive conditions, such as a line forming to pay respects at a funeral. But when individuals are concerned about missing out, some will often be inconsiderate and "impulsive." We expect that less reasonable and considerate reactions will occur under (the perceived) scarcity of resources or threats to survival.

However, traditionalists would emphasize in this case that the extreme frequency rates shown by diagnosed individuals indicate a delayed or disabled condition. Traditionalists would claim that the only reason impulsivity does not always occur is because the environment or person's interest can at times compensate for the posited inability to check unregulated responses. However, as we have discussed earlier, without *also* specifying prior to the action how much inhibition and executive functioning are required to conform to situational demands, the traditional explication is always post hoc. Moreover, it has not been established how frequently diagnosed persons behave contrary to traditional predictions, and there is no apparent data indicating how well that category system predicts the behavior of diagnosed individuals during day-to-day patterning.

It is also unclear why the frequency rate of a behavior alters its status from a conditioned response to an indication of functional delay. We could just as easily claim that diagnosed persons are frequently repeating reinforced behaviors when they respond in characteristically impulsive ways without asserting an inherent delay if frequency rates are high. Since we do not characterize excessively cautious patterns as resultant from advanced biological inhibitory systems, this approach seems reasonable and has precedence.

Thus, instead of framing particular diagnostic actions as uninhibited and under controlled, they might be understood as conditioned responses occurring in relation to situations and circumstances. By understanding who is involved, what happened before, during, and after these behaviors are emitted, the parameters that relate to increasing or decreasing the frequency rates of these behaviors could potentially be discerned.

There are, we suggest, myriad parameters that influence the frequency with which diagnostic responding takes place. Rather than focus exclusively on upholding an unproven argument in which neurology or the absence of antecedent mental actions causes those behaviors, we conjecture that (otherwise competent) diagnosed individuals learn behaviors characterized as ADHD in relation to conditioning during one's lifetime. For example, leaving toys scattered throughout the house can be reinforced when others pick up the toys, buy new toys to replace the ones that are missing or broken, or when there are too many toys. It is also difficult to neglect a child when belongings are not put away, and sometimes a child is copying others who are untidy or are punishing them when patterning in that fashion.

Likewise, intruding and interrupting can be reinforced when these behaviors allow for greater inclusion and prevent unwanted speech. These actions are not socially preferred, but the enactor gains discretionary authority and is noticed. In many instances, persons doing ADHD may get their own way more often than others. As the expression goes, "The best defense is a good offense."

The observation that this pattern occurs frequently need not mean that delayed inhibitory neurology is driving it, as the opposite socially acceptable behavior of frequently letting others go first may repeat for many individuals, and correlate with all kinds of problems such as frequently missing out, as well as self-deprivation. Therapists' client lists are filled with persons conditioned to behave in those ways. Moreover, if children who are often impulsive are less able to share and allow others to go first, then why do they move extremely slowly and prefer *not* to be first when lines form to enter the classroom?

Similarly, when more closely examining a diagnosed child's "out of control" impulsive behavior, often it does not seem as if they are as disinhibited as traditionalists want us to believe. While it is not unusual for many of these children in the midst of throwing a tantrum to be destructive (e.g., picking up objects in the room to damage), it is also not unusual for many of these children to destroy *only* the property of others. If they are so unregulated, why are they not damaging items more haphazardly, and why is it often the case that they stop when certain people enter the room?

Even in those instances when children pick up their personal belongings to damage, one could study learning history as well, and possibly coordinate particular event sequences that account for those seemingly indiscriminant acts. For example, if the child is destroying his or her own property, which objects are broken, what is the history that the child has with those objects, what might be the reaction of others when those belongings are ruined, or in what ways has that spiteful and outlandish behavior been previously reinforced and role modeled? When understanding diagnostic behaviors in this manner, it is important to explore the reactions that are evoked when destructive or other unreasonable behavior occurs. Are the objects replaced; is the child compensated in some way; do family members become upset and angry when the child breaks things the parent has paid for; do parents frequently discuss the child's tirades with other people?

While the traditional view regards impulsivity as a neurological phenomenon, the current approach identifies ADHD impulsivity as a label for risky, self-centered, inconsiderate, reckless, or rushed behavior that has been reinforced. Despite the probability of immediate and longer term adverse consequences, impulsive actions coordinate with numerous event sequences that shape and maintain those ADHD responses over time. Rather than seeing impulsivity as an instance of judgment devoid of the benefits of executive functioning, when event sequences associated with behaviors are specified, the behaviors may not look delayed.

Along these lines, it may be that in some circumstances people learn impulsive acts when being timed and evaluated if success has previously been improbable. If so, responding more rapidly can relate to a quick escape from assessment, due to the greater tendency towards self-consciousness and anxiety in these situations. They may be conditioned that others will become critical and impatient during delays. Similarly, impulsive responding can be reinforced as a proactive response to being labeled as stupid or incompetent, if the response would otherwise exceed a typical time frame. We do not yet know whether these individuals would have solved problems effectively had they taken the time, either privately or publicly, to complete preparatory work. Their conditioned reactions in these situations under these circumstances have adversely influenced error rates.

Traditionalists caution that it is important to rule out anxiety as an alternative explication prior to imposing the ADHD label, but this is a subtle problem, especially when considering that Newcorn et al. (2001) reported that over one-third of their large diagnosed sample also qualified for an anxiety disorder. We observe that individuals are sometime adversely affected by time restrictions and assessment, even if their general behavioral pattern is not otherwise characterized as anxious. They could therefore be conditioned to respond more rapidly and less systematically, or they may be reinforced to escape in situations where they are scrutinized and under pressure to achieve. Often these kinds of responses occur for many diagnosed persons when being appraised and/or tested. Diagnosed children often anticipate disapproval from others, and it is not uncommon for them to become defensive, and say, "Stop staring at me!" or "Leave me alone!"

The Reinforcement of ADHD Distractibility/Discontinuity

At this point it is worthwhile to consider another aspect of diagnostic responding: the frequent shift from one idea to the next, either vocally or mentally. We suggest that diagnosed individuals learn this unusual pattern. For example, a rapid shift from one idea to the next can be conditioned when individuals are likely to be preempted or rebuked for being wrong when they do not identify options and alternative points of view. If they say something that could be negatively received, this may also cue them to change the subject quickly and talk about seemingly unrelated topics as a way to divert the interaction from reprimand.

High rates of failure and disapproval can increase the probability that individuals will learn to second guess and shift rapidly from one idea to the next in order to anticipate potential disagreement before others can react. Many diagnosed individuals learn to waver between possibilities so as not to commit a mistake, or they worry about the accuracy of a stated fact or detail in their story or idea (e.g., "Is that right?"). However, the net result of these patterns is that individuals report feeling overwhelmed or confused when responding in those ways. All the angst pertaining to failure and expectation disrupts their focus.

While response patterns such as losing one's train of thought or having difficulty concentrating can occur frequently in relation to fatigue, depressive states, problem complexity, or various medical problems, these difficulties can also increase when they are reinforced in certain situations. For example, uncomfortable exchanges can be curtailed when those responses occur: others can rescue them, complete their sentences, and express concern by offering assistance if they lose track of the conversation.

Attention problems and lack of understanding are evident, too, when individuals are preoccupied with their own replies rather than responding to a discussion dominated by someone else. Frequent nodding at these times is often interpreted as acknowledgment or agreement, but may not at all correlate with comprehension. Nodding may be done to avoid disapproval for not listening, and also used as a way to reinforce the speaker to finish quickly.

Distracted or divergent responses can occur when the diagnosed individual hears the first coercive, disappointing, or disapproving utterance. Inattentive behaviors and listlessness can be apparent as soon as others say no, or when the diagnosed person must defer or wait. For some, these responses permit quiet escape from these conditions, thereby reducing the discretionary authority of others. In the more popular vernacular, these individuals tune out quickly when social conditions are critical, evaluative, discouraging, or limiting.

However, when these kinds of non-participatory responses happen frequently during social exchanges, it is likely that he or she will not fully comprehend what is pertinent. The individual's preoccupied thought will truncate or prevent understanding (i.e., as what may happen if one thinks about something else during a movie and subsequently loses track of the plot). Difficulty remembering and learning will also likely become evident when this pattern occurs. The individual has less opportunity to practice responding to material presented by others when more frequently lost in a solitary agenda. But the fact that these persons have not grasped the social interaction tells us nothing about the etiology or source of the difficulty; it is possible that diagnosed persons have more often been conditioned to be distracted, non-consensual, inefficient, preoccupied, rambling, or unfocused in particular situations and circumstances.

For example, talking incessantly about a multitude of events can keep one socially focal for longer periods of time, and make it less likely to forget something important. Rambling can thus be reinforced to prevent others from interrupting, disapproving, or perhaps to maintain the attention of others by embellishing stories with myriad details and interesting tidbits. Others will be conditioned to rush to jam in as much content as possible, because they have learned that some people are attentive for only short periods of time.

Flightiness and disorganization may be evident in some persons, but lack of assertiveness may account for many instances of behavioral discontinuity. This subset often responds like jellyfish carried by the current. These individuals fail to complete what they start, in that they lack forcefulness, and too easily stop what they are doing and acquiesce. However, the end result is a lack of persistence and failure to complete tasks in ways consistent with diagnostic criteria.

Thus, if individuals often do any of these patterns, the orderliness and coherence of their actions, their memory and grasp of events, and the intelligibility of their verbal responses can often decrease. The individual is conditioned to shift rapidly from one concern to another, but more often than not suffers the consequence of losing the coherence of his or her discourse or action sequence. Many of these individuals may complain that they cannot stop themselves, control their thoughts, or that external powers are making the behaviors occur (i.e., they are "driven" to distraction), but we understand that changing entrenched behavior is exceedingly difficult for most of us to accomplish.

However, in order to investigate reinforcement, it is helpful to observe whether the frequency of bewilderment, disorientation, confusion, feeling inundated, overwhelmed, or distracted alters when the person does equally difficult *self-initiated* tasks, and to what extent, if any, the frequency of those behaviors varies in relation to who is involved, along with other situational parameters. For example, if we hold task difficulty constant, is a diagnosed adolescent as likely to become as confused, overwhelmed, or distracted when impressing his new girlfriend? If not, then task complexity is not solely the source of the atypical functioning, and intervention may entail helping the adolescent repeat patterns of responding that he is already doing in different circumstances.

In a seemingly related matter it seems that many people learn behavior that cues others to say, "He tries hard" or "He does his best." Often these behaviors sequence with a reduction in both disapproval and expectation. While the behaviors might get reinforced in relation to those social responses, the achievements may have little to do with the person's upper limit of functioning. In other words, he might learn to behave in confused, agitated, frustrated, or beleaguered ways in particular situations and circumstances in relation to contingencies of reinforcement.

Rather than understand diagnostic responding as an unavoidable occurrence that happens to individuals who are less able to self-regulate, we argue that these responses are reinforced during social exchanges. Sometimes persons behaving in these ways have learned that they will not otherwise obtain assistance or permission to give up unless prominent emotional difficulty is made evident to others. They have learned that suffering leads to a reduction in expectations and justifies any relief that is received. However, when that pattern is entrenched, frequent emotional over reactivity and hyperbole is likely to be observed. Interestingly, Locke and Latham (2002, 706) report, "When people are asked to do their best, they do not do so." These authors claim that this kind of goal setting has no external reference and often the behaviors result in being defined idiosyncratically. That is, one assigns the label that the person is doing as well as possible, but these assessments can be unreliable and not predictive of what the individual accomplishes when observed at other times.

If we consider Locke and Latham's assertions, we can suggest, unfortunately, that various diagnostic responses have been conditioned, given the frequently occurring circumstances these individuals encounter. But importantly, as long as diagnostic responding is their modus operandi, it will remain difficult for an ADHD diagnosed individual to achieve, sustain concentration, interact acceptably with others, and continue with a coherent vocal or non-vocal verbal sequencing of actions, because the habits will eventually impact overall social adjustment.

When pursuing a learning explanation for ADHD patterning, observers (including the individual enacting the behaviors) begin to identify the contexts, situations, and circumstances that correlate with responses (e.g., when conditions become uncomfortable, cumbersome, difficult, complex, argumentative, simplistic, repetitious, etc.). We suggest that these are reinforced behaviors equivalent to other kinds of escape or self-protective reactions such as running away, ignoring, or more dogmatically usurping authority.

We can understand many diagnostic behaviors in terms of how individuals protect themselves from disapproval, derogatory statements, or external difficulties. Non-participatory and invasive behaviors are alternatives to persisting under negative conditions, and are similar to associating danger with particular events. The individual avoids struggle, confrontation, displeasure, or is protected from failure, denial, and other deleterious events when they do not get involved. Diagnostic behaviors are reinforced in any or all of those ways.

Some inattentive diagnostic responses also resemble the dissociative behaviors that often occur with trauma victims. Adelizzi (1998) notes that posttraumatic stress responses can be comparable to reactions emitted by diagnosed persons. While the numerous situations in which diagnosed persons behave inattentively might not seem inordinately negative to us, depending on reinforcement history, the same situation can appear extreme for some responders. Because a number of diagnosed persons have functional delays of one sort or another, many situations and circumstances would be perceived as more adverse than others, and thus account for the higher response occurrences.

ADHD behavior can therefore be viewed as a potent behavior rather than an instance of less control. Others repeat, relent, accommodate, paraphrase, and sometimes plead in response to their ADHD responses. Interactions may revolve around whether or not the diagnosed person will participate, cease aggravating, or acknowledge some form of reply. In that regard, the behaviors often monopolize the social agenda. The child can maintain his own agenda for a longer time, and others will be required to bring him up to speed, if or when he expresses an interest in joining. While the lack of engagement in a social exchange can result in the parent working harder to keep the child abreast of occurrences, when the parent becomes infuriated or must accommodate to the child's failure to stay current, we can reasonably ask *who* is in control.

When instructions, assignments, restrictions, or reprimands are not heard or responded to, accountability is lowered, and ADHD responses are usually less pernicious than saying no outright. When persons are too scattered, muddled, frazzled, confused, or overwhelmed to handle an agenda imposed by others, it is unreasonable to insist that demands be met. These behaviors could be reinforced when they sequence with increased accommodation from others, and/or acquiescence from those who insist on compliance. In some instances diagnosed persons will obfuscate, thus compelling others to work even harder to convey their points, as well as prevent them from establishing even a modicum of discretionary authority.

However, when exploring the learning history, it is of utmost importance to find out *what these persons are doing instead* when they behave in an inattentive way. We could ask them to disclose the content of their non-vocal verbal responding, imaginings, etc. when they do not respond or conform to what is identified as socially required. By so doing, we may be able to identify the reinforced behaviors in those situations (e.g., preoccupations, anxieties, preferences, hostilities, etc.). This type of inquiry is the springboard for behavioral shaping.

Inquiry can also focus on the extent to which particular diagnostic responses occur in response to mistakes, or in response to tasks associated with failure. We can ask if staying in a fog protects against adversity that feels insurmountable for many diagnosed persons. Similarly, we can ask if diagnosed individuals become disrupted when others are corrective. Are they apprehensive about the adequacy of their own achievements? Does the first imposed limit cue an escape reaction to help protect against failure to meet that expectation? Do they frequently ruminate angrily while others instruct, coerce, or direct their actions?

Relationships between diagnostic behavior and particular ongoing conflicts with teachers, parents, and peers can also be explored. We might discover a correspondence between diagnostic responding and situations where there is interpersonal discomfort. While traditionalists could claim that the resistance of the diagnosed individual is caused by their ADHD, we can easily counter-claim that ADHD behaviors are more probable once social exclusion or distress occurs (i.e., the chicken and egg problem).

For many diagnosed children and adolescents, inattentive behaviors are more extreme as their displeasure increases about submitting to other peoples' agendas. Inattentive behaviors can easily occur in an angry context, or when unsolved problems persist between family members. Instances of relentless nagging, nitpicking, and complaining between individuals also correlate with an increased frequency of disengaged responses. Inattentiveness essentially limits the diagnosed adolescent's contact with parents rather than facilitating interaction with them. Incidentally, a case could be made that this is precisely what happens for those individuals doing ADD patterning, except that this population does not have a history of expressing the more provocative/intrusive, more infantile/reliant patterns during early childhood.

In any event, ADHD inattentiveness in many situations permits individuals to avoid requirements and neglect boundaries. Much like putting one's head in the sand, limits and discomforts in the outside world need not be endured. Interestingly, Lucker, Geffner, and Koch (1996) found that diagnosed children tend to be more comfortable with lower levels of speech compared to controls. We could infer that this is a conditioned pattern that has evolved in relation to the frequency with which others often raise their voices and lecture when attempting to induce conformity.

Although even in our approach of investigating a history of reinforcement, it is always important to rule out influences such as chronic pain or other physical difficulties, such as problems seeing or hearing that could be undermining participatory behaviors. However, the most basic claim is that diagnostic patterning can be understood in relation to outcomes. While particular biological characteristics may influence the reinforcement patterns that develop, the responses that occur more frequently in particular situations are not caused by that biological substrate; they are rather a function of a particular biopsychosocial history. And what has been learned will influence what *will be* learned.

Typical ADHD Reinforcements and Diminishments

Within the framework presented here, we presume that individuals learn to discriminate similarities and differences between parameters, and that these discriminations usually become subtler and generalized over time (Werner, 1948). For example, when learning first occurs, even the most primitive discernment (e.g., distinguishing oneself from the outside world) is not initially apparent. However, individuals typically learn to make increasingly varied and complex discriminations as their behavioral repertoire widens, and what occurs over time can help us account for the changes in frequency rates of particular behaviors as various conditions are reencountered. And depending on the transducer (which includes statements about an individual's history and biology), events are responded to in various ways. What is learned differs from one individual to the next. In this sense learning is never either environmentally or biologically based. We expect that this learning model will improve on many of the shortcomings evident in the traditional view, and will more effectively predict diagnostic responses for particular individuals.

When understood as learned responses, ADHD behaviors often translate into the individual avoiding too often, wanting more than others want to give, and relying excessively on others. The behavioral pattern can greatly tax the emotional resources of one's social matrix, in that diagnosed persons are often intrusive, non-responsive to the perspectives of others, insecure, or disengaged when participation and give-and-take is highly valued.

An ADHD diagnosis is often imposed when other accounts for nonconformity do not fully explain the problem (e.g., intellectual impairment, explicit refusals, etc.). So it is not surprising that this diagnosis is ascribed quite often within a variety of child-rearing practices. Individuals with a variety of different personal characteristics and environmental exposures can eventually learn the behaviors included in the diagnostic category. ADHD behaviors can be understood as that which children first learn when initially being socialized (e.g., monopolizing and irresponsibility). For all intents and purposes, socialization becomes a process of expressing fewer and fewer ADHD behaviors over time.

The problem of socializing children to function self-reliantly and consistently with societal expectations is an ongoing concern with child rearing. Helping children coordinate their actions with others invariably requires a give-and-take resolution to the question "who accommodates to whom?" ADHD becomes the descriptor for persons who rely excessively on the labors of others, and/or continue to behave in ways characteristic of those who are chronologically younger. The ADHD diagnosed child both trespasses and evades in a pattern that is inconsistent with expectations for his or her age group.

Freud's (1961) comments pertaining to competing interests of the individual and society are relevant here, as socializing individuals requires a resolution to this problem. We could argue that diagnosed persons often defer less to group preferences when they do ADHD behaviors, and failure to accommodate also repeats when these individuals handle objects, operate machines, or complete numerous tasks. Often it seems as if behaviors are enacted in the most convenient or easiest way for the diagnosed individual, even if those actions result in poorly completed work, social disruption, damage to property, and other harm. This characterization is consistent with the Zagar and Bowers (1983) finding that there is often a rapid decline in performance of *fatigued* diagnosed individuals. That is, the more difficult it is to accommodate, the more likely it is that the behavior of diagnosed persons will be unacceptable.

Similarly, it is not surprising that early negative infant temperament, pre- and post-natal brain injuries, encoding delays, fine motor problems, and parental psychiatric diagnosis may all increase the likelihood of ADHD patterning (Barkley, 1998d), in that all of those socialization conditions hinder the ability to meet expectations and coordinate acceptably with others. For example, at one point or another, 37-43% of mothers with diagnosed children have had a mood disorder, 23-27% of these mothers have had an anxiety disorder, and there is an increase in cocaine abuse for these mothers as well (Chronis et al., 2003).

Also noteworthy is that when single mothers have little education, low socioeconomic status, and if there is father desertion, the probability that ADHD will occur earlier and become more persistent is higher (Nichols and Chen, 1981). It would be contradictory for a traditionalist to say that these variables account for the occurrence of ADHD, but we argue that this type of adverse social condition increases the probability that ADHD delays will be learned in severe and persistent forms. These problems (including individual difference, cultural pattern, economic, societal, situational, and family historical variables), increase the likelihood of difficulties adjusting and conforming to normative social practice. One could actually claim that all identified early occurring correlated problems can increase the probability that a child will learn ADHD patterning—rather than posit traditional biological determinism.

In our alternative view, early occurring correlates do not increase the early emergence of neurological ADHD, but rather that ADHD behavior is more likely to be conditioned when difficult social conditions are present. For instance, many boys show less perseverance and achievement when there is father desertion. They may develop greater insecurity regarding acceptability, they may protect themselves from further disappointment by not getting involved, and many boys may have atypical relationships with their mothers, especially if she is socially isolated (Wahler, 1980). The fact that this group shows higher base rates of ADHD is not unexpected.

In the same way, factors related to biological adversity can also increase the probability of diagnosis. Even though hypoxic/anoxic brain insults (Cruickshand, Eliason, and Merrifield, 1988), seizure disorders (Hesdorffer et al., 2004), and stroke (Max et al., 2002), can create hyperactivity and attentional problems, it remains unclear whether those impairments present in the fashion as that which occurs for the majority of diagnosed persons. With that in mind, if a person has a particular kind of brain impairment, and also patterns as more typical ADHD, it can be argued that having that kind of limited brain functioning has increased the likelihood of learning diagnostic patterns.

Instead of contending that particular disruptions to the brain create an underlying (in this case acquired) neurological condition called ADHD, we claim that ADHD behaviors are likely to be learned when biological problems hinder a person's ability to achieve and coordinate with others in the usual ways. These persons will often learn to intrude, give up, and avoid more frequently than a normative sample, as their functional limitations create adversity. Not surprisingly, it has been found that close to one-third of diagnosed persons are identified as learning disabled (Barkley, 2000).

We claim that due to their biopsychosocial circumstance some people learn ADHD responses rather than continue participation, effort, and accommodation if they encounter hardship. Even if it is true that diagnosed persons as a group are less persistent, inefficient in their responses to feedback, or more reliant on having parameters externally represented, it is still a matter of conjecture as to how to account for those findings. If loved ones habitually direct, give aid, and cue behaviors, and diagnosed persons often rush, overreact, and avoid, it is not surprising then, that diagnosed persons have greater difficulty when complex achievements are not systematized or facilitated for them. They are not learning the necessary responses to handle and resolve problems. While traditionalists claim that loved ones offer help because they react to the limitations of the diagnosed person, we could also argue that as long as the diagnosed person is presumed incompetent and treated as such, and reinforced when doing ADHD responding, behaviors that could potentially increase self-reliance and cooperation are not being shaped.

ADHD behaviors can be reinforced whenever requirements are modified or reduced after the behaviors have been emitted, and these individuals will not learn to work hard and do the preparatory work necessary to conform to situational demands. Given this frequent response pattern, it is not surprising that functioning often improves when diagnosed persons work individually with a tutor, since this arrangement permits extra assistance and extensive accommodation from the instructor. Working one-to-one increases the probability of more normative participatory behaviors and effort, in that adversity will be minimized by the increased privacy and the assistance of the tutor. Many diagnosed persons have apparently been reinforced to function fairly competently if they are the center of attention, which might also condition others not to ignore or exclude them; therefore, acceptable responding can increase by receiving individualized attention during required achievements.

Interestingly, traditionalists claim that during an initial assessment, a child's behavior with parents in the waiting area is likely to better predict patterns of behavior at home than how the child behaves with the therapist. The posited reason for this is the one-to-one interaction (Barkley and Edwards, 2006). Similarly, Draeger et al. (1986) and Steinkamp (1980) also report that diagnosed children typically function better on various attention and arithmetic tasks, depending on whether an experimenter sits in the room, even when interaction does not occur.

Situations in which the child receives undivided positive attention may frequently help to ameliorate ADHD responding. A child's insecurity pertaining to social exclusion may also diminish if given discretionary input during individual exchanges. Patterns of provoking and triangulating are also likely to lessen when one-to-one interaction takes place. Since it is usually easier to accommodate a person's initiatives (and therefore decrease disappointment) in a one-to-one situation, many parameters related to discomfort can be quickly and adequately solved during mutual interaction. Not only is competition and jealousy minimized, but embarrassment related to failure can also be kept discrete. Interestingly, because many psychological tests are administered individually, the fact that most people function better in individualized instruction compared to group instruction may be a factor in the failure of these tests to accurately discriminate diagnosed individuals from controls.

Hardships can generally be managed more effectively during one-to-one interactions. Discouragement can be redirected and dispelled constructively, the curriculum can be fine-tuned for better success rates, and explanations of misunderstandings and difficulties can also reinforce acceptable responding. However, it is also important to consider parameters that tend to increase adversity, such as the child's history with the other person, and the content of the interaction so as to predict whether ADHD behavior will be more or less recurrent during individualized sessions.

While traditionalists might hold that one-to-one interaction or having someone in the room helps make reinforcement more immediate, external, and salient to offset neurological delays, we also see that the behavior of diagnosed individuals is diverse, and sometimes subtle changes in conditions have marked influence on the frequency rates of the presumed evidence of an underlying neurological problem. Sometimes diagnosed persons show many ADHD behaviors when interacting one-to-one with a parent or examiner, depending on the history between the participants, or whether an aversive interaction is occurring.

We suggest that diverse behaviors manifest as a function of the situation or circumstance encountered. For example, what they have learned to do with their parents while waiting may differ from their learned pattern when meeting a professional (someone who focuses on them in an essentially non-critical manner) for the first time. Depending on the relationship between diagnosed person and others, and parameters such as recent prior events, what happens next, duration of activity, association of an activity with failure, and how others are acting, ADHD behavior will or will not become reinforced.

Under some circumstances, diagnosed children respond acceptably even when waiting with parents in public places, although they frequently show diagnostic responses in public places if circumstances change. As examples, a diagnosed child is likely to *not* show problematic responding when a toy is available to play with in the public situation, when prior positive attention has been given, when he wants to be left alone, when a sibling is being reprimanded in the waiting room, or when the appointment is anticipated to be enjoyable.

When diagnosed children do ADHD behaviors while with parents in public waiting areas, the current model identifies which factors sequence with ADHD behaviors under various circumstances. Those sequences often include extra parental concern, distraction from anxiety about what could happen during the appointment, the availability of an interested audience, sabotage of the parent's agenda to attend the appointment, or provoking a parent who is powerless and embarrassed to respond. Because ADHD patterning is antithetical to acceptable waiting room behavior, which requires politeness and conciliation, the behavior can be powerful in that setting. However, given such remarkable shifts in functioning, it is difficult to accept that the problem resides within a diagnosed person simply because frequency rates of particular behaviors are high under particular conditions. As a way to clarify these variations in responding and diagnostic functioning, the current paradigm shifts the locus of the problem from neurobiology to interactions between diagnosed persons and their worlds.

In that regard, we anticipate that ADHD responding will typically increase when diagnosed persons are required to accommodate to troublesome social expectations; they will typically balk if sharing and turn taking are required, or if working compatibly with other people reduces their discretionary authority. For example, it has been found that ADHD children are less likely to show reciprocity in social exchanges with their peers (Cunningham and Siegel, 1987; Landau and Milich, 1988). While traditionalists presume that these problems are caused by neurobiological disinhibition, it is currently claimed that these responses are reinforced in situations that impede discretionary authority or require more accommodating responses and respect for others.

As a rule of thumb, when a social exchange is less arduous, limiting, negative, exclusionary, unforgiving, and disapproving, we predict that ADHD behaviors will be less frequent; this may or may not always correspond with times when a diagnosed child receives one-to-one attention. For example, it has been found that fathers compared to mothers influence ADHD behavior to an appreciable extent. Barkley (2000) notes that unless mothers adopt a typically male pattern of disciplining, there is a greater likelihood that Oppositional/Defiant Disorder will also develop in fatherless households.

While traditionalists claim that fathers are more likely to compensate for ADHD, in that they become a more salient, intimidating, externally represented presence, in our view it is not surprising that fathers typically elicit more compliance in the short-term, since they are likely to resort to coercion as social training. The diagnosed child learns to conform or else! Males have historically been less concerned about being liked, and are generally focused on being right. Males may also tend to induce conformity and discipline (closely paralleling the traditional approach) by means of more extensive control of the child. Fathers will also accommodate less often when diagnosed children throw tantrums or complain about limits. Men are generally less likely to indulge or reinforce infantile behavior, and will be less swayed by protests of dissatisfaction (especially with boys). Although this does not ignore the fact that—depending on the history between a diagnosed person and mother and father—very different behavioral patterns will be reinforced during interaction with either parent.

Rather than understanding the problem as one of fathers providing more immediate and salient consequences to offset inherent delays in a more adequate fashion, the condition of having father present could cue greater compliancy rather than diagnostic functioning. It may be the case that fathers more often reinforce obedience rather than ADHD. They may be less keen to reinforce cutesy, baby-like, entertaining behaviors, or be preoccupied with protecting the child (e.g., seeing if shoelaces are tied, or when injury is possible).

Thus emotionality, immaturity, rushing, delaying, intrusiveness, provocation, reliance on others, and non-participatory behavior may not be reinforced by terse parental responses. Similar to individuals in institutional settings, compliance will increase in response to structured and coercive interventions (as long as inconsistency is not introduced) during training. While traditionalists claim that fathers do not cure ADHD, and that they only temporarily offset inhibitory delays, one could alternatively say that symptom variation with fathers demonstrates that ADHD behaviors are not reinforced when specific social patterns are introduced.

We do not suggest that fathers are more effective than mothers from the perspective of our alternative model, or that paternal methods are more advantageous over the long-term, because repetition of coerced behavior may not occur under less coercive conditions. The age-old expression "when the cat is away the mouse will play" is appropriate in this context. Moreover, to the extent that mothers frequently respond to the child's perspective, typical female patterning may be more effective in conditioning socially desirable behaviors such as empathy, creativity, and compatibility.

As a way to obtain benefit from both paternal and maternal discipline, there could be a blending of the patterns correlated with the genders; a good start is to avoid over-coercion and over-accommodation. Caretakers could strive to maintain collaboration during social exchanges (rather than focus on obtaining compliance), promote self-reliance, industriousness, and avoid patterns of indulgence. For example, instead of advising parents to put on a diagnosed child's coat to save time, whenever possible the parent might instead help the child *learn* to put on the coat with progressively less parental assistance.

In another context, ADHD impairments may be ameliorated or disappear altogether when diagnosed persons are self-employed (Barkley, 2000). We know that diagnosed individuals have difficulty coordinating behavior with others, and more problems enduring delays in gratification in the workplace, so it is claimed that diagnosed persons are likely to be immediately reinforced when working for themselves; self-employment is seen to diminish diagnostic responding.

However, this explanation introduces inconsistency with regard to other traditional beliefs, in that self-employment is less monitored than work under the direct supervision of others. Since traditionalists otherwise claim that it is necessary to manipulate contingencies at the point of performance to compensate for delays, how can self-employment provide the structure and external cueing that is likely to occur when working for an employer? Clearly with diagnosed children, traditionalists do not recommend this type of self-directedness. In some instances the self-employed receive immediate payment for work, but this is not always the case; and at times contingencies may be even more delayed compared to the formal setting where regular paychecks are the norm.

In most ways the self-employed have greater responsibility and must function more autonomously. For example, a survey appearing in *USA Today* (2001) found that the most important asset needed for self-employment is ambition and the willingness to work diligently. Given that neither of these characteristics is generally associated with the ADHD diagnosis, it is difficult to believe the traditional explanation that many self-employed diagnosed individuals function adequately.

Given the apparent contradiction that diagnosed persons can function competently during self-employment, perhaps an alternative explanation is more reasonable. Competency during self-employment is a prime example of how the behavior of diagnosed individuals seems to change when they initiate the action to achieve. Often it seems that ADHD is associated with: who maintains discretionary authority, the source of the instruction to do the action, and whether activities are associated with past successes or negative evaluations when compared to the parameters designated by traditionalists.

We could argue that self-employment typically allows greater discretionary input, less exposure to actions initiated by others, and fewer controls and restraints on one's schedule. The conditions of self-employment often insulate an individual from evaluation, disapproval or reprimand from authority figures who expect certain requirements to be met in very specific ways. For example, employers of diagnosed adults often notice the same problems at work evident when these persons attended school (Barkley, 1998f).

Given the aforementioned data, diagnosed persons have learned to do ADHD responding primarily when confronted with assignments, limits, and instructions imposed by others, which have somehow become associated with negativity. It would seem therefore that a lessening of these factors help make self-employment a more positive condition compared to working for others. Functioning that exceeds posited disability can occur during self-employment, and nothing extra has to be managed in order to stimulate competent and organized behaviors in that setting.

If diagnosed individuals sometimes function better when self-employed, these findings could be interpreted in ways consistent with our current alternative perspective rather than positing the disability model. However, and very importantly, if the *source of the instruction* to enact the achievement strongly influences whether or not ADHD behaviors will occur, it can be problematic to argue from a biological determinist's perspective. That is, how is it biologically easier to make the very same achievements simply because someone else did not instruct those actions?

Inconsistency in the traditional model is also evident in reports that many diagnosed teens complete homework adequately while simultaneously listening to music (Barkley, 2000). We ask how this finding is compatible with the belief that diagnosed individuals have relative difficulty exerting interference control when engaged in activity requiring executive functioning. What enables these diagnosed teens to frequently complete homework more competently when their favorite salient and immediately reinforcing music is available to "drive them to distraction?"

When traditionalists assert that the slightest distraction may "shatter" working memory, on what neurological grounds can playing self-selected music during homework help with this neural biological problem? When it is recommended that persons attempting to treat ADHD must avoid "sources of high-appealing distracters that may serve to subvert, pervert, or disrupt task-directed behavior . . ." (Barkley, 2000), what then is the biological justification for playing one's favorite music to improve task completion? Further, when it is recommended that those who assist diagnosed persons should substitute forms of information that are "salient and appealing," but also "directly associated with or an inherent part of the task to be accomplished" (Barkley, 2006f, 328), in what way is introducing preferred music consistent with this recommendation?

Given these apparent contradictions, the traditional model does not satisfactorily explain why diagnosed teens show improved homework performance and resistance to distraction when simultaneously playing their favorite music. The alternative learning paradigm can more easily assimilate these findings without introducing apparent contradictions. By permitting diagnosed teens to play music during homework completion, the conditions of doing assigned tasks are made less aversive and more similar to non-assigned activity. ADHD behavior is less likely to be reinforced in those situations.

Consistent with that interpretation is the finding that some diagnosed children function better when doing assigned tasks if they are also permitted to be active while doing the task (Zentall, 1993). Allowing for physical movement helps make completion seem less uncomfortable or constraining. We also notice this effect when diagnosed individuals operate computer-assisted programs (Pfiffner and Barkley, 1998; DuPaul and Power, 2000; Ota and DuPaul, 2003), as improved functioning is reported on these tasks compared to occasions when passive conformity to instruction is required.

Much like what takes place when many diagnosed children are permitted to handle objects during instruction, doing assigned work can become positive or consistent with play when conditions conform to the child's interests. Being able to listen to music, move around, or handle objects, can help make conditions less aversive; those alterations help reinforce accommodating, non-diagnostic responses. When imposed requirements are less oppressive and restrictive, or when there are allowances for self-initiated responses such as freedom to move and interact, assigned tasks will begin to show similarity to non-assigned tasks that rarely correlate with ADHD responses. Traditionalists think that computer-assisted tasks effectively offset ADHD by providing immediacy and saliency, but perhaps instead it is the parameters highlighted here which are the most influential.

If diagnosed persons behave very differently in relation to changes in conditions, it is difficult to make blanket assumptions about their degraded ability to stop behavior or resist distractions. There are many instances when they can indeed stop behaviors very effectively, while on other occasions they do not behave acceptably until conditions become threatening or intriguing. However, since the behavior of diagnosed persons may be consistent with what traditionalists call "behavioral control and longer term contingencies in some situations," it is unclear what their consistent or definable internally-caused problem or "myopia for time" actually is.

Given that ADHD delays are fleeting and inconsistent, the primary delay of the diagnosed population is that they are diagnostically responding rather than conforming to normative practice frequently and at crucial times. In this alternative view, the ADHD problem is a matter of reinforcing different behaviors rather than compensating for a permanent functional delay. If it is found that new learning eliminates diagnostic responding, it will not matter whether the temporal (not causal) source of the behavioral pattern can be traced to molecular biology. As Skinner (1953, 98) notes, "We may, indeed, have little interest in how that behavior was first acquired. Our concern is only with its present probability of occurrence, which can be understood only through an examination of current contingencies of reinforcement."

Although it has been possible to increase coercion, alter responses with medication, and simplify requirements such that ADHD responding is no longer reinforced, it is not imperative to subscribe to the notion that a permanent mental/biological delay exists. Some people in relation to different histories (including those with complicating biological problems) are more likely to learn ADHD behaviors under conditions of increased discomfort. However, given that these same persons may be less likely to do ADHD behaviors when self-initiated actions are not impeded, or when situations and circumstances remain positive, ADHD reacting is consistent with a learning model. For example, how many diagnosed persons quit when they are winning, or gaze around a room when following their own directions? Rather than understanding ADHD behaviors as motivational failure or problems with self-control, the behaviors may be a means of increasing the probability of certain event sequences: finishing sooner and escaping quickly, even if others do not enjoy what they do, are not interested in those outcomes, or do not prefer those achievements.

Immediate vs. Delayed Reinforcement

When understanding these differing reactions as conditioned, we are not offsetting ADHD by changing environmental parameters, we only show the circumstances under which different kinds of responses are reinforced to occur. However, since proponents of biological determinism claim that certain conditions may temporarily compensate for biological ineptitude, we see that the distinction between delayed reinforcement and immediate reinforcement requires further discussion. The traditional account rests on this dichotomy, as it is claimed that immediate reinforcement is necessary to offset inhibitory problems that prevent intrinsic motivation from taking place.

The lack of immediate external reinforcement allegedly makes the underlying neurological inhibitory weakness and less ability to access executive functioning evident. When not receiving the benefits of particular mental/biological acts that might help the individual continue to motivate and sustain current un-comfortable behaviors for the greater long-term good, symptomatic behaviors will presumably increase. The assertion is that some environments do not pro-vide enough immediate reinforcement to the individual to counteract ADHD motivational delay.

Porrino et al. (1983) report that differences in activity levels between diag-nosed persons and others may be less during television viewing, compared to math and reading classes. It is claimed that when ADHD individuals do highly reinforcing activities, they will often respond more typically. However, once the "schedule and magnitude of reinforcement are decreased . . ." (Barkley, 1998b, 76), it is possible to easily discriminate diagnosed children from others. Hence it is the decrease of reinforcement that worsens their behavior, and inhibitory and executive non-occurrence undermines the diagnosed person's ability to persist towards a goal over time without the immediacy provided by externally-represented consequences.

It is necessary to offer the diagnosed individual immediate consequences so that persistence and achievement will continue. Wheeler et al. (1997) posit that the prefrontal cortex (the time machine of the human brain) is likely to be cause and location of this ongoing problem. Since diagnosed persons are delayed in their ability to engage in hindsight and forethought, their awareness of time is narrower when compared to individuals who do not suffer with this develop-mental delay. Barkley (1998g) holds that diagnosed persons often fail to be in-fluenced by time in ways similar to how brain-injured persons with a neglect syndrome fail to be influenced by visuospatial information. The result of this problem is that diagnosed individuals have myopia for time and less ability to control their behavior over time. Tasks must therefore be broken into smaller units to minimize the amount of time between reinforcements.

The extrinsic reinforcement "provided" by the activity explains why diag-nosed persons sometimes persist and stay on task. That is why they show few symptoms when doing certain behaviors such as playing prefabricated games that "supply" constant reinforcement. Symptom variation is expected, as activi-ties differ in terms of how much intrinsic motivation (or executive functioning) they require for competent performance, and how much extrinsic motivation they offer. Variations in persistence and achievement in different situations in no way discounts a biological etiology (Barkley, 2000).

However, this explanation seems incomplete, in that we do not know what is inherent in a designed product such as a video game that enables reinforce-ment. Is it the introduction of certain variations, the indication that an additional turn has been lost or earned, the completion of a level, or that discretionary au-thority is permitted? It is also important to identify how those parameters differ from that which happens in school, where students also complete assignments and finish chapters in similar time frames, and are soon informed about the out-come of their academic efforts. Curiously, given that many adults apparently show ADHD patterns when playing popular video games with their children, must we then believe that the game no longer emanates reinforcement when the adult is playing?

Generally, responses to even the most popular video games can vary, depending on who plays, and the context, situation, and circumstance under which the playing takes place, including what has just happened, how long the game has been played, and what is likely to happen next. The bells and whistles that sound when completing a level, the novelty being introduced, earning additional turns, or completing a section in the game can be exciting, annoying, or unrelated to persistence. Response factors depend on the reinforcement history of the respondent and the circumstances under which the responses occur. There is wide variability in the duration, frequency, and enjoyment level of a particular game for any individual (diagnosed or not), depending on different parameters.

Some games can evoke the same responses as a typical homework assignment, regardless of the effort spent designing the game. It seems that enjoyment or interest when doing even the same activity at different times depends on a number of parameters. With this in mind, we cannot readily assert that something *inherent* in the activity accounts for the variations in the observed responses in different situations for different people, despite attempts to do so.

Similarly, if diagnosed adolescents (like non-diagnosed peers) play games that require significant working memory and strategizing compared to games predicated on rapid movements and flashing lights, on what basis can one argue that diagnosed persons require more external representation? Often a successful mission is more complex when compared to other school assignments that are either ignored or completed carelessly. Additionally, the feedback given by these games seems no different from that which occurs during daily life (including functioning within school), in that enactors know very quickly whether others are pleased, or if a game decision pays off.

Although many of the game themes played by diagnosed persons are negative and aggressive (e.g., stealing cars and gangland activity), successful game play requires actions that increase the probability of a future event, and coordination of present behaviors. For example, it is often true that protagonists cannot bully their way through the game and expect to win. If these diagnosed persons are delayed in ability to control the future, why do significant numbers of diagnosed adolescents demonstrate adequate functioning and problem solving at these times? Would it be as likely that a person with a frontal lobe injury—who has significant impairment in behavior that coordinates effectively with future events—can function as competently when confronted with the afore-mentioned problems and dilemmas?

Furthermore, many diagnosed children also read strategy guides for games without showing ADHD behaviors at these times. However, it is unclear what differs about the extrinsic motivation provided by these guides compared with assigned reading activities where robust ADHD behavior occurs. A person reading a book for school or a strategy guide may in both instances be reinforced by each completed step. Doing either activity can yield achievements of remarkable complexity in relation to numerous immediately reinforced actions.

Rather than say that reading strategy guides provides what the school assignment cannot, we suggest that different behaviors are being reinforced during one or the other activity. Some diagnosed children show fewer ADHD responses when reading some strategy guides in some situations, and more ADHD responses in some situations when reading for school, but the exact opposite patterns can also occur, depending on parameters. However, when acceptable responding has been conditioned with either activity, there is no requirement to add contingencies (or any other compensatory traditional intervention) to induce non-diagnostic behaviors—even though a respondent is diagnosed as ADHD.

We notice that explicating the occurrence of particular behaviors is more complex than insisting that some activities provide a particular effect. This is evident because we know that not all diagnosed children have problems with all school assignments all the time, even without traditional intervention; and sometimes ADHD responses occur frequently during video gaming, block building, or presumably enjoyable trips to a toy store. An activity in and of itself does not provide immediate reinforcement; with certain activities, some people, in some situations, will respond in acceptable or unacceptable ways more or less frequently than others.

Environment alone does not reinforce; the response of the individual determines whether the category reinforcement is imposed. Some individuals behave consistently with pleasing teachers, getting high grades, or completing specific academic material while in school, whereas others will consistently do the opposite. However, both patterns of behavior may be (immediately) reinforced under the conditions in which the behaviors take place. History rather than neurology can explain the response variations. The traditional model draws on a significant body of empirical work which they assume to be supportive of their theoretical biological mental model, but not only are many of their assertions problematic, but we can also reinterpret their data and substitute a learning paradigm to describe the differences between diagnosed individuals and controls.

Within the learning paradigm very different kinds of behaviors can occur when circumstances are changed in either subtle or pronounced ways. The time delay of an identified contingency, granting certain rewards, and certain variations in the design of an activity can affect behaviors, with or without an ADHD diagnosis. Adding managed contingencies or designing activities can increase instances of non-diagnostic functioning in some situations for some diagnosed (and non-diagnosed persons), but diagnosed persons also show acceptable functioning without any intervention, given their history of conditioning with a particular activity coupled with present circumstances.

Imposing the traditional intervention, such as managed contingencies, is simply a means of changing conditions to influence the frequency rates of particular behaviors. However, the frequency rates of those same behaviors can be influenced just as immediately by other contingencies. Although it is possible to induce compliance in diagnosed persons when contingency management is introduced, it is also possible to increase instances of non-diagnostic behaviors by altering parameters differently to yield comparable (or better) effects over time.

In that both the current and traditional perspectives attempt to identify parameters that correlate with ADHD behaviors, these disparate constructions identify very different influences on behavior. For example, traditionalists emphasize the frequency of provided reinforcement and external representation, and the current model focuses on such parameters as the rapport a subject has with the individual initiating the requirement to achieve, and events from the past in similar situations that have reinforced either an ADHD or more acceptable response. For example, we can denote the markedly different responses when diagnosed children are asked to write "thank you" notes for a gift, compared to writing a note to "Santa," and the likelihood of remembering when it is their turn, compared to when the turn belongs to someone else.

Diagnosed persons are often not reinforced to follow instructions imposed by others (i.e., accommodate) unless personal gain is either obvious or extreme, or when the likelihood of failure and disapproval is diminished. From a learning perspective, this is a matter of conditioning rather than neural biological delay. Not unexpectedly, when comforting situations are removed, behaviors will often revert to previous patterns, as the return of the old conditions will usually elicit the return of the old diagnostic responses. However, the individual's *history* is a way to account for the variations of diligence, politeness, participation, and more acceptably paced behavior.

As discussed earlier, immediate conditioning can occur at all times despite which response pattern is evident. We call a behavior *reinforced* when that behavior repeats frequently at specifiable times; reinforcement occurs regardless of whether punishment or reward is given. When we independently define a reinforcing contingency, Meehl (1950) claims we must first identify outcomes that increase or decrease the occurrence of behavior(s) for an organism. Once those reinforcers (and their intensities) are independently identified, we might then predict how contingencies will modify the frequency rates of particular behaviors in particular situations and circumstances.

Conditions do not provide reinforcement. Labeling a behavior as reinforced or extinguished is a *statement about the frequency rates* of the behavior in relation to conditions, not something transmitted from the outside to a person. Behaviors are characterized as reinforced when they are repeated within equivalent situations and circumstances, but conditions do not *emit* "reinforcement."

It is the result of behaving that has reinforced its repetition, and frequency rates of the behavior may change in relation to what has transpired. Although the final payoff (however this is determined) might not occur until a certain amount of time has elapsed, events that occur immediately can influence a behavior's frequency rate. While adding contingency management might maintain, increase, or decrease rates of recurrence, there are countless ways that a behavior's recurrence rate can be immediately influenced after it is emitted.

It is in that sense that behaviors consistent with increasing the probability of certain long-term events can be characterized as immediately reinforced—the same as behaviors which may consistently increase the probability of short-term outcomes. During short or long-term goal achievements, behavioral acts may be immediately reinforced when they sequence with new situations that further increase the probability or temporal proximity of attaining the specified goal. The traditional distinction between immediate reinforcement and delayed reinforcement therefore is problematic and muddy.

The argument that diagnosed persons need immediate and ongoing manipulation of their worlds by a managing party is not empirically sound. ADHD responses relate to the individual's history of reinforcement with particular conditions. Traditional intervention might alter conditions so that ADHD behaviors occur less (e.g., medicate, simplify, and manage contingencies), but this does not mean that reinforcement is *being added* where there was none. Changing conditions in those ways is merely reinforcing new behaviors.

Managing the magnitude and frequency of such contingencies as intrigue/ enticement or fear (that we know will affect an individual's behavior) is beneficial only to the extent that those interventions increase frequency rates of particular actions. However, we cannot presume that such interventions provide reinforcement when reinforcement is otherwise absent. Those inducements simply alter the conditions under which an individual functions, and not surprisingly, at those times different responses are reinforced. Reinforcement was not under-supplied when diagnosed responding was previously evident, but rather the person was not reinforced to respond non-diagnostically in the previous conditions.

The main strength of the traditional model is that its interventions condition new behaviors. Practitioners do not demonstrate that delayed functioning is being offset, nor do they provide reinforcement when none existed before. According to convention, only certain kinds of activities can provide the brain with enough stimulation to activate the frontal lobes, but that statement can be interpreted to mean that when diagnosed individuals do not show an excited reaction, it is because their past conditioning prevents them from being reinforced to react in an excited manner in that setting or situation.

While individuals might repeat different immediately reinforced behaviors in particular settings and situations, including pauses and reports of specific mental actions, a history of reinforcement can clarify the conditioned responses emitted. For example, when building a tower, keeping the blocks aligned results in fewer blocks toppling; that behavior can be immediately reinforced when building with blocks at other times. Very complex sequences of behaviors will eventuate into significant achievements over time, as each action, like its own building block, influences what takes place, which then cues subsequent (immediately reinforced) actions in the ensuing conditions.

In a statement consistent with our learning model, Skinner (1953) notes that "precurrent" behavior (i.e., behavior that creates the opportunity for other reinforcing behaviors), is reinforced by its association with other reinforced behaviors. "The stimuli generated by this precurrent behavior, therefore, become reinforcing" (p. 76). Skinner also claims that "sensory feedback" (e.g., a baby shaking a rattle) might be all that is necessary to reinforce an action, as being reinforced by the success of "manipulating nature" will be advantageous for survival. In Skinner's view, our actions are reinforced immediately when they associate with other subsequent reinforcing happenings, and "in general, behavior which acts on the immediate physical environment is consistently reinforced" (p. 99).

However, if our actions are immediately conditioned by events, it is a matter of identifying the parameters and understanding how they are immediately influencing actions. Instead of understanding traditional intervention as adding conditioning when it is insufficient, we argue that traditional interventions simply change the immediate conditioning by altering parameters to reinforce non-diagnostic behaviors.

If we adopt such an understanding, ADHD would no longer be a delay in ability to motivate when reinforcement is weak or absent. It would simply be that some individuals have been immediately reinforced to do diagnostic responding rather than immediately reinforced to do acceptable responding. Traditional intervention is one of many ways to alter parameters and (immediately) reinforce non-diagnostic responses, but they cannot prove that there had been a lack of reinforcement prior to the intervention.

When understanding behavior in this fashion, receiving a token for acceptable behavior becomes precurrent to obtaining money, which becomes precurrent to buying a toy, which becomes precurrent for assembling the toy. Each behavioral act during the playing with the toy could be characterized as precurrent for subsequent behavioral acts while interacting with the toy. Accepting this formulation means that there will always be events that immediately condition our actions; it is not that some people function better without immediate reinforcement. Moreover, this immediate conditioning of responses occurs independently from the time it takes for the posited (and seemingly arbitrary) final events to take place.

Similar to an ant colony where so much is accomplished from ongoing chemical reactions, one is always being influenced by subsequent events. Those events may influence a person to continue the same response, cease a particular response, emit a mental or motoric response, or proceed with additional behaviors that increase the probability of short or long-term eventualities. As Skinner (1953) notes:

> We are automatically reinforced, apart from any particular deprivation, when we successfully control the physical world. This may explain our tendency to engage in skilled crafts, in artistic creation, and in such sports as bowling, billiards, and tennis (p. 77).

If one accepts this possibility, then people may indeed do organized behaviors over extended time frames, and show exceptional long-term achievements without the necessity for self-motivating mental recitations about future rewards (and without being given a managed reward). We might find that people rarely do such behaviors, or that there is little correlation between long-term achievement and the frequency rates of those responses.

In this view, when people do behaviors that increase the probability of certain future outcomes, it does not necessarily mean that they more often contemplate long-term consequences than others. For example, groups such as Alcoholics Anonymous claim that the narrowing of the time horizon and living one day at a time, correlates with better long-term results, compared to obsessive thinking about controlling the future.

Automatic Responses

Current ADHD empiricism has not established that the failure to do mental recitations (at particular times) is the primary reason for the lack of socially-valued long-term achievements evident in the diagnosed population. There is apparently no data showing a relationship between the frequency of these self-directed "motivating" actions and the attainment of long-term goals. Thus, it is unclear whether a lack of occurrence, timing, or content of particular mental responses about future consequences correlates with an ADHD diagnosis. Moreover, even if diagnosed persons are not doing mental motivations like others, no one is yet providing data that establishes a lesser ability to learn those responses.

ADHD empiricism has also not established that diagnosed persons are too limited to enact more socially valued behaviors any more than a smoker is too limited to be influenced by getting cancer. In this view, diagnosed persons learn to repeat ADHD behaviors in the same way that cigarette smoking is learned. Regardless of the long-term problems associated with particular behaviors, patterns can be reinforced with enough frequency to maintain their persistence over time. While it is unavoidable that the consequences of our actions may play out well into the distant future (e.g., high grades in school, gaining weight in relation to eating, joint problems in relation to over-exercising), our actions may nevertheless be immediately reinforced at the time they occur. Whatever we do there is a benefit/risk tradeoff, as each action may increase some future probabilities and lower others (often without our knowledge).

Additionally, even if diagnosed persons are unaware of the future consequences of ADHD actions at the time of performance, increasing their awareness at strategic times, bribes, or coercion, does not necessarily mean that they are delayed. A similar result might be obtained when pressuring the workaholic to go home to family. Rather than infer that a diagnosed person's delay must be quite severe when behavioral change is difficult to achieve, we can presume that the person is reinforced to continue the old patterning, and that interventions are bound to be ineffective in the short-term unless urgency is established.

As we know, changing reinforced behaviors is a difficult proposition. If particular reactions have been conditioned for many years, those responses will persist and generalize. The circumstances may continue to be associated with either troubling or pleasurable events, and without knowing the individual's history with particular conditions, responses may seem deficient or pathological in some way. However, non-consensual responses do not indicate that the person has failed to undergo an executive process due to inherent delay, but rather that they are responding instantaneously due to past conditioning that has reinforced the atypical behaviors.

In much the same fashion, Bargh and Chartrand (1999) claim that behavior is "automatic." They assert that environment rather than antecedent mental activity cues responses. These authors agree with estimates that acts associated with "the conscious self guiding of behavior" occur perhaps 5% of the time (which in this learning view can also be seen as "automatic" conditioned responses). Bargh and Chartrand indicate that "most of daily life is driven by automatic, non-conscious mental processes" (p. 476). They maintain that it is not possible for conscious control behaviors to adequately direct a person's actions throughout most of daily life. They summarize their findings by saying:

> Automatic evaluation of the environment is a pervasive and continuous activity that individuals do not intend to engage in and of which they are largely unaware. It appears to have a real and functional consequence, creating behavioral readiness within fractions of a second to approach positive and avoid negative objects, and, through its effect on mood, serving as a signaling system for the overall safety versus danger of one's current environment. All of these effects tend to keep us in touch with the realities of our world in a way that bypasses the limitations of conscious self-regulation capabilities (p. 475).

We suggest that Bargh and Chartrand are claiming (much like this current alternative view) that individuals more typically operate in a continuously automatic manner in contrast to the intentional disability formulation proposed by the traditional two-step inhibitory process: delaying the decision to respond and engaging in subsequent executive activity which may guide the decision response. For Bargh and Chartrand, evaluative functions are always accessible; they are not made accessible by a necessary inhibitory response.

However, adoption of these premises means that behaviors can facilitate event sequences in the "not here and not now" without the added requirement that an individual inhibit or pause to only then be guided by "conscious self-controlling" mental actions which enable competent intentional responses to occur. As stated by the neuroscientist Vittorio Gallese, "This neural mechanism is involuntary and automatic," and "with it we don't have to think about what other people are doing or feeling, we simply know" (Winerman, 2005, 50).

Importantly, while Barkley (2006f, 304) argues to "decouple" the typical stimulus/response arrangement, and insert a delaying response and private self-controlling actions to account for behaviors that we deem to be adequately controlling the future, we argue in favor of that coupling. Even if a person pauses, is not derailed by distractions, or reports particular kinds of mental responding prior to other subsequent responses, all those behavioral events will still be understood as learned within a stimulus/response paradigm. Executive functioning is learned just like any other behavior (e.g., talking), and begins to occur automatically in particular situations and circumstances.

Similar to our discussion regarding behavioral "control," organization of behavior thus becomes a construct imposed upon a succession of actions, not something the person is doing *in addition to* behaving. The person is not organizing and behaving, he or she is simply behaving in a particularly organized way. Our actions are understood as cued by context and situation in a way similar to Bargh and Chartrand's "automatic" characterization.

Likewise, when individuals evaluate, predict, encourage themselves, plan, reflect on the past, discriminate differences, solve complexities, and scrutinize their own actions (or the actions of others), they are doing particular behaviors; they are not "consciously controlling" and also doing those behaviors. For example, when I move my hand carefully, I am simply doing a different kind of action, compared to when I move my hand in a typical way. When I observe myself moving my hand, it is equivalent to when I observe others moving their hands. As noted, people are doing one action not two when they behave in a self-aware, effective, or circumspect way, and people can respond acceptably without pausing to do executive functioning in most instances.

Because it is possible at times for most diagnosed persons to modulate their actions carefully, provide self-reports which include preparatory mental responses in some situations, and respond in ways that consider future possibilities, it is problematic once again to say that they are biologically less able to function in those ways. Unlike some defective individuals who consistently show difficulty if required to do careful behavioral enactments or manage the "not here and not now," the major problem for diagnosed persons is that they fail to respond acceptably when *others want them to*. History rather than disability can be invoked to account for that problem.

Interestingly, Gollwitzer (1999) also notes that *most* people do not follow through with what they have planned; time blindness can frequently occur for the majority of us. He indicates that even when people report having intentions, the relationship between intentions and behavior is very weak. According to Gollwitzer:

> The correlations between intentions and behavior are modest; intentions account for only 20% to 30% of the variance of behavior that is specified, and people's past behavior commonly turns out to be a better predictor than their

intentions. Most interesting, the weak intention-behavior relation is largely due to people having good intentions but failing to act upon them (p. 493).

In light of Gollwitzer's data, one might ask if traditionalists can argue confidently that diagnosed persons differ significantly from others when they make plans (covertly or overtly) to behave in particular ways, as they may in fact not differ markedly from their non-diagnosed counterparts. Moreover, if we consider Gollwitzer's claims, we can gain insights by investigating the times when diagnosed persons reliably follow through with stated intentions (or plans of action). For example, diagnosed persons will not forget their intention to play video games after school; they are more likely to remember their plan to meet friends for skateboarding; and they will typically not forget to remind parents about the new movie out on DVD.

One might also investigate what is different about those time organized behaviors in comparison to bringing books home from school, cleaning rooms after promising to do so earlier that day, taking out the garbage the same time each week, and feeding the dog without being reminded. Is it that the failed achievements require more executive functioning, or is it that diagnosed children are not yet conditioned to reliably complete certain chores? The view here is that diagnosed persons are not delayed in their ability to behave reliably over time; they are merely reinforced to behave in less socially acceptable ways from the vantage point of those who must coordinate with them over time.

Chapter 6

ADHD Diagnosis: Correlated Problems

Many children who express ADHD behaviors also show numerous functional problems that have, from the start, hampered their ability to succeed and coordinate effectively with others. Under these circumstances loved ones and other frequently encountered individuals will have significant difficulty socializing the child, since a pattern of monopolizing and avoidance of responsibility is likely to emerge. Many children conditioned to do ADHD patterning will not develop their resources in ways consistent with their age group. Less accommodating responding, irresponsibility, and avoidance behaviors may on the one hand shield the child from failure and denigration and provoke concern, but those patterns of response will also not assist in skill development. When a child is characteristically viewed as weak, inept, struggling, or vulnerable, it is probable that ADHD behaviors will be learned more often in different situations.

According to the biological determinist, co-occurring conditions with ADHD are a consequence of genetics. ADHD either causes additional functional problems, or problems in the diagnosed population multiply because people pair with others having similar educational backgrounds. Since many of these individuals will have functional impairments that limit academic advancement (just like ADHD), the diagnosed population is increasingly inundated with correlated problems. For instance, when there are co-occurrences between ADHD and learning problems (e.g., simple language ability, visual-spatial-constructional skills), they are understood as distinct conditions that co-occur due to selective mating (Barkley, 2000).

But we think that various co-occurring problems simply increase the probability that ADHD behaviors will be learned. When individuals show the problems that correlate with ADHD, social exchanges are altered such that the development of these skills is made significantly more arduous. Time spent with the struggling child would otherwise be intent on the shaping of autonomous functioning, if those problems were absent.

We think that ADHD behavior is likely to be reinforced when persons function under various adversarial conditions. For example, Leibson et al. (2001) report that persons diagnosed with ADHD also have a 69% increase in asthma. While it has been reported that the side effects of asthma medication do not seem to contribute to behavior problems (Stein et al., 1996), there have been noted effects (Barkley and Edwards, 2006); moreover, there could be a greater likelihood of learning ADHD behaviors if a child has asthma.

A biological determinist could argue that having asthma may be a sign of a delayed body, however, it is also possible to put forward the argument that similar to all other ADHD correlated problems (including having a depressed or single mother), ADHD behaviors may be conditioned more frequently and severely when operating under those conditions. Although we cannot be definitive about the correlation between asthma and ADHD, we can speculate that an asthmatic condition would certainly increase patterns of over-protection of the child, which could foment his resentment at being confined. Self-sufficiency and independence are also invariably impeded whenever there is enormous concern about a child's health and safety.

Particular problems such as asthma, negative infant temperament, learning difficulty, speech delays, fine motor problems, brain injuries, adoption, and depressed mothers, will complicate adaptation to normative practice. Traditionalists have identified a long list of problems and functional impairments that often co-occur with the ADHD diagnosis. Empirical studies note these correlations and suggest that ADHD behavior is concomitant of a bodily problem, but our learning model interprets those finding differently: that ADHD behaviors are *more likely* to be learned when one has functional problems that stifle the opportunity to coordinate with others or meet societal expectations. Since ADHD patterns also occur when there are no bodily troubles or other functional limitations, it remains unverified as to why ADHD causes functional anomalies only in some cases. We can assert that individuals are conditioned to do ADHD patterning, and that it is possible to learn the behaviors, regardless of whether or not a person has other complicating functional difficulties.

Sub-typing

Less than 5% of diagnosed persons have a history of prenatal or postnatal brain injury that probably disrupts their biology and subsequent behavior, but this condition is not relevant for most diagnosed individuals. For that reason alone, it is unreasonable to infer that all diagnosed persons have the same neurobiological condition—*despite that* certain brain injuries may also increase the probability that ADHD patterns will develop. Moreover, because attentional problems (and other functional disruptions) associated with brain injury may not be identical to the condition exhibited by the majority of ADHD diagnosed persons; it is unreasonable to cluster these persons with the majority of cases.

However, empirical studies often amass a heterogeneous group of diagnosed individuals and compare them to controls during the study, and thus differences between groups become evident. But these differences may not capture the patterning and characteristics of many of the individuals within the ADHD aggregate; this is referred to as the problem of *group means and standard deviations*. As noted earlier, due to the standard practice of using group characteristics to characterize ADHD, individuals with varying co-occurring problems are not sub-typed; many important variations may therefore potentially be overlooked. There is the increased risk that the correlated functional limitations ascribed to the group will inadvertently be imposed on each presenting individual—who may in fact not show the group average traits.

Given this potential problem, it would be reasonable to segregate individuals receiving diagnosis into various subgroups and begin to accumulate specific data. For example, while those with clear biological impairments (due to injury) might show problems with perseverance, concentration, and anticipation, etc., their behavior might differ starkly from diagnosed persons without these traumatic histories. The medically compromised group may show difficulties that remain static, regardless of situation—including times when contingencies are altered prior to restorative procedures.

If persons with adverse medical histories show functional problems different from the majority of persons currently receiving an ADHD diagnosis, it is not fruitful to compare them to individuals showing relatively impressive functioning in some situations and circumstances, and risk skewing the overall data by including a minority of extreme cases. Diagnosed persons could be more succinctly stratified to factor out the influences of various co-occurring problems on empirical outcomes instead of being aggregated into very heterogeneous groups.

Another approach is to *only* give the ADHD diagnosis when individuals clearly do not show evidence of physical damage or have histories of biological trauma, and to otherwise deal with this subgroup on its own strengths and weaknesses. Findings pertaining to their attentional responses and other non-normative patterns of functioning can differ markedly between the two groups. Statements about prognosis can also be made in relation to other co-occurring problems that might be present, in that treatment outcomes could correlate with the presence of the other complications.

For instance, Barkley (2000) notes that as many as one in five ADHD males have some indication of pre-natal brain injury, and sometimes ADHD occurs as a result of an event such as Reye's syndrome, near drowning, smoke inhalation, head trauma, central nervous system infection, and cerebral-vascular disease (Barkley and Edwards, 2006). Given these bodily compromising histories, it is worthwhile to investigate the extent to which inattention patterns and mistakes of commission differ from other diagnosed persons without an adverse medical history. If notable differences occur between the groups, it will be unreasonable to characterize both groups as having similar conditions, disruptions, or delays.

The prediction is that the presence of brain injury, intellectual limitation, and other pervasive developmental delays will correlate with consistent functional difficulty. We also expect that a wider range of situations will be strongly disliked by these individuals, and will therefore more often reinforce ADHD responding. In these cases of dual diagnosis, it could very well be that these individuals *have* particular delays and are also *doing* ADHD as a learned response pattern.

Conversely, we anticipate that diagnosed persons without this adverse medical comorbidity will exhibit ADHD responding in a more circumscribed range of contexts and situations, and show greater variation in their patterns of functional competency. Distinguishing situational influences on the frequency rates of ADHD responding for these individuals will also be crucial when deciding on intervention. Situational influences could indeed be quite different from one diagnosed person to the next, and identifying them will help us design effective shaping procedures.

Many of these otherwise unimpaired diagnosed persons can show acceptable organization of behavior and typical kinds of achievements without extra inducements or the externalization of parameters. They may show more age-consistent persistence, working memory, and significantly lower error rates in certain situations. Often there will be uninterrupted task persistence and significantly fewer problems with what traditionalists call interference control. All of these competencies could of course contrast markedly with behavior at other times, especially while in school, or when instructed by parents to complete particular tasks.

By studying ADHD from this alternative vantage point, we can develop a differentiated system of classifying diagnosed persons. Some might show greater shifts in functioning when responding to different settings and circumstances, while others will not. However, when we consistently factor out co-occurring problems, we will better understand how other functional disruptions influence the accumulating data pertaining to the ADHD diagnosis.

We can also sub-type diagnosed persons in terms of their frequent psychosocial interactive patterns, in that diagnosed persons vary extensively in these patterns, despite all qualifying for the DSM-IV-TR behavioral criteria. For example, some diagnosed children frequently do silly and rambunctious behaviors, meaning that they are loud and disruptive and thus monopolizing the social agenda. Others most often do ADHD in the context of reducing exposure to failure and negative evaluation. A third group does ADHD more frequently in response to the usurping of discretionary authority, while a fourth group instigates others to rescue them from discomfort at the first sign of difficulty. While a diagnosed child might do one or another of these patterns to some degree, we claim that differences in psychosocial patterns make these children more dissimilar than similar, even though it is now customary to label and cluster them into the same neural biological category.

There has been some interest and discussion about sub-typing the diagnosed group, but such discussions have occurred in relation to biological rationale. For example, Hunt et al. (1991) have outlined several types of ADHD, claiming that each type represents a different biological anomaly and/or neurotransmitter problem. Similarly, Barkley (1998d) has discussed sub-typing diagnosed children in relation to whether they show internalizing symptoms such as anxiety and depression, because these individuals have been less responsive to stimulant medication. Much like the recommendation to differentiate output ADHD from input ADD, it has been advised that sub-typing be based on biological criteria.

In contrast, our alternative approach recommends identifying diagnosed persons in relation to changes in functioning with context and circumstance, other complicating problems, or in relation to frequent psychosocial interaction patterns. We predict that this approach will identify crucial differences between diagnosed persons, help define presenting problems, and assist in designing individualized interventions for many diagnosed persons who are currently aggregated into one heterogeneous group. We expect many diagnosed individuals to show wide variations in the frequency and severity of their diagnostic responding and competencies as they encounter different contexts and situations, particularly when we exclude those with functionally-impairing biological trauma or other complications that impact on success.

Distinguishing ADHD and Oppositional Behaviors

Given the data accumulated thus far, individuals might do ADHD behaviors and never learn oppositional behaviors, because relationships do not always become acrimonious when ADHD behaviors are initially conditioned. Similarly, individuals might learn to protest and argue more vehemently when pugnacious responses are reinforced, but those social patterns can be shaped even if the more immature ADHD responding has not previously occurred.

We notice that the ADHD aggregate of behaviors subsumes a relatively large set of heterogeneous actions, especially when compared to other disruptive patterns such as *oppositional responses* that occur when individuals are rancorous, disrespectful, argumentative, and angry with each other. The contingencies of reinforcement that shape and maintain oppositional behaviors—compared to the diverse set of behaviors encompassed within the ADHD category—are often easier to identify and alter. Not surprisingly, analyses indicate that it has often been easier to change oppositional patterning during short-term psychotherapeutic intervention (Barkley, 2000).

Different from oppositional/defiant responses, ADHD behaviors are generally repeated more often, and are typically exceedingly difficult to extinguish. Practitioners report that it is easier to identify oppositional social patterning and help people resolve their animosity with others in reasonable ways over shorter term psychotherapeutic intervention. Interestingly, the earlier occurring ADHD responding seems to be reinforced in subtle and insidious ways, and psychological interventions have thus far rarely produced significant results.

While recent studies show that children with difficult behavior (including ADHD) can benefit from social skills training (Pfiffner, Barkley, and DuPaul, 2006), this intervention has not yet shown the benefit impacts more often associated with medication and stringent control over the diagnosed person. Although these results are not surprising, in that effective skill training would have to be performed over fairly long periods of time, and be tailored to address specific learning issues of each diagnosed person. Nuance and detail of communication exchanges are fundamental in any psychotherapeutic investigation: What is said, tone of voice, what is *not* said, facial expressions, slight laughter, and nonverbal gestures and communications all relate to the reinforcement of certain ADHD actions. Compared to helping individuals find solutions to specific problems that occur in very limited angry situations, we anticipate that (short-term) psychotherapeutic intervention will often result in fewer benefits or changes.

There are other parameters that distinguish ADHD and oppositional patterns. Defiant behavior generally provokes confrontation with others and seems to establish a belligerent version of discretionary authority. In contrast, ADHD behaviors provoke concerns about safety, competency, and appropriate behavior from concerned others. Sometimes after doing an ADHD action the child looks around to see if others are watching, but defiant behaviors provoke conflict and power struggles. ADHD behaviors often elicit distress, annoyance, embarrassment, concern, and apprehension.

Oppositional Defiant Disorder (ODD) behavior is domineering and combative; it often prevents others from obstructing, because anger can be very intimidating to most people. In contrast, ADHD responses seem to be indirect ways to rebel against social expectations. The pattern of responding permits individuals to avoid the adverse consequences of participating, trying and failing, and provokes the involvement of others in order to stop their perceived ineptitude, time squandering, immature infringements, or carelessness. Often it is helpful to encourage diagnosed persons to express assertiveness when discomfort seems apparent with the requirements being imposed—in contrast to the usual message to tame forceful oppositional patterning.

Rather than quarrel and dispute, ADHD children usually behave recklessly; they side-step requirements, show ineffectuality, or dominate social settings by being loud, extreme, or intrusive. ADHD children frequently elicit consternation, worry, aggravation, and irritability, but oppositional/defiant behaviors comprise bullying, which quickly escalates to arguing and fighting. Both patterns certainly provoke concern and relate to a failure to compromise, but ADHD behaviors most often seem to arouse protectiveness and assistance in others.

While oppositional/defiant behaviors are apparently reinforced in relation to dominating others and enforcing independence in a hostile and cantankerous way, ADHD diagnostic responding can be burdensome. They are typically rambunctious, amplified, immature, provocative, silly, or disconnected. Individuals qualifying for ADHD diagnosis are described as intrusive, flamboyant, inconsiderate, or impudent. They may be disruptive and exasperating, but they are less often considered to be mean or nasty.

The ADHD patterning is not only reinforced under a broad array of sometimes very subtle conditions, but as stressed here, is also more likely to be learned when the child experiences a functional problem that significantly impedes adaptation. When those situations occur, it seems that the child's opportunity to be acculturated in a typical fashion becomes markedly reduced, and success rates for these children when dealing with the outside world are likely to be lower and erratic. Psychological intervention may do little to alter that fact. For those reasons, positive treatment effects for the ADHD group might better correlate with the kind and/or degree of complications that are evident rather than be related to the problematic contention that ADHD behaviors are biological and immutable.

In our view, both patterns may be characterized as reinforced descriptions of particular *atypical* ways of responding. Both seem to occur frequently in relation to certain situations (with ADHD occurring prior to the defiant pattern) in the case where one person gets conditioned to do both behavioral sets. While those diagnosed as ADHD respond rapidly when it is preferable to be careful and considerate, and/or show non-participatory behaviors when others want involvement, the oppositional/defiant child will be saying "no" to expectations more explicitly. Despite that the forms of transgressions differ, we do not presume that one set of behaviors is biologically determined, and the other, more argumentative, set of behaviors is learned.

Although many children respond with ADHD-like patterns prior to age three, it is often not possible to accurately identify children as qualifying for the DSM-IV-TR diagnosis until age three to four. Clearly, many children normally do ADHD-related behaviors until more social training takes place. By the age of five to seven, some diagnosed children also learn to be more hostile and emphatic when conflicts of interest arise (Barkley, 2000); these children are routinely exposed to argumentativeness, inconsistent training, and volatility during interpersonal exchanges. This group of children is vulnerable to behaviors that qualify them for an ODD diagnosis (in addition to ADHD).

However, one must understand that individuals who do ADHD do not always learn oppositional/defiant responding. Moreover, traditional practitioners have asserted that learning oppositional behaviors rather than the presence of ADHD accounts for most turbulence in family relationships (Barkley, 1998d). One could say that once oppositional and defiant behaviors are conditioned, the diagnosed person does ADHD patterning within some contexts and situations and more hostile disobedient behaviors during other times.

Significantly, it has been found that when children do ADHD responding and then oppositional/defiant behavior, it is increasingly difficult to stop them from either pattern. For example, Barkley (2000) reports that "incurable" ADHD has been found to correlate with "persistent" oppositional/defiant behaviors when the two behavioral patterns co-occur. Translated into current vernacular, if a child is initially invasive and non-contributive, it is increasingly difficult to extinguish those patterns if the child has also learned to respond in intimidating ways. When angry extremes are constantly reinforced, children will also tend towards extreme forms of anti-social behaviors.

Barkley (1998d; 2000) also notes another important relationship between ADHD and ODD. He points out that if individuals show oppositional behavior only at a very early age, approximately half will cease after several years. In contrast, if individuals show *persistent* oppositional/defiant behavior, they are also likely to show a history of ADHD behavior prior to the unrelenting oppositional/defiant patterning. This correlation escalates until the child reaches the age of eight to 10, when up to 85% of all individuals presenting with ODD will also show a behavioral history consistent with ADHD. This data is quoted to support the view that underlying neurological ADHD is making it more difficult to stop oppositional behaviors.

However, in response to those data, it is not surprising that individuals showing either patterning in a less complex form will show improvement over time. The same positive outcomes that occur with uncomplicated oppositional behaviors also occur for ADHD individuals who have mild problems and no other disruptions. For example, Barkley (2000) indicates that even when taken as a conglomerate, approximately 10% of ADHD individuals outgrow their condition by adolescence with another 10% showing only borderline problems by the teenage years, despite whether or not they have received medical intervention.

Conversely, when ADHD *and* oppositional/defiant behaviors are evident for extended periods of time, one could reasonably assume that socialization has been hindered for many years, and that participants (for numerous reasons) are not finding effective solutions to promote normative functioning and positive interpersonal exchange. The fact that some children increase defiant behaviors in addition to ADHD could be interpreted to mean that these dually-diagnosed persons are learning multiple ways to operate under adverse conditions. Angry behaviors are now being reinforced along with the ADHD behaviors conditioned earlier.

We can surmise that when children show ADHD behavior at a very early age, positive change is more probable if no other functional problems are evident, and when other disruptive interpersonal patterning can be prevented. Although when ADHD emerges in early development and the child is also reinforced to be angry and resistive, it is increasingly difficult for these children to learn acceptable patterning as time passes.

We observe that the co-occurrence of both ADHD and oppositional/defiant behaviors is likely to occur in families with limited interpersonal resources for solving problems in mutually-beneficial ways; a shift from doing only ADHD behavior to hostile behavior indicates that social training has broken down. The disappointing outcomes and escalating problems of some diagnosed persons relates to limitations of families, complexity of presenting problems, and the tendency for ADHD actions to be reinforced by those involved. Psychotherapeutic intervention relies extensively on family participation, and success rates are inextricably tied to the resources of those individuals. If ineffectiveness persists, it is not surprising that psychologically-based interventions fail, and the child's patterning worsens over time.

Although if one considers the group of children showing only later onset oppositional/defiant behavior, and not the earlier ADHD patterning, it generally seems that these children have responded more favorably to the psychotherapy being offered (Barkley, 2000). When compared to the reported outcomes for those diagnosed as ADHD, the later onset oppositional problems can be ameliorated more effectively with psychologically-based intervention. Traditionalists are not surprised by these findings, as they see ADHD as genetically caused, and the more angry behaviors as having a greater correspondence with social parameters.

However, in contrast to that interpretation, we might observe that treatment for later onset oppositional/defiant behavior is simply easier to implement effectively, in that non-normative patterning has been occurring over less time. The later onset oppositional child may have been functioning reasonably well prior to the current acrimony that brought the family to treatment, and it could be easier for everyone involved to relearn acceptable behavioral patterns rather than shape acceptable responding for the very first time. For those children just beginning to show oppositional/defiant behaviors later in childhood, it may be the case that those behaviors have not yet generalized as extensively as the ADHD responding. The oppositional behaviors may also be easier to extinguish in comparison to ADHD responding, because oppositional behaviors are circumscribed and reinforced *only* during abbreviated time frames and with fewer people. With the exception of angry conflicts that intermittently flare up, many of the later onset oppositional/defiant children may very well be functioning acceptably with others on a daily basis.

If one's only problem is a high frequency of hostility in response to conditions of disagreement, disappointment, or limitation relatively late in childhood, it is not surprising that problems can be resolved relatively quickly when compared to other disruptive patterns that might exhibit in a diverse range of situations, and begin earlier in development. Many of the later onset oppositional/defiant children may show acceptable responding when not inordinately angry, and the frequent occurrence of acceptable responses makes it easier to facilitate change during psychotherapeutic intervention. Once the acrimony has dissipated, typical psychosocial patterning can resume. The doggedness of ADHD patterning can imply that most complex behavioral patterns learned early in life are exceedingly difficult to solve, especially during short-term interventions. In pursuit of help for these children, we can investigate whether non-diagnosed persons are *any better* than diagnosed children at altering highly repetitious patterns of behaviors they have learned in early childhood.

In any case, the psychosocial patterns for ADHD and ODD diagnoses are clearly very different, and each condition can be reinforced separately or together. While ADHD includes many different kinds of behaviors that may be reinforced very early in development such as over reactivity when not receiving accommodation, and/or reliance on others to complete chores and maintain schedules, oppositional behaviors seem to be conditioned when social exchange includes angry conflicts and inconsistencies that reinforce resistive responses. Despite that many toddlers show some oppositional behavior, the type of behavior in the diagnostic category ODD occurs more frequently in later childhood when erratic and angry patterns of training eventually compel malicious kinds of exchanges in order to establish discretionary control.

Despite these differences, both ADHD and oppositional/defiant behaviors can be understood as variant learned patterns of behavior. While oppositional/ defiant behaviors are overtly angry, ADHD behaviors may produce disengagement, increase attention and concern, disrupt the pacing of social exchange, or create havoc that prevents others from imposing an agenda. ADHD behaviors are typically reinforced very early in development (sometimes without acrimony), and oppositional/defiant behaviors will be reinforced (with or without ADHD) for as long as the social matrix strengthens the overtly angry interpersonal behaviors.

While ADHD is likely to be conditioned when children have problems that hinder their ability to meet age expected norms (developmental delay, cognitive problems, etc.), oppositional behaviors are likely to be learned when children reside in families where hostility, diminished monitoring, exposure to deviant peers, inconsistent training, and other social difficulties are present (Szatmari, Boyle, and Offord, 1989; Hinshaw and Lee, 2003). It is now being reported that ODD also reveals a genetic contribution that may overlap with and occur independently from ADHD (Nadder et al., 2002), but oppositional patterns are more probable when one lives in a largely negative environment.

Additionally, when discussing relationships between the two diagnostic categories, Silberg et al. (1996) emphasize that while early ADHD increases the risk of ODD, the reverse has not been found to occur to a marked extent. Traditionalists interpret these findings as supportive of the view that social conflict does not cause ADHD. However, in response, one might also claim that it is not surprising that individuals who might have behaved typically in early childhood do not *revert* to patterns of behavior characteristic of younger children. If immature and provocative behaviors were not reinforced during the child's early life, this patterning is highly unlikely to be reinforced after combative, confrontational, and domineering social patterning has already been shaped.

Hence, if we sample children diagnosed as ADHD, one will often find that they were doing those behaviors prior to behavior that would have qualified them for a diagnosis of ODD. Children intent on establishing ascendancy are not likely to revert to infantile, insecure patterning, which usually evokes concern, consternation, and rescuing from others. Conversely, if the child persists in an immature, less accommodating pattern, under conditions of increased social discord and inconsistency of training, there is the increased probability that hostile and defiant behaviors will be learned as the child develops and becomes powerful.

An escalation of hostility and defiance might not only occur because children often become insistent and resourceful as they age, but also to the extent that parents become disgruntled when the child does not conform or contribute in ways consistent with others the same age. ADHD responding becomes increasingly unacceptable as others expect more from that individual. Expressing a behavioral pattern that is a caricature of immaturity has worsening consequences as the individual grows older. Acrimony develops when older children do not assume responsibility and continue to burden the resources of the family. In contrast to infancy when others accept that they must do all of the adjusting, ADHD responding becomes increasingly problematic when there is failure to develop adequate self-reliance. Family members and friends may also be convinced that these children actually know better, and thus become less tolerant of the child's lack of consideration and contribution. For these reasons, conflict will likely follow, but not precede, ADHD patterning.

However, while many highly active children under age three might not be characterized as overtly hostile, and/or meet the full criteria of ODD, it is not reasonable to claim that their very active behavioral pattern is solely neurological hyperactivity devoid of problems of compliance. Hyperactive behaviors often pertain to activity which has been forbidden and increase when parents become critical. We argue that highly active children are often as defiant as the older children who are overtly verbally hostile, even though very young highly active children are not generally characterized as insolent or negativistic, despite frequently testing or ignoring limits, and causing deep dismay for parents.

Additionally, ODD behavior may precede or co-occur with ADHD patterning more than traditional data presently indicate. Parents might retrospectively describe their toddler as ADHD rather than oppositional, but the descriptor depends on how the parent has interpreted and formulated the child's actions. The data now being generated largely depends on the extent to which parents discriminate the child's behaviors as consistent with limit testing or disobedience, compared to parents' characterizing the behavior as hyperactive, relentless or inattentive, which are ADHD rather than oppositional descriptors.

Nevertheless, the relationship between ADHD and oppositional behavior is similar to that which occurs with most other ADHD comorbid conditions. For example, Bipolar I Disorder (Spencer et al., 2000), Post-traumatic Stress Disorder (Weinstein, Steffelbach, and Biaggio (2000), tic disorders (Gadow, Nolan,

Sprafkin, and Schwartz, 2002), Autistic Spectrum Disorders (Goldstein and Schwebach, 2004), Tourette's Syndrome (Comings, 2000), and low birth weight (Mick, Biederman, Faraone, Sayer, and Kleinman, 2002) all seem to relate to ADHD in much the same way: ADHD does not cause those disorders, but if one samples people with those problems, a larger than expected number also learns to respond with ADHD patterns.

ADHD and Negative Infant Temperament

One category, however, that traditionalists use to entrench their biological determinist argument is that of temperament. Barkley (1998f) reports that early negative infant temperament correlates with an ADHD diagnosis as a sign of limited self-control or genetic inevitability playing out. Infants who seem overly demanding, and who respond with excessive intensity are also likely to qualify for a diagnosis of ADHD when compared to normal children or other clinical control groups (Barkley, DuPaul, and McMurray, 1990; Hartsough and Lambert, 1985). Negative temperament is seen as a possible developmental precursor to ADHD.

Barkley (1998f) describes temperament as an early and dogged personality characteristic that pertains to an infant's level of activity, intensity of responding, persistence of action, attention span, and ease with which infant can be consoled. The category is used to describe the infant's typical mood such as whether the baby is demanding, irritable, easily angered, and overly emotional. Temperament includes statements about a baby's adaptability to environmental change, and the extent to which he or she might show regulated sleeping, waking, eating, and elimination patterns. In so far as temperament is understood as unlearned responding and correlates with a later ADHD diagnosis, from this perspective we can see that biological determinist views are easily reinforced.

Conversely, we allow that negative infant temperament may indeed increase the probability of atypical social patterning and learning. Early negative temperamental responses are likely to influence possibilities for socialization, and social interaction is likely to be affected by negative forms of attention and criticism from others who become stressed by the patterning. More avoidance behaviors from caretakers are also likely to occur, and in some cases, more accommodating to prevent outbursts or to quickly stop their behavior. Consistent with this view is the DSM IV-TR notation that negative temperament also correlates with oppositional/defiant behaviors.

However, we suggest that negative infant temperament is not caused by embryonic ADHD, but that these early response patterns influence how an individual coordinates with others and develops language and intimacy. Individuals doing numerous different difficult behaviors very early will often put inordinate demands on others to adjust to their troublesome response patterns. Long-standing problems are not inevitable (depending on other events), but normative adjustment will be more difficult under these problematical conditions. So it is not unusual that a high percentage of infants with negative temperaments learn atypical behavior, which includes learning ADHD and oppositional responses. Negative temperament infants will initially learn that others will help them settle down, and/or show disappointment with their behaviors, thus setting the socially disrupted patterning in motion.

In a learning perspective, the child's initial temperament is the catalyst for this social patterning. Investigators have reported that mothers not only spend less time with difficult infants, but are also less responsive to them. These mothers have indicated that they find it harder to cope with such babies, and feel less satisfied as mothers (Campbell, 1979; Hagekull and Bhlin, 1990; Maccoby, Snow, and Jacklin, 1984; van den Boom and Hoeksma, 1993).

That a demanding temperament in infancy or a developmentally delayed child correlates with ADHD patterning is therefore not surprising, since the socializing process between parent and child is taxing starting at a very young age. The child is difficult to please and socialize, and parents will also go to great lengths to soothe and facilitate for the child in order to grapple with the negativity. Moreover, other parents will withdraw until problems escalate; the probability then is that over reacting will continue, as that patterning is how the child produces environmental change. In this view, a nascent self-regulatory delay is not the cause of such problems; we hold that intrusiveness, insecurity, impatience, and reliance can be profoundly reinforced, especially when negative temperament is present.

But again, this pattern is not a necessary condition for ADHD behavior to evolve, because ADHD patterning can be learned even without that starting point; negative infant temperament simply increases the probability that ADHD behaviors will be learned. It is not inevitable or predestined that ADHD will occur when individuals show various early occurring problems. Not all "demanding" babies show ADHD years later, even though sometimes early difficulties increase accommodation problems, and correlate with obstacles to achieve mutuality and self-sufficiency. When studying this issue further, it might be interesting to determine what is different about those difficult babies who do *not* subsequently show ADHD behaviors. When conducting such investigations, we also must define negative temperament by an independent measure other than parental self-report, in that what is demanding and negative for some parents is not as much of a problem for others (i.e., goodness of fit).

For instance, some research shows that the more negative, active or inhibited infants often remain that way over time (Broberg, Lamb, and Hwang; 1990, Kagan and Snidman, 1991; Kochanska and Radke-Yarrow, 1992; Stifter and Fox, 1990; Wasserman et al., 1990). However, other studies show that negative infant characteristics shift frequently when mothers show high self-esteem, are happily married, or when they care for their babies with sensitivity, and remain negative when their fathers lack empathy and are uninvolved (Belsky, Fish, and Isabella, 1991). While the child's patterns of competency will most certainly influence events, patterns of stability in the home will significantly affect situations over time as well (Weiss and Hechtman, 1993).

Depending on "goodness of fit," including who does the training, and the safety of the environment, etc., there will be effects on the child's development. However, since socially difficult behaviors are a mismatch for situations in which conformity and calm behavior are required (e.g., classroom functioning), problems are likely to arise there due to differences between the child's typical pattern and situational demands, even with tolerant and adept caretakers and teachers.

Although adverse social behaviors (including ADHD) might be learned relative to what happens after negative infant behaviors become evident, it is unreasonable to posit that later maladjustment is inevitable. In other words, these outcomes are not predestined to sequence in that fashion. In fact, there is the greater likelihood that the early occurring negative pattern can be shifted if the psychosocial environment remains positive (as indicated by the empirical findings noted above).

ADHD and Atypical Motor Behavior

Motor coordination delays have also been implicated in the eventual development of ADHD. Kadesjo and Gillberg (2001) found that 47% of diagnosed children meet DSM-IV-TR criteria for Developmental Coordination Disorder, and Hartsough and Lambert (1985) note a slight delay in the onset of crawling within the diagnosed population. For traditionalists, these kinds of correlations are viewed as support that ADHD is caused by a delayed biological substrate. Coordination difficulties are seen as another example of an underlying self-control problem, despite that only half of the children with these problems qualify for the DSM-IV-TR behavioral criteria.

However, similar to the argument put forth for negative infant temperament, data pertaining to motor behaviors and ADHD can also be integrated into a learning paradigm. For example, children showing coordination difficulties or delayed crawling frequently elicit assistance from important others. The reinforced patterning could include a greater probability of learning that functioning more independently often results in struggle and failure. Many of these children learn to say "I can't," and complain about expectations more than a normative sample. Over-reliance on others evolves in contrast to self-reliant patterning when these delays are evident.

Since child and parent may also be responding to the higher probability of accidents, failure and dependency, the availability of the parent is crucial. These children learn that contact and accommodation from others is necessary for comfort and security, and prolonged immaturity and perceived ineffectuality by both child and parent is the frequent result of this social patterning. Therefore, it is not surprising that behaviors consistent with diagnostic patterning persist and repeat with a significant proportion of individuals who show early coordination difficulty.

Moreover, to the extent that deficits in motor skills will lower a child's status with peers, coordination problems can also significantly disrupt a child's social adjustment. The child might not be invited to play, and as a response, learn to avoid a variety of activities in order to maintain dignity; or the child could learn how to intrude and behave imprudently in response to social exclusion. Coordination problems can displace a child, impede further motoric development, and increase non-participatory and disruptive behaviors included in the ADHD diagnosis.

The effect that motoric action has on physical health and psychosocial patterning can be quite dramatic as well. For example, Biringen et al. (1991) indicate that as soon as babies begin to walk, their mothers say "no" more often than when their babies were crawling. Matheny (1992) reports that highly active and unpredictable babies will suffer from more accidental injuries between ages two and three. Goldsmith (1978) has noted that highly active low IQ scoring babies seem to impede their own early cognitive development in that they are less focused and persistent; their activity patterns interfere with opportunities to learn. These infants often respond to objects for shorter periods, and do not as frequently pursue objects which are not readily available.

Not surprisingly, early high activity levels, a short attention span, and demanding and intense emotional responses all correlate with a subsequent ADHD diagnosis (Nigg, Goldsmith, and Sachek, 2004). When these unusual response patterns are evident during infancy, the child is likely struggle into the preschool years (Campbell, 1990; McInerny and Chamberlin, 1978; Palfrey et al., 1985).

On average, when motoric activity and response intensity are out of the ordinary, or when children are thought to be in jeopardy, interaction patterns will frequently manifest as having to limit, contain, help, or protect the child. Those social patterns will increase the probability that the child will learn ADHD behaviors. When parents must monitor excessively in order to safeguard, compared to what is usually required with children showing calmer behavior, there will be learning consequences for these children.

While the only significant difference between these children and others during early functioning may be greater vigor or lack of coordination, psychosocial patterning will evolve markedly differently. The child will learn to be more insecure about competency, become accustomed to an inordinate amount of attention, and associate interactions with others with either being saved, restricted, or shunted. These learning patterns can increase the probability of qualifying for an ADHD diagnosis. However, Gandour (1989) notes that highly active toddlers may benefit from a great deal of stimulation. This can substantially reduce their activity levels and patterns of motoric exploration. We notice that a very different progression of events can occur if different socialization practices are implemented.

Incidentally, because boys are generally more motoric and less verbal compared to girls, it is not surprising that ADHD correlates mostly with males. The variations in social patterning occurring when children are unusually motoric (e.g., more danger, less opportunity for language exchange, etc.) increase troublesome social patterning, and result in the likelihood that more males will learn ADHD behaviors. If a child (typically a boy) moves and explores a great deal, it is exceedingly difficult to protect and monitor that child for his own safety. Although when any child seems at risk (e.g., poor coordination, accident prone, asthma), parents usually offer greater assistance, orient themselves as protectors, attend to their child more vigilantly, or accommodate more than normal.

Because parents are required to impede and constrain the atypically motoric child, social difficulties begin to occur; unusually motoric children learn how to prevent parents from interfering. If parents become critical or frustrated while responding to problems associated with high activity, children could react negatively, learn that doing specific motoric behaviors can effectively elicit intense reactions, and learn not to respond to the parent's directives to stop.

The probability that the child's initiatives will exceed the parent's limits increases when a child is atypically motoric, and the child is also less likely to learn cooperative behaviors. Instead of responding to a helpful or protective parent, these children might respond toward the parent as if an opponent: one who denies, criticizes, and is oppressive. When greater numbers of negative interactions occur, many children react as if they are disliked rather than safeguarded. The child might also repeat the behaviors in retaliation when parents are vehement or critical. Under these circumstances, the child is likely to be reinforced to *not* respond positively to parental instruction. Rates of ADHD-like patterns will increase rather than lower, in that their behavior reduces the ability for others to impose an unwanted agenda.

Generally, diagnostic responding is probable under distressful socialization conditions. The degree and quality of activity expressed by the infant/toddler (and other temperamental characteristics and patterns of initial responding) can profoundly influence how psychosocial patterns are learned. An individual who is restless, intense, and fidgety presents a unique set of problems for socialization compared to the contented infant/toddler. Many initially negative responders are ultimately diagnosed as ADHD, *especially* if parenting is negative (Belsky, Hsieh, and Crnic, 1998). However, we emphasize that even agile and (very healthy) children can be diagnosed as ADHD.

Delays in the Finer Skills

Within a very different set of presumptions ADHD patterning is likely to be conditioned when we observe the difficulty for an individual to be reinforced by normative practice or to develop age-consistent patterns of cooperation. As Barkley has pointed out (1998f), educated mothers, intellectually competent and healthier infants, and improved language skills and family stability help guard against the advance of ADHD and its persistence during preschool years. Conversely, negative interactions between a parent and child correlates with tenacious diagnostic patterning (Campbell, 1987).

When examining the data, we are not surprised that language skill and family stability enable self-reliance and mutually-acceptable patterning to be realized. Social integration is enjoyable when one can articulate verbally. In addition, when children have problems with language encoding, motoric activity (including crying and whining) can become the primary way to establish social contact or increase the probability that others will accommodate them. In those circumstances, why is it surprising that hyperactivity and over reactivity become probable?

Children with encoding problems cannot easily convey to others information that they do understand. Helpers thus have difficulty determining what they were able to comprehend, and which alternatives they will accept. Parents will either frequently pardon the child due to this ambiguity, or else work very hard to determine the child's needs, and, more often than not, provide the child with the required solution. Such accommodations reinforce ADHD responses including a pattern of under-utilizing personal resources (executive functioning).

Moreover, when trying to encourage language development, some parents will also permit the child to determine the content of verbal exchanges more than they would typically allow. In some scenarios, parents might be less inclined to steer their child towards conformity to their agenda, or less frequently emphasize that the child take turns during verbal exchanges. Such over-accommodations truncate the learning of typical interaction patterns, which would invariably help the child function acceptably and be better prepared to function in school. Additionally, if a child has trouble speaking in public, he or she is also likely to have problems when required to express non-vocal verbal behaviors when those responses are helpful during problem solving. Clearly, individuals with less expressive language development have greater difficulty with tasks that would be easily solved if there was linguistic competence.

Given the social patterns that often evolve with speech-delayed children; we are not surprised when a greater proportion of these children eventually learn unacceptable patterns of social behavior such as ADHD. Although depending on myriad events (including the behavior of primary caretakers), there will be a wide variety of psychosocial outcomes. In the end, some problematic speech-delayed children will learn ADHD behaviors while many others will not.

But rather than take this position, traditionalists choose to interpret problems that correlate with diagnosis as biological determinism at work. For instance, when fine motor and language fluency problems are seen within the diagnosed population, Barkley (2000) identifies such problems as "inability" to self-control. He notes that 60% of diagnosed children show problems with handwriting, which Sleator and Pelham (1986) and Marcotte and Stern (1997) describe as immature. Similarly, others emphasize that diagnosed children often show difficulties with drawing (Hoy et al., 1978; McGee et al., 1992), and have trouble organizing speech and coherent dialogue, especially during story retelling (Tannock and Schachar, 1996).

Barkley (1998c) interprets all of these problems as indicators that the biological underpinning of diagnosed persons interferes with the ability for quick and intricate fine motor sequences. Although it is well known that the development of less normative fine motor and language fluency responses is indeed influenced by learning, once a person is diagnosed with ADHD, competence problems are invariably understood as consequences of a fixed neural biological condition.

However, even though significant numbers of diagnosed children lag behind their peers in some aspects of functioning, we simply do not know how much change in each of these competencies is possible through the introduction of new learning. A common example is the influence of situation and circumstance on fine motor and language behaviors evident when people show a deterioration of language and motoric functioning when reporting self-consciousness while talking, dancing, or playing group sports. Both fine and gross motor behaviors can be significantly influenced by context, situation, and circumstance in obvious and subtle ways; psychology may therefore be very important.

Because learning is influential in the development of finer and intricate skills, it seems prudent to investigate patterns of conditioning and provide opportunities to practice skills before we conclude that a permanent delay in neurobiology will always impede. For example, some studies indicate that diagnosed adults are not showing evidence of fluency problems (Kovner et al., 1997) unless larger samples are used (Johnson et al., 2001), so we cannot argue that incipient ADHD prohibits competency in an appreciable way.

The possibility remains that the fine motor and encoding difficulties sometimes evident in the diagnosed population are significantly influenced by conditioning. Roizen et al. (1994) argue that self-help skills such as buttoning and zipping are the hallmarks of ADHD neurological delay, but even individuals with missing fingers or other deformities learn to do what diagnosed children purportedly cannot do because of ADHD.

For example, rather than being shaped to accurately attend to detail and complete tasks with increased agility, some diagnosed children may continue to show clumsiness, imprecision and irregular sequencing, in that those behaviors are being reinforced in ways not immediately identifiable by participants. Some might respond as if the child is cute when blundering, and others might offer to "rescue" too rapidly. Some parents might be more effective than others in shaping particular competencies, even when children initially show many problems when learning intricate skills.

A parent's characterization of the problem can also affect how competency is built; parents who assume that their child cannot succeed will intervene very differently from parents who presume that their child can eventually learn to become agile by struggling and receiving only enough help to prevent the stagnation of progress. For example, if family members rush to assist, and frequently zip a child's coat without promoting that skill development, the child will not, over the long-run, master the art of how to use a zipper.

Incidentally, and in contrast to biological reductionism, the discipline of Graphology, as described by Jacoby (1948), also posits a relationship between fine motor sequencing movements and the way a person patterns during the lifetime. Similarly, Gilbert (1978) follows the well-accepted practice of using visual spatial tests such as the Bender Gestalt and/or Human Figure Drawings to make predictive statements about frequency rates of particular emotional responses and interpersonal behaviors. To the extent that these approaches help us make reliable predictions about behavior, Barkley and Edwards (2006) report that diagnosed children are likely to exhibit problems with sloppy handwriting, or react carelessly to tasks, tells us nothing about the extent to which biology is antecedent and impairing those behaviors, or the extent to which these atypical behaviors are likely to occur when specific conditioning has taken place over time.

Biological determinists might understand fine motor sloppiness in the diagnosed population as a neurological problem, but it is difficult to distinguish cause from consequence when explicating problem behaviors. That is, if one is doing ADHD behavior, one is also less likely to accommodate and practice when responding to assigned tasks. Likewise, if one is having particular difficulty doing fine motor behaviors, it is probable that one will learn ADHD responding as soon as those particular adversities are encountered (i.e., finish quickly, depend on help, give up, and avoid). However, the development of skill competency will be impeded whenever the child learns to rush, delay, or evade requirements that have become associated with difficulty, negative evaluation, and failure.

For example, a significant number of diagnosed children become defensive when others impose instructional assistance, such as teaching strategies to help them stay within the lines, or exercises to help them move a pencil with greater agility across a page, and so on. Many such children become disrupted if directed, corrected, or scrutinized during instructional exchanges. Rather than practice so that their writing skills improve, they presume futility, rush, or shun requirements. It is as if an invitation to assist is interpreted as an attempt to coerce, belittle, or insinuate incompetence. While there seems to be agreement that significant numbers of diagnosed children show messy handwriting and less dexterity, the issue is how to account for those responses and the continuance of delays.

We can, however, observe that one can have no neurobiological problem whatsoever and still have illegible handwriting; there are many such persons with poor handwriting who are not diagnosed as ADHD. To make matters even worse for biological determinists, some individuals report that their handwriting becomes more illegible the more they write (e.g., doctors' prescriptions, therapy progress notes, etc.), and significant numbers of people with exemplary penmanship are diagnosed with ADHD. Given these distributions, we see that neurological ADHD is not causing poor fine motor skill development, but that problematic fine motor functioning occurs in relation to atypical biological parameters and various psychosocial histories, and both can be altered by changing contingencies of reinforcement.

In this view, problems with writing or coloring do not invariably reduce to statements about delayed neural biology when those patterns are evident within the diagnosed population. For example, some individuals write or color recklessly, because elsewhere their actions rarely conform to limits or parameters. They have learned to frequently respond in non-conventional ways, and overstep boundaries so as not to permit others to impede upon them; such patterns could repeat during coloring.

Other diagnosed persons are reinforced to enact behaviors carelessly, in that this permits the rapid completion of stipulated tasks associated with negativity. Some diagnosed persons also give up quickly, in that those behaviors correlate with extra assistance, and diminish the amount of work that others expect from them. In many ways it is possible for us to account for the poor quality of fine motor skills without ascribing the variability to neurobiology when these behaviors are evident in the context of an ADHD diagnosis.

Also noteworthy is that in a significant number of cases many diagnosed individuals do not form their letters and numbers in the classical way; this type of patterning may also contribute to their writing difficulties. While many of these children might, due to bodily hindrance, have greater difficulty producing the necessary fine motor movements demonstrated by the teacher, a divergent writing pattern may also be related to repetitive behavior associated with imprecisely following instructions of others. Many will expect the system to accommodate to them instead of conforming to it. Diagnosed children who show no apparent fine motor delays will frequently draw lines upward rather than downward, start the letter at the wrong point, or construct letters in idiosyncratic ways wholly different from the teacher's demonstrations.

While reversals and variations are usually regarded as instances of neurological difficulty with self-control that prevent accuracy of imitation, we could also posit that these non-normative handwriting patterns often occur in relation to a non-accommodating, insecure, or avoidant behavioral pattern. The person frequently does not precisely modulate behavior to the bidding of others, in that the individual is conditioned such that others adjust and adapt, and that conformity is associated with negativity (e.g., regret, admission of shortfall, disapproval, neglect, etc.). One might ask whether these individuals are less able to contour their productions to an external model and follow instructions because of neurological ADHD, or are these irregular patterns related to an unreceptive or evasive behavioral pattern. However, if these individuals do not practice handwriting, it is not surprising that they often fall farther behind with each passing year.

Conversely, when activities are iterated consistently, we might observe, for example, that that same "delayed" child who has problems forming letters and numbers has learned to operate a video controller adeptly, or handles collectibles in a careful and confident manner. Fine motor actions *can* be more adroit, and the precision of their imitations can be impressive in certain situations, compared to what is evident during school work, requests to tie shoes, or other assigned tasks.

The importance of investigating whether failures to accurately imitate exhibit in consistent ways, as tacitly implied within a biological determinist account, cannot be overstated. A possible way to tease out a current best-case scenario of what diagnosed persons can do in some situations might be to observe their fine motor behaviors during various self-initiated actions (e.g., when building with blocks, copying movements demonstrated by friends, and when copying the gestures of musicians). The motoric and imitative competencies seen then could be quite discrepant from what we observe during assigned conditions, or when context and circumstance cue immature, insecure, and awkward responses.

If significant differences are found in relation to these parameters, the competent responses indicate that positive results have already been obtained with similar skills in other situations. While this does not mean that neurobiology is not influential or at times delaying, and/or that neurology may impede the rate at which new learning takes place, the implication is that it may be possible to improve the quality of functioning for many diagnosed persons through behavioral conditioning.

We understand that many children have shown problematic functioning during infancy, which seemed unrelated to contingencies of reinforcement, but we must now ask whether their subsequent history of conditioning is facilitating competency or immaturity (and ADHD responding) when they are given opportunities to learn. Since many diagnosed children have initially shown problematic functioning that made age-consistent achievement difficult, it is not surprising that many of these children struggle and remain the focal point of the family as they receive extra help learning important skills. However, if we observe that diagnosed children are *not* being shaped to function in competent ways when given opportunities to do so, our observations of current incompetence will tell us precious little about the child's learning potential over time. We maintain that a history of conditioning influences the development of the "finer skills" when many diagnosed persons show particular kinds of problematic responses. As stated earlier, if we presume that the occurrence of fine motor and intricate language behaviors are predominantly contingent on behavioral shaping, it seems that conditions to reinforce skillful speaking and fine motor movements for many diagnosed persons can be introduced, and become effective over time.

Although if a child, for example, expects failure when pouring a drink, or is fearful of spilling something, her muscles may tense awkwardly. Regardless of whether she expresses a consistent fine-motor delay during intricate movements, the particular response during the pouring task can significantly impede performance and, for all intents and purposes, apparently be a direct result of bodily ineptitude. If the child has *also* learned that awkward movements elicit rapid approach, hyperbole, and assistance from others, those responses could very well be reinforced to the detriment of other movements that would help the child realize achievement.

Moreover, once a child is characterized as a "klutz," all behaviors consistent with that label are increasingly associated with her. The level of expectation will begin to influence the frequency rates of maladroit actions, and the notion of self-fulfilling prophecy comes into effect. As soon as the child receives attention for awkwardness and physical incompetence, she will dwindle in her ability to develop fine or gross motor skills. The more a parent comments on miscues and worries about their occurrence, or preempts clumsiness, the more those behaviors will be emitted. If the child is also interrupted mid-action by an adult in order to prevent a miscue, that particular parental intervention can worsen the situation as well.

In a similar scenario, children who are reinforced to behave in loud or outlandish ways (e.g., making exaggerated motor movements, banging toys) will also have fewer opportunities to learn fine motor behavior. A child who is reinforced to be noisy will elicit concern from others, but will simultaneously reduce the probability of becoming dexterous. Similarly, if a child frequently rushes to be first or acts quickly before other people intervene or obstruct, it is also likely that the child will stumble and fall and break things.

Frequent mishaps will convince others that the child cannot control his movement, but importantly, those behaviors may be getting reinforced. Reckless, boisterous, accident-prone behavior often motivates adults to maintain vigilance when the diagnosed child is nearby. Diagnosed children may do these behaviors in more extreme ways immediately as the parent redirects his attention to something else. But if the situations and circumstances of problematic functioning can be identified, we cannot accept the argument that the origin of immature motor behaviors resides solely in a diminished ability to manage complex action sequences.

Interestingly, a profound way in which social patterning influences fine and gross motor presentation is evident when an individual "comes out of the closet," and begins to be increasingly explicit about, for example, being an effeminate homosexual. When this transformation takes place, verbal patterning, voice tone, posturing and gesturing can change extensively. Body mass may appear to be markedly different, more feminine, compared to previous observations. While nothing has changed biologically, fine and gross motor behaviors can indeed alter when social conditions change.

In many ways the same observation can be applied when evaluating the ineffectual, loud, provocative, and very immature diagnosed child, particularly when pervasive developmental delays are not evident. For many of these children, it is not uncommon to observe their initial awkwardness when they first learn new activities. Although when they function away from an audience or after a number of successes and notoriety for achievement has occurred, they will often show greater adeptness within in a fairly short period of time.

Some diagnosed children also climb stairs like elephants (the louder the better); although when trying to move secretly, or if being heard would be disadvantageous, their movements up stairs will be surprisingly coordinated. When changes occur in relation to circumstance, is it neurology that dictates whether they are clumsy or delicate on their feet? If spills and accidents occur in predictable settings and circumstances (and much less frequently at other times), how well does a biological explanation account for those findings?

ADHD and Delays in Language Encoding

When listing other co-occurring problems with an ADHD diagnosis, Barkley (1998c) also notes that diagnosed children are often quite delayed in developing private speech. In Barkley's view, self-speech permits individuals to formulate questions, privately label, describe, and consider before responding. In the traditional view, it is believed that neurological ADHD impedes private actions from occurring and developing at a normative pace.

Berk (1992) also notes that impulsive children do more task-irrelevant responses and less mature speech as problem difficulty increases. Those observations are seen as further examples of ADHD individuals not doing precursor speech behaviors that would help them solve problems effectively. Barkley (1998c) reports that the immature forms of externalized self-speech are maintained longer by diagnosed individuals; he notes that these speech patterns remain in public form rather than the internalized (mature) form.

It also seems possible, however, to account for the apparent disparities in the self-speech of diagnosed children relative to others by invoking a learning perspective. If their general pattern is to rely on others to facilitate achievement, and work is usually completed in the presence of others, we suspect that the non-vocal forms of self-speech will not be practiced or reinforced as often. Diagnosed children are likely to continue behaving in ways that are more observable and effective in eliciting social responses; they would be less inclined to do quieter self-directed speech or any other behavior correlated with autonomous functioning. Despite the speech difficulties associated with that pattern, this does not differ from what normally happens when we learn to respond in a particular way and then repeat the behavior—regardless of its advantage.

For instance, if a child is reinforced to behave like a much younger child, the result will be loud behavior, and sometimes, the louder the better. Often the loudest person in the room will dominate, monopolize, and be less restricted than those who maintain social propriety. Talking overtly rather than thinking quietly is also likely to be reinforced, in that hearing one's own voice is like having company; this may be preferable to functioning in silence or feeling alone. Some diagnosed children also become uncomfortable or anxious when a hush or pause settles over a room. They often conclude that something must be wrong when interactions cease. That patterning can also reduce the frequency of quieter self-speech, and increase fidgeting, among other diagnostic responses.

There may be countless examples where diagnosed children are inadvertently encouraged towards audible self-speech behaviors because they will be noticed and because self-commentary can ward off potential criticism. This pattern can become conditioned, but have little to do with an "inability" to act covertly. Moreover, if it could (somehow) be determined that under some conditions diagnosed children engage in quieter self-speech, traditional notions of disability would conflict with those findings.

For example, we observe that many diagnosed individuals can be more private when preferring that others not know what they are doing. One could ask if their self-directed speech changes significantly when assessed across a wide range of circumstances. Let us not presuppose that diagnosed children have less ability to inhibit speech behaviors or to engage in mature forms of private speech; let us investigate if they have not yet been conditioned towards quieter, mature patterning in particular situations, and let us work to facilitate the acquisition of the quieter self-speech.

In addition to showing patterns of immature self-speech, reports indicate that diagnosed persons will also show problems with expressive language. They purportedly have enormous difficulty stating and explaining ideas, reiterating, clarifying, summarizing, and organizing. According to Barkley (1998c, 102), explanatory speech is difficult to accomplish, and generally requires "more careful thought and organization" in comparison to "spontaneous speech." While "10% to 54%" of diagnosed children show speech problems, only "2% to 25%" of non-diagnosed children show language-based difficulties.

The traditional view posits that the speech difficulties of diagnosed children are indicative of their problems with complex forms of thinking, organizing, and monitoring one's own behavior. ADHD children often have difficulty during verbal problem-solving tasks; they seem less capable of communicating important information to peers during shared activity. The information that they provide is often less substantial and disordered when they must outline a story narrative, for example, and they often struggle when asked to inform others about the strategies they use when completing tasks. However, when there is no stated goal or specified task, their language discourse does not depart markedly from that which occurs with non-diagnosed children.

While traditionalists rely on the model of disinhibition and difficulty with executive functioning to account for the aforementioned speech and verbal fluency problems, a learning paradigm could potentially account for these difficulties too. For example, it has been reported that the incidence of speech problems is as high as 90% among outpatients and in-patients in psychological distress (Rousey and Toussieng, 1964; Page and Page, 1941). Likewise, Cohen et al. (1998) report that as many as 64% of children with speech and language disorders have a psychiatric diagnosis, and it is also quite common for speech disturbances to fade as psychological functioning improves (Kernberg and Rousey, 1970; Flemming and Rousey, 1974).

In that atypical language behaviors correlate with many diagnostic categories, and often resolve fortuitously when individuals cease the diagnostic behaviors, it is thus problematic to argue that there is something unique or causal about the finding that a number of diagnosed individuals show atypical speech patterns. As is often the case when explicating behavior, differentiating cause from consequence seems relative to one's metaphor of understanding rather than linked to facts.

With this data it appears that speech anomalies are often correlated with non-normative behavioral patterns, but that they decrease in frequency when individuals become less troubled or eccentric in their social behaviors. Because language behavior corresponds directly with psychosocial functioning to a large degree, we do not yet know whether problems with fluency, discourse organization, coherence of communication, and the quality of encoding during explanatory speech is a result of neurological delay, or if it is essentially related to living in the world in specific ways. That is, if one *behaves* in an immature, reliant, less accommodating, and inconsiderate way, one will *speak* in an immature, reliant, less accommodating, and inconsiderate way. The fact that language anomalies are evident within the diagnosed population does not point to the root cause of such problems or inform us about the extent to which those patterns can be adapted.

In that early parent/child interactions also profoundly influence language development, traditionally posited ADHD neurological delay is not our only interpretive option when we attempt to explain correlations between an ADHD diagnosis and inadequate language behaviors for diagnosed persons. For example, linguistic incompetence can occur during limited or inconsistent shaping of infant vocalizations, and if there is failure to provide the child with language that corresponds with particular ostensive events.

Encoding delays may also occur if the social context is one in which loved ones are compelled to organize the actions of diagnosed children, tell them what to do next, and articulate and clarify, rather than guide and assist them to learn more on their own. How can we expect them to acquire verbal fluency and explanatory speech when socialized in that way? Obviously, if any parent maintains a tight rein over a child's development of communication techniques, that particular child will not learn age-consistent patterns of fluency.

While traditionalists may reply to these assertions by claiming that parents and siblings are only reacting to a delayed child who is more active than verbal, or is not performing the necessary language behaviors competently, we cannot be assured about the extent to which it might be possible to shape greater language competency within the diagnosed population through an adjustment in reinforcement history. Rather than take over the verbal exchange, go to extremes in order to pressure communication, or presume that the diagnosed child cannot succeed, family and caretakers can focus instead on shaping the child to articulate competently with progressively less reliance on others.

However, we observe the possibility that when a less effectual verbal interaction pattern evolves, a vicious cycle ensues in which others must increasingly take action to communicate. This is when diagnosed children learn to rely on others to facilitate rather than learn to initiate those behaviors themselves. Some may eventually rely on parents and siblings to do significant amounts of their communication for them (including articulating), and will balk at the laborious chore of explaining content to someone else.

Other diagnosed children will often be reinforced to remain quiet in order to avoid the annoyance of having to accommodate to a verbal interaction initiated by someone else. These interactions will end abruptly when the initiator stops trying to evoke a response. Some diagnosed persons learn that they are unlikely to please others when they express ideas, opinions, and feelings. They become conditioned to talk less at these times, and non-responsive behaviors become reinforced to the extent that they correlate with quickly ending an interaction. Sometimes a parent will harangue, but then immediately accommodate the child —even though he has not spoken a word.

In many instances diagnosed children are conditioned to say, "You know," "Maybe," "Sort of," "Kind of," "Yep," or "I don't know," rather than struggle to be understood. They might avoid responding that could potentially prolong the verbal exchange or force them to make a commitment they might not like. Mumbling will also be more frequent, as it seems to permit ideas to be retracted easily and also allows one to avoid the work needed to articulate clearly. The infamous yawn could indeed immediately occur.

It is also not unusual that diagnosed children say the word "what" after others speak. We expect that constant disengagement from social exchanges will increase the likelihood of persons replying in that way, but saying "what" may also afford individuals extra time before responding. The individual may have the luxury of being involved in a personal agenda, and others are saddled with the responsibility of having to accommodate and repeat. There may also be an increase of concern received, since the response often results in others reiterating, simplifying, or clarifying to bring the individual up to speed. The predictable result is that the entire interaction comes to a complete halt to accommodate the diagnosed person. Instead of struggling to digest what has been spoken, the child effectively recruits others to rectify the situation simply by emitting a single word. However, in some other context, saying "what" innocently could reduce accountability; and when emitted angrily or defensively, others are likely to retreat rather than insist on a contribution.

Because many of these interactions fail to help the child develop language competence, the parental role could be to exercise patience: wait before repeating so the child has time to understand what has taken place with less external help. Parents might also speak less disapprovingly and more concisely—so that verbal exchange is cooperative. This will potentially help to develop turn taking, increase instances of comprehension and attentiveness, and shape verbal interactions which help shape genuine discussion. By changing patterns of verbal exchange, fluency, comprehension, attunement to the listener, and intricacy of diagnosed persons' communication will likely increase over time.

Furthermore, over trials the child can become better at figuring out what transpires (from context), and what is likely to occur next by deriving those possibilities for himself. If he obtains benefit from a personal agenda instead of modulating to group concerns, it makes little sense for others to work diligently to keep him informed. Those responses may only exacerbate the child's failure to stay current. Parents can also facilitate group participation by inviting the child to lend his point of view. They might also avoid interaction patterns that reinforce disconnection (e.g., interrogations, badgering), and formulate ways to clearly express complicated ideation so that it is understandable to him.

Ultimately, if significant numbers of diagnosed children are locked into particular interaction patterns that do not help them develop language proficiency; we should not expect a wide range of language competencies to develop. Perhaps they remain quiet while others talk, lecture, or direct conversation. If asked a question, or when required to pay attention, they may be easily distracted, change the subject, and contribute little. Loved ones do most of the talking, while the diagnosed person is disengaged, uninspired, and detached, and agreeable only in order to end the interaction.

However, we also observe that diagnosed persons are eager to talk when not coerced to do so. Some parents complain about the difficulty in stopping their diagnosed child from talking when the child initiates it. Apparently diagnosed persons are significantly more verbal when talking about their own interests. Diagnosed persons lack motivation when dealing with impositions from outside their worlds, but those non-participatory behaviors juxtapose with their incessant talking and increased arousal when they define the content and trajectory of a social exchange. Often they light up when talking about their own interests or agenda and also show competence. For instance, when instructing the parent to follow a directive (e.g., will you get me some juice), words are stated emphatically and clearly; the child is likely to talk with less restraint and greater intelligibility in those situations.

Taking an alternative approach, we encourage further analyses of verbal exchanges in order to identify interaction patterns that facilitate competent verbal functioning. A concerted effort to develop proficient language exchanges can become the priority. It then becomes an empirical question as to whether diagnosed individuals will show improvement in verbal fluency and explanatory speech when social exchanges are adjusted towards reinforcing those competencies. Traditionalists have not yet provided us with the means to determine how much neurological ADHD is causing particular speech problems, the extent to which particular speech problems increase the probability of learning ADHD, and the extent to which particular patterns of speech are probable when one has learned to do ADHD.

We might find that when history of reinforcement is altered language behavior will also change. For example, Eskimos have many words to differentiate kinds of snow, because these distinctions are fundamental to decisions having critical importance during day-to-day functioning; however, other social groups do not have dozens of words that refer to snow, since such variations are unrelated to contingencies of reinforcement. In this sense, language develops in relation to the world in which we live.

In the same way we anticipate that altering the worlds of diagnosed persons will elicit shifts in language behaviors. For instance, diagnosed persons can begin to talk about events in the distant future frequently and thoroughly when reinforced by concerns for the future. Given anecdotal observations, we observe that many diagnosed persons already show increased concern for future-oriented events when events relate to what they initiate and enjoy. Obviating their delay will probably only entail that we get the same behaviors to repeat under widespread conditions and diverse content.

Alternative assessments of language competency will also help to establish a best-case scenario for behaviors that traditionalists see as requiring higher cognitive functioning. By identifying this positive benchmark, we might avoid the problem of defining their verbal competency based solely on instances of logorrhea, "mindless attention seeking" behaviors, instances where avoidant behaviors are occurring, or when reliance on the resources and efforts of others has been reinforced. If improvements in verbal fluency are evident in some situations even prior to additional training, this could indicate that delays may not be as pernicious as implied by the biological perspective.

In order to seek the best psychological starting point, it is advisable to postpone categorizing diagnosed persons as inherently disabled until more diverse sampling of their behavior is obtained. By increasing *the sampling of behavior to include actions that diagnosed persons frequently initiate and enjoy* (that occur apart from directives, evaluations, and efforts of others), competencies which are already occurring may come to light.

According to conventional practitioners, the spontaneous or self-initiated talking of diagnosed children requires less executive functioning, because requirements for organization and explanation are less complex than the demands imposed by the school. But when responding to content initiated by others, there is a loss of discretionary authority and a greater probability of evaluation. To the extent that those parameters also influence their responses, it is crucial to observe improvements in their verbal fluency when they initiate explanatory speech, orient to defend their points of view in an argument with their parents, and attempt to convince others about something. We may see that the quality of their explanatory speech advances when they are not jabbering aimlessly or reacting to external authority.

While it is improbable that all language discrepancies will immediately vanish under varying sets of conditions, in that diagnosed persons do not constantly use their resources, and do not practice communicating in more age-consistent ways in as many situations, their speech quality may still vary in ways that should not be ignored. However, even if problems are rigorously observed over time, we may still not know how much change is possible when we alter how these children are reinforced during day-to-day functioning.

For many diagnosed persons plenty of new learning is possible, but reinforced response patterns are adversely influencing their rate of acquiring new language skills. For example, some diagnosed children develop less verbal competency because they are reinforced to present themselves as innocent, cute, baby-like, and naïve. Immature or poorly constructed speech and articulation are aspects of this pattern of relating to others. Those verbal responses will often sequence with the compliance of others to their requests, and forgiveness when mistakes are committed. These children are less often reinforced to demonstrate maturity and verbal skill. Puerile incompetent behaviors may be reinforced in numerous ways, and will thus impede the development of language fluency for many of these children.

When diagnosed children talk in ways that sound quite infantile (e.g., Rug Rats), the naiveté may often result in others remarking, smiling and enjoying the apparent innocence. Diagnosed children with this patterning might frequently miscomprehend, mispronounce, make grammatical mistakes, and reverse word sequences. Instead of struggling to articulate their ideas, they will likely offer a vague nondescript utterance. It gradually becomes incumbent on others to speak for them and work harder to comprehend the speech. In some instances parents reinforce immature language patterning by speaking with the child in "baby talk" as well. Children who orient in this way can also avoid learning how to read, and instead will depend on their parents to read to them.

Parents may not be aware of how strongly they are influencing language development; nor will they realize that many different parental responses can hinder language fluency. The child may elicit assistance when inarticulate, be filled with self-doubt during verbal exchange, and have insufficient opportunities to learn language competence.

As a way to address this matter, parents might avoid reinforcing the seemingly incompetent and sometimes humorous infantile verbalizations by talking with the child in a mature fashion, and not express amusement when the child shows infantilism. Parents can exercise greater patience while their child tries to communicate, instead of anticipating what he or she is trying to say. They can also be less accommodating or reproachful when the child shows immature speech patterns, as this can help to build the child's confidence. Parents can become responsive and impressed when the child is composed and emits more age-consistent verbalizations, and furthermore, can provide the child with substitute language forms in a non-judgmental way. Since immature speech behaviors become markedly problematic in school, where competence is rewarded (in contrast to naiveté or whining), these kinds of family interventions are important.

Generally in cases where it is observed that diagnosed children repeat the same linguistic mistakes, we can ask whether responses to those behaviors are reinforcing the atypical verbalizations rather than extinguishing them. Frequent disapproval and non-responsiveness from both parent and child are likely to hamper the child's linguistic development. Ideas might not be exchanged very often because parties will often maintain negative characterizations about the other. Defensiveness, rigidity, and insistence can occur more often than attempts to solicit ideas, or resolve concerns through joint efforts and creativity. All of those patterns are ultimately unlikely to help the child learn to use language in subtle and sophisticated ways.

Delays in Sustaining Effort

When discussing another correlated problem with the ADHD diagnosis, Barkley (1998c) notes that diagnosed individuals have great difficulty sustaining effort over time, and maintaining adequate performance when delays are introduced. He asserts that diagnosed persons have motivation problems.

However, from the learning perspective, it may be that poor persistence of effort equates to an association between certain actions and exposure to failure, disapproval, and negativity. One could posit that giving up when delays are encountered is reinforced in the same way as when people learn to persist. That is, depending on what happens when sustained effort occurs, those responses are either reinforced or partially extinguished.

For example, if diagnosed children learn that others lower their expectations and requirements, and offer assistance in response to their lack of persistence, they seem to get reinforced to work less whenever they encounter discomfort. This pattern occurs most often after conflict about required tasks. Poor persistence when hindered can repeat in other contexts, and giving up will likely be shaped when a disappointment or hardship occurs, especially if negativity is associated with continued participation.

But the fact that diagnosed persons do not persevere or maintain quality of performance when having to wait does not by default prove that they are delayed in their ability to generate motivation, that an underlying mechanism is inadequate, or that they are less able to suppress, moderate, or regulate the prepotent reactions to stop persisting. Diagnosed persons could in reality be managing quite effectively when they show diminished persistence and impatience. This alternative view is lent further support when we see that some diagnosed persons are adept at self-denial when behaving spitefully; the notion of a reduced ability to delay or wait seems illogical given that pattern of response.

Generally, a lack of persistence may be reinforced in that it sequences with a diminution of adversity. Non-persistent behaviors might also be retaliatory, in that incomplete work will disrupt those who have assigned the task. Abandoning an activity also permits more time for enjoyable activities, and delays the disappointment that can occur when tasks are concluded or evaluated. However, sometimes lack of task completion permits an individual to avoid unsettling problems. He may think about the work that was not completed rather than focus on more troubling concerns. A failure to finish can also increase concern and coaxing from others, and therefore reinforce the individual that others *do* care. Finally, if the individual is also conditioned to work primarily in the company of others, as soon as they stop attending, persistence will also stop. Lack of persistence is then reinforced, because that response keeps others close at hand.

It seems that lack of persistence can be reinforced whenever the consequences of not finishing are less extreme than the consequences of grappling with and completing the task. Because lack of persistence seems to occur more often under conditions of less discretionary authority, emotional upset, evaluation, or failure (i.e., work cannot be wrong if it is incomplete), it is difficult to ascribe the problem *solely* to inner biological delay. It is reasonable to presume that many of us do fewer participatory behaviors when we fail to succeed, or when it does not matter much if we do succeed, when we are troubled, or if our opinions are disregarded. The possibility exists that diagnosed persons are simply conditioned to do those responses more than most due to their biopsychosocial circumstance.

Since it is also typical for diagnosed persons to show patience and improved task persistence under certain conditions, it is reasonable to understand instances of diagnostic functioning as reinforced in relation to what occurs when those responses are emitted rather than as evidence of delay. Particular diagnostic and non-diagnostic responses can repeat in myriad ways as particular sequences of events are encountered through day-to-day functioning. It is not that diagnosed persons are less able to persist because of motivational delays, but rather that they have been reinforced to lack persistence under some conditions with some content, and not do that response pattern in other contexts and circumstances, such as when they nag parents for something specific.

Conventional practice urges that we must remediate lack of persistence by increasing controls and through external motivation, but there are ways to increase persistence without the limitations and side effects of intervening as aforementioned. For example, we can increase the individual's opportunity for success, incrementally shape greater tolerance when others are not attending, and condition the individual to accommodate others by shaping collaborative interactions.

Nevertheless, it is not surprising that individuals with depressed mothers and various functional difficulties persist less during daily activity. As a group, individuals who operate under these conditions learn to give up faster than others, since the probability of success is lower. When requirements are complicated to master, and when individuals are difficult to reach and to please, perseverance and sustained effort might not be appreciated, and thus not reinforced very often. In this regard, traditionalists have not yet demonstrated that non-diagnosed persons are more adept at persisting when encountering activities associated with adversity given their reinforcement histories in comparison to the ADHD group. For example, what kind of persistence is evident when a "book worm" is required to do sports-related activity?

When examining the behaviors of diagnosed persons, there are numerous reinforcement histories that relate to patterns of low persistence. The distinction between a neurological persistence failure and learned non-persistence does not emanate from the data, but is inferred in relation to the assumptions and tacit presumptions being imposed. We observe that traditionalists have found ways to interpret data so that instances of diagnostic functioning may be subsumed within their disability formulation, but alternative accounts remain plausible.

Diminished Delay of Gratification

When attempting to explain another correlated problem for diagnosed persons called "diminished delay of gratification," it is posited that they have less ability to be cognizant of the long-term consequences of their indulgences. However, it is also possible to account for this behavior within a learning paradigm, and *not* posit a lesser ability. In particular, if we presume that diminished delay of gratification is another way to say that some people behave in a way that increases the probability of immediate rather than future events—and we can specify the parameters that reinforce the behavior—the responses can be understood as conditioned rather than as signs of delay.

On what grounds do we make the additional claim that the immediate pattern is delayed, and not merely a pattern that has been reinforced compared to the longer term pattern? Traditionalists have not shown that diagnosed persons are "less able" to be conditioned to do the longer term reward behaviors; they have only shown that diagnosed persons are often likely to behave with shorter term considerations for socially valued achievements.

The data shows only that diagnosed persons often do not work for particular long-term socially valued rewards. The explication of those data is a matter of interpretation, not facts, as historical parameters might explicate those same data just as reasonably as a biological determinist view that posits disability. A difference model might be utilized to explicate the more frequent occurrence of the shorter term reward behaviors. Individuals may learn how to live in relation to increasing the probability of either immediate or less immediate gratification. Both patterns may be conditioned and shaped by one's history of reinforcement.

If diagnosed persons show higher levels of intolerance and impatience, and these behaviors are also coordinated with specific outcomes such as the more rapid acquisition of particular objects, reduction of coerced activity, or receiving conciliatory behavior from others, we can reasonably argue that this patterning is being reinforced. But to date we still do not know whether the individual is less able to learn alternative responses, or if particular contingencies are preventing the behaviors from being extinguished.

Consistent with this interpretation, if parents are less keen to allow their developmentally-delayed children to endure suffering, then why are we surprised that these children can also be conditioned to expect immediate rectifications, and not respond positively when that social response does not occur? Ostensibly, it is more difficult to sustain limits when we observe children in distress, and such situations occur when children function under difficult circumstances such as functional delay. However, this patterning may be inadvertently conditioning the child to fuss, complain, and not learn to work for longer term outcomes.

On the other hand, one need not be neurologically delayed to learn those responses. When we observe individuals acting annoyed and irritated when disappointed, it does not mean that we should assume that they are unable to show opposite responses. Moreover, it is even more of a misnomer to say that they are "less able," since many diagnosed persons who spend money frivolously have been known to save for extensive periods of time to acquire particular objects (e.g., a car, a video game, etc.).

While traditionalists claim that lack of inhibition prevents the person from recognizing contingencies that would reinforce the tolerant long-term behaviors, it might also be claimed that diagnosed persons are simply reinforced to behave in order to satisfy immediate desires. For example, some diagnosed children may be conditioned that they are important to others when hyperbole and crisis surround their irresponsible short-sighted actions. If the child is rescued when consequences for *not* fulfilling longer term achievements occurs, it will thus become improbable that long-term goal achievement behavior will be conditioned. The child will instead rely on behaviors that increase the probability of immediate acquisitions, and not encounter the adversity that takes place for most when striving for future achievement. As touched on earlier, many children are careless with their toys if they have plenty, or when toys are quickly replaced or repaired. A diminished delay of gratification can be reinforced when children (diagnosed or not) are rescued or protected from every form of adversity and disappointment that comes their way.

However, traditionalists alternatively posit that diminished delay of gratification for the diagnosed person is a result of a neural biological limitation that will not disappear. Their recommended treatment is to impose immediate contingencies to stop the unacceptable behaviors, presuming that diagnosed persons only respond to those kinds of consequences. More time-delayed attainments are only to be accomplished by leading the diagnosed person step by step assisted by immediate manipulated contingencies.

Although when intervening in this fashion, it seems that diagnosed persons are invariably put on a schedule of managed reinforcement without extensive time delays between the required behaviors and added gifts or retributions. The intervention does not reinforce behavior which is not followed by immediate extra reward or punishment administered by someone else. While the individual will incrementally achieve the desired longer term outcome, the approach maintains the exact patterning that is most important to assuage. The presumption of disability further undermines the potential of the person to effectively learn how to operate *without* an immediate reward.

Moreover, when we examine ADHD behavior within a learning paradigm, the formulation that diagnosed persons are inherently deficient at delaying gratification is problematic. The social acceptability of a behavior tells us nothing about whether that behavior is immediately gratified. For example, some people learn that frequent complaining results in others accommodating or reassuring; while others learn that complaining delays accommodation and results in much discomfort. Others are conditioned such that calm and concerted conversation allows them to obtain what they want, while others learn that it accomplishes nothing. However, it is not that one pattern delays gratification relative to the other, but that each behavior is immediately reinforced in relation to a particular history.

One might also ask if individuals who work persistently for long-term rewards that have a low probability of happening are any better at managing their futures than those who work for predictable short-term rewards. Despite being trained that "good things happen to those who wait and work hard," these individuals can nevertheless suffer for inordinate amounts of time, even though the likelihood of actually obtaining the anticipated reward will be nearly nonexistent (e.g., effort to become a movie star). A common response to individuals with these types of aspirations is that they are deluding themselves and wasting time, despite having long-term goals.

There are other problems with traditional views regarding statements about delayed gratification as well. For instance, it may seem relatively easy to gain consensus about a behavioral act having a particular beginning and endpoint, but these discriminations are always arbitrary. What, for example, is the endpoint of playing and practicing the piano? Statements about the time delay of gratification after a behavior always depend on the formatting that the observer imposes on the ongoing sequencing of actions. Deciding that gratification is delayed is always a function of determining its beginning and end, as well as the consequential event seen as the gratifier.

As noted earlier, when we say that a person does delayed gratification behavior, we are identifying reinforcers that occur after a long period of time has elapsed that seems to account for the increased frequency rates of particular actions. We are not saying that some people are more ascetic, therefore more capable than others to endure delays in gratification. Nor are we saying that they can better withstand not being immediately reinforced, or that they did more preparatory activity for that action sequence. We are simply saying that we can coordinate particular distant future consequences with the frequency rates of the behavioral acts.

Individuals accomplishing long-term goals may be gratified just as readily as those who seldom accomplish long-term goals, and there might not be significant correlations between the amount of mental preparatory activity and the time interval of the posited gratification. Immediately occurring sequences of contexts and circumstances may immediately reinforce responses that we characterize as delaying gratification (e.g., enjoying playing and practicing the piano and eventually becoming proficient).

In this view we can assert that persons may be reinforced to do the long-term pattern without also positing that they are doing a delaying action of some sort, or that they have to inhibit other responses that would otherwise be immediately gratified. People work for less impending, larger rewards just as automatically (or without thinking of long-term consequences) as when they work for shorter, fast-approaching rewards. Patterns of longer term achievements may be just as immediately gratified as patterns described as impatient or indulgent.

Nor should we doubt that, at times, facilitating the occurrence of imminent events entails more intricate mind machinations than that required to facilitate distant future outcomes. Behaving to increase the probability of accomplishments in the future does not necessarily mean that enactors are undertaking many more complicated mental antecedent actions as compared to behaviors that coincide with immediate accomplishments.

We also cannot presume that it is more complex to identify distant future consequences that might occur in relation to one's current behavior trajectory compared to identifying immediately occurring future consequences. Both types of identifications may be equally or differently complex according to some imposed criteria. For example, it is possible that one can do non-vocal verbal responding or imagining about the immediate benefits related to reading a magazine compared to doing homework. Likewise, one can also think about long-term benefits related to learning about content in the magazine as compared to doing the homework, or think about doing homework and attaining a high grade on a report card weeks later as compared to reading a magazine.

All of these actions may require approximately the same number of interdependent steps, discriminations, or other imposed criteria to determine complexity (including statements about brain activity). While the social acceptability of the content of these mental actions may differ, the degree of difficulty and intricacy of the sequence of responses related to unacceptable content could be greater than what occurs with acceptable content. We do not presume that fecklessness equates with incompetent mind functioning.

To use traditional vernacular, individuals may act in relation to events within a restricted time horizon, and still do as much (if not more) inhibitory and executive activity as those who seem to take action to enhance the probability of events occurring in the distant future. The time interval between a current response and a designated outcome event cannot enlighten us about the complexity of actions involved when achieving either a near or distant future goal. The width of a person's time horizon does not inform us about the competency of inhibitory or executive systems.

Moreover, there are discrepancies with the idea that diagnosed persons have a constricted time horizon when responding to current circumstances, in that sometimes non-immediate events influence their actions. For example, they reliably remember that their parents owe them money, and can remember a transgression that a parent committed long ago when trying convince them to conform to their current demands. Similarly, after receiving a treat during a visit several weeks earlier, they remember to request a treat again before leaving. Situation and circumstance may adequately account for the width of a diagnosed person's time horizon.

Since our presumption here is that contingencies of reinforcement can be identified to account for the increase in the smaller reward short-term pattern evident for otherwise competent diagnosed persons, it is reasonable to alter patterns of reinforcement before settling on a disability model. Conditioning rather neurological delay might reasonably explicate the differing patterns—assuming equal competence in other areas of functioning. In the common vernacular, one could say that it has not been worthwhile for diagnosed persons to work for particular distant future outcomes, in that working for smaller short-term results has been influenced by the past.

There may be numerous and very different histories of reinforcement that either reduce or increase the frequency rates of working for long-term larger socially valued rewards in one's social matrix. For example, persons may be reinforced when not doing behaviors that others value when relationships are unsettled or conflicted (Skinner, 1953). When interactions are frequently negative, uncooperative, overly indulgent, and/or unreliable, individuals might be reinforced less often to participate in activities that require extended interaction, protracted synchronization of resources, or prolonged waiting responses. Frequent disharmony or the ongoing permission of exploitation reduces the probability that the long-term reward pattern will take hold.

When loved ones often forget, give in, fail to keep promises, and behave erratically, there is a reduction in the frequency of behaviors that increase the probability of particular distant future event sequences. Under these social conditions future outcomes will rarely transpire in predictable ways and reinforce particular systematic sequences of actions over time. When there is routine indulgence and unpredictability, obtaining rewards more quickly will be reinforced. The more frequent occurrence of capriciousness, uncertainty, leniency, and irregularity frequently extinguishes responses that are conditioned when there is formula, consistent structure, and credibility. It seems that most of us change as we learn to perceive our worlds in particular ways, as for example, when an elderly person jokingly states that he is too old to buy green bananas.

Generally, it is likely that behaviors will be organized around increasing the occurrence of future-oriented achievement when the individual realizes success while doing interrelated steps in a routine fashion, and when that same individual's history of reinforcement includes instances of reliable follow-through from others. Under predictable conditions, effort towards fulfilling larger, distant future accomplishments is likely to be reinforced. There will be fewer instances of interference, discouragement, and unforeseen disruptions to obstruct and thus extinguish incremental achievements. While conditions of *relative* certainty can be perceived as trustworthy, certainty can equate with statements about predictability of event sequences; these conditions will nevertheless be likely to reinforce long-term accomplishments for both diagnosed and non-diagnosed persons.

In sum, if it is confirmed that certain problems and disappointments are frequently encountered when doing socially valued achievements in particular situations and circumstances, we cannot reasonably argue that failure to enact socially valued behavior is due to a biological inability to self control. If repetition of a short-term reward pattern reduces the probability of adverse outcomes in predictable ways, we say that a person is in control. The problem then becomes how to determine which outcomes actually influence the frequency rates of less valued behaviors.

Before adopting the view that some people can better withstand fewer gratifications because they have a superior neurobiology, it seems important to study the individual's history of reinforcement. We argue that people are simply learning to gratify themselves in different ways due to their history of conditioning. Perhaps diagnosed persons can learn acceptable patterning if we systematically change what they have learned.

Problems with Hyper-responsiveness and Variability of Performance

Finally in our list of correlated problems, traditionalists also report that diagnosed persons show signs of disinhibition when they demonstrate greater variability of behavior and work performance, and hyper-responsiveness to environmental events (Douglas, 1972; Rucklidge and Tannock, 2002). Variability of response is taken as evidence of a lesser ability to regulate oneself.

However, when diagnosed persons show exaggerated responses, crisis of existence behaviors, or excessive drama in their social patterning, these behaviors may sequence with others noticing and accommodating rather than ignoring. Interestingly, those subsequent reinforcing consequences can occur not only within the ADHD population, but also for those who qualify for a Histrionic Personality Disorder. Although when persons reveal a histrionic pattern, we are less likely to posit that they are "driven" to overreact. We more often claim that melodramatic behaviors have been reinforced in relation to particular historical parameters.

If neurobiology is not seen as the determining factor for the histrionic personality, on what grounds can we impose this account for the ADHD pattern? In what ways is the greater variability of behavior and hyper-responsiveness of the diagnosed person any different from the behavior of the histrionic (or for that matter) any child who has frequent temper tantrums? What might account for times when the diagnosed child does *not* show over reactivity; isn't it sometimes found that diagnosed persons are under aroused and minimally responsive?

Even if it is argued that sometimes conditions compensate, this may simply be another way to say that certain over reactive behaviors are not always reinforced. Might we gain greater precision and scope simply by claiming that over reactivity and variability of performance are reinforced response patterns that occur under particular sets of conditions such as when diagnosed persons become inconvenienced, and when they mobilize others to either retreat or show increased concern?

Despite the difficulties that occur when excessive behaviors repeat in various situations (similar to histrionic patterns) the overstated responses might be reinforced on numerous occasions and role modeled by other family members. Moreover, while over reactions can appear to be defective from an observer's standpoint, once we have discerned history of reinforcement, heightened responses can often seem fairly reasonable. For example, if a spouse explodes upon seeing the toothpaste tube squeezed from the "wrong end," our knowing what has led to that response will often shed a very different light on that seemingly irrational behavior; this is known as understanding "old bruises."

In conclusion, traditionalists claim that diagnosed children lag behind because of ADHD, but we suggest that many individuals within this group show a variety of other problems and environmental exposures that enhance the probability that ADHD will be learned. Once ADHD behaviors are learned it then becomes even less probable that other skills will develop. As the child continues to steer clear of certain requirements and relies on others to permanently ease discomforts, he or she is not as likely to develop particular competencies. However, because there are some diagnosed individuals who do not express correlated problems (including atypical responses during infancy), it is pointless to argue that ADHD is the root cause of the problems that can co-occur within the diagnostic category.

Chapter 7

Reinterpreting Laboratory Findings

Significantly, traditionalists impose the same biological account whenever differences in functioning on tasks are evident between groups of diagnosed persons and controls. Whenever relatively poor performance is shown by groups of diagnosed individuals on particular tasks, neural biological delay is said to be the cause. Traditionalists often point to this accumulation of data to bolster their claim that ADHD is a "real" disorder, and not mere misbehavior.

However, it is also possible to interpret the behavior of diagnosed persons both in and out of the laboratory in a very different way from the traditional construct of neurological delay. For example, while traditionalists see laboratory research as uncovering cognitive delays related to limited neurobiological functioning, these empirical studies can also be seen to only show correlations between learning to do ADHD behaviors and functioning in particular ways on particular tasks. When one learns to do ADHD behavior in various circumstances, it is probable that those behaviors will repeat when required to complete other different tasks, including those assigned in a laboratory setting. The fact that some or many diagnosed individuals sometimes function poorly on laboratory measures, does not tell us the extent to which the problem might be related to learning, and/or a posited self-regulatory delay that makes them less capable of more adequate functioning; the etiology of the problem behaviors is not established by those data. For example, when Hoza et al. (2001) report that diagnosed children are likely to stop working during laboratory experiments, is it that they have self-regulatory problems, or have they *learned* to escape when encountering particular adversity in particular situations?

Despite the possibility of numerous interpretations, traditionalists assert that diagnosed persons do not adequately inhibit when mistakes are made on laboratory tasks. Due to inhibitory failures, mental actions such as anticipating, planning, imagining, rehearsing, evaluating, coordinating sequential steps, or reconfiguring variables (in mental form) will occur less often. The diagnosed person is therefore susceptible to distraction, is non-reactive to essential feedback, and is generally impaired when required to solve complex problems in the lab. Traditionalists insist that empirical work performed in the lab shows consistency with those views.

We might alternatively begin to explore the possibility that the relatively poor performance of some diagnosed persons during some laboratory tasks relates to past learning, and to learning that has not *yet* occurred. Particulars of each case vary extensively, but it is probable that many diagnosed individuals have not yet been conditioned to respond in accommodating ways when receiving feedback; nor have they been shaped towards innovative responding in certain circumstances. Data showing less ability is neither presented, nor gives us insights into addressing ADHD reactions.

Rather than interpret laboratory findings as the unveiling of inner delays, findings can be understood as exemplifying instances of behavioral shaping and the repetition of conditioned responses. Accounting for relationships between diagnosis and task performance is a matter of conjecture, inference, and interpretation made in relation to an individual's particular set of assumptions and tacit presumptions. The account proposed by traditional interpretation is not inherent in those data, but is instead a function of the way the data is *represented* by those interpreters.

In the view presented here outcomes of laboratory experiments are interpreted such that when a person has entrenched ADHD behavior, he is likely to repeat particular kinds of responses when particular kinds of tasks are presented in particular situations. If for example, one screams when others do not comply, we will not be surprised if the person also screams at a video game when results do not meet expectations. The fact that those behaviors occur in both situations does not tell us whether delayed neurology is causing those responses, or whether those responses might be reasonably explicated in alternative ways, including a learning paradigm.

Important Concerns when Interpreting Laboratory Data

We suggest that laboratory findings are simply demonstrating the consequences of having learned to respond with ADHD patterns. Experimental findings may be understood as demonstrating the consequences of past learning, or showing that persons who learn ADHD responding are also likely to generate other kinds of problematic responding that impedes performance on various laboratory tasks. Moreover, in that many of these correlated problems are seldom accounted for empirically when laboratory data are analyzed, it is not always clear to what extent lack of success on laboratory tasks relates to other functional problems, or to the fact that individuals manifest a sufficient number of the different behaviors described in the DSM-IV-TR manual under the heading of ADHD.

When comorbidity is not an issue, the failure to respond acceptably in the laboratory might not be associated with a posited inhibitory problem that prevents individuals from doing necessary preparatory activity, but may actually refer to other complications. As noted earlier, the undertaking of empirical work must be utterly vigilant in factoring out the influences of these problems. Without such caution the end result is unawareness of the extent to which correlated problems and/or ADHD contribute to laboratory outcomes. For example, Shaw and Brown (1990) did *not* find that highly intelligent diagnosed children had creativity deficits.

While there is agreement that diagnosed persons show more problems compared to controls (on average), if they must meet the requirements of a multitude of laboratory tasks, individuals from the ADHD population are also more likely than controls to show pre- and post-natal brain injuries, lower intelligence, expressive language delays, anxiety, depression, problems with reading and math, fine motor problems, various biological conditions, and other difficulties. Therefore, they generally function poorly during laboratory tasks.

It seems important to determine whether diagnosed persons without co-occurring complicating problems show the same kinds of difficulties and weaknesses during the completion of various laboratory tasks compared with group averages for the ADHD aggregate. If the ADHD group as a whole is compared to a control group, and these co-occurring problems are not considered in the interpretation of results, we might be sidetracked by reporting more on problems other than the presence of ADHD when we observe group differences. We may often find that the existence of *other problems* succinctly explains who will express the most difficulty on laboratory experiments.

However, even for diagnosed persons without co-occurring problems, we can invoke history of reinforcement to account for less acceptable functioning in the lab. This includes slower mental calculations, problems estimating time intervals, decreased competence during problem solving, and less flexibility and learning from mistakes. Reduced performance in the denoted areas of functioning can occur if individuals have learned to respond with ADHD patterns.

Our view here is that when some people (for different reasons) learn to do ADHD frequently and severely, they do not develop particular skills as a consequence of having learned ADHD patterning. Subsequently, they perform poorly when assessed in the laboratory. We observe that individuals learn to respond to the directives of others, assigned complex tasks, limitations, the absence of assistance, and/or loss of discretionary authority in particular ways. The responses can then repeat in multiple settings—including during laboratory experiments.

The claim is that many diagnosed persons have been reinforced to do ADHD when encountering adversity, particularly during unsettling circumstances which were assigned or initiated by others. ADHD responding is often reinforced in relation to the provision of assistance, or with a reduction of time and effort spent conforming to these problematic conditions. The consequences of learning unique behavioral patterns can therefore become apparent for some diagnosed persons during laboratory tasks.

When ineffectuality, non-adherence, defensiveness, and reliance on others becomes conditioned in various situations (e.g., immediate complaints about assigned task difficulty), we see that these individuals gradually become less adept at expressing themselves, and solving problems that require persistence, imitation, estimation, responsiveness to feedback, as well as planning, rehearsing, and imagining future events prior to acting. Even when factoring out known comorbidities, the issue is whether poor laboratory functioning of diagnosed persons is an expression of their posited neurological ADHD delay, and/or is derived from having been conditioned to do ADHD responding.

If we accept the latter view, learning ADHD response patterns affects performance on a multitude of tasks. What these children seem to most often learn are ways to increase the probability that others will provide answers, and reduce requirements. Because many of these individuals have often learned to rely on others to rectify, and have also learned to avoid, disregard, rush, and delay in response to tasks associated with negativity, the probability of their mastering presented material is expected to be low.

When feedback from others is associated with negativity and/or is not received because of negligence, we do not think these individuals will respond in typical ways in difficult situations (including those in the lab). If less conscientious responding permits avoidance of work, we cannot be surprised when many tasks are completed rapidly rather than accurately. Greater effort and creative responses that could interfere with escape from adversity, or that would slow the pace of task completion are less likely to be reinforced, whereas ADHD responding under similar conditions will have utility.

In that distractibility often results in the removal of a requirement, protection from denigration, extra help, and/or more time available to do other activities that correlate with higher success rates, those responses may often be reinforced for some people, given their particular histories of living in the world. However, if individuals learn to respond with distractibility, they are also not as likely to learn alternative responses that would help them succeed on various laboratory tasks; failure rates will thus remain high.

Unfortunately, the sometimes less adequate functioning of diagnosed persons may relate to particular reinforcement histories that insidiously shape passive and ineffectual responses which repeat in and outside laboratory settings for individuals (who are otherwise unimpaired). For example, if loved ones often tie their shoes, and advise them how to act step-by-step (e.g., "Take off your coat," "Say thank you," and "Sit down," and so on), we see that diagnosed persons do not practice those steps in order to become proficient and increasingly autonomous. Physical and mental self-reliance will not develop.

Many persons who interact with diagnosed children quickly become accustomed to directing and monitoring as if dealing with a toddler; such a reaction allows for the minimization of danger and as a means of facilitating rapid acceptable patterning. However, this interactive style tends to instigate increasing reliance on parental cues; the parent solves most problems related to self-organizing behavior by urging the child to "Slow down," "Think," "Try hard," "Brush your teeth," "Put that down, then unzip your jacket." The responsibility for anticipating time parameters, specifying problem solving steps, and remembering is shifted to others. These persons will thus solve problems, maintain schedules, systematize, provide cues, recognize associated problems, correct, and "direct traffic." Parents and teachers become the "executives" who lead and arrange the actions of the diagnosed child. Moreover, because traditionalists presume that self-reliance and self-control for ADHD diagnosed individuals is impossible, an overly dependent arrangement is encouraged by conventional practitioners and is expressed as necessary for handling the child's inherent and permanent reduced capability. Parents are actually encouraged to further tighten controls and micromanage.

We acknowledge that compensatory interventions might increase current performance for the duration under which those strategies are administered, but worryingly, it is not clear how such interventions also impede the long-term development of competent self-reliant behaviors, including particular mental actions in response to managing future contingencies. We hold that laboratory data may be understood in relation to a particular biopsychosocial history.

One has only to observe the many achievements evident within the diagnosed population in order to recognize that they can indeed master many problem solving tasks when they are not responding with ADHD patterns. When we consider those competencies, rather than assert that they cannot resist the urge to escape when mental effort is required, we suspect that they have learned the distractible responses only in specific situations and circumstances. As noted, the distinction between being "driven to distraction," compared to not reacting in a more concerted way due to past learning, is unclear.

Diagnosed persons may be fairly competent at self-evaluation and notice errors whenever *they* are the initiators of the instruction. For example, they might show greater persistence and identify potential solutions when rescuing a video game character from a dilemma, when doing car mechanics, or when assembling their bikes. However, those same competencies may be absent when they respond to typical school assignments or laboratory tasks that draw on similar proficiencies. Because these variations in functioning seem to occur, we are reluctant here to interpret instances of poor laboratory functioning as evidence of a fixed disability. Lack of responsiveness to feedback, less competent responses during tasks with interdependent steps and precursory actions, problems duplicating, sensing time, driving safely, and competency at mental calculation may all be reasonably understood within a paradigm that relates history to current responding.

We also suggest that the purportedly large gap in performance between diagnosed persons and controls will also become less apparent by manipulating parameters that are usually not considered during typical laboratory investigations. In particular, do diagnosed persons show "resistance to distraction" when collaboration has occurred prior to carrying out the assigned task? Does the person show enhanced performance when

- he or she retains more discretionary input/authority/autonomy,
- when there is increased similarity between the assigned task and tasks the individual frequently initiates and enjoys,
- and when there is the probability of success?

Diagnosed persons might not be incurably incompetent; they merely may not be appropriately conditioned to function acceptably in the lab.

For instance, if diagnosed persons learn that their actions instigate others to acquiesce or mollify, they may function poorly on many laboratory tasks because the inanimate tasks will not accommodate or yield to their reactions. The problem is evident when diagnosed children yell and scream at video games, or complain that the game is cheating them. Blaming the game in no way addresses their own dilemma, but if blaming the environment is continuously reinforced on varied occasions, similar behaviors will repeat in many settings, including the lab.

In addition, there are instances where diagnosed persons are conditioned to do the easier rather than the more accurate response, or to rely on luck to solve problems. These behaviors run parallel to their excessive reliance on others to perform work, and their tendency to gloss over the requirements of others and avoid situations that threaten self-esteem. Given this conditioning, they will frequently show problems when independent problem solving skill or self-evaluation of errors is assessed. However, if conscientiousness has not been conditioned in response to obligations, then reasonably, these individuals will not learn the necessary skills to succeed during laboratory studies. They may lack the conditioning to engage in precise, imitative, insightful, systematic, persistent, meticulous, and methodical work.

Importantly, since current functioning does not tell us about the etiology of the problematic behaviors, or how much behavioral change is possible, we advise proceeding as if altering contingencies of reinforcement can shape new behaviors. Although it is recognized that responding with ADHD patterns will result in delayed performance, this less acceptable current functioning does not enlighten us about achievements that are possible were those ADHD responses to be extinguished, and typical responses developed. Who could have predicted that pigeons can be trained to play ping-pong as some behaviorists have demonstrated?

It is also worthwhile to investigate whether peculiarities occurring during laboratory experiments are influencing the reported results. An analysis of task parameters could highlight alternative explications when problematic functioning is observed. For example, do a significant proportion of diagnosed persons become disrupted when evaluated by others, in that they have learned to anticipate disapproval? Their performance during evaluation might differ markedly when compared to functioning when they solve similar problems without the scrutiny of others. They may be reinforced to behave differently when being assessed or judged. Individuals who are exposed to frequent berating or correction will associate evaluation with significant unpleasantness.

The problem of criticism is evident, for example, when children learn to read, as reading is often a public activity when first being learned. Children are asked to read aloud in front of the class, in small groups, and one-to-one with a teacher. Some children apparently become conditioned to avoid reading in order to avoid the embarrassment of failure, especially if it is associated with poorer performance compared to peers during learning.

Moreover, although laboratory tasks are specifically designed to assess competency in certain areas or domains of functioning, the achieved scores can have little to do with what the evaluator actually sets out to measure. For example, on the Wechsler Intelligence Scale a subtest called Block Design requires individuals to arrange blocks into a particular pattern. Many respond as if this subtest informs the evaluator about aspects of visual spatial functioning, even though the tabulations do not explain the failures and successes achieved. There can be a host of different problematic responses that occur during task performance. The final point total may provide scant information about the person's behavior progression while completing the task. Ultimately, subjects with identical scores could have obtained the scores by exhibiting very different behaviors; their functional difficulties might also be dissimilar.

Some individuals might show problems when trying to recreate even the most simplistic spatial relationships between the blocks. When evidence of brain injury accounts for functional difficulties, we will readily accept that biological impairment limits their performance. This assessment seems even more reasonable when data shows that the individual had functioned well prior to an injury, and when the functional problem is consistent, regardless of situation.

Other individuals respond to the Block Design Subtest as if it were insurmountable. These individuals might express a similar pattern when asked to feed the dog, complete homework assignments, or manage household chores. For these persons, a low score relates to shunning the activity, not learning alternative ways of responding to assigned complexity, or not utilizing developed skills, in that they anticipate unfortunate results. It is therefore possible for them to obtain the exact score as the group which is apparently functionally impaired due to brain injury.

Another set of individuals will not have practiced doing puzzle tasks requiring a systematic approach (i.e., manipulating one variable at a time). Given a lack of experience, they may also function just as poorly as individuals with starkly different problems and response patterns. These individuals might turn the blocks rapidly instead of turning them methodically 45 degrees at a time, or perhaps they will move them past their correct positions. By not systematically approaching the task, their scores are reduced appreciably. Their total points could also be exactly the same as that of the other two groups, despite that the solution to their problem could be as straightforward as demonstrating a method or strategy.

Many other respondents lose credit because they are not conditioned to check their own work. They may repeatedly indicate that they have finished even though one (or more) of the blocks is incorrectly placed. These individuals can easily rectify mistakes if encouraged to check their work once more; but it may be the case that they associate competence with rapid completion, depend on others to remedy problems, and avoid any activity that expects them to face their mistakes directly (including when their parents express a desire to check schoolwork).

Another subgroup may indicate extreme emotional reactions during item presentations. They will become frustrated if unable to solve the task immediately, or when encountering the first disappointment. Intense responses to obstacles can lower scores, despite that many of them know that a display of histrionics will provide them with relief.

There could also be individuals who become exceedingly anxious or self-conscious when they are evaluated and timed. As noted by Tannock (2000), anxiety disrupts performance when individuals must solve complex tasks; functioning becomes disrupted because being watched and scrutinized is disconcerting. Their first mistake or difficulty will cue fretful rushing or giving up.

Finally, other respondents will be reticent throughout the evaluation. Their scores will be lower because they feel that they have been coerced to participate. These individuals orient as if they are establishing authority and protecting themselves when they do not perform as directed. They will often be averse to evaluation by others because they already expect disapproval, and resent situations that they feel undermines them.

Given these possibilities scoring on a task that ostensibly measures visual spatial functioning can be influenced by a multitude of factors. Even when individuals achieve the same score, it is reasonable to account for the scores that are achieved in unrelated ways. These concerns also apply when diagnosed persons are evaluated with inventory scales and various tests that purportedly assess inhibition and executive functioning.

Individuals might score poorly on these measures, but the explanation given is a postulation not a fact. Traditionalists will interpret many laboratory findings to be consistent with their own beliefs, despite that those same data can also be understood as consistent with other accounts. Most importantly, rejecting the null hypothesis that diagnosed persons do not differ from controls is not the same as proving the existence of a delayed inhibitory response. The debate is not that significant numbers of diagnosed individuals show intense frustration, rigidity, disinterest, less creativity, distractibility, and less efficient responsive-ness to feedback when tested in the lab. The controversy revolves around whether or not the observations confirm a medical problem that can be cogently explicated within traditional psychology.

Delays in Responding to Feedback

It has been reported that diagnosed persons function relatively poorly on continuous performance tasks (Frazier, Demaree, and Youngstrom, 2004). Sergeant and van der Meere (1988) note that diagnosed persons are likely to continue committing errors after giving receiving feedback on these tasks. It is thought that diagnosed persons have difficulty stopping a behavior once it is initiated, and that they perseverate due to lack of inhibitory control. They are presumed to have difficulty accessing their executive functions, in order to re-evaluate present circumstances and have command over changed circumstances. This limitation in functioning means that they often fail to keep working when necessary, or fail to coordinate their actions when change is introduced. Problems with self-regulation allegedly hinder their ability to profit from feedback as quickly as others, and to maintain consistency of achievement when interference occurs.

Here too we suggest that perseverating in the context of an ADHD diagnosis is a reinforced pattern; not responding to others permits the retention of discretionary authority. When there is non-responsiveness to feedback others cannot impede, criticize, or thwart; and aversive (assigned repetitious tasks) can be completed quickly when perseverating takes place. We assert that it is not that diagnosed persons are unable to respond to feedback or learn from mistakes, but that if they do *not* respond, they have learned that they are less likely to be interrupted or derailed by others. Shallice et al. (2002) assert that diagnosed persons show perseverative responses, but that reactive pattern also permits the continuance of self-initiated activity. Persistent self-initiated action will then become habitual, and the individual can resist the adversity associated with shifting set or rule recognition.

The finding that diagnosed persons do not respond to feedback as readily as other people does not tell us whether the source of those behaviors is history of reinforcement and/or neurobiological delay. For example, it seems that many younger children perseverate in many different ways when interacting; they might tell a joke repeatedly or continue a behavior numerous times simply because others laughed at first. It seems that frequent repetition occurs not only because children (generally) are less adept at identifying appropriate, humorous, tiresome, or intrusive behavior due to lack of experience, but also because many children (especially those who behave immaturely) are reinforced when others respond enthusiastically.

If this behavioral pattern is frequently reinforced outside the lab, we expect that perseverative responses will also occur regularly in the lab. These children may be conditioned to monopolize, or compel others to relent; they will nag parents all day about doing a particular activity, repeat behaviors that "push buttons," or repeat a phrase over and over that was initially amusing. They might be reinforced whenever a failure to stop has created powerful effects.

In addition, some diagnosed individuals are less willing to accept the instruction to change, since discriminating and correcting errors has until now been the domain of those who have compensated for inadequate functioning (i.e., they rectify problems). The unrelenting behavior of diagnosed persons can mean that they do less while others do more. A pattern of non-responsiveness to feedback can thus encroach, which subsequently yields greater frustration from adults who plead and are distressed by the extra work as the child continues to do wrong behavior. It is therefore not unusual to hear a parent remark, "No matter how many times I tell him, he keeps doing it," but the parent nevertheless continues to compensate.

While traditionalists recognize neurological ADHD as causing these patterns of perseveration, such response patterns may also be understood as conditioned responses. Rather than believe that diagnosed children repeat the same mistakes that constantly upset their parents because they have inhibitory delays, we might instead think that when doing those behaviors diagnosed children become the center of their parent's world. They effectively disengage them from everything else, or are otherwise limiting the extent to which their parents can exercise parental authority.

Many diagnosed persons do not respond to feedback effectively because it is typical for them to be non-accommodating when given a command. For example, a parent might pose a question to obtain particular information, or nitpick frequently and direct the child's actions throughout the day. This child may consequently learn to ignore what the parent says, and persist in self-initiated behavior. Disregard can be learned and can occur just as effortlessly as conformity occurs for others.

We could argue that in general, people become frustrated and defensive when required to change behavior when others remark on our mistakes (e.g., back-seat driving). Another illustration is the moaning and sighing of a child (diagnosed or not) when he has to clean his room a second time after "missing a spot." For most people, hearing others repeatedly offer unsolicited "constructive" criticism will eventually generate non-compliance. The fact that some diagnosed persons repeat non-compliant behaviors more often when given feedback need not mean that a neural biological delay is the culprit, nor is it the only reasonable interpretation of those data.

In sum, there are innumerable situations and circumstances where continuing an unacceptable behavior is reinforced compared with changing or stopping a particular action. Individuals might learn to be non-responsive to feedback from others in relation to power struggling for discretionary authority or soliciting greater concern. They self-initiate longer when comments and directives made by others are ignored. When feedback is not addressed, required activity may very likely be completed swiftly, with greater ease, and with fewer obstacles, as the non-responder need not contend with additional requirements resulting from feedback and the necessity to adjust action accordingly. Persons may also be conditioned to associate feedback with disapproval. They might be reinforced to be less responsive; the neglect allows them to avoid admitting that they have been responding inadequately.

Consequently, while it is noted that diagnosed persons often neither respond to external warning stimuli for upcoming responses nor adjust responses after errors (Barkley, 1998c), such reactions may be accounted for within a learning paradigm. If less responsiveness to feedback is regularly reinforced in daily living, we can expect the response pattern to also repeat in the laboratory (i.e., the way one practices is the way one plays the game). Diagnosed persons may be reinforced to not adjust their actions in response to others. For example, if we observe that diagnosed children function poorly during a game of "red light/ green light," we cannot immediately assume that they have neurological delay in the immediacy of their reactions. A number of these children could have pervasive motor problems, thus complicating the overall assessment. There may be children who are reinforced by responses that occur when getting caught, or when others chide their ineptness. Some will expect to win more often by not stopping, and some will not try to stop in that they do not expect to win.

As a way to investigate alternative hypotheses, it could be insightful to change the rules of the game, and for example, give bonus advancement points for every correct stopping response; we could then observe whether some diagnosed children show improvement under the new conditions. However, if positive changes are evident, it would be fruitless to assume that their neurology now permits them to stop more efficiently even though traditionalists will counter argue that stopping is now more salient, and thus discount the apparent gains.

Non-responsive patterning and actions that lead to problems (e.g., repetitiously ruining other children's toys with scissors), can indeed become habituated within a variety of circumstances. Those behaviors will repeat frequently if conditioned early in childhood—if we do not assume neurological delay. When investigating these possibilities, one might ask why, if the responses are unrelated to psychology, so many diagnosed persons persist at activities that others want stopped, and also show little persistence for activities that others want started, completed, and finished correctly.

Douglas (1983) claims that diagnosed persons have less ability to inhibit enough to profit from a warning stimulus that helps in the preparation of new items, but we can alternatively presume that diagnosed persons repeat behaviors that have been conditioned. Non-responsiveness can be reinforced in many families of origin if parents adapt more to the child rather than vice versa, or if disengagement between family members is frequent. These interactional patterns can become so habituated and automatic that even when it is very important to be responsive and compliant with an imposed directive, it is extremely difficult to do. Much like a troublesome marriage where spouses learn to ignore each other, individuals can also become conditioned to be less responsive to the feedback from others.

A common interpretation is that diagnosed persons are not able to benefit from past mistakes, and are hampered in their ability to change by integrating feedback. But we suggest that many diagnosed individuals have learned to respond in these particular ways when being corrected, coerced, nagged, directed, solicited, or criticized. The upshot, however, is that this behavior precludes their learning effective, efficient and acceptable ways to react to feedback or ways to act within other social contexts.

Furthermore, if changing one's actions is perceived as equivalent to admitting wrongdoing and having one's acceptability threatened, then individuals will learn to not shift readily as a function of that history. Individuals learn defensiveness when others give (helpful) advice or point out mistakes, and they also learn to not comply immediately. For example, how often do we observe that people will argue a point doggedly, despite being fully aware that their position is erroneous, in that they seem reluctant to lose face?

Defensiveness rather than conciliation with regard to negative comments about the suitability of their actions can logically lead to these individuals not altering behavior in response to mistakes highlighted by others, and the frequency rates of the noted responses could potentially increase. The person is thus protected by unyielding rigidity as when, for example, a spouse leaves the toilet seat up regardless of partner's constant complaints. However, by changing parameters in systematic ways we may be able to identify the conditions that influence response to advice, directives, feedback, and pointers from others in various contexts, on specific tasks, with particular content, at given times, with some people. We first need to understand and confirm systematically whether diagnosed persons respond to feedback differently, depending on whether advice is beseeched or non-solicited.

Some diagnosed persons show consistent delays when required to respond to feedback, but their current patterns do not predict what might happen if their history of conditioning were to change, or inform us about the origins of current less responsive patterns. For example, we know that sprinters train to become more responsive to the starter's gun. Responsiveness to feedback can be significantly influenced by the shaping of tactical procedures. Given that diagnosed persons are not practicing proficient responding to feedback, we do not yet know how they can develop greater responsiveness. Although in this regard, the University of Rochester reports that young adults will "sharpen" their "visual processing skills" simply by frequently playing video games (*USA Today*, 2003). If those finding are relevant, we can investigate whether diagnosed children show similar sluggishness when responding to feedback emanating from activities they initiate and enjoy, and whether improvement is apparent when social interactions are congenial.

In total, rather than conclude that diagnosed individuals cannot stop themselves, inhibit their urge to react, self-monitor previous responses and results, and that they have an inherently slow and inconsistent motor preparation response (Barkley, 2000; 1998c; 1998g), their inefficient and ineffective responses to feedback can instead be understood in relation to historical parameters: diagnosed persons have not yet been reinforced to respond when exposed to instruction, direction, and attempts to limit or change their behavior. The disapproval of others is a powerful disincentive to respond, both in and outside the lab. Therefore, before we agree to adopt a disability model, we need to investigate their lack of response gradient when we say yes and when we say no. We can gauge their efficiency of response when they receive compliments, when they are charming a parent, and when helping hastens the beginning of enjoyable activity.

ADHD and Delays in Creativity and Arousal when Problem Solving

As has been the case throughout, cause and consequence are apparently inverted when comparing traditional and current views. While traditionalists espouse that ADHD is antecedent and creator of evident problematic responses, the alternative view puts forward that particular conditioning accounts for the less acceptable performance of diagnosed persons in the lab. For many diagnosed persons, entrenched, less innovative solutions are reinforced during daily functioning. For example, if a parent commands a diagnosed child to "put the radio away!", and the diagnosed child places it on the nearby table without shutting it off, is he only capable of "literal" thinking (i.e., the parent didn't say to shut it off), or is he merely being rebellious? Is he promoting self-interest by leaving the radio on, or is he unable to respond thoughtfully?

If it has been the case all along that diagnosed individuals are shirking obligation or patterning in a non-accommodating way, we should not be surprised by their energetic, ambitious, creative, thoughtful, or accommodating, albeit less impressive, solutions to assignments. Apparent deficits may be coherently related to how they have been living in the world. We have often observed diagnosed children complain, "It is too hard" prior to exerting a modicum of effort, even with an easy assignment. As advised by Cowen, Wiener, and Hess (1953, 103), when studying problem solving rigidity (and controlling for intelligence, age, etc.), it is always advisable to "specify precisely a wide range of conditions and to examine the relationship between problem solving rigidity and other designated personality variables, under these measurable conditions."

Since diagnosis reduces the person to not performing what is known more frequently than others, rather than not being able to learn, other thoughtful or novel problem solving behaviors are already evident for many diagnosed persons in some situations. Parents have remarked on the achievements of their diagnosed children when they become absorbed in self-initiated tasks. Some diagnosed individuals may demonstrate reasonable competency and patterns of arousal when problem solving under these conditions.

Rather than presume a delayed arousal system, we need to evaluate their arousal patterns in varying contexts (i.e., not only continuous performance laboratory tasks). It is not clear to what extent their patterns of arousal may or may not change as we examine them across circumstances. For example, Elias (2004) points out that magnetic resonance imaging (MRI) shows that blood flow in the brain is different for Democrats and Republicans, depending on whether the observer has the same or other political affiliation. We might therefore alternatively claim that diagnosed individuals are not aroused enough when others require greater input and subject them to scrutiny, and are perhaps aroused very differently when others require greater calm.

Delays in Rule Following

Another correlated ADHD problem is that diagnosed persons have trouble engaging in rule-governed behavior. According to traditionalists, this kind of behavior depends on having "mental representations of past events in working memory. . . ," (Barkley, 1998g, 238). The notion is that these mental representations will enable rules to preside over behavior and connect the time intervals between behavior and contingencies; this helps keep behavior organized, systematic, and consistent with rules. The capacity to access rules in working memory purportedly assists in inhibiting prepotent and irrelevant responses (Zelazo, Reznick, and Pinon, 1995). Allegedly diagnosed individuals have difficulty keeping behaviors consistent with rules, particularly when other rewarding activities are available because they are not being influenced by covert speech that pertains to the rules. Therefore, diagnosed children are purportedly less biologically equipped than others to resist prohibited temptations. Rule following is particularly difficult for them whenever rules are counter to the gratification that is available when violating the rules (Barkley, 2006c).

Diagnosed children are supposedly less able to allow rules to direct their behavior; their delay makes it problematic for them to adhere (Greve et al., 1996). For those who believe the assertions, in order to behave consistent with particular rules, one must adequately inhibit and do the mental act of remembering a rule. Diagnosed persons are presumed to have trouble following rules because they cannot inhibit well enough to do executive action that would permit them access to the information contained in the rule.

However, less rule-governed behavior or instruction-following and less sensitivity to punishment and reinforcement (Barkley, 1998a) can be accounted for within a very different metaphor of understanding. Individuals may also be *con-*

ditioned to not behave in ways consistent with rules and instructions. While ADHD responses are not overtly resistive, other subtle types of reluctance and non-conformity may be occurring when diagnosed persons fail to comply with instructions, rules, or to adjust their behavior to prevent transgressions.

We could inquire, for example, into whether diagnosed persons follow more rules when they direct the game, if a loophole in the rule is advantageous, or when the rule can help them win. We need to identify whether diagnosed persons have the same inability to behave consistently with rules if they are the ones instructing others to conform to rules, or if they have designed them.

Rather than presuming delay, we can also posit that diagnosed persons are conditioned to deny themselves less often. For example, if a diagnosed child opens a bag of candy while asking permission (instead of asking prior to acting), is it that he cannot stop himself or remember the rule, or has he been reinforced so that others have greater difficulty stopping him if he behaves in that way?

We have observed that some diagnosed children excel when playing games that require strategizing (e.g., Magic cards, Yu-Gi-Oh Card Games). During these activities diagnosed children not only learn how to play, but they also rarely show problematic functioning apparent as when conforming to rules pertaining to assigned activities (i.e., no one must remind them of the rules). Some of these children also demonstrate competent memory for event sequences when they accurately recall the progression of moves occurring during the game, and sometimes they are quick to highlight when others break rules during the game. In some respects, these picture card games seem are more complex in their rules and procedures than the requirements, for example, of church or school (e.g., raise your hand; do not call out).

In addition, while diagnosed persons may not initially object to a rule when it is first introduced (which, according to traditionalists, would be oppositional behavior), it is possible that they stop behavior that is consistent with rules in response to the subsequent conditions they encounter as a result of abiding by the rules. This pattern of responding occurs, for example, when they notice that they are failing or experiencing other discomforts *during* rule compliance. We must ask whether patterns inconsistent with rule conformity or endurance have been reinforced in relation to these circumstances.

We cannot readily accept a disability interpretation when we observe that the same diagnosed persons show behaviors consistent with rules when enacting some non-assigned tasks, and when competently reciting particular rules at the point of performance when correcting others. Moreover, even if it were confirmed that diagnosed persons do not remember particular rules and consequences as well as others, we cannot insist that they have less access to those memories due to a defective inhibitory mental mechanism; they may be cued by working memory to act otherwise. They could be reinforced in ways that interfere with remembering rules, if past experience has shown that distress and surrender will occur when behaving in ways consistent with rules.

This is not to say that diagnosed children are pretending to not know the rules, but rather that they could be reinforced to not *remember* or learn certain rules because they have learned something other than rule conformity. Diagnosed individuals could be conditioned to behave inconsistently with rules in the same way that they learn greater compliance to rules that promote their successes. However, a noteworthy complication is that failure to behave consistently with rules can occur so frequently that the responses are emitted even when it is advantageous to comply. For example, a diagnosed child may resort to cheating when he could have won the game fairly, in that he anticipates losing. The same notion can apply when he expects parents to say something negative when it was not the case.

Moreover, how is it determined that *non*-diagnosed persons behave such that they are consistent with rules because of frequent *rule recitation*, or that an inhibitory response permits these recitations to occur? When addressing these matters, Ryle (1949, 46) notes that when we say a person knows how to do something, there are "observances of rules or canons or the applications of criteria, but they are not tandem operations of theoretically avowing maxims and then putting them into practice." For Ryle, people do not first recite the rule (vocally or non-vocally), and then behave consistent with those recitations. Instead, people learn to do behaviors consistent with rules, principles, and standards.

At first these rules may be repeated (vocally and non-vocally)—especially when questions arise about the legitimacy of a committed response—or concerns are voiced about the permissibility of an action in a new situation. Although after enough practice, it is increasingly unusual for anyone to recite rules in any form prior to behaving consistently with them. For example, after learning a card game, precursory activity is seldom required in order to function adequately in rule-consistent ways.

In Ryle's view, actions are consistent with rules after people have learned "how." People do not "follow rules" in the sense that their behavior must be "guided" by the ability to sense or restate a rule prior to acting consistently with it. People learn through practice to behave consistently or inconsistently with certain rules; however, after this conditioning takes place (and unless unique or dubious circumstances occur and there is time for prefatory responses), these behaviors are enacted without the additional requirement of also having to access a working memory of the rule in mental form prior to doing rule-consistent behaviors. As emphasized here, much of daily life happens without rule recitation, and only under unique and very circumscribed conditions do any of us mentally prepare to remember rules once we learn "how."

Thus it is difficult to believe that individuals are given an ADHD diagnosis based on the relatively small sample of circumstances when people frequently recite rules to enable them to behave consistently with rules. As noted earlier, Bargh and Chartrand (1999) claim that conscious self-guiding responses occur only 5% of the time during daily life. Moreover, no data exists where it is established that diagnosed persons do less rule recitation than others; therefore, those frequency rates cannot be used to empirically account for their ADHD patterns.

Less Ability to Organize

It has also been reported that ADHD children are less likely to use rules to organize and strategize during laboratory memory tasks. That finding is used to support the claim that biological ADHD interferes with executive functioning that would help success rates on complex memory tasks. Barkley (2006c) notes that diagnosed persons will generally have more problems when greater amounts of information and/or complex forms of information must be retained (in mind) over periods of delay. It is believed that diagnosed persons are biologically less able to implement tactics to help them organize and remember effectively.

However, learned patterns of responding might also impede the development of doing more strategic responses on complex memory tasks (assuming equal intellectual competence). For example, if many diagnosed individuals are conditioned to rely on others to cue, sort out, remind, and discriminate procedures for them, they would not learn those behaviors when doing laboratory memory tasks. Moreover, less use of organizational strategies when required to remember particular kinds of content is not unique to diagnosed children, and sometimes diagnosed children show systematic remembering under on specific occasions with specific content.

For example, diagnosed individuals have shown significantly different competency in using organizational rules and strategies when content pertains to a Christmas list or to their collections. Time and again we find examples where diagnosed children talk with others about non-assigned activities (e.g., television series, snakes, dinosaurs, etc.); we typically notice their methodic responding and noteworthy memory categorizations at these times. They recall information specific to each character, including physical characteristics and unique behaviors. They have notably little difficulty with grouping schemes, the recall of significant events, and the correct ordering of those occurrences when asked questions about such content.

If it is true that diagnosed persons are less able to systematize, how is it that some organize and remember complex information in such detail and with such precision? Why would the capability of their neurological system alter in relation to the specific items being remembered? For example, what makes it neurologically easier to remember the names of each wrestler, their weights, managers' names, special moves, past losses and triumphs, the history of matches, and memberships in associations, compared to remembering the same number of items, categories and interrelationships presented during biology class? If we could persuade diagnosed persons to spend as much time studying their biology books as they do learning about their hobbies, they would likely develop similar competency with school-related content.

Empirical work demonstrates that more practice time helps. For example, Lorch et al. (2004) found that diagnosed children benefited more than controls from assistance in study methods that helped them learn to produce coherent story recall. Once again, it may be that diagnosed people have not yet learned the competent methodical responses with content that is socially valued, expected, evaluated, and assigned by others.

Delays in Responding to Time Intervals

Barkley (1998c) also notes that diagnosed persons significantly overestimate relatively short time intervals when asked to determine how long they have waited. He claims that diagnosed persons show problems related to temporal delays interposed within tasks, or when temporal uncertainties are introduced. He concludes that diagnosed individuals have delays with "sense of time, timing of responses, and the cross-temporal organization of behavior" (p. 115). Other studies reveal that diagnosed persons exhibit problems reproducing presented time intervals in comparison to controls (Barkley, Edwards, et al., 2001; Bauermeister et al., 2005; Meaux and Chelonis, 2003). Since those time sensing tasks *seem* to require access to working memory, this empiricism is assumed to be consistent with the inhibitory model.

However, if one adopts the view that diagnosed persons are conditioned to react atypically to inconvenience, hindrance and the requirement to hurry or wait, they are not learning to respond to "time" in normative ways. Faulty estimates during empirical studies may simply be measuring those learned patterns along with the consequences of not interacting with others in routine and synchronized ways. If diagnosed persons are also conditioned such that others coordinate time parameters, they will have trouble learning to solve problems relating to time perception, because someone else has attended to time frames, maintained the itinerary, planned future activity, and perceived the time intervals for them. It is therefore not surprising that their sensing of time is deficient. The finding that diagnosed persons have problems sensing time intervals (Barkley, Murphy, and Bush, 2001) may only reveal that diagnosed people often do not learn the skills necessary to accurately perceive time, or that time sensing delays will increase the probability of learning ADHD patterns.

However, when addressing concerns about time, it might be informative to design an experiment to see whether diagnosed children will still over-estimate time intervals when they are the source of the directive to endure a time delay, as when a parent asks "How long has it been since I called you for dinner?" Even if we presume that some time sensing tasks require more working memory than others, there could nevertheless be a confounding of unmeasured influences that diminish the scores of diagnosed persons, depending on how experiments are designed (e.g., requiring them to use a flashlight to recreate a demonstrated time interval, etc.). As with many other skill deficits, we might observe that these children can learn to respond effectively to time sensing tasks by exposing them to new training, and that their measured competence varies significantly with circumstance.

If we also evaluate how diagnosed persons help themselves remember upcoming events that relate to non-assigned activity, this might help us determine the parameters of possibility, given the current status of their behavioral repertoire for time management. If some exemplars of effective time management exist, why not refer to these impressive scenarios when discussing their purported disabilities and delays with them? For example, many diagnosed persons can be punctual and reliable during a courtship; that they frequently reveal problems in other situations with time-related behavior only indicates that they more often repeat non-normative time-related responses.

Juxtaposed with these interpretations is the claim that ADHD interferes with a person's ability to organize actions through time (Barkley, 2000; Barkley et al., 1997). A competent sense of time requires executive functioning, which helps the individual to better understand the past and potential future. It is generally posited that diagnosed persons cannot readily access memories that inform them of particular sequences of past events, and which help them better recognize what will likely occur. With the availability of such information, behaviors might be adequately navigated via executive functioning in time regulated ways, and likely to control wider time horizons. Since diagnosed persons frequently act before they can consider additional information that might otherwise be available through working memory, future goal accomplishment may not occur, and previously planned behaviors may not happen. Commitments are often neglected and the individual's behavior has less continuity, organization, consistency, and predictability when viewed over time.

However, traditionalists have not established a correspondence between the amount of working memory required and the time horizons being recalled. It has not yet been proved that it invariably takes more working memory to remember events from the distant past, compared to recall of recent events. We could alternatively claim that sometimes remembering distant past events is easier than remembering recent events, depending on the associations evoked by present and current conditions. For example, memories of the past often take place when one examines memorabilia, hears a song from youth, or recognizes a store and remembers purchases made years earlier. Because these interludes occur, we can investigate whether there is always a direct relationship between having the time to remember (i.e., a better inhibitory system), and the time interval between the act of remembering and the remembered event.

For the traditional account to be tenable, designers of that view must also prove that individuals with punctual, reliable, and very organized patterns of behavior have patterns of biology opposite to that of diagnosed individuals. They also need to show that the quality of access to working memory (however that might be established) correlates with punctuality, reliability, vigilance towards achieving long-term goals, and better preparedness at the time of performance throughout the day.

But to date those data have not been presented. Traditionalists have not shown that individuals with accessible and very competent working memories do exemplary behavior in relation to time; they have *not shown that such capacities protect a person from an ADHD diagnosis.* Additionally, since not all diagnosed persons express problems during measurements of working memory, or have difficulties estimating and reproducing time intervals, individuals might still qualify for the ADHD behavioral criteria and not show any such functional deficits.

Because not all appointments and commitments are missed, traditionalists are further obliged to account for those inconsistencies too. Diagnosed individuals sometimes show an adequate sensing of time, so there has to somehow be a means, a capacitor, for their neurology to permit such behaviors. While traditionalists may try to account for these inconsistencies by positing extenuating circumstances such as interest, saliency, etc., as noted from the outset, those forms of explication are merely tautological; if they behave acceptably, then they must be interested or else the events must have been salient to them.

However, if we can show that instances of punctuality and failure to be timely relate to contingencies of reinforcement, a learning paradigm becomes the more logical model. Perhaps diagnosed persons are simply showing the consequences of learning different priorities, or in this alternative vernacular, different behaviors have been reinforced to occur reliably through time. As Skinner (1953, 115) points out, if one is attempting to distinguish between a "reflexive" sneeze and a "facsimile" sneeze, it is recommended that we establish conditions to see if incompatible behaviors can be induced. In Skinner's view "If we offer him candy and the sneezing stops, we may be pretty sure that it was not a reflex." Likewise, if we can establish that changing conditions alters the extent to which time organized behavior occurs, we may be fairly confident that the disorganized pattern is not a result of a fixed delay.

When studying time-related behaviors we can identify the conditions under which diagnosed individuals show acceptable punctuality and reliability such as when returning home on time to meet a friend, and note the conditions under which they do *not* maintain schedules, including a missed doctor's appointment. Consistent with the view that attentiveness to time is influenced by conditioning, it is remarkable how adroitly and frequently diagnosed children watch the clock while enduring an assigned activity, but will profess to ignore time while doing self initiated and enjoyable tasks.

In light of these competencies, we would expect that they can learn to use a watch rather than a timer set by someone else, as well as learn to check their watch routinely in order to resolve scheduling problems and improve punctuality. Since the behaviors that improve punctuality already occur in some situations, the solution may be as simple as obtaining response repetition in new circumstances. For example, checking their watch routinely to facilitate conforming to the family's eating schedule just as they look at the clock continuously during school. Arguing that an inherent delay prevents them from stopping enjoyable activities and remembering socially valued schedules and time parameters is actually a strange context-specific bodily disorder.

Rather than posit such a disability, we alternatively claim that diagnosed persons learn patterns of response that impede punctuality. In contrast to many non-diagnosed individuals, who might enact specific behaviors to help them conform to scheduled events, persons doing ADHD patterning rarely carry out simple routine solutions. For example, while many non-diagnosed persons will record appointments at the moment of scheduling, place necessary objects for the maintenance of stipulated routines in predictable places, put mail by the door, and invariably put a watch on while getting dressed in the morning, diagnosed persons do not usually act in ways that would increase the probability of compliance.

When these behaviors are not conducted in a customary or routine fashion (diagnosed or not), the likelihood of time effective organized behavior decreases; this problem is not unique for the diagnosed group and applies to most of us. It may therefore be interesting to evaluate the extent to which diagnosed persons (who complain of an inability to maintain schedules) conduct very simple protocols to solve the problems they report. If we discover that they are not doing these very simple routines, then how do we account for the fact that they invariably do not forget to put on their baseball hats in the morning? What neurological event allows them to learn that routine but prevents the routine of putting on a watch? Are we to believe that they are not doing *enough* inhibiting and executive functioning to consistently wear a watch, or are they behaving in a reinforced way based on their history of living in the world? For example, if they do not wear a watch they will be less accountable to time parameters.

When diagnosed persons do not do the most basic solutions to solve time management problems, such as keeping an appointment book, it is reasonable to ask if they are physically less able to do these behaviors, but it is also reasonable to explore the possibility that continued disorganized behavior, a limited time horizon, and failure to coordinate with others "in time" is reinforced. This approach resembles Freud's (1963) conceptualization that problem behaviors can be understood as psychological solutions; forgetting often has its advantages.

Even when diagnosed persons complain that they miss out due to poor time management, it is interesting to observe whether they change their behavior in order to diminish the probability of the same outcome once again. For example, do they set an alarm, or write a note and place it where they can find it before an appointment? It is reasonable to pursue a more psychologically-based explication when they sometimes demonstrate the required competencies, and when they do not enact these apparently simple solutions.

Despite their insistence that *they want* to change (which is reinforced such that others are less disapproving when they insist), close examination of their actions and the simplicity of the available solutions—that they do not do—

suggests that old behaviors are still reinforced. One might logically inquire whether diagnosed persons are reinforced by normative practice, but limited due to biological delays, or if they are reinforced to continue responding with ADHD patterns.

Interestingly, some diagnosed persons try to maintain a schedule by putting notes all over the house, or by employing an atypical system to externally represent the required activity, but the chosen methods are frequently incoherent and not very helpful. In fact, the remedies would not benefit most people who want to better organize their time. The conventional claim may be that ADHD causes these ineffective problem solving behaviors, but perhaps these individuals are still reinforced to do non-normative practice rather than conform; the outcomes occurring in relation to their chaotic approaches (i.e., avoidance) could be reinforcing the continuance of the ineffective actions.

There are numerous ways to account for problems with time organization, and many different reinforcement histories correlate with ostensibly the same non-normative behaviors. For these reasons, biological determinism is not put forward to account for the kinds of non-normative patterns with time evident in the diagnosed population. Time management behavior in the diagnosed population could also be explained in the same way as we account for individuals who run late due to lack of assertiveness.

The way in which this interpretation diverges from convention is especially evident when Barkley (2000) attempts to illustrate the devastating effects of having ADHD by recounting the story of a man who missed a prearranged date (which, in Barkley's view) is forgotten due to an ADHD-constricted time horizon. While this male is portrayed as a victim of his delayed "time awareness," a learning paradigm can investigate the contingencies of reinforcement in this case.

For example, what has happened with other prearranged dates, and any other possible historical outcomes related to situations where past disapproval and disappointment with females has occurred. We can inquire about competing activities that may have been available to reinforce a response other than abiding by the scheduled rendezvous. Despite the possibility that this man's learning history can reasonably account for his failure to attend his "blind date," we notice that once a person qualifies for diagnosis, psychological factors are ignored. Biology takes precedence and it is claimed that the man lacked the necessary internal equipment to remember and organize his actions appropriately over time.

Similarly, Barkley also describes being picked up at the airport by a diagnosed individual who purportedly has learned to compensate for his ADHD by placing "sticky notes" all over his dashboard (including his speedometer) as a way to manage his disorganization. Barkley concludes that the individual's ADHD prevents him from recognizing the future consequences of covering his speedometer with reminder notes, but we can also make the case that covering the speedometer is reinforced behavior that permits him to speed without the feedback that he is doing something wrong.

In the current conceptualization of ADHD there is an ongoing attempt to identify the conditions that relate to the frequency rates of either maintaining or not maintaining schedules, responsibilities, or completion of assignments over long time periods. The organizational characteristics of behaviors are accounted for by identifying what happened when diagnosed persons behave in an orderly or disorganized way, if they are otherwise intellectually competent. It is not that diagnosed persons cannot perform what they know, but that what they know (or what behaviors are reinforced for particular situations and circumstances) differs from what most people have been conditioned to do. Even if involved participants do not initially identify contingencies of reinforcement that can reasonably account for their actions, ADHD responding may nonetheless be related to historical parameters. As noted by Skinner (1953):

> When a discriminative stimulus has an effect upon the probability of a response, we see that the present environment is indeed relevant, but it is not easy to prove the inevitability of the control without an adequate account of the history of reinforcement and deprivation (p. 112).

Punctuality and keeping appointments are not expected to occur when considering the reinforcement histories of many diagnosed people. Diagnosed or not, if otherwise competent persons generally do not relate with people in integrated and courteous ways, over time they will realize problems dealing with scheduling, deadlines and appointment-keeping. For example, if an individual has been reinforced to play a card game on the computer for long periods of time, it is less likely that she will curtail game playing in order to do school work, chores, and keep appointments—unless those more socially-valued behaviors have also been reinforced. However, that same person (diagnosed or not) will show little difficulty coordinating in time with others to play a card game within a designated time frame.

The accepted belief is that neurological ADHD wreaks havoc on the ability to sense time and organize through time, which reduces the probability that school assignments will be completed, the family pet will be fed, or that curfews will be kept, but this current learning paradigm rejects that formulation. We can observe that this same individual engages in other habitual behaviors including turning on the television when entering the house, and checking the sports page when the home team has played the previous day. It is therefore puzzling that their disability prevents them from carrying out socially preferred routine behaviors such as brushing teeth before bed, taking out the garbage on a designated day of the week, arriving home on time to eat with the family, and washing the dishes when it is their turn.

What kind of disability prevents one from starting homework when entering the house, but simultaneously does not interfere with immediately reading a magazine? Is there something less neurologically complex about going upstairs and reading a magazine that could be a continuation from the day before, compared to starting a homework assignment placed on a table directly in front of them (with pencil ready) by a concerned parent? Moreover, even if diagnosed persons are less able to consider the long-term consequences of their actions, no one has yet established that they would change behavior if that information were made available; perhaps they will remain reinforced to read the magazine rather than do homework.

Procrastination can be reinforced in a number of ways: others help and show concern as deadlines become imminent; deadlines are sometimes shifted to the future; anticipated difficulty with an assigned task is avoided longer; failure to succeed may be attributed to insufficient time to complete the work; other self-initiated behavior may be enacted for longer periods of time; adequate role modeling may not be occurring; and last-minute functioning may be more desirable because the thrill of it induces effective and vigilant responding, and completion of it yields a greater sense of relief.

When conditioned to neglect future concerns, diagnosed persons learn that required activity is unnecessary unless dire circumstances prevail; many will not carry out household instruction, responsibilities, or assignments until their parents reach a boiling point (e.g., parent becomes stern, raises his or her voice, counts to ten or makes threats). Not surprisingly, that same individual may therefore also not conform to homework assignments until grades are imminent and a crisis encroaches.

In many instances parental worry and consternation about unfinished assignments (or self-care) reinforces diagnosed individuals to procrastinate. The parent reassures the child about his or her importance whenever showing anxiety about looming adverse consequences, and in so doing, parents could be inadvertently conditioning laxity by providing excessive assistance just prior to a project's due date. The diagnosed person is thus is able to escape and is protected from the jeopardy associated with missing deadlines. However, if these individuals do not learn to enact consistent routines, as is necessary for most of us, they will frequently fail when scheduling is required.

In our view, nonconsensual *habits* rather than neurological inability to remain organized account for the time-related problems often seen in the diagnosed population. For example, many individuals develop such consistent sleep habits that they no longer require an alarm to wake at precisely the same time each morning. Similarly, many therapists eventually sense when the clinical hour is about to end, since they have a consistent pattern of one-hour blocks of time. We have no data that these individuals maintain such precise time-related responding because they do more executive activity at crucial moments.

Another important question is why do diagnosed persons interact within acceptable time horizons while achieving on non-assigned tasks over time, but not when others *expect* achievements over broad time spans? For example, we observe that it is rare for a diagnosed person to procrastinate when required to arrange for a non-assigned event such as inviting friends for a sleep over, paintball game, or trading card tournament. Here, they will often call friends in *advance*, secure transportation, ensure access to enough money, and so on. Because the planned event will sometimes occur later compared to a due date for a school assignment (not begun until the last moment), it is puzzling that a limiting bodily condition should interfere with their perception of time and their ability to organize over time.

Moreover, if "time" is conceptualized as a parameter that imposes limitations, it is not surprising that many diagnosed individuals will relate to "time" differently than the majority. The absence of alacrity, problems maintaining schedules, failure to keep commitments, and lack of punctuality and promptness can all be related to how diagnosed individuals have learned to respond to the limits, demands, requirements, and expectations of others. Rather than biological inferiority in coordinating within time parameters, these individuals have been conditioned to integrate behavior with other people in uniquely unacceptable ways. Their response to time-based parameters can be consistent to how they react in general to restrictions, imperatives, denials, impediments, demands, and impositions. They may rely too often on others or disapprove of the schedules that usurp much of their parents' time, and thus prevent them from relaxation and enjoyment. Any social pattern that is rigid and harried is potentially rejected by diagnosed individuals with this type of patterning.

Non-verbal Memory Delays

In furthering our laboratory findings review, other reports indicate that diagnosed persons show more short-term memory problems when asked to imitate hand movements (Mariani and Barkley, 1997). Barkley (1998c) assumes that this is indicative of problems with non-verbal working memory, which produces impairment in ability to imitate intricate sequences of behaviors novel to the subject. Difficulty in copying hand movements means that diagnosed persons have problems gaining access to these memories because of inhibitory failures (Barkley, 2006c).

However, a reasonable approach to this assumption is to investigate other ways to account for the failure of diagnosed children to succeed on these tasks. For example, to what extent are diagnosed persons intimidated when the demonstration is given? Past failure with other similar tests could be the trigger of those responses. Instead of reacting in order to help them perform adequately, such as watching a demonstration intently, they may do less positive, more anxious reactions before the examiner completes the full range of movements. Not being fully involved while the items are initially presented, coupled with a lack of participation from the outset can, for some, guarantee a relatively poor performance. Additionally, others will have learned that when they feel overwhelmed, various forms of relief are offered.

Diagnosed children with motor difficulties might also have problems during the hand copying memory test, simply due to functional impairment (Barkley, 2006c). They will also associate failure with any task requiring dexterity. Perhaps functioning is disrupted because of negative past experiences when performing physically in front of others. Performance may be awkward if they feel inadequate to the expectation. As always, a possible way to draw out these alternative explanations would be to investigate whether competence changes as a result of practice and with recognition of successes.

We could also observe whether the child enacts the same or similar competencies when conditions are less evaluative. We can observe how they learn to operate a control pad for a video game when instructed by a peer. We might inquire whether they reveal imitative difficulty when doing karate movements, car mechanics, and doing the sequence of hand movements for a special handshake. Given the possibility of discrepancies in competency as conditions change, it is important to assess functioning in many situations, and note how the extent of variation in the content of the activity, the people involved, and the source of the instruction for the task influences success rates of imitating presented motor sequences.

It may be the case that some diagnosed persons exhibit problems with copying tasks (in general), in that imitation is associated with losing discretionary authority. If they must imitate exactly as others, then it is the other person who maintains all authority. Tasks requiring rigid conformity may be less likely to elicit an unreserved accommodating reaction. Some diagnosed individuals may be conditioned to not acquiesce to situational demands, or mimic if instructed to do so. As noted earlier, if non-conciliatory responding takes place on a daily basis, fewer instances will occur in which they practice contouring their actions to external parameters, and there will be fewer instances of precise imitative enactments.

Rather than point to poor working memory as the way to account for the lackluster imitative performance of otherwise unimpaired diagnosed persons (Barkley, 1997), perhaps they have learned other responses that impede the quality of their imitations. If conditioned responses push these individuals to evade compulsory tasks and guard against loss of discretionary authority and exposure to failure, it would seem that imitative behavior or any other conforming response is not repeated in a typical way for this population. Moreover, before we adopt the view that diagnosed persons are unable to imitate, we need first to consider the facility with which some of these individuals can parody their parents word for word (using exact tone of voice and inflection) after the parent has, for example, behaved critically towards them, even if the criticism took place days or weeks before.

If diagnosed individuals frequently deflect from tasks instead of doing more conciliatory responding, they are unlikely to become adept in their imitative skills. The failure to imitate may become evident when first learning to form letters and numbers, and when asked to perform a task in a particular way. The initial and continuing pattern is to *not* abide by specific directives, demonstrations, and instructions. They apparently "buck" or disregard the system without ever saying no directly; although the end result is a greater number of errors in relation to standards.

Incidentally, because diagnosed children did not demonstrate problems with remembering sequences when asked to recreate patterns emitted by a "Simon" toy (Barkley, Edwards, et al., 2001), we also think that (depending on the task used in the experiment), different manifestations of competence can be obtained. Since diagnosed adults showed problems during a similar experiment (Murphy, Barkley, and Bush, 2001), the age of the population sample can therefore also influence the results obtained. Again, very subtle changes in parameters can sometimes yield very different outcomes.

One example of how context influences imitative competence for some adults is evident when they attempt to learn simple dance routines. If they approach the task presuming they "cannot" dance, their learning curve will seem inordinately wide. Each movement during the instruction is carried out in a tentative and self-conscious manner. Although they make the same physical movements with ease in other contexts, during dance class they nevertheless express delayed competency.

While many diagnosed persons may indeed have functional delays that impede competence on imitative memory tasks (which may also increase the probability of learning ADHD responding), we think that when conditioned to do ADHD responding, individuals are also less likely to learn how to adequately meet most expectations. The empirical question then arises as to which extent these individuals can be conditioned to show improved imitative behaviors.

Delays in Solving Complex Problems

When exploring other functional difficulties in the lab, traditionalists also report that an aggregate of diagnosed persons will have greater difficulty compared to controls when they have to construct complex spatial models such as "The Tower of London" and "The Tower of Hanoi," which require the anticipation of a sequence of interdependent steps (Brady and Denckla, 1994; Pennington, Grossier, and Welsh, 1993; Weyandt and Willis, 1994). They conclude that ADHD prevents diagnosed persons from using mental representations to help them envision the steps. They are, according to Barkley (1998c), biologically less able to do forethought and planning before enacting the actual motor movements.

However, in that diagnosed persons may show other functional complications, and various counterproductive responding can impair performance (including presumed incompetence), it is essential to determine who shows relative difficulty on tower-building tasks, and who functions in typical ways. Other response patterns may hinder their success on tower building tasks, even when learning problems, low intelligence, and depression are factored out of the analysis. Since tower-building does not discriminate ADHD for diagnostic purposes, one can still meet the behavioral criteria and adequately build the towers. Such an inquiry could highlight what, other than qualifying for the ADHD behavioral criteria, accounts for relatively poor functioning of some diagnosed persons.

As noted, many diagnosed persons become agitated when they realize that they must coordinate multiple steps; they respond as if the problem is inscrutable and that success is unattainable much like when instructed to clean the mess in their room (e.g., they complain about not knowing where to start). While these conditioned behaviors may frequently sequence with others helping or removing requirements, these children are not learning the necessary skills to adequately solve even fairly simple day-to-day cleaning tasks. Peevishness, moaning, and exasperation can become conditioned instead of the more systematic responses. Given these patterns, we would not expect success on the complicated tower-building task.

A subset of diagnosed persons may also respond poorly to the tower-building tasks because they are expected to conform without allowance for mistakes. These tasks require that they build towers with the fewest possible steps so that the product exactly matches the experimenter's design. Some diagnosed individuals might react more negatively than others in the intolerant and highly circumscribed situations. They might presume that participation will only expose them to failure and diminishment.

If these influences are operative, it is reasonable to explore whether changing task parameters significantly alters performance for some diagnosed individuals. Examiners can, for example, increase the number of permissible options (while still controlling for task complexity), and increase task difficulty by increments. The outcome could reduce concern about the failure to meet perfectionist standards (Harticollis, 1968), and expose the child to preliminary success that ameliorates the expectation that task completion is insurmountable.

We could also explore whether functioning improves by allowing the children greater discretionary input into the design of the towers. For example, some diagnosed children may perform better when allowed to select the parts of the model rather than respond to a rigidly formatted item. Similarly, we can investigate whether diagnosed children perform better when they build the towers with familiar materials compared to using unfamiliar disks and pegs. Those modifications could potentially evoke positive associations, and help make the tasks seem achievable. If we see that these changes relate to improved performance, we may later discover that the use of the new content will cue the repetition of increasingly competent behavior rather than return observers to the notion of neurological weakness.

Another inquiry could examine whether diagnosed children improve markedly when permitted to talk out loud or draw ideas on paper to stepwise represent the problem, as has been advised by conventional practice. In order to coincide with traditional views, diagnosed persons would have to improve in these tasks compared to non-diagnosed persons, given that traditional belief posits that the diagnosed person's only problem is a deficiency in mental capability to do these tasks. While we cannot know the exact number of diagnosed persons who respond favorably to the aforementioned interventions, and whether their performance improves more than is the case for most of us, this is one way to explore the traditional explication in detail.

Nevertheless, it remains contradictory that diagnosed persons can function competently on tasks specifically designed to cull the problems traditionalists insist embody the ADHD delay. The fact that diagnosed individuals do not show consistent weaknesses on tasks purportedly requiring preparatory mental action prior to an overt response could be seen as profoundly at odds with the disability assertion. For example, certain studies indicate that diagnosed children do not show poor performance when asked to complete maze tasks, despite that these tasks require the functioning predicted to be delayed when someone has neurological ADHD inhibitory delay (Barkley, Godzinsky, and DuPaul, 1992; Grodzinsky and Diamond, 1992; Mariani and Barkley, 1997; McGee et al., 1989; Milich and Kramer, 1985; Moffit and Silva, 1988).

In an attempt to retain a disability model, Barkley (1998c; 2006c) posits that sample size and age of the participants is likely influencing the results of these investigations. He also claims that maze tasks do not require as much mental planning as tower-building tasks, or that the solutions are evident within the maze, and only have to be discovered by the subject. That is, while maze puzzles require individuals to imagine an escape route within the externally-represented design, the tower-building tasks provide less external representation; the subject has to rely heavily on imagination. As is often the case, it then becomes possible to identify parameters that offset ADHD whenever problematic responding is absent.

However, one may reach very different conclusions regarding the data on maze tasks. The traditional perspective that diagnosed individuals also have problems with impulse control runs counter to the fact that diagnosed persons can often competently solve maze puzzles. Since the movement of a pencil in a wrong direction results in loss of points, it is better to cease all motor movements and imagine the path of the pencil prior to a physical response. While the correct response is discoverable by viewing the maze design and coordinating a sequence of correct movements, performance would clearly improve by imagining prior to a motoric response. However, this is precisely what diagnosed persons should *not* easily be able to do, according to traditional dogma, which also purports that diagnosed persons have less ability to stop themselves, to brake sufficiently for this kind of functioning to take place.

This presumed inability becomes *the reason* for darting into traffic and blurting out inappropriate responses. Not finding a consistent problem for all diagnosed persons when solving maze problems (even by not factoring out co-occurring problems) is a notable inconsistency with traditional beliefs about

ADHD, and a problem that is difficult to ignore. Even if we accept that tower-building problems tax the executive functions more than maze tasks, successful performance in both tasks seems to require imaginative activity prior to motoric response, as well as discriminating and remembering correct and incorrect imagined responses. We recognize that the interpretation and application of data is a key factor in our study.

In consideration of the shortcomings discussed here, we suggest that the non-delayed functioning of significant numbers of diagnosed individuals on maze tasks, for example, might be best explained by invoking psychosocial categories. Escaping from a maze can often be familiar to some diagnosed children because they solve these kinds of problems regularly when responding to various obstructions, restrictions, and confinements throughout the day. Much like a video game character trapped in a dilemma (and in typical social relationships), diagnosed children have plenty of experience working out solutions to escape predicaments. They may therefore be better trained for success when functioning on maze tasks.

Moreover, fascination can play a part; the maze task evokes very different responses compared to tower building, although both apparently require mental action prior to motoric responding. For instance, it may be more exciting to figure out how to break free from boundaries, compared to building a tower, which requires conformity to a particular standard. The maze task might seem less coercive or restrictive, and in contrast to tower building tasks that require much preparatory activity, children can initiate their solutions quickly. Consistent with this interpretation is the observation that it is usually not difficult to convince children (diagnosed or not) to participate, show effort, and persist when maze designs are presented; they often seem delighted to do those activities.

Perhaps we will also find, for example, that diagnosed children who frequently climb rocks also learn to anticipate pathways that either increase or decrease the ease or likelihood of reaching the desired goal without delays and setbacks. It might be interesting to evaluate whether diagnosed "rock climbers" differ from controls in their anticipatory behaviors related to this recreational activity. If functioning is assessed in relation to familiar activity, do diagnosed children (without other co-occurring problems to limit functioning in pervasive ways) show typical competency? Will we find that their posited inner problems vanish when functioning is evaluated in relation to activities in which they immerse themselves?

Problems with Driving and Touching

To continue our list of laboratory findings, we observe that diagnosed persons (as an aggregate) also express difficulty with the task of driving an automobile (actual and lab-simulated) compared to non-diagnosed persons (Barkley, 2004; Barkley, Murphy, and Kwasnik, 1996; Barkley, Guevremont et al., 1993).

Barkley (2000) points to biological determinism as causal for this outcome because diagnosed persons have problems with interference control, impulsivity, distractibility, and the anticipation of the future, which all contribute to their high accident rates. Clumsiness with car pedals and controls is also seen as consistent with their fine motor sequencing problems.

However, observations of driving difficulties can be accounted for very differently; driving can also be construed as a social behavior, not solely as a manifestation of neurobiology. Driving requires coordination with others, turn taking, and acquiescence. Not everyone is conditioned to operate acceptably as drivers. When persons are reinforced to take risks, or that they must be first relative to others (even at the expense of others), such individuals are likely to speed and suffer accidents. Individuals showing this patterning may be less obliging, not only to other people, but also to the physical limitations of the car, pedals and other controls (even without delays in coordination).

They might be insensitive with the controls in the same ways that they bang, provoke, intrude, or behaved boisterously in social situations. These behaviors need not be neurologically delayed. Many of these children have obtained benefits throughout childhood when not heeding parental instruction to be careful with themselves and with objects in their environments. A case could be made that diagnosed persons simply repeat conditioned social behaviors while operating a vehicle. Since diagnosed persons are frequently not integrating their actions with the perspective of others, and often doing behavioral acts that require others to accommodate to them, one might claim that they are not conditioned to be collaborative out of the car, in the car, or with the car.

That same learning paradigm can also be used to interpret findings derived from observations of diagnosed children in "laboratory playrooms" (Roberts, 1979). For example, while these studies indicate that diagnosed children touch more objects during periods of free play (Barkley and Ullman, 1975; Routh and Schroeder, 1976; Zentall, 1985), and are less likely to sustain attention during play (DuPaul et al., 2001), the interpretation of the findings is a matter for debate. These behaviors are consistent with the inhibitory model, according to convention, but we can interpret those same observations in various ways.

First, it is important to note that even within these relatively unstructured settings, symptom variation is often apparent. Diagnosed children do not always touch, provoke, or do non-normatively paced behavior relative to controls. Once an object is found that resembles objects that the child has been reinforced to play with, the diagnosed child may not differ from controls in any appreciable way. Rather than lack of inhibition, one could argue that many diagnosed children have been conditioned to increase touching under certain conditions, in that this accelerates the probability of finding an acceptable toy.

In the playroom setting many diagnosed children might have also learned to discard a toy quickly, and touch another toy as soon as disappointment or difficulty with the toy is encountered. Such behavior can also be reinforced because it increases the probability that something less disappointing will be found. Like people who frequently move residence in order to resolve problems, diagnosed children may be reinforced to change toys rather than adjust behavior to deal with the shortcomings of the toy they currently handle. By manipulating many objects the diagnosed child is perhaps reassured that he or she is not missing out or settling for less. As noted throughout, the more active the pattern, the less the associated constraint, limitation, denial, or restriction.

Consistent with a pattern of reaching boredom very quickly, many diagnosed children orient as if external sources will solve their problems. Many learn that their parent's job is to resolve unhappiness and discomfort. Like opening the refrigerator, trying one food after another, and hoping that eventually a satisfying taste will be found, diagnosed persons can be conditioned to shift from one object to the next until a more delightful object is found. Diagnosed or not, many people learn to self-gratify in this way (e.g., channel surfing with the television remote, etc.).

Interestingly, a very similar pattern of reliance on external change is frequently evident during couple's therapy. Participants will complain that their problems would be resolved if only their spouses would change. In the same way, it could be said that when diagnosed children disrupt, fail to sustain attention, whine, or pester until the world changes to their liking, they are orienting with an extreme form of external locus of control (i.e., the acquisition of a new or different toy will produce happiness).

More rapid touching of objects can, however, also take place when adults are transitioning the child away from an enjoyable activity or stipulating a certain action. Being directed towards a stipulated agenda can often correlate with an increase in hyperactive touching, as the rapid touching might counter the deprivation that the transition imposes, as well as impede the adult's attempts to pull the child to another setting or activity.

Touching may also divert the attention of others in the context where people are talking together without including the child, or when parents compliment a sibling. Here, the diagnosed child will look around and then begin fidgeting and touching nearby objects. Touching may, however, occur less frequently when the child is preoccupied with an activity that she initiates and enjoys, and when she maintains complete discretionary authority during a social exchange.

Generally, frequent touching behaviors seem to elicit concern from others, waiting decreases, change becomes easier and more rapid, and limits may be disregarded, etc. However, it seems that diagnosed children rapidly touch objects differently from what occurs when a blind person regularly touches (permissible) objects more than others as a way to compensate for a bodily disability. We observe that diagnosed children touch objects one after the other very frequently, but it is not clear how it has been decided that doing these behaviors offsets a diminished ability to imagine (Barkley, 2000), especially when they often touch only the most forbidden objects in the room, create a mess that is difficult to ignore, and less often behave in this manner when situations are more settled and enjoyed.

Moreover, we observe that diagnosed children often report that they fantasize about future possibilities such as what might happen during recess, after school, or on the fishing trip with father several weeks hence. When considering those reports, it seems inconsistent to claim that these children lack the ability to imagine future content. Additionally, for traditional account to be tenable, it seems that proponents would not only have to establish that diagnosed children are less able to imagine as competently as others, but also to confirm that non-diagnosed children do not touch objects as frequently because they are imagining instead.

One might also ask if there is something about a forbidden object, acting out in public, a telephone call, or having a parent talk with a sibling that cues these purportedly delayed responses, or if these behaviors have been reinforced in relation to the increased probability that others will be distracted and turn to attend to the child who behaves that way. We can reasonably ask whether children have difficulty imagining possibilities, or have they been conditioned to do particular kinds of frequent touching, in that the outcomes of those actions increase the probability that social exclusion, denial, or constraints will be eliminated. Although when considering those benefits, why would anyone settle for imagining when touching is available, unless conditioned to defer?

Abandoning the Disability Model

Before we assume delay, there must be consistency to that explanation. Many diagnosed pre-teens and adolescents regularly go online and use the Internet to research various self-selected topics. When engaged on the computer ADHD responding is often less apparent. Persistence in a search, the ability to integrate past and present, as well as anticipate future outcomes, along with methodical and organized behavior is present (in contrast to a school assignment requiring very comparable behaviors). One diagnosed teen, for example, researched various cell phone plans on several different Internet sites, and compared and contrasted the benefits and detriments of each plan. In an attempt to persuade his parent to buy one of the plans, he presented each in great detail and had no apparent difficulty remembering costs, number of permitted minutes, and many other subtle differences between the contracts.

It seems disingenuous to insist that research on the Internet, or complex video games often played by diagnosed persons are inherently more interesting and provide the external representation and immediate reinforcement than what usually occurs with school assignments. We observe that very similar immediate feedback does not prevent diagnostic behaviors from occurring when diagnosed children provoke parents and teachers, or when required to complete school assignments.

Moreover, in contrast to simplistic video games where parameters are observed on the screen, the advanced video games and activities on the Internet require hindsight, planning, and anticipation as is required for the completion of many school assignments. Getting to the desired endpoint may require reconfiguration, conjecture, and significant working memory. Correct solutions often require preparatory activity before giving a response, and some responses must take place before actually seeing physically represented parameters. Yet, significant numbers of diagnosed persons often show reasonable competency doing these tasks.

Very similarly, when initiating playing chess or card games, diagnosed persons demonstrate planning, rehearsing, imagining possibilities, and show competent working memory. Even though these individuals might meet diagnostic behavioral criteria during school and family functioning, they will show significantly less symptomatic behavior during these non-assigned activities. Moreover, it is reasonable to ask how some diagnosed persons can play a game like chess, given their posited neurobiological delay. What enables these diagnosed persons to behave in ways consistent with the rules of chess or a challenging card game (that many *non-diagnosed* persons will have difficulty learning), when they are told that they need signs on their desks to externally remind them of the fixed school rules?

From these observations we see that the response patterns of many diagnosed persons change significantly with context and situation. Although they may continue to overreact (e.g., throw the game controller, show overly-excited moving, rely on enhancement codes, or blame the game when losing), a squirming response, reliance on others, and erratic responses when fulfilling tasks are less frequent. Instead, greater persistence, care, success with complexity, and accurate and positive response to external feedback all occur more often when the child initiates the action to achieve.

If, however, diagnosed individuals demonstrate age-consistent problem solving skill and working memory when doing activities they initiate and enjoy, it may only be necessary to alter parameters to make assigned activity consistent with those activities in order to facilitate better functioning. For example, when teaching writing skills, parents and children might playfully write notes to each other about content that is familiar and appealing to the child.

Traditionalists claim that ADHD responses will prevail unless they are prevented by stimulant drugs, contingency management, and external representation, but the biologically-delayed argument crushes the possibility for learning solutions to be explored. Additionally, if diagnosed persons have learned nonproductive, unavailing ways to respond to material that others impose, we must ask whether traditional disability intervention is our best (or the only way) to proceed, since it is inadvertently reinforcing dependence on external resources: the exact behaviors that are important to change. The self-fulfilling prophecy that ADHD actions will recur as soon as traditional interventions are withdrawn may only mean that we have not yet helped the person learn to respond effectively with less medication and directive assistance in situations that correlate with diagnostic responding.

One might also surmise that the continuance of diagnostic patterns is a "chicken and egg" problem. ADHD responding reinforces the provision of assistance, and this interactional pattern compels others to identify mistakes and derive solutions without first urging the individual to develop autonomy by contributing to the problem solving. The evolving social patterns will impede the learning of self-reliance and skill. When this psychosocial arrangement between individuals repeats across contexts and circumstances, recipients are not only frequently receiving comfort and aid in relation to errors and incompetence, but are also deprived of the opportunity to problem solve, self-evaluate, assume responsibility, and learn strategies to help them function effectively.

The question remains: Are they less *able* to learn from mistakes or to show mental proficiency, or are they to some unknown extent, *not learning* those behaviors because of insufficient training or because others are doing those behaviors for them and not fostering self-reliance? Reported laboratory studies also do not tell us the extent to which some diagnosed individuals are disabled and reacting problematically because of their insidious underlying neurological delay, or are enacting particular conditioned responses (e.g., "learned helplessness") that serve them very poorly in the lab. We as yet do not know the extent to which psychosocial history has shaped the less acceptable responding compared to the shaping of behaviors that can help them effectively meet task demands.

In response to these concerns, the approach used here avoids locating the problem inside the child or the parent; we instead advise a case-by-case study of the lifestyle patterns that have occurred over time for particular diagnosed persons. While diagnosed persons are not responding effectively, we do not know *a priori* how different their behavior might be were we to introduce different conditions of socialization. In this regard, Barkley et al. (2002) report that functional delays are not evident for those diagnosed persons who stop ADHD responding later in development.

To facilitate such improvements, we attempt to shape diagnosed children to respond effectively to "what if" statements, and to learn strategies to help them solve tasks requiring coordination of interdependent steps. We avoid the presumption that permanent compensation is necessary, and that diagnosed persons invariably need parameters in externalized form (Barkley and Edwards, 2006).

To avoid underwriting ineffectual responding, diagnosed children can be asked to clarify what they think is problematic for them before giving them the solution. They can be asked to recall as much material as possible before providing the answer. The objective is to develop initiative and contributory behavior, rather than to perpetuate avoidant and futile behavior. By conditioning diagnosed persons to use their own resources effectively when tasks are presented, improved competence may slowly be shaped—despite the assumption that reconditioning is futile.

By increasing problem complexity incrementally, we anticipate that diagnosed persons will eventually effectively manage intricacies and multi-step problems that might have formerly cued unhelpful diagnostic responses. Their functioning in subsequent laboratory study might then reflect the influence of this new learning. Given anecdotal observations, we hold that it is possible for diagnosed individuals to learn mental problem-solving responses—just as they would other sequences of actions (provided they are otherwise competent) and reinforced to do so.

Chapter 8

A Proposed Alternative: Developing Self-reliant and Collaborative Interacting

Despite widespread use of quick-fix remedies used today for ADHD diagnosed children, alternative, ongoing efforts can instead be taken to promote mutual respect and participation between the diagnosed child and others during social interactions, as well as to encourage greater self-reliance in problem solving and functioning. The objective is to help children learn to be more successful alone and in collaboration with others. A detailed presentation of these methods is discussed in Wiener (2007); this chapter provides an overview of the approach.

We suggest—rather than to select the traditional-style intervention of inculcating compliance, with prescription medication as its first line of intervention, and increased directive assistance to counter internal bodily delay—that professional health practitioners consider alternative interventions that can over the long-term, potentially outperform traditional remedies. For the most part, these alternative recommendations will contrast markedly with the traditional approach.

For instance, while the status quo aims to increase externally-induced compliance, our alternative approach is designed to increase personal initiative and cooperative acts. While the status quo focuses on inducing certain behaviors by adding extra contingencies and more stringent management of the diagnosed person's resources, our approach is designed to help the child learn to function competently with less parental coercion and assistance.

For these kinds of reasons, there will be numerous occasions where it is difficult to combine both methods. The selection of our approach means that participants are committed to inquiring into long-term behavior change. For example, rather than presume a response to be due to a less regulated or delayed behavior, one might ask what is being accomplished by an emitted ADHD response. The apparent advantages or event sequences that increase in frequency in relation to the ADHD behaviors can be identified, and ADHD acts become more like clues to solutions rather than problems. The so-called traditional "less capable" responses are transformed into *learned* behavioral events and given psychosocial meaning: for example, hyperactivity provokes concern, impulsivity prevents denial, and inattentiveness reduces discomfort. The increased frequency rate of the behaviors within particular equivalent conditions is thus explicable in the domain of *social* science.

However, psychotherapeutic approaches based primarily on treating the child in isolation, such as play therapy are not recommended here. Treatment of a child in isolation can truncate the awareness needed to recognize the interaction patterns between family members that are reinforcing ADHD behaviors. Without the knowledge of which cues may be reinforcing ADHD behaviors within the social matrix, it is nearly impossible to introduce alternative effective procedures to modify persistent ADHD behavioral patterns.

It is recommended that we use *in vivo* forms of intervention to help alter the ongoing responses of diagnosed persons; this is essentially a way to reinforce substitute behavioral patterns within a larger array of contexts, situations, and circumstances. While this recommendation is similar to the traditional approach of acting into the biological processes of the diagnosed person, we are not claiming that *in vivo* work is necessary to offset inherent delays. This method of intervention is, however, designed to be an effective way to shape diagnosed persons towards successful, appropriate, and correct behavior within a larger set of conditions over longer periods of time. Those who interact with diagnosed persons on a daily basis are in the best position to help accomplish this task.

Because parents are involved in the child's social matrix they are enormously significant. However, to shift the locus of the problem to either environment or poor parenting offers no more enlightenment than does locating ADHD in one's biological framework. We are merely advocating that we can understand ADHD as a biopsychosocial event accounted for by historical rather than antecedent biological parameters. Conceptualizing ADHD as a conditioned response pattern is *not* an attempt to blame parents, but it *is* a way to understand the parameters that are reinforcing diagnostic behaviors.

The model encourages facilitators to work together with the diagnosed person so that his or her discretionary input is not diminished when incongruities between individuals occur. While the more commanding traditional intervention will probably yield quicker results (especially with younger children), and earn high marks during empirical short-term studies measuring compliance and conformity, the side effects and outcomes may be less acceptable over the long-term compared to what can be achieved with self-reliant/collaborative intervention. For example, ordering children at every step may later lead to problems when parental behavior is interpreted as disrespect (i.e., "they don't care enough to ask"). Children may then learn to disregard whatever the parent stipulates.

With the possibility of these adverse effects, we recommend conditioning diagnosed persons by using fewer threats and intrusive demands. Acceptable actions can eventually resemble the competent self-initiated non-coerced actions by being the activities the person *wants* to do, not *has to* do. In addition, by increasing the diagnosed person's skill set so that success is probable in relation to effort, the requirement to frequently govern (and medicate) may also decrease.

Although the current approach is geared towards the use of less medication and stringency, diagnosed persons are nevertheless not passively allowed to fail. Intervention is highly proactive; it undertakes the sometimes cumbersome task of shaping and extinguishing behaviors, and works to alter conditions that elicit particular ADHD responses. The recommendation to facilitate joint contribution and reciprocal exchange does not mean that we are to sit idly by and watch the child needlessly and haphazardly struggle without obtaining assistance from others.

As a general policy there is an attempt to shape self-reliant/collaborative patterns from the earliest possible age as a way to maximize the occurrence of those behaviors. Because we observe that many diagnosed individuals apparently do not consider the perspectives of others, or use their resources in age-consistent ways, such socialization patterns are essential to develop. Moreover, since many diagnosed persons also have various functional problems that impede their quest for autonomy and cooperation, the goals of increasing self-efficacy and give-and-take during social exchanges may be especially beneficial for this subgroup. In that traditional interventions seem less likely to condition reciprocity, empathy, or the exchange of ideas that would eventually help these children interact with others in the family, school, and work in a more appreciated, non-diagnostic fashion, why endorse such methods?

Moreover, it seems advantageous in any society for participants to develop harmonious ways to arbitrate differences rather than induce compliance through use of coercive methods. Those with discretionary power may get their own way less often with fewer authoritarian approaches, but collaborative exchange can allow for more participants to have some discretionary authority when perspectives, concerns, and interests differ. By socializing diagnosed persons using fewer pressure tactics, we may eventually observe how differences between individuals can be settled through negotiation where cooperation is established.

In many ways the current approach moves closer to the recommendations of the "Montessori Method." Diagnostic responses may be extinguished by increasing mutual agreement, and by allowing the child to learn by doing, including of course, making mistakes without immediately being told explicitly what to do. Different from traditional intervention, the child's discretionary input is encouraged, autonomy is shaped, and integrative solutions (rather than obedience) are promoted. For example, in order to derive agreeable arrangements about what to do in various circumstances, the parent might ask the child what he would do if friends began behaving dangerously, or if people began to tease. The parent would then guide the child by responding in a Socratic fashion to the child's proposals; solutions that the child can enact independently are promoted whenever possible.

We believe that competent self-reliant/collaborative interacting is the best antidote for ADHD patterns, since persons receiving the label usually contribute less than most others in their age group. The approach requires a basic shift— from inducing calm and submission—towards fostering the development of the child's resources to solve problems. To implement these procedures, diagnosed persons will be asked if they would *like* to solve problems in order to meet various expectations; they are also asked if they are comfortable with the status quo. As a way to encourage participation, they are informed that their input will reduce the necessity for unilateral solutions. When it becomes necessary to impose a unilateral solution, rather than act critically or angrily, loved ones can instead assert that they are solving *their* own dilemma. The facilitator role models flexibility and makes clear that multiple perspectives and possibilities are valued. The diagnosed person is invited (not obliged) to participate in problem solving.

Over time diagnosed persons also learn that rules and limits are designed to prevent exploitation and harm, and are best used to facilitate self-reliance rather than to impose restrictions on others in order to gratify those who wield authority. The expectation is that there will be an increased probability of mutually acceptable patterns of interaction as social discourse becomes less coercive and accusatory. Participants are encouraged to negotiate and reassure others that they have been heard.

Facilitators take an assertive role, but remain open to compromise and are willing to promote mutually-agreed solutions. Although they are not asked to acquiesce or submit to something they deem unacceptable, they are urged to respond positively to the diagnosed person's attempts to be constructive. It is crucial that they role model the kinds of behaviors they prefer others to repeat. All participants are encouraged to tone down intrusive and coercive behaviors and gradually become attentive to each other's concerns. If diagnosed children begin to solve problems effectively rather than overreact, complain, or look to others to urgently solve problems for them, we expect that they will also learn that nothing terrible will happen if immediate accommodation does not occur, that problems are eventually resolved, and that their contribution is beneficial in family functioning.

As always, a mitigating factor is that shaping new behaviors requires numerous learning trials, and without medication, the intervention depends entirely on the resources of everyone involved. For example, even when participating in traditional parent training, parents may become familiar with the new skills, but neglect to change what they themselves do in appreciable ways in daily interactions with their children (Hechtman et al., 2004). Moreover, additional problems arise when some family members are reluctant to participate.

Since loved ones are primary instigators in this alternative intervention, altering ADHD behaviors in this way can be a knotty problem. Parents have unwittingly been participants in the conditioning of the ADHD patterning for many years, and the probability of improvement often relates to how parents modulate the child's history of reinforcement. However, we expect that significant numbers of parents can effectively help diagnosed persons respond with less ADHD responding through self-reliant/collaborative interacting, despite limitations in their own reinforcement history, and the reinforcement history between themselves and their diagnosed child. But it will not be an easy road to travel.

Despite our optimism, we observe that the intervention methods used nowadays have consistently outperformed other treatment approaches that rely more on the *assets* of the participants. This situation is highlighted when we compare the use of medication and contingency management to our current less dramatic forms of intervention during early stages of treatment. Typically, the use of both medication and coercion will produce the most visible results the most quickly for the greatest number of people. Most often, it will be easier for parents to stringently manage the child in comparison to persuading mutually acceptable interactions.

Frequently diagnosed persons will not obtain professional help until parents, teachers, spouses or employers complain vehemently, or when increased achievement is vital. Diagnosed persons are often less interested in changing their patterning, unless conditions are more personally unsettling. However, by that time, ADHD patterning is entrenched, and despite a desire to change, it is usually very difficult to alter many years of repetitive responses, even when they correlate with significant problems such as divorce, school failure, and health concerns.

It is therefore expected that change will be slow, and many will be resistant to stop previously conditioned responses. When addressing this problem, Skinner (1953, 87) indicates that interventions are simply changing the "future probability of responses in the same class . . ." of responses by changing what happens after those behaviors are emitted. This often entails a period of reconditioning where there are multiple attempts to shape and extinguish behaviors before results become evident.

However, despite that these variant recommendations can be slow and arduous; we anticipate that some people will nevertheless regard these methods as reasonable, intriguing, and worthwhile to enact long enough to substantially reshape diagnostic behavior patterns. The goal is to shape diagnosed persons to initiate acceptable functioning and diminish the need for others to direct or coerce their actions. Our aim is to focus on disentangling conflicts of interest through collaborative interacting, rather than through actions chosen merely to enhance submissiveness. We believe that efforts to develop self-reliance will mentally equip diagnosed persons to deal with situations when their parents are powerless to rescue, which occurs gradually with increasing frequency as they age. Unless diagnosed persons learn to operate effectively apart from a parentally-contrived world, they are certainly likely to have numerous problems when they are "all grown up."

The Basic Approach

When employing this alternative intervention we attempt to help diagnosed persons solve problems and dilemmas that they are amenable to solving. Loved ones work together with diagnosed persons to decide on a mutually-acceptable social arrangement that minimizes harassment and inconvenience for each participant. For example, rather than cook on demand an alternative meal when the diagnosed child complains about the menu of the family meal, the parent can instead encourage the child to prepare his own meal, or eat food that requires no extra preparation, as long as the child cleans up any additional mess.

By so doing, we might see significant improvements in participation and reliability. For example, Meyer (2001) reports that clients are likely to attend scheduled therapy appointments when *they* initiate the scheduling of the appointment, and when the therapist enables the client to talk "without losing face" about why he or she failed to attend a previous session.

These findings indicate that cooperation and reliability or follow through improves for most of us when coercion is decreased, and when problems are resolved collaboratively. Rather than assume that punishment and disapproval will develop acceptable responding, we can work with the child to better understand what is bothersome, what might be interfering, and what seems to be reinforcing objectionable acts. Only then can we help the child figure out alternatives that promote positive results. If pressure tactics are used in the attempt to coordinate behavior with diagnosed children, there is the potential risk towards conditioning avoidance and acquiescence, which is simply a means of getting others to cease haranguing. Independent follow through is unlikely to be observed when children are socialized towards passivity in the face of domination.

Due to a typically long history of negative interpersonal patterning, it is not surprising that many diagnosed persons are not forthcoming when others attempt to get affirmation or a frank reply. Reluctance can be reinforced in that the child will avoid saying the "wrong thing" and the outcome of having his or her actions constrained by others; schedules and agreements are regarded as equivalent to incarceration. Often numerous trials will need to take place before the diagnosed person responds positively.

It is therefore essential that family members distinguish between collaborative interacting and times when the child placates or attempts to avoid. This requires that caregivers be keen observers, listen closely to tone of voice, and identify other behaviors that reveal indifference, despite overt agreement or acquiescence. For example, parents often report that their diagnosed child says all the right things, but does not change at all.

When using a less coercive approach, diagnosed persons are asked to clarify what is problematic whenever they are required to accommodate to others. By encouraging discussion, it is possible to derive mutually satisfactory resolutions more often. We expect that over time diagnosed persons will speak freely about their concerns rather than act defensively or wait for others to problem solve. They will less often say what others "want to hear" in order to end the interaction, or say as little as possible to avoid incrimination. By altering relationships so that individuals have greater input, and by changing social patterning so that interactions are mutually acceptable rather than obstructive or indulgent, we anticipate fewer ADHD patterns to be emitted.

It is, however, anticipated that unforeseen problems will arise during the course of our intervention. Until those problems are resolved, the child is unlikely to effectively follow through. A failure to engage in socially acceptable behaviors following collaborative interacting is not evidence of an inherent condition, nor does it justify a more authoritarian approach, or prove that diagnosed individuals need incessant compensations in order to offset delay. The failure is understood as a *signal* that additional problem solving is required. Given the vicissitudes of living, this is an expected necessity for all of us much of the time.

When application of training or discussion does not occur, rather than posit that neurological delay is preventing further progress, disappointing outcomes may only mean that new learning has not yet taken hold, or that newly encountered situations have changed to make previous solutions obsolete. Unanticipated problems can appear at any time, and circumstances can change in ways that necessitate additional problem solving and different solutions.

We can confidently assert that by socializing diagnosed children to behave in acceptable ways with less coercion and reliance on others, problems over the long-term will be circumvented to a greater extent. These alternative recommendations will help children learn to behave effectively apart from the particular pressures and involvement brought to bear by others (e.g., pestering, bribing, controlling). Self-reliance will be shaped more than "mommy" or "daddy" reliance. Like the proverb, "give a person a fish and he eats a meal, but teach him to fish, and he eats for a lifetime," the current alternative approach orients to shape autonomy.

As noted, ADHD patterning seems like a prolongation of the interactions that occur during infancy and early childhood. The diagnosed individual continues to behave in ways that demand intense involvement and accommodations from others (Johnston and Mash, 2001), similar to when a new baby is brought into the household. The child often has functional difficulties that increase the probability of this occurring; the evolving social patterning often means that loved ones go to great lengths to protect or control the child who shows behavior that requires extensive management.

The lure of medicating, bribing, and simple solutions might make the child more advantageous, reduce his error rates, and make non-compliance unappealing, but there is a significant risk that those interventions will also condition the diagnosed child's dependence on medication inducements and need for assistance. Moreover, additional contingencies and compensations are relatively difficult to remove, in that the individual learns to behave acceptably only if enticed by extras and reduced work, but does not learn to respond acceptably in typical situations. Proponents of biological determinism interpret recidivism to mean that ADHD is incurable, but it may also be that at present traditional intervention accounts for the low long-term treatment success rates.

We suggest that traditional intervention may increase a reliance on those treatments; the respondent learns to rely on directives, enhancements, a reduction in difficulties and intricacies, and the effects of a stimulant medication. Since diagnosed persons are not learning to respond to encountered adversities without traditional facilitation, it is not surprising that there is an increase in ADHD patterns when traditional remedies are retracted.

Consequently, although commands (and medication) might rapidly effect changes, our choice of alternative intervention is determined to facilitate collaborative transactions where diagnosed children progressively enact acceptable behaviors with less coercion, enticement, or cues from others. For example, parents could gradually stop insisting that the child leave a toy in the car before entering a restaurant with the intention that he does not forget the toy in the restaurant or have a problem with it during the meal. When the parent works together with the child to identify problems associated with particular behaviors, he will less frequently learn to depend on the parent to designate the actions to be performed, or become focused on countering what the parent imposes.

Many attempts to promote self-sufficiency and personal responsibility exist by offering the child options. The child can be asked to think about problems that could occur if the toy were taken into the restaurant. The focus is to help the child anticipate what might happen to the toy rather than think for the child. Depending on circumstance or in cases where insistence is necessary, it is possible to decrease the alternatives given, and to raise issues (for the child) that occur in relation to bringing a toy into the restaurant. Parents can also talk with the child about possible steps to be taken if playing with the toy during mealtime becomes problematic, including (as a last resort) having to remove the toy to end the annoyance for restaurant patrons. There will also be occasions when it is simply not permissible to bring the toy along.

We know that in many circumstances unilateral coercion will be less necessary, but that negotiated mutually acceptable responses will be difficult to figure out. However, it will often be possible for parent and child to derive an agreeable alternative instead of either agreeing to the child's demand to bring the toy into the restaurant, or commanding the child to leave the toy behind. By requesting the child's input, he will use his personal resources in ways that he cannot if commanded; plus the child receives the message that the parent cares enough not to dictate.

If it is decided that the child will bring the toy into the restaurant, and he leaves the toy behind, the parent can also (at times) find it helpful to *not* retrieve it (especially if this is a repetitious pattern and others would be inconvenienced). The unfolding of those consequences can increase the future probability that the child will behave responsibly with less parental involvement when the next similar situation occurs.

By allowing the scenario to unfold (rather than avoid the situation altogether by coddling the child who is not allowed to bring the toy into the restaurant), greater input from the child in the decision making process can be encouraged. We expect that interventions of this quality will help diagnosed children learn to discriminate and enact plans of action and therefore increase the probability of playing with the toy in an acceptable fashion, and also remember to take the toy with them when leaving the restaurant without relying on external cues.

Parent as mentor rather than controller or provider of solutions, can help the child identify behavior patterns that strengthen his or her focus and memory. Asking children to describe what has worked well for them in the past will help them think in ways that lead to success in new instances. It will not always be possible to discover options that all participants find acceptable, but we presume that this approach allows for further collaborative exchanges and the development of the child's resources.

Some might find this collaborative/self-reliant model to be too permissive (especially as many diagnosed persons are already conditioned to expect frequent accommodations). However, many diagnosed persons will discover that they are exposed to an increased number of limits within this alternative pattern of discipline; the proposed changes in conditioning are to reinforce consideration of other perspectives, as well as more completed work with less dependence on external help. Hence, for many diagnosed persons, this approach is far less permissive and indulgent than previous social patterns.

Rather than act as satellites around which the child's happiness is the center, whereby parents accommodate excessively, this approach develops cooperative, and less monopolizing or entitled patterns of behavior that nevertheless help to instill the child with the importance of meeting obligations. It does not logically follow that a discipline system is lax if behaviors are less often induced with medication, unilateral control, or perpetual reliance on external directives and reminders.

Compared with our current approach, both authoritarianism and permissiveness may be less effective in conditioning a balanced sensibility. For example, if a caretaker provides mere authoritarian discipline, the message is: "you do what I say, or you are unacceptable." Conversely, when being merely permissive, the message becomes "I do what you say, or do whatever you want." The individual in either case is not learning mutually-accommodating behaviors, or learning to differentiate between different points of view.

However, when implementing this alternative form of discipline, parents work to reduce the problems and hardships which each family member identifies. The expectation is that diagnosed children in conjunction with other family members will gain increased dignity within the family structure. A collaborative model is not, however, a submissive approach. For example, the parent will stop buying junk food if problems continue with food consumption and sharing. A parent will sometimes find it necessary to ask the child to wait for a later time to discuss a problem when there will be ample time to derive a solution in a less unilateral way, or when emotions are more settled. However, rather than a first option (often the case in traditional interventions), unilateral decision making is generally employed as a last resort out of practical necessity.

As we begin to learn that we are separate from the outside world, and later learn that the perspectives of others differ from our own and have value, different patterns of socialization can either accelerate or impede acceptance and coping. It is the aim of this current intervention to increase the probability that diagnosed children will learn to understand and coordinate multiple perspectives in agreeable ways during socialization, and function in ways that less often usurp the time and energy of others. Hastening the conditioning of those social patterns is a primary focus, in that diagnosed persons are usually less likely to pull their own weight and conform to acceptable boundaries.

Our recommendation for self-reliant/collaborative interacting is not synonymous with leniency, permitting the child to behave inappropriately, not assisting the child enough, or changing limits in order to please certain individuals and exploit others. Interacting with the child in this manner is not meant to stop the parent from giving necessary assistance, disallow the child to be the focal point in certain situations, or impede parental protection of the child. Our socialization is an attempt to help children gain competence while simultaneously considering the perspectives of others.

Although efforts to extinguish ADHD will often require parents to reduce their shielding, it is crucial at this juncture to convey that in no way do we condone that the child suffer extreme and permanent adverse consequences. Traditionalists presume that the natural environment is insufficient for training a disinhibited person, but these alternative solutions can be tested first with relatively benign behaviors in order to check their effectiveness in reducing ADHD frequency rates. By allowing diagnosed persons the opportunity to experience problems that relate to their hyperactivity, impulsivity, and inattentiveness, very useful lessons can take place. Loved ones are encouraged to examine how they shelter, compensate, or save diagnosed individuals from the consequences their ADHD patterns; many such responses are ultimately counterproductive over the long-term.

For example, when a diagnosed child protests that he didn't hear the parent say, "If you get a milk shake, you can't have the sundae," was he "driven to distraction," or has he been inadvertently conditioned to *not* attend to parental statements related to *limits*? When the parent concedes to the child's claims of ignorance and gives the child both the milk shake and the sundae, the parent risks conditioning even more "inattentive" responses. Like the recommendations of Webster-Stratton and Herbert (1994) when intervening with families of troubled children, there is greater emphasis on developing patterns of teamwork.

Moreover, when diagnosed children begin to see their parents as over protective, and are receiving infantile treatment and undue worry about events that are highly unlikely to occur, they may also learn to disregard parental advice. Over protectiveness will only reinforce ADHD inattentive responding and lead to a cycle of repetition. The child learns to see parental directives as worthless, unbelievable, obstructive, and overly cautious. The child is conditioned not to respond to feedback or instructions, and ends up characterizing the parent as unreasonably anxious about physical harm, emotionally fragile, or excessively worried that a certain object might break. The parents can lose credibility if they cling to beliefs the child no longer endorses.

For example, it is not that the child will catch a cold if she goes outside without a hat or a buttoned coat, but rather that the child will be cold until she learns to behave differently. When her own actions result in her being uncomfortably cold, she may follow parental recommendations rather than ignore them. Perhaps she will discover the weather conditions prior to leaving the house, as well as learn how to button her coat under her own cue. As the behaviors are learned and routinely performed, they will be increasingly integrated with the future in acceptable ways without any point of performance involvement from the parent.

When socializing diagnosed children in this alternative manner, it becomes the child's prerogative to initiate, even if he or she is not behaving in ways the parent recognizes as the best choice (e.g., handling personal funds, care of toys, etc.). Loved ones can induce behavioral change in an indirect fashion by continuing to alter conditions to increase non-diagnostic responses. For example, if the parent prefers that the child be less of a spendthrift, he might ask her to contribute to certain purchases, stop commenting about money burning a hole in her pocket, and be more consistent about the amount of money she is given each week. As Katharine Whitehorn writes, "The easiest way for your children to learn about money is for you to not have any."

Facilitating self-efficacy sometimes requires diagnosed children to endure adversity even though parents should not abdicate their responsibility to help the child. When problems do not present an unacceptable risk to self or others (as determined by the family members who must live with the consequences), it is reasonable to allow diagnosed persons to live with the consequences of their own actions to promote future competent behaviors. Parents can think about what might happen if they were to allow particular events to play out without harboring, compensating, or coercing the child. As has often been advised, don't sweat the small stuff.

There is also an ongoing effort to decrease special accommodations made by others and when feasible, decrease medication as well. Diagnosed persons can learn to do non-diagnostic responding in typical conditions where they will be reinforced by personal accomplishments and improved social relationships, rather than conditioned to rely on medications and parental cues and coercion. Traditionalists claim that diagnosed persons are less able to be motivated by the world at large, but this assertion has not been proven; we suggest that diagnosed persons have not yet been conditioned to respond in acceptable ways to typical socio-cultural expectations.

Moreover, we hold that traditional intervention does little to rectify the problem without the necessity to impose medicinal intervention, markedly reduce expectation, and implement a reward/punishment approach that requires dependency on parent action. Dominating patterns of socialization and relentless management impedes the conditioning of self-efficacy and mutuality if used throughout childhood into adolescence; it is also possible that such methods will not improve diagnosed persons' neurobiology over the longer term as well.

When diagnosed persons are conditioned to operate with extra contingencies that are frequent and immediate, a case for lack of persistence can also be made. It has been empirically shown that a variable-interval schedule of reinforcement is an effective way to produce behaviors that are difficult to extinguish (Skinner, 1953), so it is expected that a rapid decline in the persistence of the conditioned behavior will ensue when the continuous reinforcement schedules recommended by traditionalists are removed.

Promoting Longer-term Change

While self-reliant/collaborative interacting is often easier to accomplish with older diagnosed children, these approaches can be modified to match the behavioral repertoire of younger participants as well. With young children it remains possible to set limits in a courteous way, direct the child's actions in order to elicit accord, and orient in ways that increase the child's self-reliance.

Even though it might be necessary for facilitators to be specific, less abstract, and demonstrate repeatedly when interacting with younger diagnosed children, showing consideration of the younger child's point of view can potentially increase the probability of an agreeable reaction and reduce the necessity to impose coercion. One need not presume that an autocratic style is the only option even for the very young diagnosed child. Coordination of behavior with others over time might alternatively be increased by affording younger diagnosed persons some discretionary input and the opportunity to realize small, albeit important successes. Moreover, since behaving in ways characteristic of a younger child usually becomes increasingly less tolerable the longer the patterning occurs, fostering these changes early in development has its advantages.

As diagnosed children grow older, events that sequence their ADHD responding change from what may have happened early on when the behaviors were initially learned. Their social matrix will often become impatient with their failures to behave appropriately. Behaviors conditioned during early childhood years will often exacerbate problems at school, and the increased expectation for mature behavior is now pressing for change to take place. With each passing year the ADHD behaviors that have been reinforced in numerous situations are now resulting in escalating negative consequences. The monopolization of social resources and constant monitoring done previously is now less possible, burdensome, inconvenient, and unreasonable. By the time problems become disruptive enough for participants to seek professional help, they are extremely difficult to extinguish. Relationships can be so strained that some find it more suitable to avoid the child rather than risk further disappointment by trying to work together.

However, the contingencies that have reinforced the behaviors may also be occurring often enough to maintain exceptionally high frequencies. For example, one diagnosed child was asked what he most liked doing with his mother. He indicated that playing the games "Monopoly" and "Trouble" were his favorite activities. Another diagnosed child, who tested limits and provoked others, often directed conversation to his collection of fuses, which would "blow up" at differing rates. Given the characteristics of ADHD patterning, those responses seem to fit neatly into our presumption of learned responses.

Nevertheless, it is conventional practice to urge others to give frequent rewards and punishments to compensate for the child's "lesser ability" to use good judgment. Stimulant medication is a necessity, they say, in order to help regulate bodily deficiencies that would otherwise interfere with work productivity and methodical procedure. They recommend that until diagnosed children reach age seven, contingency management must be consistent, immediate and literal in order to keep ADHD children motivated. Parents are advised to apply these strategies whenever the child must pay attention for a prescribed period of time. For instance, Barkley (2000) recommends that parents count out loud to give the child an external basis for understanding that a behavior has to be enacted immediately.

Despite the absence of substantial long-term benefits and the potential for untold side effects, countless numbers of diagnosed persons (and growing) continue to undergo such aforementioned prescribed remedies. They are believed to be mandatory for the child with ADHD delays, and given the ease with which it is possible to dominate a child, they usually result in short term compliance. Success rates are always understood as an outgrowth of compensating for the *posited* neural biological problem. It is believed that no reasonable treatment can fully rely on the diagnosed person to enact acceptable behaviors without ongoing management from outside sources.

As long as there is compliance, treatment is regarded as successful. Even when there are allowances for cooperative problem solving, and positive communication training during adolescence, as advised by Robin (2006), loved ones are nevertheless encouraged to monitor, manage, reward, and punish diagnosed persons, depending on the extent to which they comply. For example, in Robin's approach parents are explicitly told to administer positive and negative consequences that have been "agreed-upon" when homework is not completed. They are recommended to remain at home to oversee the adolescent, structure home-work, remind and monitor the teen to ensure that work is accomplished, as well as set the stage for him or her to remain honest. In all those ways we can observe that reliance on parental monitoring, reminding, and intimidation are fostered, despite recommendations during family discussions to increase effective com-munication, self-reliance, and consensus.

Consequently, while the adolescent is permitted some discretionary input during scheduled family deliberations in Robin's intervention, the teen is still being conditioned to function against continuous parental tracking and addi-tional contingency management that requires ongoing parental supervision and unilateral coercion. We notice that contexts in which the shaping of self-reliant and collaborative functioning in diverse sets of contexts and circumstances are scant. Diagnosed teens are conditioned to rely on parental initiatives and unwav-ering surveillance; all participants are persuaded to operate within the belief system that the diagnosed teen has even less self-control than his or her counter-parts.

The empirical basis (with possible side effects) of those recommendations is not provided, but parents are nonetheless encouraged to continue coercive inter-vention even when engaged in mutual patterns of communicating at other times. Traditionalists seem reticent to decrease the use of coercion for this diagnostic group. In fact, Robin claims that restoring "parental control" should be a pri-mary treatment goal, and if outpatient intensive work has not accomplished that outcome, then other placement options should be considered.

The belief is that recidivism will occur because of neurological delay, but traditionalists have also *not* investigated whether diagnosed children react to the withdrawal of contingency management training any differently from other groups. Despite the empirical shortcomings, they continue to believe that diag-nosed persons must be governed by others due to an inherent disability. At-tempts to shape more self-reliant/collaborative interacting are circumscribed, infrequent, or abandoned altogether, and often those strategies are presumed to be beyond the realm of feasibility for this population.

Although the traditional approach can induce certain behaviors quickly, there are many side effects when socializing children in such a way. For exam-ple, many parents of diagnosed children complain that after using contingency management, their child has been less helpful without the promise of an extra reward. They also report that acceptable behaviors diminish after the child has obtained the reward, and that the child frequently responds to a failure to offer a reward as if being cheated or denied.

Once contingencies are added, it may be necessary to keep administering the extra contingencies simply to avoid a precipitous drop off in the frequency with which particular behaviors are emitted. These kinds of problems are often notable when loved ones first attempt to remove contingency systems that have been operative for long periods of time. While traditionalists interpret increases of ADHD behaviors in response to the easing of contingencies (and medication) as further proof that inherent delays must be offset, one can also argue that the return of old behavior almost invariably occurs for most people when the conditions of training (employed for a long time) are revoked and replaced with substantially different sets of conditions.

When behavior is induced with the use of extra contingencies, one may ultimately increase the risk that the behavior will only occur in the presence of the added contingencies. Even if the behavior had previously been conditioned without supplements or atypical contingencies, when they are added and then removed, the behavior may quit. In many instances the removal may also depress the behaviors frequency rate to a point that is lower than its initial baseline (Lepper, Greene and Nisbett, 1973). While traditionalists claim that ADHD returns because contingencies must be externally represented, others think that contingency management frequently has these side effects; ADHD is not a special case.

If we consider this as a possibility, the limited training results obtained for diagnosed persons could actually relate to what is being learned rather than to neurobiological delay. The introduction of traditional contingency management (and medication) may have undesirable repercussions for this diagnostic group. Increased reliance on such forms of assistance can potentially worsen the ability to shape autonomous functioning once those interventions are introduced. Traditional methods may make it even less likely that ADHD can be cured when evaluated over the long-term.

Once a commitment to the traditional approach is made, there is significantly less focus on shaping self-managing behaviors that repeat at points of performance without the involvement of the manager. For example, rather than having the diagnosed child decide for himself when or if to remove his coat, or try to find out about weather conditions, the child will instead continue to react to parental directives or commands to wear or not wear a jacket. Directing the child will mean that specific tasks are completed more often *as long as supervision occurs*, but problems crop up immediately as attempts are made to reduce overseeing. In effect, development of the child's autonomy has been curtailed.

The reasonable alternative is to increase self-reliance and collaborative interacting in order to reduce side effects of traditional treatments. We anticipate that this new formulation will provide a consistent and coherent account for ADHD behaviors, as well as promote treatment that yields long-lasting positive results without reliance on medication and an assigned manager. Treating ADHD patterning within a learning paradigm is preferred over presuming futility because heritable quotients for ADHD are high, or because past attempts to change behavior through psychotherapeutic intervention have not been very successful.

ADHD treatment may shift to conditioning less reliance on directive assistance and/or various kinds of medications. Intervention may often only entail helping diagnosed persons repeat competent behaviors that they already have been doing. For example, if the diagnosed person has difficulty organizing school work, it is worthwhile to inquire into whether similar organizational behavior is shown, in particular, when doing self-initiated tasks or hobbies.

The facilitator can then help the child identify similarities between the two activities and solve whatever problems impede replication of the non-diagnostic functioning with the troublesome activity. Since diagnosed persons respond less often with diagnostic patterns during actions they initiate and enjoy, it may be possible to induce improvements simply by facilitating response generalization. Instances of non-diagnostic functioning are the starting point for the current intervention. For example, if non-diagnostic responding is evident when the child builds models, she can be encouraged to duplicate those response patterns during tasks that have previously correlated with overreacting or lack of persistence.

This alternative intervention orients proactively and seeks to alter the contexts and circumstances that typically elicit ADHD responses so that they gradually converge with non-ADHD conditions and help increase the probability of cueing non-diagnostic behaviors. One way may be to use the child's collectibles while doing a school math assignment, play catch while learning multiplication tables, or have the individual design a showcase displaying the collectibles in order to develop organization and planning skills. Discretionary input can be highlighted and maintained, thus making assigned tasks seem even more self-directed.

However, conventional thinking focuses on changing conditions so that diagnosed children and adults function continuously within a more externally represented and immediately reinforcing environment. Most often, there is a recommendation to increase supervision and decree. For practical reasons, many adults will have to construct this kind of world for themselves, as it is problematic to find someone to continuously help them meet expectations (although some adults now hire coaches).

For example, Murphy (2006) encourages diagnosed adults to train in prioritizing, time management, and organizing. They are encouraged to be consistent by making lists, using appointment calendars, and posting reminders where they will be easily seen. They are instructed to break large tasks into smaller units, and to ensure that they give themselves smaller rewards when doing longer projects (taking life one day at a time). Many will also benefit from learning anger control so that better decisions can be made. Diagnosed adults are advised to reflect on their own actions so that their ways of thinking can help them be efficient at work. They are also advised to practice consistently until the new skills become automatic and routine.

However, it seems that once those kinds of recommendations are made, traditionalists shift to an interpretation closer to this current alternative view. Murphy seems to be suggesting that normative behaviors may be learned and then enacted in an automatic fashion, without a necessary inhibitory response and activation of executive behaviors, *as long as enough practice* has occurred. If this is the case, then it seems that Murphy accepts the view that routines may increase the probability that one will "perform what is known" even for those with ADHD.

We might then ask if diagnosed persons are biologically delayed, or whether they have simply not been reinforced to do acceptable behaviors routinely enough. If we help diagnosed individuals become aware of the conditions that cue diagnostic responding, and also help them identify alternative routines, we may well facilitate different patterns of behavior and achievements. If a diagnosed person agrees to Murphy's recommended strategies (imperatives for everyone in order to organize activity over time), much of the problem is already solved. The individual is receptive to new automatic routines that will prevent him or her from qualifying for the ADHD disorder.

With the choice to medicate less and develop self-reliant/collaborative behavior, we can help family members pool resources and change how behavior is synchronized and routinely enacted. Participants are encouraged to identify ways to change their own actions in order to encourage different outcomes. Telling others what to do, or waiting for others to change first is discouraged. For example, if parents want their children to show improved listening, the therapist might ask the parents what they would do differently in order for that to happen. Similarly, diagnosed children might be asked to identify changes they can make to increase the likelihood that their parents will talk with them more congenially.

Since it is often reported that diagnosed persons fault others inordinately, and seldom recognize how their behavior affects others, these collaborative interactions can highlight how to reduce the occurrence of problems rather than locate blame. We expect that these collaborative exchanges will reduce power struggles, accusations, and defensive reactions between diagnosed persons and loved ones. A child might be asked, "What can you do to take better care of yourself when you are in that situation?" The adult helps the child explore possible complications that relate to plans of action, and helps the child identify solutions that are more positive to the child.

The ultimate aim is to increase the contribution of diagnosed persons, and we again urge that parents must not refuse to give guidance. Parents will sometimes find it necessary to suggest alternatives, indicate what has worked for them in the past, and specify and demonstrate possibilities when the child is mired, and when the child does not have the experience to derive a reasonable solution. However, interventions are likely to be deemed successful when acceptable responding occurs with less answer giving or reward with the managed contingencies that seem to maintain child/parental enmeshment.

When shaping greater self-reliance, the parent might ask the child, "Would you like to complete this on your own, so in case I'm not around you will still be able to do it?" Parents impart the message that they want their children to be self-reliant because it is better for their survival, not because they don't want to take care of them. As a way to impart that message, parents can facilitate independent functioning in an encouraging way rather than sound as if helping the child is a burden or inconvenience.

Our basic empirical question is whether this alternative approach can lead to improvements in treatment outcomes compared to the traditional intervention for some clients and therapists, over varying time frames. We are not insisting that medication or other directive interventions recommended by traditionalists do not have limited efficacy in the short-term; we merely seek to develop a different way to intervene with the expectation of improving on the traditional handling of the problem. We observe that diagnosed persons usually do more non-diagnostic responding during positive situations and circumstances, so the goal is to help them repeat those same behaviors in situations that include external instruction and limited access to assistance. The expectation is that they can be shaped to progressively master assigned tasks (e.g., schoolwork) in the same ways they have advanced with other content. The important goal is to emancipate the child.

Although medicinal and contingency treatment interventions sometimes work relatively quickly, we regard the decision for medication, easements, and increased cueing and coercion to be a practical matter, which is based on the resources of participants, safety concerns, and urgency—rather than a decision necessitated by the posited nature of ADHD. However, when selecting a treatment option, one must consider that traditional interventions can potentially truncate long-term results and impede self-reliance and collaboration. We argue that changed conditions of socialization, including sharing of resources rather than competing for them, and mutual agreement on behavior rather than unilateral control, will reduce helplessness and impetuosity in ADHD diagnosed individuals in the long-term.

Moreover, a win/win negotiation can help diagnosed persons practice anticipating possibilities, and may also help individuals improve on their non-vocal verbal responding. Much like first reading to others and then repeating those behaviors but without vocalizing, if diagnosed persons initially learn to manage the future acceptably when talking with others, they can, with practice, repeat those behaviors when doing what traditionalists have called "self-speech" —if such responses help with adaptation.

More self-reliant private responses can replace complaining, rushing, neglecting, giving up, and other behaviors that increase the probability of receiving assistance and lowering expectation. Much like what often happens when a tutor shows improved functioning after having instructed others about particular subject matter, the diagnosed person will also benefit from being active and participatory during collaborative interaction. By asking diagnosed persons to consider various perspectives, encouraging them to make decisions pertaining to themselves and others, and by helping them identify likely consequences of their actions, we recognize that they are being requested to do the behaviors that traditionalists *assert occur infrequently* in the diagnosed population.

This intervention encourages the child to be inquisitive, creative and philanthropic, and there is greater emphasis on flexibility during problem solving so that diagnosed persons can learn new skills. Parents are also advised to speak kindly with the child rather than use a dogmatic or coercive approach and also treat the diagnosed child as honorable and competent. Instances of unacceptable behavior can be addressed through inquiring about what is troubling the child; maliciousness and "disability" is less often presumed.

While it is always possible to coerce the child into doing the desired behavior by employing contingency management in highly specific ways when one has dominance over another (e.g., do it or sit in that chair), it is also possible to increase the likelihood of desirable behavior by working through obstacles, understanding the child's perspective, and deciding on possible compromises. Some parents will initially be more adept at this kind of activity compared to others, and find it easier to persuade the child without introducing coercive conditions. For example, instead of commanding the child to wear a coat, the parent says, "You can always leave it in the car if it gets warm."

Parental training under this new approach focuses on developing negotiating skills; strategies are designed so that parents become impressed with their child's initiatives and acts of kindness. The hope is that family members can appreciate each other, and behave in ways that encourage ongoing give-and-take when resolving problems.

People will agree to anything with a "gun at their head" and know what to do when others tell them, but that does not ensure acceptable behavior in the absence of pressure or guidance. This alternative intervention will be advantageous for many diagnosed persons when they function apart from their parents. Traditional intervention sometimes works exceedingly well in the short-term when parents can supervise, medicate, and coerce the younger diagnosed child. The choice is merely whether parents prefer confident, self-reliant adult children or instead want to foster dependence over the long-term. The fact remains that most diagnosed people continue to show problematic behaviors throughout their lives even though a significant percentage have received traditional treatments at one time or another (if only to obtain medication).

We acknowledge that long-term solutions require long-term involvement and thus developing mutually acceptable patterns of interacting can be a very complicated activity, and the required discriminations can be very subtle. For example, how does a parent rephrase a comment so that it is helpful rather than judgmental, pressuring, or critical? How does the parent avoid demanding compliance when uncooperative behaviors occur? How does a parent protect a child, and at the same time not become obstructive? What might a parent do to facilitate self-reliant functioning, inventiveness, and initiative?

The shaping procedures recommended here can be intricate and time consuming, and we expect that some diagnostic behaviors will continue to be reinforced in understated ways that make them resistant to extinction. Grandparents and siblings can also unwittingly continue to condition ADHD responding even when the parent works diligently to shape new behaviors in ways consistent with these current alternative views.

The Subtleties of Psychosocial Intervention

In many instances it is not easy to distinguish between what reinforces one behavioral pattern, but does not reinforce some other pattern. Quite often the participants do not know what cues the emission of a particular response. We are not always able to identify, as complex as they can potentially be, the conditions that determine behavior. In some instances people seek professionals to help them clarify their behaviors.

The objective when investigating learning possibilities is to figure out what maintains or reinforces symptom behaviors within particular situations, and to alter the dynamics so that substitute responses are introduced and reinforced. It may be necessary to study interaction patterns in detail before it is possible to identify the parameters that influence the frequency rates of the responses that are emitted.

In this regard, Skinner (1953) remarked that it is not very reliable to ask a person what reinforces him or her. It is "only in retrospect that one's tendencies to behave in particular ways are seen to be the result of certain consequences" (p. 75). Moreover, on many occasions that relationship may be obvious to others, but is still not acknowledged by the enactor. In Skinner's view, "we can improve our understanding of human behavior and greatly strengthen our control by designing alternative practices which recognize the importance of reinforcement as well as other variables of which behavior is a function" (p. 116). The current approach is an attempt to follow this recommendation.

Diagnosed persons are studied in relation to reinforcement history: the conditions under which ADHD behaviors occur for each individual. It need not be necessary that the diagnosed person be aware of or agree with the constructed history. However, and as noted throughout, we expect that after identifying a history of reinforcement, behaviors that initially seemed disordered will begin to seem reasonable within a newly derived framework.

Consistent with these assertions, Skinner advises that we have no way of knowing what might constitute a reinforcing stimulus "before we have tested its reinforcing power upon a given organism." In Skinner's view, "we must therefore be content with a survey in terms of the effects of stimuli upon behavior" (p. 84). We argue throughout this work that traditionalists have not made this kind of survey a priority, and thus have been underestimating environmental influences.

Skinner also recommends that we first assess the frequency of a given response, make an event contingent upon it, and then observe if there are any frequency changes. He argues that if there is a change, "we classify the event as reinforcing to the organism under the existing conditions" (p. 73); those changes in frequency rates indicate a correspondence with a learning paradigm. For example, if the frequency rates of ADHD behavior increase when the behaviors sequence with impatience from loved ones, or if the behaviors become more frequent when others lessen, remove requirements, or fix after the behaviors occur, a learning paradigm seems to fit those data as well. If ADHD responses change in frequency in relation to such stimuli as having troublesome assignments imposed by others, during negative parental lecturing and reprimand, or when diagnostic responses reduce the probability of social exclusion and denial, then it seems that these behaviors are consistent with this current view. That is, the recurrence of diagnostic responding becomes predictable in relation to the consequences that have followed similar behaviors in the past.

If Skinner's pattern of study is adopted, one orients to obtain a highly detailed survey of the presenting diagnosed person's reinforcement history with the hope of understanding how particular ADHD behaviors have been shaped for particular diagnosed persons in particular classifications of contexts and situations. This very thorough analysis of a diagnosed person's psychosocial history sheds light on how event sequences have inadvertently reinforced responses. For example, what does the parent do when the child becomes rambunctious during phone calls, when the child does not respond to directives, when toys are not put away, when teeth are not brushed, and when school assignments are not brought home?

Everyone is encouraged to identify the conditions in which ADHD behaviors occur. For example, older diagnosed persons might be asked, "What was happening before you behaved in that way?" After more clearly specifying context and situation, diagnosed children may feel sufficiently confident and capable of enacting other behaviors that could promote mutually acceptable patterning.

We suspect that it will usually be necessary to focus on altering how a diagnosed person responds to assignments, instructions, and activities imposed by others. These are the situations that are likely to correlate with significant ADHD responding for the majority of diagnosed persons. We can, for example, notice how easily diagnosed persons are distracted by other activity in the room when having to conform to a required agenda, compared to the difficulty of distracting them from actions they have initiated—even if those tasks are complex or intricate.

If we set about understanding ADHD as a conditioned set of responses, we might question whether the child will stop doing hyperactivity if he constantly overhears his parent(s) talking to others about how active and uncontrollable he behaves. Often "the mother who complains that her three-year old child whines and cries for attention in an annoying way may not realize that her own reinforcing practices are responsible" (Skinner, 1953, 97). In that same vein, Azerrad (1997) discusses the ways in which a parental attention may influence the frequency rates of certain behaviors during child rearing.

Rather than label a child as neurologically impeded, the new approach is to understand what the child *is doing* when not responding to the preferred agenda, and what has *possibly* conditioned less acceptable behavior rather than cultivate the desired participatory behaviors. The approach might inquire into whether the child is preoccupied with something else, or whether she is withholding because of anger. We can look into whether the child is avoiding failure, disapproval, and whether she is patterning in ways that increase attention from others when disengaged in particular situations. We can also ask if this response pattern occurs when others negate her initiatives.

Similarly, when diagnosed persons respond more rapidly than the norm, including doing risky behavior, what could be reinforcing that pattern of responses? Are these reactive behaviors resultant from imposed restrictions and constraints? Is the child frequently disturbed by parental overprotection and barriers? Have these behaviors frequently correlated with dramatic provocations whenever others are busy and non-attentive? One could also ask if carelessness or rapid responding correlates with loved ones more often solving problems for the individual, thus reducing expectations. Perhaps these abrupt behaviors have also enabled the person to escape with minimal effort and without repercussions. All of these questions are important in a learning paradigm.

Endorsing a learning perspective presumes that ADHD responses are reinforced when they result in certain outcomes, or when they reduce instances where others can interfere, evaluate, criticize, impede, exclude, win, or deny. Often ADHD behaviors correlate with finishing faster, getting it sooner, and escaping from adversity, and by responding thus, the likelihood of doing other self-initiated activities is increased. Rather than construe ADHD behaviors as evidence of impairment, the behaviors become functional or reinforced in relation to these subsequent events.

Although rather than provide continuous point of performance intervention (which gets the job done in the short-term), our alternative intervention operates to avoid the side effect of inadvertent conditioning of diagnosed persons to rely on others for quick assistance, or depart from the importance of developing personal responsibility. For example, even if it is decided that it would be helpful for a short period of time to place a sign as a reminder for the diagnosed person to do a behavior at a particular time (Robin, 2006), the diagnosed individual can create the sign and place it wherever it is helpful, rather than rely on the parent to decide.

In that diagnosed persons will eventually have to function autonomously as adults, one could therefore argue that traditional intervention will impede long-term adjustment. Since empirical work to date indicates that diagnosed children show an external locus of control compared to non-diagnosed children (Linn and Hodge, 1982), this alternative approach is particularly relevant. In order to facilitate an internal locus of decision making, parents might ask the child if he or she *wants* to follow through rather than pressure the child to *promise* to follow through.

In a related matter, Campbell, Douglas, and Morgenstern (1971) have reported that many diagnosed individuals show greater field dependence in their cognitive styles. More recently, Diener and Milich (1997) also highlight that many ADHD children are developing a depressive patterning, in that they often feel inadequate about their reduced ability to achieve. In each example we suspect that diagnosed individuals (in general) are labile, reliant on environmental changes, and characterizing themselves as ineffectual. What have traditionalists been doing to address these concerns?

In many instances diagnosed persons are discouraged, a condition that Skinner (1953, 103) calls "abulia." Many diagnosed persons report that they have stopped obliging and initiating because they presume that others will not like what they will do. They may be characterized as lazy, but alternatively, they may be quite dispirited. They learn that if there are no commitments, attempts to please, or goals, then failure and disappointment cannot take place. Given such a depletion of human resources, it seems important to counter this negativity by role modeling receptivity towards the child's vantage point, and to discuss successes and personal concerns.

Within our approach discipline still occurs, albeit subtly, by means of consistent parental concern and mentoring. This is true even when parents respond less negatively (or not at all) when diagnostic responses are emitted. Facilitators can redirect, discuss, and at times seemingly ignore objectionable diagnostic patterns; however, intervention is still taking place, even if coercion and disapproval are decreasing. Moreover, we might find that when stringency is lessened, it is safer for the diagnosed person to risk failure during evaluated activity; this is a major benefit for many of these individuals.

Parents are advised to avoid power struggles and critical undermining of each other. It is very important for them not to make overt (or subtle) negative comments or hints about each other in front of the children, which can result in the children running the household or copying the same behaviors. At times when it is not feasible to compromise, it is crucial that the diagnosed person recognize that non-negotiable limits are imposed in order to prevent escalation of harm or danger.

When such preemptive discipline is necessary, parents are encouraged to remain calm and explain the reasons for imposing the non-negotiable limits. This might minimize animosity, resentment, and retreat when the child experiences a sudden absence of discretionary authority. However, on these occasions the parent can also ask the child to consider another possible resolution to the dilemma in order to keep the child engaged.

While it is sometimes necessary to introduce discipline which is unacceptable to the child (viewed as coercive), these actions can cease as soon as a mutually acceptable arrangement is found. When feasible the diagnosed child has an opportunity to promote a different solution at any time. For example, while the parent may initially think it necessary to remove toys to alleviate problems attendant to them, the parent and child may subsequently find it mutually acceptable that the child put toys away by a certain time each day, or keep them in a confined area.

Parents must still impose limits in order to reduce significant exploitation and risk, even if the focus of interaction is not primarily to reestablish parental control. The intervention is designed above all to incorporate the child's concerns into the social patterning. Diagnosed persons are redirected or dissuaded from behaving for personal gain (i.e., what's in it for me) or with disregard for others, and encouraged towards behavior that is consistent with mutual interest (i.e., what's in it for both of us). By coordinating with others acceptable behaviors can eventually be forged to replace diagnostic responses. Rather than not participate at all (i.e., inattentiveness), or participate in a disruptive manner (i.e., impulsivity and hyperactivity), acceptable functioning is shaped over time by the positive event sequences that occur when the child works alone on tasks, as well as with others.

As a result of these efforts, we expect that participants will be reinforced by reciprocity when coordinated behavior takes place. Participants learn that compromising is more advantageous than inducing compliance through intimidation. As this new learning takes place, it is anticipated that behavior will be reliably integrated with others over long time spans, in that diagnosed persons will less often jeopardize the camaraderie they have established. Investment in the family is reinforced, and those patterns can potentially repeat in a variety of settings, including school and work.

We anticipate that this alternative psychological intervention can effectively alter the biological system as well. For example, Schmidt (2004) reports that when individuals feel greater self control and reduced stress in a situation, there is less activation of an enzyme in the brain called protein kinase C. The release of this enzyme is associated with impairment in short-term memory and prefrontal cortex functioning, increases in impulsiveness and distractibility, and interference with abstract reasoning and working memory: problematic functioning that traditionalists typically ascribe to ADHD.

Since it is increasingly difficult to maintain a watchful eye over any individual as they mature, the goals of the current intervention are worth pursuing even if multiple trials are needed to attain acceptable behavioral changes. We can observe that individuals in general become increasingly adept at circumventing restrictions and coercion. An example of this problem is evident in many penal institutions where it is typical for an underground society to develop which includes drug use, violence and sexual abuse—despite the presence of guards—who ostensibly have greater control than what seems possible for most parents of school age children. While it is usually the case that younger individuals spend most of their time in direct contact with their caretakers, this is not the case as we age. It becomes problematic to monitor those who have lived with the interventions proposed by traditionalists, even when they are sensitively implemented.

Based on that limitation alone, it is reasonable to shape self-reliance as much as possible for diagnosed children, even if they are presumed to suffer from a neurological delay that limits possibilities for independent functioning. Despite our most vigilant efforts, with increasing age, we cannot expect to monitor or coerce anyone; and diagnosed children must eventually function more independently despite whether we like what they do. Shaping more self-reliant/collaborative interacting in early childhood will increase the probability that diagnosed children will competently learn socially acceptable behaviors as they approach adulthood, and thus function independently.

The evident shortcomings of the traditional intervention become problematic as older diagnosed individuals are difficult to continuously supervise (and persuade to take their medication regularly). Traditionalists have tried to address this problem when the diagnosed child approaches adolescence; this is the first instance when we notice that they *allow* the interventions which our alternative approach would implement in early childhood. However, despite meager attempts at self-reliant/and collaborative interaction with teenagers, it could take many trials before such behaviors are effectively conditioned—compared to what could have been accomplished had they been reinforced much earlier. This highlights an additional problem brought about by traditional procedures.

Moreover, prior to obtaining professional help, many diagnosed persons have apparently been living in situations where forced compliance socializing methods were used extensively. While traditionalists work diligently to reduce inconsistency of training, and extreme forms of negativity and permissiveness—significant numbers of diagnosed persons are, we observe, already subjected to patterns of socialization resembling traditional approaches. In that sense, we do not recognize a substantial shift away from the socialization techniques used during a traditional intervention. The lack of significant departure from prior socialization patterns may help account for the relatively unimpressive long-term results.

We can therefore understand that even before seeking consultation from an expert, the majority of families already engage in traditional training methods in varying degrees. For example, many families frequently discipline children for example, by forcing them to sit in chairs while watching timers, subjecting them to grounding, counting to a certain number and then coercing. The introduction of stimulant medication may be a new intervention, and the consistency of discipline may be improved, but we do not observe that the format for solving problems has changed substantially.

Disciplining with Less Coercion and Parental Reliance

The primary emphasis for those who design ADHD interventions appears to be on achieving compliance. Barkley (2000) recommends that contingency management should be applied with greater consistency, and that ADHD problems will be best managed by imposing more limiting forms of discipline to supplement the benefits of psychotropic medications. Collaborative exchanges geared towards helping diagnosed persons develop self-reliance, especially with pre-adolescents, are negligible or non-existent. Greater focus is instead given to intensifying supervision and extending the parental mandate. In order to redirect the trend towards self reliance, the current learning paradigm offers a number of practical suggestions.

Diagnosed children can be asked to give their opinions on plans of action, as well as to discuss the difficulties they would have were particular solutions to be tried. When identifying a plan of action, it is also helpful for the child to specify a time line, and to then note which situations will cue the planned responses. By so doing, parents and children learn to organize the designated sequence of actions within a structure.

These interventions are contoured to match the intellectual and linguistic functioning of the participants. Diagnosed children learn about the advantages and disadvantages of their current patterning, as well as how to respond differently in situations that had formally cued diagnostic patterns; this can be done to promote changes that they want to make. When intervening in this fashion, the child might be asked, "Let's say no one is going to punish or pressure you. When do you want to complete your homework during the weekend?", and "What will help to remind you to do your work?" The child might also be asked, "If you get unhappy while doing your work, how much do you want to complete before you stop?"

The child also has the opportunity to learn conciliation and compromise when socialized in this alternative fashion; parents are the role model for these behaviors. For example, a parent can ask, "When the advertisement comes on, would you pick up the toys on the floor?" instead of giving a command that negates the child's interest. Similarly, the parent can say, "I'm sorry to interrupt what you are doing, but it is important that you come with me." Parents (and diagnosed children) are advised to operate like skillful ambassadors rather than army generals.

We notice that many diagnosed children already show problems with sharing and accommodating to the perspectives of others, so why should parents and health professionals continue to role model autocratic responding? Dogmatism only increases the probability that younger diagnosed children will copy those behaviors, and learn to mitigate the chance of being dominated; that is, they will learn clandestine behaviors, avoidance, and withdrawal from sharing feelings, ideas, and interests. It is therefore preferable to help these children learn to interact directly with parents and be explicit about what they want.

Depending on the child's level of linguistic functioning, the parent can also initiate a verbal exchange pertaining to the child's actions; during a collaborative interaction, both parent and child can identify what may have cued unacceptable responding, and what alternative would be mutually acceptable behavior the next time a similar situation occurs. The parent asks the child, "What can we do so that our basketball game works out the next time?" "What if you talked with me about what you would like to see happen instead of doing something to irritate me?" and "What if you believed that I would like to make things better, and asked me to play with you in a different way?" Since there are countless ways for parent and child to respond differently to similar circumstances, by identifying and carrying out substitute actions, mutually acceptable behaviors are likely to recur the next time similar situations arise. For example, the parent might discover that the child dislikes instruction and scrutinizing during game play.

Additionally, rather than inadvertently reinforcing the child to make outlandish statements (e.g., wanting to have the teacher's head fall off) by overreacting and criticizing, parents can condition less drama and amplification by remaining calm. Parents can let the diagnosed child know that others will respond in empathic and helpful ways if the child's feelings are expressed in a less exaggerated or aggressive manner. With a less extreme pattern, the child will effectively speak for himself, when for example he says, "I get really angry when the teacher criticizes me in front of others."

Behaviors, in our view, are shaped by consequences. In many instances the behaviors can be interpreted as indirect ways of saying no to directives, and ways to antagonize, avoid, increase social inclusion, or retain discretionary authority in response to external interference. The ever present question is: which event sequences increase in frequency when the aforementioned responses are emitted? For example, we observe that ADHD annoyances can be reinforced when participants reconcile after a disagreement. The attempts to punish, the subsequent talking about the problem behaviors, complaining to others, attempts to offer restitution, and reestablishment of intimacy (initiated by either diagnosed child or parent) reinforces similar diagnostic patterning in the future. The over reactive parent can at times report remorse, and then over-compensate in order to reestablish a positive rapport with the indignant child. The child may then be reinforced to withhold, be accusatory of the parent, and remain angry. Such responses punish the parent and subsequently sequence with a continuance of consolation or acquiescence in order to please the child.

Other scenarios reinforce diagnostic responding as well. For example, after a diagnosed child has angered one parent, the other parent will compensate and defend the child in order to ward off the parent who is overreacting and behaving negatively. These triangulations occur quite frequently when the diagnosed child and one of the parents share the same complaints about the other parent's actions. However, to once emphasize again, these patterns do not cause ADHD; these *kinds of patterns* may condition ADHD behaviors.

Diagnostic patterning can also be reinforced when adults are preoccupied with a quest for perfection. Rather than curtail diagnostic functioning that is not dangerous or exploitative by not responding or pretending as if the behaviors were invisible, there is instead excessive correction, direction, and disapproval by the parent(s). If, instead of kindly redirecting the child towards positive action and shifting old behavioral patterns by speaking congenially with the child, participants become irritable and domineering, ADHD behaviors will be reinforced. What better way to be noticed than to usurp discretionary authority, induce guilt, or retaliate by continuing to instigate extreme responses from the other person?

Within that backdrop, rather than use coercive methods to increase acceptable responding via rewards/punishments, the treating professional can inquire into the dissatisfactions, preoccupations, apprehensions, concerns, and priorities of the diagnosed individual. For example, on some occasions we see that diagnosed children do not acknowledge an interaction, even if it is apparent that they heard every word spoken. In these instances, it is important to identify problems with the relationship, and adversities associated with particular social exchanges. Non-responsiveness can be due to a child's discontentment; we need not always presume that the child is delayed, perseverating, etc.

However, the current recommendation is not an attempt to permit unreasonable behavior without censure. For example, there might be occasions when parents turn off the television if the child does not conform to a necessary agenda. In other scenarios, parents will also unilaterally decide to prevent the child from extracurricular activity in an attempt to facilitate better prioritizing (i.e., develop better habits). Similarly, if the child continues to intrude into a family member's bedroom, he or she will be required to pay for a lock for the door. Under extreme circumstances, the parent will also find it necessary to request outside help to protect family members against harmful acts. If participants continue exploitative or dangerous behavior to self or others, it is of course necessary to firmly get those behaviors to stop.

At times when it is impractical or unfeasible to compromise due to extenuating circumstances, including time constraints, religious beliefs, social customs, or risks, parents can nevertheless urge diagnosed children to endorse enacting particular behaviors by emphasizing situational urgency and the requirement for everyone to behave in a certain manner. For example, obedience is necessary for safety reasons during a bike riding trip, and when social propriety dictates very specific limitations on behavior such as the social protocol during a funeral. However, while behavior might be non-negotiable at these times, it would nevertheless help if parents can obtain the child's *affirmation* that he is willing to comply before proceeding.

Parents might also find that it is sometimes necessary to leave a child at home with a babysitter or parent (who is careful to not indulge), and not extend an invitation to join the family, in that the child has repeatedly been unreasonable in similar situations in the past. The family can also require that a child pay for breakage resultant from a destructive tirade or carelessness that could have easily been avoided (even if this means selling toys or video games, or offering labor as reparation). However, enacting these solutions is not a means of penalizing the child so that she will learn to not repeat certain behaviors; these consequences compensate others for unreasonable acts *exactly* as what the diagnosed person would expect others to do if she were mistreated. Parents converse with the child in ways that help her to willingly repair the situation for the harmed party in order to reconstruct a positive relationship.

Similarly, if a diagnosed child has committed petty theft (despite whether the child agrees with the intervention), it is necessary to return the item to the store and pay the clerk. Parents are invariably encouraged to help the child understand reasonable ways to rectify harm done to others. However, it may not be necessary to induce further suffering on the child by adding punishment to further deter him from stealing in the future. In our view, attempts to punish only risk distracting the child from the main concern: that it is best to treat others in a kind and respectful manner. Parents should of course take action in a firm (rather than) an angry way so that the child can observe problem solving behaviors worth repeating, but interactions are to be kept as positive as possible, even when it becomes necessary to impose unilateral remedies.

These approaches are designed to prevent a cycle of punishment where participants continue to teach each other "lessons" by inducing suffering. For example, if a diagnosed teen uses all the hot water when showering, a parent can first ask the teen to offer possible solutions to the problem. While the parent might unilaterally turn off the hot water, this particular solution will strain the relationship significantly less if the teen also acknowledges that it is a reasonable solution when all else fails. In these approaches parents strive to maintain positive relationships. When they do take a unilateral stand they enact the behavior calmly and in the spirit of resolving dilemmas.

Parents can also reduce the adverse side effects of introducing coercive solutions by emphasizing that, were they to behave in a comparable way, they would receive the same responses imposed upon them. Intrusive, dangerous, or exploitative behavior is not tolerated or permissible for any family member, regardless of age. Clarification helps the child recognize that the limits apply to everyone. However, because calling the police, filing a "stubborn child" complaint, or placement outside the home cannot be rescinded, such extreme coercive solutions as these (viewed as betrayal) are best avoided *whenever* possible.

The current alternative model largely coincides with the work of Alfred Adler (1958) who coined the term "Gemeinschaftsgefuebl" or "social interest", and Rudolph Dreikurs (Dreikurs, 1971; Dreikurs and Soltz, 1964; Dreikurs and Grey, 1968; Dreikurs, Grunwald and Pepper, 1971; Dreikurs, Corsini and Gould, 1974). Both authors advocate socialization that endorses the development of personal responsibility, concern for the perspectives of others, and an interest in contributing to society in general. Similarly, Nelsen (1987) and Kvols (1998) also provide a detailed account of possible ways to socialize (even very young) children so that they can learn self-reliance and increased concern for others.

When coupled with systematic effort to stop reinforcing diagnostic responding, it also seems that the "Authoritative" approach described by Baumrind (1967) has a higher probability of training the kinds of patterning being recommended here, compared to either a "Permissive" or "Authoritarian" child rearing method, all else being equal. In addition, Shure's (1994) "Raising a Thinking Child," Leman's (1984) "Reality Discipline," Chapman and Campbell's (1997) "Five Love Languages," Glasser and Easley's (1998) "Nurtured Heart Approach," and Green's (2001) collaborative methods with the "Explosive Child" dovetail with many of the recommendations noted here.

Concluding Remarks

Although it is probable that only some diagnosed persons will benefit from the interventions proposed here (for various reasons), it is still heuristic to raise questions about the traditional way of conceptualizing and treating ADHD so that new possibilities can be explored for greater numbers of diagnosed persons. Perhaps new ways of thinking about the set of behaviors will address the apparent contradictions evident within traditional understanding, and coherently explicate empirical findings that are inconsistent within the disability framework.

A number of people will object to any potential undermining of the traditional formulation, but others will be attracted to the current learning paradigm. They will regard it as an opportunity to improve on the disappointing long-term outcomes presently being reported. However, the fact that past psychosocial interventions have not produced a great deal of change in response patterns of diagnosed persons could be due to limitations related to the type of *intervention* rather than to biological disability. There is no clear reason to stop seeking behavioral events simply because previous attempts have only been minimally successful: the skill set of therapists, problems associated with using parents as change agents, and the time taken to shape new behaviors will each have been limits to success.

Depending on one's metaphor of understanding, we see that very different conclusions can be drawn from the same observations. While the current model invokes history of reinforcement as a way to account for ADHD patterns, the traditional approach invokes a delayed inhibitory mechanism. It has been the expectation of this current work to show that a learning paradigm is consistent with ADHD empirical findings. The model currently being proposed does not see ADHD as something separate from the behaviors being observed; the *many behaviors associated with the ADHD* become the disorder in total.

Our alternative model has very different presumptions compared to the traditional approach: ADHD behavior becomes a way for some individuals to learn to adapt to socio-cultural expectations, and behaviors are seen as functional in relation to a reinforcement history. Accounting for the frequency rates of those behaviors entails the coordination of context, situation and circumstance, and response interactions. There is no attempt to locate ADHD within particular individuals as an antecedent biological limitation *or* as an instance of poor parenting. While traditionalists attempt to change ADHD behavior by imposing interventions that compensate for inner delay, the current model works to shape self-reliance, and takes a compromising stance when training diagnosed persons to coordinate acceptably with others. We avoid pressurizing, medicating, and manipulating resources until diagnosed persons acquiesce, since such methods rarely produce generalized effects.

The current view is that ADHD patterning is expressed in ways very unlike other biologically-determined problems. For example, even though it may be possible to improve on one's delay or limitation with remediation over time, we do not know what these categories mean if individuals are potentially able to exceed their boundaries prior to rehabilitation. When invoking a biological account for atypical functioning, the usual assertion is that individuals have a particular restriction in functioning that cannot be transcended without at least some evidence of systemic change. Conversely, ADHD is a unique medical problem that may be obviated immediately simply by introducing an enticement or threat.

According to the traditional view, individuals can be characterized as pervasively delayed with ADHD and yet function in ways that contradict the posited functional impairment. The delay assessment is imposed without empirical evidence that the diagnosed population has a consistent restriction in functioning. The typical reaction is to push aside these contentions, claim that it is the disorder's nature to be inconsistent, and argue that particular compensations must be offsetting the ever-present inner problem, including the assertion that the individual may simply be interested in functioning well.

Because we observe that significant numbers of diagnosed persons are engaging in behaviors that they *should not* be able to do (given their disability), we cannot support the notion that their biology is the limiting factor. Clearly they are not doing the more acceptable responses consistently enough at the appropriate times, but much of the controversy surrounding the diagnostic category relates to the observation that diagnosed persons *can and do* function quite well on some occasions, such as when they initiate or engage in activities they enjoy.

Those who endorse biological determinism will often admonish others who focus on social patterning as a way to better understand the diagnostic category. They assert that as long as an individual is not subjected to atypical extremes, socialization will generally account for few of the differences apparent between those who are diagnosed and those who are not. However, despite such assertions, we notice that traditionalists have not investigated the detailed learning histories of diagnosed persons, and may thus be jumping to conclusions that have not been adequately tested.

The current learning paradigm does not assert that psychosocial events cause ADHD, as this would be equivalent to using the same mechanistic construction of the traditional view. There is no attempt here to discount the influence of biology, but rather the model is simply unseating biology from a position of having primary antecedent causal status in accounting for apparent situational behaviors that change in relation to subsequent events. Since diagnosed persons may already be doing the required acts some of the time, in some places and under certain circumstances, it is not necessary to completely reengineer these individuals to effect the desired change. In traditional vernacular, their inhibitory function may already be good enough.

Diagnosis within this view becomes a matter of how frequently, at what point, and under what conditions are troublesome behaviors emitted. ADHD becomes reinforced behavior most often learned when people encounter social discomfort, lack of success, or denial. Those with particular functional difficulties are more likely to respond with ADHD patterns, but this is not always the case. This alternative understanding departs from the traditional view and presents an alternative that coherently accounts for the variations in diagnostic functioning which seem so contradictory and poorly explained by biological determinism. The vicissitudes and variations of problem behaviors can often be better explicated by detecting, noting, and addressing the recurrence of particular situations and circumstances that cue the behaviors rather than accepting a neurobiological categorization.

Works Cited

Abikoff, H. "An Evaluation of Cognitive Behavior Therapy for Hyperactive Children." in *Advances in Clinical Child Psychology* 10 (p. 171–216) edited by B. Lahey and A. Kazdin, New York: Plenum, 1987.

Achenbach, T. M., S. H. McConaughy, and C. T. Howell. "Child/Adolescent Behavioral and Emotional Problems: Implications of Cross Informant Correlations for Situational Specificity." *Psychological Bulletin* 101 (1987): 213–32.

Ackerman, P. T., R. A. Dykman, P. J. Holcomb, and D. S. McCray. "Methylphenidate Effects on Cognitive Style and Reaction Time in Four Groups of Children." *Psychiatry Res.* 7 (1982): 199–213.

Adelizzi, J. U. *Shades of Trauma.* Plymouth, MA: Jones River Press, 1998.

Adler, L. A. *What Life Should Mean to You.* New York: Putnam & Sons, 1958.

Adler, L. A., T. J. Spencer, D. R. Milton, R. J. Moore, D. Jones, and D. Michelson. "Long-Term, Open-Label Safety and Efficacy of Atomoxetine in Adults with Attention Deficit Hyperactivity Disorder." *Journal of Clinical Psychiatry* 66, no. 3 (2005): 294–99.

Alberts-Corush, J., P. Firestone, and J. T. Goodman. "Attention and Impulsive Characteristics of the Biological and Adoptive Parents of Hyperactive and Normal Control Children." *American Journal of Orthopsychiatry* 56 (1986): 413–23.

Amen, D. *Healing ADD: The Breakthrough Program That Allows You to See and Heal the Six Types of Attention Deficit Disorder.* New York: Berkley Books, 2001.

American Psychiatric Association. *Diagnostic and Statistical Manual of Mental Disorders, 4th ed.* Washington, DC, 1994.

——. *Diagnostic and Statistical Manual of Mental Health Disorders, Test Revision, 4th ed.* Washington, DC, 2000.

Anastopoulos, A. D., L. H. Rhoads, and S. E. Farley. "Counseling and Training Parents." in *Attention Deficit Hyperactivity Disorder: A Handbook for Diagnosis and Treatment* (p. 453–78, 3d ed.) edited by Barkley, R. A., New York: Guilford Press, 2006.

Anastopoulos, A. D., J. M. Smith, and E. E. Wien. "Counseling and Training Parents." in *Attention Deficit Hyperactivity Disorder: A Handbook for Diagnosis and Treatment* (p. 373–93, 2d ed.) edited by Barkley, R. A., New York: Guilford Press, 1998.

Aoki, N. "Brain Chemical Linked to ADHD." *Boston Globe*, March 13, 2001, D2.

Azerrad, J. *Anyone Can Have a Happy Child.* London: Evans, 1997.

Baranski, J. V., R. Pigeau, P. Dinich, and I. Jacobs. "Effects of Modafinil on Cognitive and Metacognitive Performance." *Human Psychopharmacology* 19, no. 5 (2004): 323–32.

Barber, M. A., and R. Milich. "The Effects of Reinforcement Schedule and Task Characteristics on the Behavior of Attention Deficit Hyperactivity Disordered Boys." Paper presented at the annual meeting of the Society for Research in Child and Adolescent Psychopathology, Miami, Fla., February 1989.

Bargh, J. A., and T. L. Chartrand. "The Unbearable Automaticity of Being." *American Psychologist* 57, no. 7 (1999): 462–79.

Barkley, R. A. "A Review of Stimulant Drug Research with Hyperactive Children." *Journal of Child Psychology and Psychiatry* 18 (1977): 137–65.

———. *Hyperactive Children: A Handbook for Diagnosis and Treatment.* New York: Guilford Press, 1990.

———. "ADHD: What Do We Know?" New York: Guilford Press (Film), 1993.

———. *ADHD and the Nature of Self-Control.* New York: Guilford Press, 1997.

———. "History." in Barkley, R. A. *Attention Deficit Hyperactivity Disorder: A Handbook for Diagnosis and Treatment* (p. 3–55, 2d ed.) New York: Guilford Press, 1998a.

———. "Primary Symptoms, Diagnostic Criteria, Prevalence, and Gender Differences." in Barkley, R. A. *Attention Deficit Hyperactivity Disorder: A Handbook for Diagnosis and Treatment* (p. 56–96, 2d ed.) New York: Guilford Press, 1998b.

———. "Associated Problems." in Barkley, R. A. *Attention Deficit Hyperactivity Disorder: A Handbook for Diagnosis and Treatment* (p. 97–138, 2d ed.) New York: Guilford Press, 1998c.

———. "Comorbid Disorders, Social Relations, and Subtyping." in Barkley, R. A. *Attention Deficit Hyperactivity Disorder: A Handbook for Diagnosis and Treatment* (p. 139–63, 2d ed.) New York: Guilford Press, 1998d.

———. "Etiologies." in Barkley, R. A. *Attention Deficit Hyperactivity Disorder: A Handbook for Diagnosis and Treatment* (p. 164–85, 2d ed.) New York: Guilford Press, 1998e.

———. "Developmental Course, Adult Outcome, and Clinic-Referred ADHD Adults." in Barkley, R. A. *Attention Deficit Hyperactivity Disorder: A Handbook for Diagnosis and Treatment* (p. 186–224, 2d ed.) New York: Guilford Press, 1998f.

———. "A Theory of ADHD: Inhibition, Executive Functions, and Time." in Barkley, R. A. *Attention Deficit Hyperactivity Disorder: A Handbook for Diagnosis and Treatment* (p. 225–60, 2d ed.) New York: Guilford Press, 1998g.

———. *ADHD in Children, Adolescents and Adults: Diagnosis, Assessment, and Treatment.* New England Educational Institute, Cape Cod Summer Symposia (Audio cassettes). New England Educational Institute, Pittsfield, MA, 2000.

———. *ADHD: An Intensive Course on the Nature and Treatment of Children and Adolescents with Attention Deficit Hyperactivity Disorder.* New England Educational Institute, Pittsfield, MA, 2001.

———. "Mental Health Outcomes of Attention Deficit Hyperactivity Disorder." *University of Massachusetts Medical School: Grand Rounds Lecture Series* 17 (January), 2002.

———. "Driving Impairments in Teens and Adults with Attention Deficit Hyperactivity Disorder." *Psychiatric Clinics of North America* 27, no. 2 (2004): 233–60.

————. "History." in Barkley, R. A. *Attention Deficit Hyperactive Disorder: A Handbook for Diagnosis and Treatment* (p. 3–75, 3d ed.) New York: Guilford Press, 2006a.

————. "Primary Symptoms, Diagnostic Criteria, Prevalence, and Gender Differences." in Barkley, R. A. *Attention Deficit Hyperactive Disorder: A Handbook for Diagnosis and Treatment* (p. 76–121, 3d ed.) New York: Guilford Press, 2006b.

————. "Associated Cognitive, Developmental, and Health Problems." in Barkley, R. A. *Attention Deficit Hyperactive Disorder: A Handbook for Diagnosis and Treatment* (p. 122–83, 3d ed.) New York: Guilford Press, 2006c.

————. "Etiologies." in Barkley, R. A. *Attention Deficit Hyperactive Disorder: A Handbook for Diagnosis and Treatment* (p. 219–47, 3d ed.) New York: Guilford Press, 2006d.

————. "ADHD in Adults: Developmental Course and Outcome of Children with ADHD and ADHD in Clinic-Referred Adults." in Barkley, R. A. *Attention Deficit Hyperactive Disorder: A Handbook for Diagnosis and Treatment* (p. 248–96, 3d ed.) New York: Guilford Press, 2006e.

————. "A Theory of ADHD." in Barkley, R. A. *Attention Deficit Hyperactive Disorder: A Handbook for Diagnosis and Treatment* (p. 297–334, 3d ed.) New York: Guilford Press, 2006f.

Barkley, R. A., G. J. DuPaul, and M. B. McMurray. "A Comprehensive Evaluation of Attention Deficit Disorder with and without Hyperactivity." *Journal of Consulting and Clinical Psychology* 58 (1990): 775–89.

Barkley, R. A., and G. Edwards. "Diagnostic Interview, Behavior Rating Scales, and the Medical Examination." in Barkley, R. A. *Attention Deficit Hyperactivity Disorder: A Handbook for Diagnosis and Treatment* (p. 337–68, 3d ed.). New York: Guilford Press, 2006.

Barkley, R. A., G. Edwards, M. Laneri, K. Fletcher, and L. Metevia. "Executive Functioning, Temporal Discounting, and a Sense of Time in Adolescents with Attention Deficit Hyperactivity Disorder and Oppositional Defiant Disorder." *Journal of Abnormal Child Psychology* 29 (2001): 541–56.

Barkley, R. A., M. Fischer, L. Smallish, and K. Fletcher. "The Persistence of Attention Deficit Hyperactivity Disorder into Young Adulthood as a Function of Reporting Source and Definition of Disorder." *Journal of Abnormal Psychology* 111 (2002): 279–89.

Barkley, R. A., G. Grodzinsky, and G. DuPaul. "Frontal Lobe Functions in Attention Deficit Disorder with and without Hyperactivity: A Review and Research Report." *Journal of Abnormal Child Psychology* 20 (1992): 163–88.

Barkley, R. A., D. G. Guevremont, A. D. Anastopolous, G. J. DuPaul, and T. L. Shelton. "Driving-Related Risks and Outcomes of Attention Deficit Hyperactivity Disorder in Adolescents and Young Adults: A 3–5-Year Follow-up Survey." *Pediatrics* 92 (1993): 212–18.

Barkley, R. A., S. Koplowicz, T. Anderson, and M. B. McMurray. "Sense of Time in Children with ADHD: Effects of Duration, Distraction, and Stimulant Medication." *Journal of the International Neuropsychological Society* 3 (1997): 359–69.

Barkley, R. A., K. R. Murphy, and T. Bush. "Time Estimation and Reproduction in Young Adults with Attention Deficit Hyperactivity Disorder (ADHD)." *Neuropsychology* 15 (2001): 351–60.

Barkley, R. A., K. R. Murphy, and D. Kwasnik. "Motor Vehicle Driving Competencies and Risks in Teens and Young adults with ADHD." *Pediatrics* 98 (1996): 1089–95.

Barkley, R. A., and D. G. Ullman. "A Comparison of Objective Measures of Activity Levels and Distractibility in Hyperactive and Non-Hyperactive Children." *Journal of Abnormal Child Psychology* 3 (1975): 213–44.

Bauermeister, J. J., R. A. Barkley, J. V. Martinez, E. Cumba, R. R. Ramirez, G. Reina, et al. "Time Estimation and Performance on Reproduction Task in Subtypes of Children with Attention Deficit Hyperactivity Disorder." *Journal of Clinical Child and Adolescent Psychology* 34 (2005): 151–62.

Baumrind, D. "Child Care Practices Anteceding Three Patterns of Preschool Behavior." *Genetic Psychology Monographs* 75 (1967): 43–88.

———. "The Average Expectable Environment is not Good Enough: A Response to Scarr." *Child Development* 64 (1993): 1299–307.

Baxter, L. R., J. M. Schwartz, K. S. Bergman, M. P. Szuba, B. H. Guze, J. C. Mazziotta, et al. "Caudate Glucose Metabolic Rate Changes with both Drug and Behavior Therapy for Obsessive-Compulsive Disorder." *Archives of General Psychiatry* 49 (1992): 681–89.

BBC News Online. "Taxi Drivers' Brains 'Grow' on the Job." Retrieved April 19, 2004, http://news.bbc.co.uk/1/hi/sci/tech/677048.stm.

Belkin, L. "Office Messes." *New York Times Magazine.* July 18, 2004.

Belsky, J., M. Fish, and R. Isabella. "Continuity and Discontinuity in Infant Negative and Positive Emotionality: Family Antecedents and Attachment Consequences." *Developmental Psychology* 27 (1991): 421–31.

Belsky, J., K. Hsieh, and K. Crnic. "Mothering, Fathering, and Infant Negativity as Antecedents of Boys' Externalizing Problems and Inhibition at Age 3 Years: Differential Susceptibility to Rearing Experience?" *Development and Psychopathology* 10 (1998): 301–309.

Benson, E. S. "Behavioral Genetics: Meet Molecular Biology." *Monitor on Psychology* 35, no. 4 (April 2004): 42–5.

Berk, L. E. "Children's Private Speech: An Overview of Theory and the Status of Research." in Diaz, R. M., and L. E. Berk (eds.) *Private Speech: From Social Interaction to Self-regulation.* (p. 17–54). Hillsdale, NJ: Erlbaum, 1992.

Bernstein, B. "Social Class and Linguistic Development: A Theory of Social Learning." in Halsey, A. H., J. E. Floud, and C. A. Anderson (eds.) *Education, Economy and Society: A Reader in the Sociology of Education.* New York: Free Press, 1961.

Berry, N., V. Jobanputra, and H. Pal. "Molecular Genetics of Schizophrenia: A Critical Review." *Journal of Psychiatry and Neuroscience* 28 (2003): 415–29.

Bespalova, I. N., and J. D. Buxbaum. "Disease Susceptibility Genes for Autism." *Annals of Medicine* 35 (2003): 274–81.

Biederman, J., R. J. Baldessarini, V. Wright, D. Knee, and J. Harmatz. "A Double-Blind Placebo-Controlled Study of Desipramine in the Treatment of Attention Deficit Disorder: I. Efficacy." *Journal of the American Academy of Child and Adolescent Psychiatry* 28 (1989) 777–84.

Biederman, J., S. V. Faraone, K. Keenan, J. Benjamin, B. Krifcher, C. Moore, et al. "Further Evidence for Family Genetic Risk Factors in Attention Deficit Hyperactivity Disorder: Patterns of Comorbidity in Probands and Relative in Psychiatrically and Pediatrically Referred Samples." *Archives of General Psychiatry* 49 (1992): 728–38.

Biederman, J., S. V. Faraone, E. Mick, T. Spencer, T. Wilens, K. Kiely, et al. "High Risk for Attention Deficit Hyperactivity Disorder among Children of Parents with Childhood Onset of the Disorder: A Pilot Study." *American Journal of Psychiatry* 152 (1995): 431–35.

Biederman, J., S. V. Faraone, S. Milberger, S. Curtis, L. Chen, A. Marrs, et al. "Predictors of Persistence and Remission of ADHD into Adolescence: Results of a Four-Year Prospective Follow-Up Study." *Journal of the American Academy of Child and Adolescent Psychiatry* 35 (1996): 343–51.

Biederman, J., K. Keenan, and S. V. Faraone. "Parent-Based Diagnosis of Attention Deficit Disorder Predicts a Diagnosis Based on Teacher Report." *Journal of the American Academy of Child and Adolescent Psychiatry* 29 (1990): 698–701.

Biringen, Z., R. Emde, and J. Campos. "Infant Walking Onset: Home Observations of Affectivity and Autonomy." Paper presented at the Biennial meeting of the Society for Research in Child Development, Seattle, WA. April, 1991.

Block, G. H. "Hyperactivity: A Cultural Perspective." *Journal of Learning Disabilities* 110 (1977): 236–40.

Blum, K., J. G. Cull, E. R. Braverman, and D. E. Comings. "Reward Deficiency Syndrome." *American Scientist* 84 (1996):132–45.

Bonham, V., E. Warshauer-Baker, F. Collins. "Race and Ethnicity in the Genome Era." *American Psychologist* 60 (2005): 9–15.

Boyle, M. H., and E. L. Lipman. "Do Places Matter?: Socioeconomic Disadvantage and Behavioral Problems of Children in Canada." *Journal of Consulting and Clinical Psychology* 70 (2002): 378–89.

Brady, K. D., and M. B. Denckla. "Performance of Children with Attention Deficit Hyperactivity Disorder on the Tower of Hanoi Task." Unpublished manuscript. Johns Hopkins University School of Medicine, Baltimore, 1994.

Broberg, A., M. Lamb, and P. Hwang. "Inhibition: Its Stability and Correlates in Sixteen-to Forty-Month Old Children." *Child Development* 61 (1990): 1153–1163.

Bronowski, J. *Human and Animal Languages: A Sense of the Future* (p. 104–31). Cambridge, MA: MIT Press, 1977.

Brown, R. T., and H. C. Quay. "Reflection-Impulsivity of Normal and Behavior-Disordered Children." *Journal of Abnormal Child Psychology* 5 (1977): 457–62.

Brown, T. E. (ed.) *Attention Deficit Disorders and Comorbidities in Children, Adolescents and Adults.* Washington, DC: American Psychiatric Press, 2000.

Bruns, J. H. *They Can but They Don't: Helping Students Overcome Work Inhibition.* New York: Viking Press, 1993.

Bussing, R., F. Gary, D. M. Mason, C. E. Leon, K. Sinha, and C. W. Garvan. "Child Temperament, ADHD, and Caregiver Strain: Exploring Relationships in an Epidemiological Sample." *Journal of the American Academy of Child and Adolescent Psychiatry* 42 (2003): 184–92.

Cadoret, R., and M. Stewart. "An Adoption Study of Attention Deficit Hyperactivity/ Aggression and their Relationship to Adult Antisocial Personality." *Comprehensive Psychiatry* 32 (1991): 73–82.

Cahill, L., B. Prins, M. Weber, and J. L. McGaugh. "b-Adrenergic Activation and Memory for Emotional Events." *Nature* 371 (1994): 702–704.

Campbell, S. B. "Hyperactivity: Course and Treatment." in Davids, A. (ed.) *Child Personality and Psychopathology: Current Topics* (vol. 3). New York: Wiley, 1976.

———. "Mother-Infant Interactions as a Function of Maternal Ratings of Temperament." *Child Psychiatry and Human Development* 10 (1979): 67–76.

———. "Parent-Referred Problem Three-Year Olds: Developmental Changes in Symptoms." *Journal of Child Psychology and Psychiatry* 28 (1987): 835–46.

———. *Behavioral Problems in Preschool Children.* New York: Guilford Press, 1990.

Campbell, S. B., V. I. Douglas, and G. Morgenstern. "Cognitive Styles in Hyperactive Children and the Effect of Methylphenidate." *Journal of Child Psychology and Psychiatry* 12 (1971): 55–67.

Campbell, S. B., M. Endman, and G. Bernfield. "A Three-Year Follow-up of Hyperactive Preschoolers into Elementary School." *Journal of Child Psychology and Psychiatry* 18 (1977): 239–49.

Campbell, S. B., and L. J. Ewing. "Follow-up of Hard to Manage Preschoolers: Adjustments at Age 9 and Predictors of Continuing Symptoms." *Journal of Abnormal Child Psychology and Psychiatry* 31 (1990): 871–99.

Cantwell, D. *The Hyperactive Child.* New York: Spectrum, 1975.

Caspi, A., J. McClay, T. E. Moffitt, J. Mill, J. Martin, I. W. Craig, et al. "Role of Genotype in the Cycle of Violence in Maltreated Children." *Science* 297 (August 2002): 851–53.

Castellanos, F. X. in "Family Circle." (February 2003) 128.

Castellanos, F. X., J. N. Giedd, W. L. Marsh, S. D. Hamburger, A. C. Vaituzis, D. P. Dickstein, F. X. Sarfatti, et al. "Quantitative Brain Magnetic Resonance Imaging in Attention Deficit Hyperactivity Disorder." *Archives for General Psychiatry* 53: (1996): 607–16.

Chapman, G., and R. Campbell. *The Five Love Languages of Children.* Chicago: Moody Publishing, 1997.

Chronis, A. M., B. B. Lahey, W. E. Pelham Jr., H. L. Kipp, B. L. Baumann, and S. S. Lee. "Psychopathology and Substance Abuse in Parents of Young Children with Attention Deficit Hyperactivity Disorder." *Journal of the American Academy of Children and Adolescent Psychiatry* 42 (2003): 1424–32.

Clark, M. L., J. A. Cheyne, C. E. Cunningham, and L. S. Siegel. "Dyadic Peer Interactions and Task Orientation in Attention Deficit Disordered Children." *Journal of Abnormal Child Psychology* 16 (1988): 1–15.

Cohen, N. J. "The Earth Is Round (p < .05)." *American Psychologist* 49, no. 12 (1994): 997–1003.

Cohen, N. J., R. Menna, D. D. Vallance, M. A. Barwick, N. Im, and N. Horodezky. "Language, Social Cognitive Processing, and Behavioral Characteristics of Psychiatrically Disturbed Children with Previously Identified and Unsuspected Language Impairments." *Journal of Child Psychology and Psychiatry* 39 (1998): 853–64.

Comings, D. E. "Attention Deficit Hyperactivity Disorder with Tourett Syndrome." in Brown, T. E. (ed.) *Attention Deficit Disorders and Comorbidities in Children, Adolescents, and Adults* (p. 363–92). Washington, DC: American Psychiatric Press, 2000.

Conners, C. K., C. Casat, T. Gualtieri, E. Weller, M. Reader, A. Reiss, et al. "Bupropion Hydrochloride in Attention Deficit Disorder with Hyperactivity." *Journal of the American Academy of Child and Adolescent Psychiatry* 35 (1996): 1314–21.

Connor, D. "Other Medications." in Barkley, R. A. *Attention Deficit Hyperactivity Disorder: A Handbook for Diagnosis and Treatment.* (p. 658–77, 3d ed.) New York: Guilford Press, 2006.

Connor, D. F., K. E. Fletcher, and J. M. Swanson. "A Meta-Analysis of Clonidine for Symptoms of Attention Deficit Hyperactivity Disorder." *Journal of the American Academy of Child and Adolescent Psychiatry* 38 (1999): 1551–59.

Conrad, P. "The Discovery of Hyperkinesis: Notes on the Medicalization of Deviant Behavior." *Social Problems* 23 (1975): 12–21.

Cook, E. H., M. A. Stein, and D. L. Leventhal. "Family-Based Association of Attention Deficit Hyperactivity Disorder and the Dopamine Transporter." in Blum, K. and E. P. Noble (eds.) *Handbook of Psychiatric Genetics* (p. 297–310). CRC Press, Boca Raton, FLA., 1997.

Cowen, E., M. Wiener, and J. Hess. "Generalization of Problem-Solving Rigidity." *Journal of Consulting Psychology* 17, no.2 (1953): 100–103.

Crawford, N. "ADHD: A Women's Issue." *Monitor on Psychology* 34, no. 2 (2003): 28–30.

Cruickshank, B. M., M. Eliason, and B. Merrifield. "Long-Term Sequelae of Water Near-Drowning." *Journal of Pediatric Psychology* 13 (1988): 379–88.

Cunningham, C. E. "A Large Group Community-Based, Family-Systems Approach to Parent Training." in Barkley, R. A. *Attention Deficit Hyperactivity Disorder: A Handbook for Diagnosis and Treatment* (p. 394–412, 2d ed.) New York: Guilford Press, 1998.

Cunningham, C. E., and R. A. Barkley. "The Interactions of Hyperactive and Normal Children with Their Mothers During Free Play and Structured Tasks." *Child Development* 50 (1979): 217–24.

Cunningham, C. E., and L. S. Siegel. "Peer Interactions of Normal and Attention Deficit Disordered Boys During Free-Play, Cooperative Task, and Simulated Classroom Situations." *Journal of Abnormal Child Psychology* 15 (1987): 277–68.

Cunningham, C. E., L. S. Siegel, and D. R. Offord. "A Developmental Dose Response Analysis of the Efforts of Methylphenidate on the Peer Interactions of Attention Deficit Disordered Boys." *Journal of Child Psychology and Psychiatry* 26 (1985): 955–71.

———. "A Dose-Response Analysis of the Effects of Methylphenidate on the Peer Interactions and Simulated Classroom Performance of ADHD Children with and without Conduct Problems, 2" *Journal of Child Psychology and Psychiatry* 32 (1991): 439–52.

Curry, D. R. "Case Studies in Behavior Modification." *Psychology in the Schools* 7 (1970): 330–35.

Davis, K. L., R. S. Kahn, G. Ko, and M. Davidson. "Dopamine and Schizophrenia: A Review and Reconceptualization." *American Journal of Psychiatry* 148 (1991): 1474–86.

Davison, G. C., and J. M. Neale. *Abnormal Psychology: 17th Edition.* New York: Wiley, 1998.

DeGrandpre, R. *Ritalin Nation: Rapid-Fire Culture and the Transformation of Human Consciousness.* New York: W. W. Norton & Company, 1999.

Dick, D. M., and T. Foroud. "Candidate Genes for Alcohol Dependence: A Review of Genetic Evidence from Human Studies." *Alcoholism: Clinical and Experimental Research* 27 (2003): 868–79.

Diener, M. B., and R. Milich. "The Effects of Positive Feedback on Social Interactions in Children with ADHD: A Test of the Self-Protective Hypothesis." *Journal of Clinical Child Psychology* 26 (1997): 256–63.

Diller, L. "Bitter Pill." *Psychotherapy Networker.* (Jan/Feb. 2005): 56–72.

Douglas, V. I. "Stop, Look, and Listen: The Problem of Sustained Attention and Impulse Control in Hyperactive and Normal Children." *Canadian Journal of Behavioural Science* 4 (1972): 259–82.

———. "Attention and Cognitive Problems." in Rutter, M. (ed.) *Developmental Neuropsychiatry* (p. 280–329). New York: Guilford Press, 1983.

Douglas, V. I., and P. A. Parry. "Effects of Reward and Non-Reward on Attention and Frustration in Attention Deficit Disorder." *Journal of Abnormal Child Psychology* 22 (1994): 281–302.

Douglas, V. I., and K. G. Peters. "Toward a Clearer Definition of the Attentional Deficit of Hyperactive Children." in Hale, G. A., and M. Lewis (eds.) *Attention and the Development of Cognitive Skills* (p. 173–248). New York: Plenum Press, 1979.

Draeger, S., M. Prior, and A. Sanson. "Visual and Auditory Attention Performance in Hyperactive Children: Competence or Compliance?" *Journal of Abnormal Child Psychology* 14 (1986): 411–24.

Draganski, B., C. Gaser, V. Busch, G. Schuierer, U. Bogdahn, and A. May. "Neuroplasticity: Changes in Grey Matter Induced by Training." *Nature* 427 (2004): 311–12.

Dreikurs, R. *Social Equality: The Challenge of Today*. Chicago: Contemporary Books, Inc., 1971.

Dreikurs, R., and V. Soltz. *Children: The Challenge*. New York: Hawthorn Books, Inc., 1964.

Dreikurs, R., and L. Grey. *A New Approach to Discipline: Logical Consequences*. New York: Hawthorn Books, Inc., 1968.

Dreikurs, R., B. Grunwald, and F. Pepper. *Maintaining Sanity in the Classroom*. New York: Harper & Row, Inc., 1971.

Dreikurs, R., R. Corsini, and S. Gould. *Family Council*. Chicago: Henry Regnery, 1974.

DuPaul, G. J., R. A. Barkley, and D. F. Connor. "Stimulants." in Barkley, R. A. *Attention Deficit Hyperactivity Disorder: A Handbook for Diagnosis and Treatment*. (p. 510–551, 2d ed.) New York: Guilford Press, 1998.

DuPaul, G. J., and R. A. Ervin. "Functional Assessment of Behaviors Related to Attention Deficit Hyperactivity Disorder: Linking Assessment to Intervention Design." *Behavioral Therapy* 27 (1996): 601–22.

DuPaul, G. J., K. E. McGoey, T. L. Eckert, and J. Van Brakle. "Preschool Children with Attention Deficit Hyperactivity Disorder: Impairments in Behavioral, Social, and School Functioning." *Journal of the American Academy of Child and Adolescent Psychiatry* 36 (2001): 1036–45.

DuPaul, G. J., and T. J. Power. "Educational Interventions for Students with Attention Deficit Disorders." in Brown, T. E. (ed.) *Attention Deficit Disorders and Comorbidities in Children, Adolescents, and Adults* (p. 607–35). Washington, DC: American Psychiatric Press, 2000.

Eberhardt, J. "Imaging Race." *American Psychologist* 60 (2005): 181–90.

Ebstein, R. P., O. Novick, R. Umansky, B. Priel, Y. Osher, D. Blaine, et al. "Dopamine D4 Receptor (D4DR) Exon III Polymorphism Associated with Human Personality Trait Novelty Seeking." *Nature Genetics* 12 (1996): 78–80.

Egerton, John. "The Misuse of IQ Testing: An Interview with Leon Kamin." *Change* (October 1973): 40–43.

Elia, J., B. G. Borcherding, W. Z. Potter, I. N. Mefford, J. L. Rapaport, and C. S. Keysor. "Stimulant Drug Treatment of Hyperactivity: Biochemical Correlates." *Clinical Pharmacology Therapy* 48 (1990): 57–66.

Elias, P. "Brain Scans a Political Tool?" *Telegram & Gazette*. October 29, 2004, A13.

Elkins, I. J., M. McGue, and W. G. Iacono. "Genetic and Environmental Influences on Parent-Son Relationships: Evidence for Increasing Genetic Influence During Adolescence." *Developmental Psychology* 33 (1997): 351–63.

El-Sayed, E., J. O. Larsson, H. E. Persson, and P. Rydelius. "Altered Cortical Activity in Children with Attention Deficit Hyperactivity Disorder During Attention Load

Task." *Journal of the American Academy of Child and Adolescent Psychiatry* 41 (2002): 811–19.

Erickson, K., W. Drevets, and J. Schulkin. "Glucocorticoid Regulation of Diverse Cognitive Functions in Normal and Pathological Emotional States." *Neuroscience and Biobehavioral Reviews* 27 (2003): 233–46.

Ernst, M. "Neuroimaging in Attention Deficit Hyperactivity Disorder." in Lyon, G. R., and J. M. Rumsey (eds.) *Neuroimaging: A Window to the Neurological Foundations of Learning and Behavior in Children.* (p. 95–118). Baltimore: Brookes, 1996.

Ernst, M., A. S. Kimes, E. D. London, J. A. Matochik, D. Eldreth, S. Tata, et al. "Neural Substrates of Decision Making in Adults with Attention Deficit Hyperactivity Disorder." *American Journal of Psychiatry* 160 (2003): 1061–70.

Faraone, S., J. Biederman, W. J. Chen, B. Krifcher, K. Keenan, C. Moore, S. Sprich, and M. Tsuang. "Segregation Analysis of Attention Deficit Hyperactivity Disorder: Evidence for Single Gene Transmission." *Psychiatric Genetics* 2 (1992): 257–75.

Faraone, S. V., and A. E. Doyle. "The Nature and Heritability of Attention Deficit Hyperactivity Disorder." *Child and Adolescent Psychiatric Clinics of North America* 10 (2001): 299–316.

Faraone, S. V., A. E. Doyle, E. Mick, and J. Biederman. "Meta-Analysis of the Association between the 7-Repeat Allele of the Dopamine D4 Receptor Gene and Attention Deficit Hyperactivity Disorder." *American Journal of Psychiatry* 158 (2001): 1052–57.

Fingerman, K. L., and M. Perlmutter. "Future Time Perspective and Life Events Across Adulthood." *Journal of General Psychology* 122 (1994): 95–111.

Fischer, M. "The Persistence of ADHD into Adulthood: It Depends on Whom You Ask." *ADHD Report* 5, no. 4 (1997): 8–10.

Fischer, M., R. A. Barkley, L. Smallish, and K. Fletcher. "Young Adult Follow-up of Hyperactive Children: Self-reported Psychiatric Disorders, Comorbidity, and the Role of Childhood Conduct Problems." *Journal of Abnormal Child Psychology* 30 (2002): 463–75.

Fisher, S. E., C. Francks, J. T. McCracken, J. J. McGough, A. J. Marlow, L. MacPhie, et al. "A Genome-Wide Scan for Locu Involved in Attention Deficit Hyperactivity Disorder." *American Journal of Human Genetics* 70 (2002): 1183–96.

Flemming, P., and C. Rousey. "Quantification of Psychotherapy Change by Study of Speech and Hearing Patterns." in Rousey, C. (ed.) *Psychiatric Assessment by Speech and Hearing Behavior.* Springfield, Ill.: Charles C. Thomas, 1974.

Frank, Y., R. G. Pergolizzi, and M. J. Perilla. "Dopamine D4 Receptor Gene and Attention Deficit Hyperactivity Disorder." *Pediatric Neurology* 31, no. 5 (2004): 345–48.

Frazier, T. W., H. A. Demaree, and E. A. Youngstrom. "Meta-Analysis of Intellectual and Neuropsychological Test Performance in Attention Deficit Hyperactivity Disorder." *Neuropsychology* 18 (2004): 543–55.

Freud, S. *Civilization and Its Discontents.* (J. Strachey, ed. and trans.) New York: Norton (Originally published 1930), 1961.

———. *General Psychological Theory.* New York: Macmillan Co., 1963.

Frontline. " Medicating Kids," PBS, 2001.

Fuster, M. M. *The Prefrontal Cortex* (3d ed.) New York: Raven, 1997.

Gadow, K. D., E. E. Nolan, J. Sprafkin, and J. Schwartz. "Tics and Psychiatric Comorbidity in Children and Adolescents." *Developmental Medicine and Child Neurology* 44, no. 5 (2002): 330–38.

Gammon, G. D., and T. E. Brown. "Fluoxetine and Methylphenidate in Combination for Treatment of Attention Deficit Hyperactivity Disorder and Comorbid Depressive Disorder." *Journal of Child and Adolescent Psychopharmacology* 3, no. 1 (1993): 1–10.

Gandour, M. J. "Activity Level as a Dimension of Temperament in Toddlers: Its Relevance for the Organismic Specificity Hypothesis." *Child Development* 60 (1989): 1092–98.

Gardner, R. A. *Hyperactivity, the So-Called Attention Deficit Disorder, and the Group of MBD Syndromes*. New Jersey: Creative Therapeutics, 1987.

Gaser, C., and G. Schlaug. "Brain Structures Differ between Musicians and Non-Musicians." *The Journal of Neuroscience* 23, no. 27 (2003): 9240–45.

Gastfriend, D. R., J. Biederman, and M. S. Jellinek. "Desipramine in the Treatment of Attention Deficit Hyperactivity Disorder in Adolescents." *Psychopharmacology* 21 (1985): 144–45.

Gilbert, J. *Interpreting Psychological Test Data: Associating Personality and Behavior with Responses to the Bender-Gestalt, Human Figure Drawing, Wechsler Adult Intelligence Scale, and the Rorschach Ink Blot Test*. New York: Van Nostrand Reinhold Company, 1978.

Gittelman, R., D. F. Klein, and I. Feingold. "Children with Reading Disorders-II: Effects of Methylphenidate in Combination with Reading Remediation." *J. Child Psychol. Psychiat.* 24 (1983): 193–212.

Glasser, H., and J. Easley. *Transforming the Difficult Child: The Nurtured Heart Approach*. Center for the Difficult Child Publications: Arizona, 1998.

Golden, G. S. "Controversial Therapies." *Pediatr. Clin. North Am.* 31 (1984): 459–69.

Goldsmith, H. *Behavior-Genetic Analyses of Early Personality (Temperament): Developmental Perspectives from the Longitudinal Study of Twins during Infancy and Early Childhood*. Unpublished doctoral dissertation, University of Minnesota, 1978.

Goldstein, S., and A. J. Schwebach. "The Comorbidity of Pervasive Developmental Disorder and Attention Deficit Hyperactivity Disorder: Results of a Retrospective Chart Review." *Journal of Autism and Developmental Disorders* 34 (2004): 477–90.

Gollwitzer, P. "Implementation Intentions: Strong Effects of Simple Plans." *American Psychologist* 57, no. 7 (1999): 504–15.

Goodman, R., and J. A. Stevenson. "Twin Study of Hyperactivity-II: The Aetiological Role of Genes, Family Relationships and Perinatal Adversity." *J. Child Psychol. Psychiat.* 30, no. 5 (1989): 691–709.

Gordon, M., and R. A. Barkley. "Tests and Observational Measures." in Barkley, R. A. (ed.) *Attention Deficit Hyperactivity Disorder: A Handbook for Diagnosis and Treatment* (p. 294–311, 2d ed.) New York: Guilford Press, 1998.

Gordon, M., R. A. Barkley, and B. J. Lovett. "Tests and Observational Measures." in Barkley, R. A. *Attention Deficit Hyperactivity Disorder: A Handbook for Diagnosis and Treatment* (p. 369–88, 3d ed.) New York: Guilford Press, 2006.

Gottesman, I. I., and T. Gould. "The Endophenotype Concept in Psychiatry: Etymology and Strategic Intentions." *American Journal of Psychiatry* 160 (2003): 636–45.

Gould, S. J. *The Mismeasure of Man*. New York: Norton, 1996.

Green, R. *The Explosive Child*, 2d ed." Harper Collins, 2001.

Greve, K. W., M. C. Williams, and T. J. Dickens Jr. *Concept Formation in Attention Disordered Children*. Poster presented at the meeting of the International Neuropsychological Society (February 1996) Chicago.

Grodzinshy, G. M., and R. Diamond. "Frontal Lobe Functioning in Boys with Attention Deficit Hyperactivity Disorder." *Developmental Neuropsychology* 8 (1992): 427–45.

Hagekull, B., and G. Bohlin. "Early Infant Temperament and Maternal Expectations Related to Maternal Adaptation." *International Journal of Behavioral Development* 13 (1990): 199–214.

Haight, S. "Caffeine's Latest Buzz." *Vogue* (2003): 321 (magazine).

Hallowell, E. M., and J. J. Ratey. *Driven to Distraction*. New York: Touchstone, 1995.

Halperin, J. M., J. H. Newcorn, V. H. Koda, L. Pick, K. E. McKay, and P. Knott. "Noradrenergic Mechanisms in ADHD Children with and without Reading Disabilities: A Replication and Extension." *Journal of the American Academy of Child and Adolescent Psychiatry* 36 (1997): 1688–97.

Hart, E. L., B. B. Lahey, R. Loeber, B. Applegate, and P. J. Frick. "Developmental Changes in Attention Deficit Hyperactivity Disorder in Boys: A Four Year Longitudinal Study." *Journal of Abnormal Child Psychology* 23 (1995): 729–50.

Harticollis, P. "The Syndrome of Minimal Rain Dysfunction in Young Adult Patients." *Bulletin of the Menninger Clinic* 32 (1968): 102–14.

Hartsough, C. S., and N. M. Lambert. "Medical Factors in Hyperactive and Normal Children: Prenatal, Developmental, and Health History Findings." *American Journal of Orthopsychiatry* 55 (1985): 190–210.

Hathaway, W., J. K. Dooling-Litfin, and G. Edwards. "Integrating the Results of an Evaluation: Eight Clinical Cases." in Barkley, R. A. *Attention Deficit Hyperactivity Disorder: A Handbook for Diagnosis and Treatment* (p. 312–44, 2d ed.) New York: Guilford Press, 1998.

Heath, A. C., M. C. Neale, J. K. Hewitt, L. J. Eaves, and D. W. Fulker. "Testing Structural Equation Models for Twin Data Using LISREL." *Behavior Genetics* 19 (1989): 9–36.

Hechtman, L., H. Abikoff, R. G. Klein, G. Weiss, C. Respitz, J. Kouri, et al. "Academic Achievement and Emotional Status in Children with ADHD Treated with Long-Term Methylphenidate and Multimodal Psychosocial Treatment." *Journal of the American Academy of Child and Adolescent Psychiatry* 43 (2004): 812–19.

Herrnstein, R. J. *IQ in the Meritocracy*. Boston: Atlantic Monthly Press, 1973.

Hervey, A. S., J. N. Epstein, and J. F. Curry. "Neuropsychology of Adults with Attention Deficient Hyperactivity Disorder: A Meta-Analytic Review." *Neuropsychology* 18 (2004): 495–503.

Hesdorffer, D. C., P. Ludvigsson, E. Olafsson, G. Gudmundsson, O. Kjartansson, and W. A. Hauser. "ADHD as a Risk Factor for Incident Unprovoked Seizures and Epilepsy in Children." *Archives of General Psychiatry* 61 (2004): 731–36.

Hinshaw, S. P., and S. S. Lee. "Conduct and Oppositional Defiant Disorders." in Mash, E. J., and R. A. Barkley (eds.) *Child Psychopathology* (2d ed., p. 144–98). New York: Guilford Press, 2003.

Hofstadter, A. "Objective Teleology." *Journal of Philosophy* 37 (1941): 29–39.

Hoy, E., G. Weiss, K. Minde, and N. Cohen. "The Hyperactive Child at Adolescence: Cognitive, Emotional, and Social Functioning." *Journal of Abnormal Child Psychology* 6 (1978): 311–24.

Hoza, B., A. C. Gerdes, S. P. Hinshaw, L. E. Arnold, W. E. Pelham Jr., B. S. G. Molina, et al. "Self-Perceptions of Competence in Children with ADHD and Comparison Children." *Journal of Consulting and Clinical Psychology* 72 (2004): 382–91.

Hoza, B., W. E. Pelham, D. A. Waschbursch, H. Kipp, and J. S. Owens. "Academic Task Persistence of Normally Achieving ADHD and Control Boys: Performance, Self-

Evaluations, and Attributions." *Journal of Consulting and Clinical Psychology* 69 (2001): 281–83.

Hull, A. M. "Neuroimaging Findings in Post-Traumatic Stress Disorder: Systematic Review." *British Journal of Psychiatry* 181 (2002): 102–10.

Hunt, R. D., L. Mandl, S. Lau, and M. Hughes. "Neurobiological Theories of ADHD and Ritalin." in Greenhill, L. L., and B. B. Osman (eds.) *Ritalin: Theory and Patient Management.* Larchmont, NY: Mary Ann Liebert, 1991.

Hynd, G. W., M. Semrud-Clikeman, A. R. Lorys, E. S. Novey, and D. Eliopulos. "Brain Morphology in Developmental Dyslexia and Attention Deficit Disorder Hyperactivity." *Archives of Neurology* 47 (1990): 919–26.

Jacoby, H. J. *Analysis of Handwriting.* London: Allen & Unwin Ltd., 1948.

Jinks J. L., and D. W. Fulker. "A Comparison of the Biometrical-Genetical, MAVA and Classical Approaches to the Analysis of Human Behavior." *Psychological Bulletin* 73 (1970): 311–49.

Johnson, D. E., J. N. Epstein, L. R. Waid, P. K. Latham, K. E. Voronin, and R. F. Anton. "Neuropsychological Performance Deficits in Adults with Attention Deficit Hyperactivity Disorder." *Archives of Clinical Neuropsychology* 16 (2001): 587–604.

Johnston, C., and E. J. Mash. "Families of Children with Attention Deficit Hyperactivity Disorder: Review and Recommendations for Future Research." *Clinical Child and Family Psychology Review* 4 (2001): 183–207.

Kadesjo, B., and C. Gillberg. "The Comorbidity of ADHD in the General Population of Swedish School-Age Children." *Journal of Child Psychology and Psychiatry* 42 (2001): 487–92.

Kagan, J., and N. Snidman. "Infant Predictors of Inhibited and Uninhibited Profiles." *Psychological Science* 2 (1991): 40–4.

Kanaya T., M. H. Scullin, and J. S. Ceci. "The Flynn Effect and U.S. Policies: The Impact of Rising IQ Scores on American Society via Mental Retardation Diagnoses." *American Psychologist* (October 2003): 778–90.

Keown, L. J., and L. J. Woodward. "Early Parent-Child Relations and Family Functioning of Preschool Boys with Pervasive Hyperactivity." *Journal of Abnormal Child Psychology* 30 (2002): 541–53.

Kernberg, P., and C. Rousey. "Variations in Speech Sounds During Psychotherapy: An Independent Indicator of Change." *Journal of the American Academy of Child Psychiatry* 9 (1970): 762–77.

Kirsch, I., and S. J. Lynn. "Automaticity in Clinical Psychology." *American Psychologist* 57, no. 7 (1999): 504–15.

Knox, R. A. "Musicians' Brains are Distinctive, Imaging Shows." *Boston Globe.* (February 3, 1995) 10.

Kochanska, G., and M. Radke-Yarrow. "Inhibition at Toddlerhood and the Dynamics of the Child's Interaction with an Unfamiliar Peer at Age Five." *Child Development* 63 (1992): 325–35.

Kolb, B. "Brain Development, Plasticity and Behavior." *American Psychologist* 44 (1989): 1203–12.

Kovner, R., C. Budman, Y. Frank, C. Sison, M. Lesser, and J. M. Halperin. *Neuropsychological Testing in Adult Attention Deficit Hyperactivity Disorder: A Pilot Study.* Unpublished manuscript, North Shore University Hospital, Manhasset, NY, 1997.

Kvols, K. J. *Redirecting Children's Behavior.* Parenting Press: Seattle WA, 1998.

LaHoste, G. J., J. M. Swanson, S. B. Wigal, C. Glabe, T. Wigal, N. King, et al. "Dopamine D4 Receptor Gene Polymorphism is Associated with Attention Deficit Hyperactivity Disorder." *Molecular Psychiatry* 1 (1996): 121–24.

Lam, P., C. Y. Cheng, C. J. Hone, and S. J. Tsai. "Association Study of Brain-Derived Neurotrophic Factor (Val55Met) Genetic Polymorphism and Panic Disorder." *Neuropsychobiology* 49 (2004): 178–81.

Lambert, N. M., J. Sandoval, and D. Sassone. "Prevalence of Hyperactivity in Elementary School Children as a Function of Social System Definers." *American Journal of Orthopsychiatry* 48 (1978): 446–63.

Landau, S., E. P. Lorch, and R. Milich. "Visual Attention to and Comprehension of Television in Attention Deficit Hyperactivity Disordered and Normal Boys." *Child Development* 63 (1992): 928–37.

Landau, S., and R. Milich. "Social Communication Patterns of Attention Deficit Disordered Boys." *Journal of Abnormal Child Psychology* 16 (1988): 69–81.

Langley, K., L. M. Marshall, H. van den Bree, M. Thomas, M. Owen, M. O'Donovan, et al. "Association of the Dopamine D4 Receptor Gene 7-Repeat Allele with Neuropsychological Test Performance of Children with ADHD." *American Journal of Psychiatry* 161 (2004): 133–38.

Lawrence, V., S. Houghton, R. Tannock, G. Douglas, K. Durkin, and K. Whiting. "ADHD Outside the Laboratory: Boys' Executive Function Performance on Tasks in Video Game Play and on a Visit to the Zoo." *Journal of Abnormal Child Psychology* 30 (2002): 447–62.

Lehrman, D. "Semantic and Conceptual Issues in the Nature-Nurture Problem." in Aronson, L. R., et al. (eds.) *Development and Evolution of Behavior* (p. 18–53). San Francisco: Freeman & Co., 1970.

Leibson, C. L., S. K. Katusic, W. J. Barbaresi, J. Ransom, and P. C. O'Brien. "Use and Costs of Medical Care for Children and Adolescents with and without Attention Deficit Hyperactivity Disorder." *Journal of the American Medical Association* 285 (2001): 60–6.

Leman, K. *Making Children Mind without Losing Yours.* Dell Publishing. New York, 1984.

Lepper, M. R., D. Greene, and R. E. Nisbett. "Undermining Children's Intrinsic Interest with Extrinsic Rewards: A Test of the Over-Justification Hypothesis." *Journal of Personality and Social Psychology* 28 (1973): 139–87.

Lewontin, R. C. "Race and Intelligence." *Bulletin of the Atomic Scientists* (March, 1970): 2–8.

———. *Inside and Outside: Gene, Environment, and Organism.* Worcester, Massachusetts: Clark University Press, 1994.

Levy, F., and D. A. Hay. *Attention, Genes, and Attention Deficit Hyperactivity Disorder.* Philadelphia: Psychology Press, 2001.

Linn, R. T., and G. K. Hodge. "Locus of Control in Childhood Hyperactivity." *Journal of Consulting and Clinical Psychology* 50 (1982): 592–93.

Locke, E. A., and G. P. Latham. "Building a Practically Useful Theory of Goal Setting and Task Motivation." *American Psychologist* (September, 2002): 705–17.

Lorch, E. P., K. O'Neill, K. S. Berthiaume, R. Milich, D. Eastham, and T. Brooks. "Story Comprehension and the Impact of Studying on Recall in Children with Attention Deficit Hyperactivity Disorder." *Journal of Clinical Child and Adolescent Psychology* 33 (2004): 506–15.

Luckner, J. R., D. Geffner, and W. Koch. "Perception of Loudness in Children with ADD and without ADD." *Child Psychiatry and Human Development* 26 (1996): 181–90.

Luk, S. "Direct Observation Studies of Hyperactive Behaviors." *Journal of the American Academy of Child and Adolescent Psychiatry* 24 (1985): 338–44.

Luman, M., J. Oosterlaan, and J. A. Sergeant. "The Impact of Reinforcement Contingencies on AD/HD: A Review and Theoretical Appraisal." *Clinical Psychology Review* 25 (2005): 183–213.

Maccoby, E., M. Snow, and C. N. Jacklin. "Children's Dispositions and Mother-Child Interaction at 12 and 18 Months: A Short-Term Longitudinal Study." *Developmental Psychology* 20 (1984): 459–72.

MacCorquodale, K., and P. E. Meehl. "On a Distinction between Hypothetical Constructs and Intervening Variables." *Psychological Review* 55 (1948): 95–107.

Maguire, E. A., D. G. Gadian, I. S. Johnsrude, C. D. Good, J. Ashburner, R. S. Frackowiak, and C. D. Frith. "Navigation-Related Structural Changes in the Hippocampi of Taxi Drivers." *Proceedings of the National Academy of Sciences*, USA 97 (2000): 4398–403.

Marcotte, A. C., and C. Stern. "Qualitative Analysis of Graphomotor Output in Children with Attentional Disorders." *Child Neuropsychology* 2 (1997): 1–10.

Mariani, M., and R. A. Barkley. "Neuropsychological and Academic Functioning in Preschool Children with Attention Deficit Hyperactivity Disorder." *Developmental Neuropsychology* 13 (1997): 111–29.

Matheny, A. *Neonatal Temperament Predicts Children's Unintentional Injuries During 1-3 Years.* Paper presented at the annual meeting of the American Psychological Association, Washington, D.C. (June, 1992).

Matthys, W., J. M. Cuperus, and H. van Engeland. "Deficient Social Problem-Solving in Boys with ODD/CD, with ADHD, and with Both Disorders." *Journal of the American Academy of Child and Adolescent Psychiatry* 38 (1999): 311–21.

Max, J. E., P. T. Fox, J. L. Lancaster, P. Kochunov, K. Mathews, F. F. Manes, et al. "Putamen Lesions and the Development of Attention Deficit Hyperactivity Symptomatology." *Journal of the American Academy of Child and Adolescent Psychiatry* 41 (2002): 563–71.

Mayberg, H., A. Silva, S. Brannan, J. Tekell, R. Mahurin, S. McGinnis, and P. Jerabek. "The Functional Neuroanatomy of the Placebo Effect." *American Journal of Psychiatry* 159 (2002): 728–37.

McGee, R., S. Williams, and M. Feehan. "Attention Deficit Disorder and Age of Onset of Problem Behaviors." *Journal of Abnormal Child Psychology* 20 (1992): 487–502.

McGee, R., S. Williams, T. Moffitt, and J. Anderson. "A Comparison of 13-Year Old Boys with Attention Deficit and/or Reading Disorder on Neuropsychological Measures." *Journal of Abnormal Child Psychology* 17 (1989): 37–53.

McGuffin, P., and P. Huckle. "Simulation of Mendelism Revisited: The Recessive Gene for Attending Medical School." *American Journal of Human Genetics* 46 (1990): 994–99.

McInerny, T., and R. W. Chamberlin. "Is it Feasible to Identify Infants Who Are at Risk for Later Behavioral Problems? The Carey Temperament Questionnaire as a Prognostic Tool." *Clinical Pediatrics* 17 (1978): 233–38.

Meaux, J. B., and J. J. Chelonis. "Time Perception Difference in Children with and without ADHD." *Journal of Pediatric Health Care* 17 (2003): 64–71.

Meehl, P. E. "On the Circularity of the Law of Effect." *Psychological Bulletin* 47 (1950): 52–75.

————. *Clinical Versus Statistical Prediction: A Theoretical Analysis and a Review of the Evidence.* Minneapolis: University of Minnesota Press, 1954.

Meyer, W. S. "Why They Don't Come Back: A Clinical Perspective on the No-Show Client." *Clinical Social Work Journal* 29, no. 4 (2001): p. 325–39.

Mick, E., J. Biederman, S. V. Faraone, J. Sayer, and S. Kleinman. "Case-Control Study of Attention Deficit Hyperactivity Disorder and Maternal Smoking, Alcohol Use, and Drug Use during Pregnancy." *Journal of the American Academy of Child and Adolescent Psychiatry* 35 (2002): 1470–76.

Milich, R., A. C. Ballentine, and D. R. Lynam. "ADHD/Combined Types are Distinct and Unrelated Disorders." *Clinical Psychology: Science and Practice* 8 (2001): 463–88.

Milich, R. A., and J. Kramer. "Reflections on Impulsivity: An Empirical Investigation on Impulsivity as a Construct." in Gadow, K., and I. Bialer (eds.) *Advances in Learning and Behavioral Disabilities* (vol. 3, p. 57–94). Greenwich, CT: JAI Press, 1985.

Moffit, T. E., and P. A. Silva. "Self-Reported Delinquency, Neuropsychological Deficit, and History of Attention Deficit Disorder." *Journal of Abnormal Child Psychology* 16 (1988): 553–69.

Morrison, J., and M. Stewart. "The Psychiatric Status of the Legal Families of Adopted Hyperactive Children." *Archives of General Psychiatry* 28 (1973): 888–91.

Murphy, K. R. "Psychological Counseling of Adults with ADHD." in Barkley, R. A. *Attention Deficit Hyperactivity Disorder: A Handbook for Diagnosis and Treatment,* 3d ed (p. 692–703). New York: Guilford Press, 2006.

Murphy, K. R., R. A. Barkley, and T. Bush. "Executive Function in Young Adults with Attention Deficit Hyperactivity Disorder." *Neuropsychology* 15 (2001): 211–20

————. "Young Adults with ADHD: Subtype Differences in Comorbidity, Educational, and Clinical History." *Journal of Nervous and Mental Disease* 190 (2002): 147–57.

Murphy, K. R., and M. Gordon. "Assessment of Adults with ADHD." in Barkley, R. A. *Attention Deficit Hyperactivity Disorder: A Handbook for Diagnosis and Treatment,* 2d ed (p. 345–69). New York: Guilford Press, 1998.

————. "Assessment of Adults with ADHD." in Barkley, R. A. *Attention Deficit Hyperactivity Disorder: A Handbook for Diagnosis and Treatment* 3d ed. (p. 425–50). New York: Guilford Press, 2006.

Nadder, T. S., M. Rutter, J. L. Silberg, H. H. Maes, and L. J. Eaves. "Genetic Effects on the Variation and Covariation of Attention Deficit Hyperactivity Disorder (ADHD) and Oppositional Disorder/Conduct Disorder (ODD/CD) Symptomatologies across Informant and Occasion of Measurement." *Psychological Medicine* 32 (2002): 39–53.

Neale, M. C., and L. R. Cardon. *Methodology for Genetic Studies of Twins and Families.* London: Kluwer, 1992.

Neisser, U. *Cognitive Psychology.* New York: Appleton-Century-Crofts, 1967.

Nelsen, Jane. *Positive Discipline.* New York: Ballantine Books, 1987.

Newcorn, J. H., J. M. Halperin, P. Jensen, H. Abikoff, E. Arnold, and D. P. Cantwell. "Symptom Profiles in Children with ADHD: Effects of Comorbidity and Gender." *Journal of the American Academy of Child and Adolescent Psychiatry* 40 (2001): 137–46.

Nichols, P. L., and T. C. Chen. *Minimal Brain Dysfunction: A Prospective Study.* Hillsdale, NJ: Erlbaum, 1981.

Nigg, J.T. "Is ADHD a Disinhibitory Disorder?" *Psychological Bulletin* 127, no.7 (2001): 571–98.

Nigg, J. T., H. H. Goldsmith, and J. Sacheck. "Temperament and Attention Deficit Hyperactivity Disorder: The Development of a Multiple Pathway Model." *Journal of Clinical Child and Adolescent Psychology* 33 (2004): 42–53.

Norman, D. A., and T. Shallice. "Attention to Action: Willed and Automatic Control of Behavior." in Davidson, R. J., G. E. Schwartz, and D. Shapiro (eds.) *Consciousness and Self-Regulation* (vol. 4, p. 1–18). New York: Plenum Press, 1986.

Ota, K. R., and G. J. DuPaul. "Task Engagement and Mathematics Performance in Children with Attention Deficit Hyperactivity Disorder: Effects of Supplemental Computer Intervention." *School Psychology Quarterly* 17, no. 3 (2002): 242–57.

Palfrey, J. S., M. D. Levine, D. K. Walker, and M. Sullivan. "The Emergence of Attention Deficits in Early Childhood: A Prospective Study." *Developmental and Behavioral Pediatrics* 6 (1985): 339–48.

Pauls, D. L. "Genetic Factors in the Expression of Attention Deficit Hyperactivity Disorder. *Journal of Child and Adolescent Psychopharmacology* 1 (1991): 353–60.

Pearl, R. L., R. E. Weiss, and M. A. Stein. "Medical Mimics." *Annals of the New York Academy of Sciences* 931 (2001): 97–112.

Pennington, B. F., D. Grossier, and M. C. Welsh. "Contrasting Cognitive Deficits in Attention Deficit Disorder Versus Reading Disability." *Developmental Psychology* 29 (1993): 511–23.

Peters, R. S. *The Concept of Motivation.* New York: Humanities Press, 1960.

Pfiffner, L. J., and R. A. Barkley. "Treatment of ADHD in School Settings." in Barkley, R. A. *Attention Deficit Hyperactivity Disorder: A Handbook for Diagnosis and Treatment* 2d ed. (p. 458–90) New York: Guilford Press, 1998.

Pfiffner, L. J., R. A. Barkley, and G. DuPaul. "Treatment of ADHD in School Settings." in Barkley, R. A. *Attention Deficit Hyperactivity Disorder: A Handbook for Diagnosis and Treatment* 3rd ed. (p. 547–89, 3d ed.) New York: Guilford Press, 2006.

Piaget, J. *Play, Dreams, and Imitation in Childhood.* New York: The Norton Library, 1962.

Piaget, J., and B. Inhelder. *The Psychology of the Child.* New York: Basic Books, Inc., 1969.

Pliszka, L. R., J. T. McCracken, and J. W. Maas. "Catecholamines in Attention Deficit Hyperactivity Disorder: Current Perspectives." *Journal of the American Academy of Child and Adolescent Psychiatry* 35 (1996): 264–72.

Porrino L. J., J. L. Rapoport, D. Behar, W. Sceery, D. R. Ismond, and W. E. Bunney. "A Naturalistic Assessment of the Motor Activity of Hyperactive Boys I: Comparison with Normal Controls. *Archives of General Psychiatry* 40 (1983): 681–87.

Prince, J. B., T. E. Wilens, T. J. Spencer, and J. Biederman. "Pharmacotherapy of ADHD in Adults." in Barkley, R. A. *Attention Deficit Hyperactivity Disorder: A Handbook for Diagnosis and Treatment* (p. 704–36, 3d ed.) New York: Guilford Press, 2006.

Quay, H. C. "Attention Deficit Disorder and the Behavioral Inhibition System: The Relevance of the Neuropsychological Theory of Jeffrey A. Gray." in Bloomingdale, L. M., and J. Sergeant (eds.) *Attention Deficit Disorder: Criteria, Cognition, Intervention* (p. 117–26). New York: Pergamon Press, 1988.

Quinn, P. O., and J. L. Rapoport. "One-Year Follow-up of Hyperactive Boys Treated with Imipramine or Methylphenidate." *American Journal of Psychiatry* 132 (1975): 241–45.

Ratey, J., M. Greenberg, and K. Lindem. "Combination of Treatments for Attention Deficit Disorders in Adults." *Journal of Nervous and Mental Disease* 176 (1991): 699–701.

Rauch, S. L., and M. A. Jenike. "Neurobiological Models of Obsessive-Compulsive Disorder." *Psychosomatics* 34 (1993): 20–30.

Roberts, M. A. *A Manual for the Restricted Academic Playroom Situation.* Iowa City, IA: Author, 1979.

Robertson-Souter, C. "Teicher Explores the Brain Development Effects of Child Abuse." *Massachusetts Psychologist* (July 3, 2001) 10.

Robin, A. L. "Training Families with Adolescents with ADHD." in Barkley, R. A. *Attention Deficit Hyperactivity Disorder: A Handbook for Diagnosis and Treatment* (p. 499–546, 3d ed.) New York: Guilford Press, 2006.

Roizen, N. J., T. A. Blondis, M. Irwin, and M. Stein. "Adaptive Functioning in Children with Attention Deficit Hyperactivity Disorder." *Archives of Pediatric and Adolescent Medicine* 148 (1994): 1137–42.

Ross, D. M., and S. A. Ross. *Hyperactivity: Research, Theory, and Action.* New York: Wiley, 1982.

Rousey, C., and P. Toussieng. "Contributions of a Speech Pathologist to the Psychiatric Examination of Children." *Mental Hygiene* 48 (1964): 566–75.

Routh, D. K. "Hyperactivity." in Magrab, P. (ed.) *Psychological Management of Pediatric Problems* (p. 3–48). Baltimore: University Park Press, 1978.

Routh, D. K., and C. S. Schroeder. "Standardized Playroom Measures as Indices of Hyperactivity." *Journal of Abnormal Child Psychology* 4 (1976): 199–207.

Rucklidge, J. J., and B. J. Kaplan. "Attributions and Perceptions of Childhood in Women with ADHD Symptomatology." *Journal of Clinical Psychology* 56 (2000): 711–22.

Rucklidge, J. J., and R. Tannock. "Neuropsychological Profiles of Adolescents with ADHD: Effects of Reading Difficulties and Gender." *Journal of Child Psychology and Psychiatry* 43 (2002): 988–1003.

Rutter, M. "Brain Damage Syndromes in Childhood: Concepts and Findings." *Journal of Child Psychology and Psychiatry* 18 (1977): 1–21.

———. "Introduction: Concepts of Brain Dysfunction Syndromes." in Rutter, M. (ed.) *Developmental Neuropsychiatry* (p. 1–14). New York: Guilford Press, 1983.

Ryle, Gilbert. *The Concept of Mind.* New York: Barnes & Noble, 1949.

Ryu, S. H., H. J. Lee, J. H. Cha, B. J. Ham, C. S. Han, et al. "Association between Norepinephrine Transporter Gene Polymorphism and Major Depression." *Neuropsychobiology* 49 (2004): 174–77.

Sawyer, A. M., E. Taylor, and O. Chadwick. "The Effect of Off-Task Behaviors on the Task Performance of Hyperkinetic Children." *Journal of Attention Disorders* 5 (2001): 1–10.

Scarr, S. "Environmental Bias in Twin Studies." *Eugenics Quarterly* 15 (1968): 34–40.

———. *Mother Care, Other Care.* New York: Basic Books, 1984.

———. "Developmental Theories for the 1990s: Development and Individual Differences." *Child Development* 63 (1992): 1–19.

Scarr S., and K. McCartney "How People Make their Own Environments: A Theory of Genotype-Environment Effects." *Child Development* 54 (1983): 424–35.

Scheibel, A. B., L. A. Paul, I. Fried, A. B. Forsythe, U. Tomiyasu, A. Wechsler, A. Kao, and J. Slotnick. "Dendritic Organization of the Anterior Speech Area." *Experimental Neurology* 87 (1985): 109–17.

Schmidt, R. "Stress Makes People Forget." *Telegram & Gazette.* (October 29, 2004): A13.

Schrag, P., and D. Divoky. *The Myth of the Hyperactive Child.* New York: Pantheon, 1975.

Schultz, W., P. Dayan, and P. R. Montague. "A Neural Substrate of Prediction and Reward." *Science* 275 (1997): 1593.

Sergeant, J. A. "A Theory of Attention: An Information Processing Perspective." in Lyon, G. R., and N. A. Krasnegor (eds.) *Attention, Memory, and Executive Function* (p. 57–69). Baltimore: Paul H. Brookes, 1995.

Sergeant, J. A., and J. van der Meere. "What Happens when the Hyperactive Child Commits an Error?" *Psychiatry Research* 24 (1988): 157–64.

Shallice, T., G. M. Marzocchi, S. Coser, M. Del Savio, R. F. Meuter, and R. I. Rumiati. "Executive Function Profile of Children with Attention Deficit Hyperactivity Disorder." *Developmental Neuropsychology* 21 (2002): 43–71.

Sharp, W. S., R. F. Gottesman, D. K. Greenstein, C. L. Ebens, J. L. Rapoport, and F. X. Castellanos. "Monozygotic Twins Discordant for Attention Deficit Hyperactivity Disorder: Ascertainment and Clinical Characteristics." *Journal of the American Academy of Child and Adolescent Psychiatry* 42 (2003): 93–7.

Shaw, G. A., and G. Brown. "Laterality and Creativity Concomitants of Attention Problems." *Developmental Neuropsychology* 16 (1990): 227–42.

Shaywitz, B. A., and S. E. Shaywitz. "Comorbidity: A Critical Issue in Attention Deficit Disorder." *The Journal of Child Neurology* 6 (1991 Supplement): S13–S22.

Shaywitz, S. E., B. A. Shaywitz, P. R. Jatlow, M. Sebrechts, G. M. Anderson, and D. T. Cohen. "Biological Differentiation of Attention Deficit Disorder with and without Hyperactivity: A Preliminary Report." *Annals of Neurology* 21 (1986): 363.

Shelton, T. L., R. A. Barkley, C. Crosswait, M. Moorehouse, K. Flecher, S. Barrett, et al. "Psychiatric and Psychological Morbidity as a Function of Adaptive Disability in Preschool Children with High Levels of Aggressive and Hyperactive-Impulsive-Inattentive Behavior." *Journal of Abnormal Child Psychology* 26 (1998): 475–94.

Sherman, D. K., M. K. McGue, and W. G. Iacono. "Twin Concordance for Attention Deficit Hyperactivity Disorder: A Comparison of Teachers' and Mothers' Reports." *American Journal of Psychiatry* 154 (1997): 532–35.

Shure, M. B. *Raising a Thinking Child.* New York: Pocket Books, 1994.

Silberg, J., M. Rutter, J. Meyer, et al. "Genetic and Environmental Influences on the Covariation between Hyperactivity and Conduct Disturbance in Juvenile Twins." *Journal of Child Psychology and Psychiatry* 37 (1996): 803–16.

Sinha, G. "Out of Control?" *Popular Science* (June, 2001): 48–52.

Skinner, B. F. *Science and Human Behavior.* New York: The Macmillan Company, 1953.

———. *About Behaviorism.* New York: Alfred A. Knopf, 1974.

Sleator, E. K., and W. E. Pelham. *Attention Deficit Disorder.* Norwalk, CT: Appleton-Century-Crofts, 1986.

Smalley, S. L., J. J. McGough, M. Del'Homme, J. New Delman, E. Gordon, T. Kim, et al. "Familial Clustering of Symptoms and Disruptive Behaviors in Multiplex Families with Attention Deficit Hyperactivity Disorder." *Journal of the American Academy of Child and Adolescent Psychiatry* 39 (2000): 1135–43.

Solano, M. V. "Neuropsychopharmacological Mechanisms of Stimulant Drug Action in Attention Deficit Hyperactivity Disorder: A Review and Integration." *Behavioral Brain Research* 94 (1998): 127–52.

Spencer, T. "Antidepressant and Specific Norepinephrine Re-uptake Inhibitor Treatments." in Barkley, R. A. *Attention Deficit Hyperactivity Disorder: A Handbook for Diagnosis and Treatment* (p. 648–57, 3d ed.) New York: Guilford Press, 2006.

Spencer, T., J. Biederman, J. Heiligenstein, T. Wilens, D. Faries, J. Prince, et al. "An Open Label Doe-Ranging Study of Atomoxetine in Children with Attention Deficit

Hyperactivity Disorder." *Journal of Child and Adolescent Psychopharmacology* 11 (2001): 251–65.

Spencer, T. J., J. Biederman, and T. Wilens. "Pharmacotherapy of ADHD with Antidepressants." in Barkley, R. A. *Attention Deficit Hyperactivity Disorder: A Handbook for Diagnosis and Treatment* (p. 552–63, 2d ed.) New York: Guilford Press, 1998.

Spencer, T. J., J. Biederman, J. Wozniak, and M. Harding-Crawford. "Attention Deficit Hyperactivity Disorder with Mood Disorders." in Brown, T. E. (ed.) *Attention Deficit Disorders and Comorbidities in Children, Adolescents, and Adults* (p. 79–124). Washington, DC: American Psychiatric Press, 2000.

Sprague, R. L., and E. K. Sleator. "Methylphenidate in Hyperkinetic Children: Differences in Dose Effects on Learning and Social Behavior." *Science* 198 (1977): 1274–76.

Sprich, S., J. Biederman, M. H. Crawford, E. Mundy, and S. V. Faraone. "Adoptive and Biological Families of Children and Adolescents with ADHD." *Journal of the American Academy of Child and Adolescent Psychiatry* 39 (2000): 1432–37.

Stein, M. A., M. Krasowski, B. L. Leventhal, W. Phillips, and B. G. Bender. "Behavioral and Cognitive Effect of Methylxanthines: A Meta-analysis of Theophylline and Caffeine." *Archives of Pediatric and Adolescent Medicine* 150 (1996): 284–88.

Steinkamp, M. W. "Relationships between Environmental Distractions and Task Performance of Hyperactive and Normal Children." *Journal of Learning Disabilities* 13 (1980): 40–5.

Sternberg, R., E. Grigorenko, and K. Kidd. "Intelligence, Race, and Genetics." *American Psychologist* 60 (2005): 46–59.

Stevenson, J. *Genetics of ADHD.* Paper presented at the meeting of the Professional Group for ADD and Related Disorders (June, 1994).

Stifter, C., and N. Fox. "Infant Reactivity." *Developmental Psychology* 26 (1990): 582–88.

Szatmari, P., M. H. Boyle, and D. R. Offord. "ADHD and Conduct Disorder: Degree of Diagnostic Overlap and Differences among Correlates." *Journal of the American Academy of Child and Adolescent Psychiatry* 28 (1989): 865–72.

———. "Ontario Child Health Study: Prevalence of Attention Deficit Disorder with Hyperactivity." *Journal of Child Psychology and Psychiatry* 30 (1989): 219–30.

Talbot, M. "Too Much." *New York Times Magazine.* (November 2, 2003): 8–9.

Tannock, R. "Attention Deficit Hyperactivity Disorder with Anxiety Disorders." in Brown, T. E. (ed.) *Attention Deficit Disorders and Comorbidities in Children, Adolescents, and Adults* (p.125–70). Washington, DC: American Psychiatric Press, 2000.

Tannock, R., and R. Schachar. "Executive Dysfunction as an Underlying Mechanism of Behaviour and Language Problems in Attention Deficit Hyperactivity Disorders." in Beitchman, J. H., N. J. Cohen, M. M. Konstantareas, and R. Tannock (eds.) *Language Learning and Behavior Disorders: Developmental, Biological, and Clinical Perspective* (p. 128–55). New York: Cambridge University Press, 1996.

Taylor, E., S. Sandberg, G. Thorley, and S. Giles. *The Epidemiology of Childhood Hyperactivity.* London: Oxford University Press, 1991.

Thelen, E. "Motor Development." *American Psychologist* (February, 1995): 79–95.

Thompson, R. A., and C. A. Nelson. "Developmental Science and the Media: Early Brain Development." *American Psychologist* 56, no. 1 (2001): 5–15.

Timimi, S. "A Critique of the International Consensus Statement on ADHD." *Clinical Child and Family Psychology Review* 7 (2004): 59–63.

Trites, R. L. *Hyperactivity in Children: Etiology, Measurement, and Treatment Implications.* Baltimore: University Park Press, 1979.

Turner, D. C., L. Clark, J. Dowson, T. W. Robbins, and B. J. Sahakian. "Modafinil Improves Cognition and Response Inhibition in Adult Attention Deficit Hyperactivity Disorder." *Biological Psychiatry* 55, no. 10 (2004): 1031–40.

USA Today. "Be Visually Adept: Play a Video Game." (May 29, 2003): 10D.

USA Today. "Snapshots." (August 13, 2001): B1.

van den Boom, D., and J. Hoeksma. *The Interaction of Mothers and Their Irritable and Non-Irritable Infants.* University of Leiden, The Netherlands: Manuscript, 1993.

van den Oord, E. J. C. G., D. I. Boomsma, and F. C. Verhulst. "A Study of Problem Behavior in 10- to 15-Year-Old Biologically Related and Unrelated International Adoptees." *Behavior Genetics* 24 (1994): 193–205.

Vangelova, L. "True or False? Extinction is Forever." *Smithsonian* (June 22, 2003): 24.

Wahler, R. G. "The Insular Mother: Her Problems and Parent-Child Treatment." *Journal of Applied Behavior Analysis* 13 (1980): 207–19.

Wakefield, J. C. "The Concept of Mental Disorder: On the Boundary between Biological Facts and Social Values." *American Psychologist* 47 (1992): 373–88.

———. "Normal Inability Versus Pathological Disability: Why Ossorio's Definition of Mental Disorder is Not Sufficient." *Clinical Psychology: Science and Practice* 4 (1997): 249–58.

Wasserman, R., C. DiBlasio, L. Bond, P. Young, and R. Colletti. "Infant Temperament and School-age Behavior." *Pediatrics* 85 (1990): 801–07.

Webster-Stratton, C. W., and M. Herbert. *Troubled Families–Problem Children: Working with Parents: A Collaborative Process.* Chichester, England: Wiley, 1994.

Webster-Stratton, C. W., J. Reid, and M. Hammond. "Social Skills and Problem-solving Training for Children with Early-onset Conduct Problems: Who Benefits?" *Journal of Child Psychology and Psychiatry* 42 (2001): 943–52.

Weinstein, D., D. Steffelbach, and M. Biaggio. "Attention Deficit Hyperactivity Disorder and Post-Traumatic Stress Disorder: Differential Diagnosis in Childhood Sex Abuse." *Clinical Psychology Review* 20 (2000): 359–78.

Weiss, G., and L. Hechtman. *Hyperactive Children Grown Up: ADHD in Children, Adolescents, and Adults* (2d ed.) New York: Guilford Press, 1993.

Werner, H. *The Comparative Psychology of Mental Development.* New York: International Universities Press, 1948.

Werry, J. *Pediatric Psychopharmacology.* New York: Breunner/Mazel, 1978.

Weyandt, L. L. (ed.) *Executive Functioning in Children, Adolescents, and Adults with Attention Deficit Hyperactivity Disorder.* Lawrence Erlbaum, 2005.

Weyandt, L. L., and W. G. Willis. "Executive Functions in School-aged Children: Potential Efficiency of Tasks in Discriminating Clinical Groups." *Developmental Neuropsychology* 19 (1994): 27–38.

Whalen, C. K., B. Henker, B. E. Collins, S. McAuliffe, and A. Vaux. "Peer Interactions in a Structured Communication Task: Comparisons of Normal and Hyperactive Boys and of Methylphenidate (Ritalin) and Placebo Effects." *Child Development* 50 (1979): 388–401

Wheeler, M. A., D. T. Stuss, and E. Tulving. "Toward a Theory of Episodic Memory: The Frontal Lobes and Autonoetic Consciousness." *Psychological Bulletin* 121 (1997): 331–54.

Whitaker, J. "A Proposal Before the Florida Legislature: Stop Drugging Our Kids." *Health & Healing.* (June, 2005): 1–2 (magazine).

Wickelgren, I. "Getting the Brain's Attention." *Science* 278 (1997): 35–37.

———. "Teaching the Brain to Take Drugs." *Science* 280 (1998): 2045–47.

Wiener, C. *Attention Deficit Hyperactivity Disorder as a Learned Behavioral Pattern: A Less Medicinal More Self-Reliant/Collaborative Intervention.* Lanham, MD: University Press of America, 2007.

Wiener, M. "Schizophrenia: A Defective, Deficient, Disrupted, Disorganized Construct." in Flack, W. F., D. R. Miller, and M. Wiener (eds.) *What is Schizophrenia?* Springer-Verlag, N.Y., 1991.

Wigal, T. J., J. M. Swanson, V. I. Douglas, S. B. Wigal, C. M. Wippler, and K. F. Cavoto. "Effect of Reinforcement on Facial Responsivity and Persistence in Children with Attention Deficit Hyperactivity Disorder." *Behavior Modification* 2 (1998): 143–66.

Wilens, T. E., J. Biederman, D. E. Geist, R. Steingard, and T. Spencer. "Nortriptlyline in the Treatment of Attention Deficit Hyperactivity Disorder: A Chart Review of 58 Cases." *Journal of the American Academy of Child and Adolescent Psychiatry* 34 (1993): 110–12.

Wilens, T. E., J. Biederman, J. Prince, et al. "Six-week, Double-blind, Placebo-controlled Study of Desipramine for Adult Attention Deficit Hyperactivity Disorder." *American Journal of Psychiatry* 153 (1996): 1147–53.

Wilens, T. E., B. R. Haight, J. P. Horrigan, J. J. Hudziak, N. E. Rosenthal, D. F. Connor, et al. "Bupropion XL in Adults with Attention Deficit Hyperactivity Disorder: A Randomized, Placebo-controlled Study." *Biological Psychiatry* 57, no. 7 (2005): 793–801.

Wilens, T. E., and T. J. Spencer. "The Stimulants Revisited." *Child and Adolescent Psychiatric Clinics of North America* 9, no. 3 (2000) 573–603.

Wilens, T. E., T. J. Spencer, and J. Biederman. "Pharmacotherapy of Adult ADHD." in Barkley, R. A. *Attention Deficit Hyperactivity Disorder: A Handbook for Diagnosis and Treatment* (p. 592–606, 2d ed.) New York: Guilford Press, 1998.

Willis, T. J., and I. Lovaas. "A Behavioral Approach to Treating Hyperactive Children: The Parent's Role." in Millichap, J. B. (ed.) *Learning Disabilities and Related Disorders* (p. 119–40). Chicago: Yearbook Medical Publications, 1977.

Winerman, L. "The Mind's Mirror." *Monitor on Psychology* 36, no. 9 (2005): 48–50.

Winsler, A. R., M. Diaz, D. J. Atencio, E. M. McCarthy, and L. A. Cabay "Verbal Self-Regulation over Time in Preschool Children at Risk for Attention and Behavior Problems." *Journal of Child Psychology and Psychiatry* 41 (2000): 875–86.

Wright, K. "Can Custom-Made Video Games Help Kids with Attention Deficit Disorder?" *Discover* 22, no. 3 (March, 2001).

Yeo, R. A., D. E. Hill, R. A. Campbell, J. Vigil, H. Petropoulos, and B. Har, et al. "Proton Magnetic Resonance Spectroscopy Investigation of the Right Frontal Lobe in Children with Attention Deficit Hyperactivity Disorder." *Journal of the American Academy of Child and Adolescent Psychiatry* 42 (2003): 303–10.

Zagar, R., and N. D. Bowers "The Effect of Time of Day on Problem Solving and Classroom Behavior." *Psychology in the Schools* 20 (1983): 337–45.

Zametkin, A. J., T. E. Nordahl, M. Gross, A. C. King, W. E. Semple, J. Rumsey, S. Hamburger, and R. M. Cohen "Cerebral Glucose Metabolism in Adults with Hyperactivity of Childhood Onset." *New England Journal of Medicine* 323 (1990): 1361–66.

Zametkin, A. J., and J. L. Rapoport. "Neurobiology of Attention Deficit Disorder with Hyperactivity: Where Have we Come in 50 Years?" *Journal of the American Academy of Child and Adolescent Psychiatry* 26 (1987): 676–86.

Zelazo, P. R., J. S. Reznick, and D. E. Pinon. "Response Control and the Execution of Verbal Rules." *Developmental Psychology* 31 (1995): 508–17.

Zentall, S. S. "A Context for Hyperactivity." in Gadow, K. D., and I. Bailer (eds.) *Advances in Learning and Behavioral Disabilities.* (vol. 4, p. 273–343). Greenwich, CT: JAI Press, 1985.

Zentall, S. "Research on the Educational Implications of Attention Deficit Hyperactivity Disorder." *Exceptional Children* 60, no. 2 (1993): 143–53.

Zentall, S., J. C. Cassady, and J. Javorsky. "Social Comprehension of Children with Hyperactivity." *Journal of Attention Disorders* 5 (2001): 11–24.

Author Index

Subject Index

twin studies, 80, 87, 90–91, 92, 97–98

university example, 124–25
University of Virginia, 97
USA Today, 167

"Vanessa" case study, 18
video games, 21–22

Wechsler Intelligence Scale, 225

"what" as response, 206
Whitehorn, Katharine, 265
who accommodates, 162
women and learned helplessness, 147
work and play, 50
work/play dichotomy, 50
Wright's study, 109

Zametkin study, 12